POPULAR
MEASURES

POPULAR MEASURES

Poetry and Church Order in Seventeenth-Century Massachusetts

Amy M. E. Morris

DELAWARE

Newark: University of Delaware Press

© 2005 by Rosemont Publishing & Printing Corp.

Extracts from Edward Taylor, *Christographia,* ed. Norman S. Grabo (New Haven: Yale University Press, 1962) are reprinted with permission of Yale University Press.

Associated University Presses
2010 Eastpark Boulevard
Cranbury, NJ 08512

The paper used in this publication meets the requirements of the American National Standard for Permanence of Paper for Printed Library Materials Z39.48-1984.

Library of Congress Cataloging-in-Publication Data

Morris, Amy M. E., 1972–
Popular measures : poetry and church order in seventeenth-century Massachusetts / Amy M.E. Morris.
       p.   cm.
    Includes bibliographical references and index.
    ISBN 0-87413-865-5 (alk. paper)
    1. American poetry—Massachusetts—History and criticism.   2. American poetry—Colonial period, ca. 1600–1775—History and criticism.   3. Christianity and literature—Massachusetts—History—17th century.   4. Popular literature—Massachusetts—History and criticism.   5. Christian poetry, American—History and criticism.   6. Massachusetts—Intellectual life—17th century.   7. Puritans—Massachusetts—Intellectual life.   8. Puritan movements in literature.   I. Title.
PS253.M4M67   2005
811'.1093823—dc22   2004025272

PRINTED IN THE UNITED STATES OF AMERICA

Contents

5

Acknowledgments

I am grateful to the Houghton Library, Harvard University for permission to publish extracts from Joseph Tompson's journal (ms am 92), and to the R. Stanton Avery Special Collections Department of the New England Historic Genealogical Society for permission to publish extracts from the Wigglesworth Family Papers (Mss 71). Extracts from *Edward Taylor's* Gods Determinations *and* Preparatory Meditations: *A Critical Edition,* ed. Daniel Patterson (Kent, Ohio: Kent State University Press, 2003) are reprinted with permission of The Kent State University Press.

I am indebted to my teachers and colleagues at Cambridge University, the University of Wisconsin-Green Bay, and Harvard University for their advice and encouragement while I worked on this project. Richard Gooder introduced me to seventeenth-century New England, and Sacvan Bercovitch thoughtfully directed me to the Halfway Covenant. From Jean Gooder and Susan Manning I learned the courage to begin and from Paul Giles the focus and discipline to finish. I thank Susan Castillo and Colin Burrow for their input on the manuscript, and I am grateful to the many early Americanists whose books I have read but whom I have not yet met. I hope I have done you justice. A Frank Knox Memorial Fellowship during my dissertation study enabled me to consult rare books and manuscripts at Harvard, Yale, the Massachusetts Historical Society, and the New England Historic Genealogical Society, and to visit the seventeenth-century church at Hingham, Mass. My final thanks go to my students and family for their practical and moral support, especially Sophie Wallace-Hadrill, Anna Hobbs, Matthew Sangster, Olivia Sheppard, Brendan Cooper, Karen Attar, my parents, and, most of all, my husband, Lawrence, who probably now knows more than he would care to about seventeenth-century New England poetry.

TEXTUAL NOTE

When quoting seventeenth-century texts in modern editions, I have followed the spelling and punctuation of the editors in each case.

When quoting from early printed books, facsimiles, and manuscripts, I have normalized the long *s* and the letters *i* and *j, u* and *v, vv* and *w* to modern usage. In quotations from texts that are fully italicized in the original, such as prefaces, I have kept the emphases but reversed the italicization. In direct quotations from manuscripts, I have also capitalized the personal pronoun *I* and expanded most of the abbreviations. Any additional special editing on my part is clearly marked in the text.

POPULAR
MEASURES

Introduction

In the 1918 Cambridge *History of American Literature*, Vernon Lewis Parrington confessed that to the modern reader, the leading ministers of seventeenth-century New England must seem like "crabbed theologians," "strange, perverted, scarce intelligible beings." "We should be inclined to dismiss them as curious eccentricities," he continued, "were it not for the amazing fact that those old preachers were not mere accidents or by-products, but the very heart and passion of the times."[1] Although not quite the "heart and passion" of modern scholarship, New England Puritan writings have enjoyed a resurgence of scholarly interest since Perry Miller's seminal work in the mid-twentieth century.[2] Miller demonstrated the value of an approach to early New England studies that was both empathetic and rigorous. While Miller's work remains the most comprehensive study of the intellectual culture of New England Puritanism, many of his findings have been usefully challenged by succeeding generations of scholars, to the extent that it is barely possible today to write of New England "Puritanism" without observing that the word is used loosely and for want of a better. On the one hand, the term has been undermined by what is now understood about its paradoxical imprecision in reference to Protestant groupings in England, and on the other, by the theological directions subsequently taken by the colonial migrants, making "post-puritan" possibly a more accurate label.[3] Nevertheless, because the term "Puritan" has become conventional in American literary scholarship I continue to use it as a convenient way of denoting the Congregationalist Protestantism that dominated New England religious culture in the seventeenth century.

To give a broader sample of recent critical trends: Miller's emphasis on the dominance of rationality and intellect in New England Puritan culture has been countered in studies by Larzer Ziff and Andrew Delbanco, who have highlighted the role played by pragmatic responses to the New World environment and politics in the development of New England Puritanism; Norman Pettit, Charles Lloyd Cohen, David Leverenz, and Charles Hambrick-Stowe have underlined the importance of Puritanism's affective dimension. New England Puritanism's factiousness and fragmentation (in contrast to the relative homogeneity portrayed by Miller) has been brought into sharper focus by Philip Gura, Janice Knight, and Michael Winship; Sacvan Bercovitch, Patricia Caldwell, and Lisa Gordis have highlighted the rhetorical complexity in Puritan speech and writing, revising Miller's more direct treatment of his written sources, and David Hall has significantly broadened the field of study by addressing popular print culture. In addition to evaluating a wider range of cultural media, recent scholarship including work by Gordis, Ann Kibbey, and Jane Kamensky has also become more nuanced in its engagement with the oral/aural and performative contexts in which much Puritan writing was produced.[4] This of course is to name but a handful of the many scholars who have shaped the study of New England Puritan writing since Miller. Yet in all this revisionist research, a question originally raised by Miller's work persists, namely, how did the humanistic and rational side of New England Puritanism jibe with the zeal and pietism that even Miller acknowledged as also characteristic of the faith. In some form or other, this question has inspired many literary critical attempts to interpret New England Puritanism, and it also forms a starting point for this one.

RECONSTRUCTIVE CRITICISM AND PURITAN AESTHETICS

In my investigation into early New England poetry and poetics I consider the design of the verse as reflecting not simply the conscious intentions of the Puritan writers, but also their underlying sense of how the world worked, and therefore of how their act of spiritual communication through this medium was best achieved. Such an effort of sympathetic contextualization is of course not an original approach: Miller's research brought home the fact that the seventeenth-century Puritan writer's sense of the world was profoundly different from that of a modern reader. Given the difficulties it has presented to modern literary critics, the difference is arguably nowhere more apparent than in the poetry. Yet the scale of the difference has become if anything one of the most attractive features of the genre to critics of the postmodern era, for whom otherness holds a special fascination. Ivy Schweitzer, for instance, has been intrigued by the otherness of "redeemed subjectivity," which, as she shows, was a difference that was expressed in gendered terms in early New England lyric verse.[5] In another context, Philip Gura (following David Perkins) has celebrated "defamiliarization" as one of the key goals of the literary historian, which he argues is inherent to the kind of "reconstructive" approach he recommends to the scholar of early American litera-ture.[6]

Empathetic approaches to early New England verse thus seem to have been curiously enabled by the increased awareness in recent years of the interpretive problems it poses. Jeffrey Hammond's work on New England Puritan verse best illustrates the application of Gura's ideal of reconstructive and interpretive criticism. Hammond has encouraged a transcultural understanding through highlighting and explicating the "forbidding otherness" that early New England poetry presents to a modern reader.[7] By trying to strip away post-Ro-mantic readerly expectations and reconstruct the "forgotten" frame-work of interpretation, Hammond has explicitly sought to recreate, albeit in the abstract, "the Puritan experience of poetry." For Ham-mond, the key to appreciating early New England poetry lies in understanding the colonists' fervent belief in the spiritually trans-forming power of words, which he explores through their practice of reading and listening to edifying texts. While following Bercovitch and Miller in his portrayal of a word-centered and relatively homoge-neous culture, Hammond has nevertheless emphasized the psychic divisiveness inherent in New England religious practice and its liter-ary and pietistic consequences, namely, the development of poetry that was designed like "spiritual workbooks" to help move the read-er's "sinful self" closer to the goal of a "saintly self." Using an "an-thropological" approach that examines the interaction between Puritan readers and poetic texts, Hammond has shown that "the Pu-ritan aesthetic was militantly functional" so that the value of poems (like sermons) lay not in any formal beauty but in "their capacity for moving readers further along the *ordo salutis*." But as Hammond ac-knowledges, this modern assessment is not without a twist, in that for the Puritan readers "divine truth *was* beauty." Moreover, Hammond equates the Puritan aesthetics of functionality with an understanding of language antithetical to Puritan thought when he concludes that what his research has uncovered is the "ritual dimension" of Puritan poetry—a paradox that invites further exploration of precisely what uses of language New England Puritans considered to be "ritualistic" and why.[8]

The idea of the performative function of Puritan texts, building on Stanley Fish's notion of the "self-consuming artifact," is central to an understanding of how Puritans squared the composition of poetry with their iconoclastic beliefs, though as Hammond's conclusions show, it leaves some questions unresolved. In exploring the relationship between religious poetry and Puritan meditative practices, Ursula Brumm, Norman Grabo, and Charles Hambrick-Stowe have also highlighted the importance of the affective religious function of Puritan poetry.[9] Robert Daly developed the notion in what was the first book-length study of New England Puritan poetry and poetics, arguing that poetry shaped by the Puritan "fear of idolatry" still included imagery and symbolism because the symbols were created by God not the poet, and because poetry could participate in God's ministry and have a salvific function: poets could use the figural value of this world to turn their readers' attention and affections to the next. Daly's interpretation, while accounting well for Bradstreet's and Taylor's poetry as exploiting the earthly senses for heavenly ends, fails to account for Wigglesworth's.[10] By focusing more fully on reader response instead of images and imagery, Hammond resists more completely than Daly the tempting dichotomy of "too Puritan to be good or too good to be Puritan," but in so doing also risks dismissing the aesthetic tensions too easily.[11]

The scattered comments about poetry in seventeenth-century New England writing certainly do not add up to a coherent poetics (as Daly pointed out); but they do convey aesthetic tensions and anxieties which have perhaps been too readily set aside by the dominant argument about the misalliance of theory and practice in Puritan culture, which has been put forward by Norman Grabo, Patricia Caldwell, and Willis Barnstone among others. "The Puritan as literary theorist has all but shouted down the Puritan as practicing poet," warns Hammond, before going on in his subsequent research to identify what he describes as a compensatory ritualism in Puritan poetic techniques.[12] While critics are right to note the potential disparities between ideology and practice, the marvelous collection of Puritan comments arrayed in Hammond's introduction to *Sinful Self, Saintly Self* cannot but convey the conflicted position of poetry in early New England religious culture. To give a sample of some of the inherent contradictions: the preface to the 1640 New England translation of the Psalms (which I shall refer to from now on as the Bay Psalm Book) famously spurned "poetry" and "elegance"; in 1726, an elderly Cotton Mather urged young would-be ministers to "preserve the chastity of your soul from the dangers you may incur by a conversation with muses that are no better than harlots"; and sometime in between, Jonathan Mitchel wrote a commendatory poem to deny that the verses written by his colleague Michael Wigglesworth were akin to the "Toyes" or "Fables" that he conceded to be "Poets wonted

Crimes."[13] On the other hand, Wigglesworth's *The Day of Doom* was obviously written within a long-established *Dies Irae* tradition of popular narrative verse; Cotton Mather obtained some of Edward Taylor's poetry to use as an epigraph to one of his treatises, and was therefore evidently aware of his contemporary's "passionate and measured pages" and extended "conversation" with muses; and the writers of the Bay Psalm Book preface may have dismissed "poetry" and "elegance" but they did so with a memorable flourish that half-rhymed the pair with their more worthy rivals, "fidelity" and "conscience."[14] Finally, early New England settlers overcame their misgivings sufficiently to write a huge quantity of poetry, though much has only found publication in any substantial form in twentieth-century anthologies.[15] Noting that Edward Taylor conducted sensitive religious self-examination through the medium of verse, Hammond suggests that Puritan objections were merely to the wrong kinds of poetry, since such serious matters as Taylor addressed were "scarcely to be entrusted to a suspect genre."[16]

Michael Clark has reminded us that the American Puritan "suspicion" of poetry was related to a larger British movement to reject "Ciceronian formalism" and "elaborate tropes."[17] As Hammond has explained, New England poets were simply following in the footsteps of Michael Drayton and George Herbert who set out to redeem the genre from its "fiction and false hair," or as Drayton put it, the "wanton and adultrate conceits," the "lothsome ordure" that "polluted" the Muses' "sweet and pleasant fields."[18] According to Clark and Hammond, the New England writers successfully focused or reconfigured their own aesthetic so as to distance their work from all such dangers of self-referentiality, paganism, and wantonness. And yet the continued equivocation and inconsistency of New England Puritan comments about poetry suggest that the dangers were felt to be ever close.[19] Anne Bradstreet's verse may indeed have been owned and read by many New England households, including Edward Taylor's.[20] But the "lavish, if patronizing praise" of the commendatory verses, Bradstreet's own self-deprecating "Prologue," and the prefatory affidavit by her brother-in-law that "these poems are the fruit but of some few hours, curtailed from her sleep and other refreshments," do not paint a particularly comfortable picture.[21] Moreover, if attention is directed at New England verse itself, rather than at comments about it, the ambivalence is still insistent. However empathetically the context is reconstructed and the element of performativity emphasized, much of the poetry is still inherently conflicted: significant moments of aesthetic resistance remain.

The long-running debate about the flawed quality of Edward Taylor's verse is one illustration of this aesthetic resistance. Taylor's startling use of domestic imagery and colloquialisms, for example, in his descriptions of how the Eucharist is "disht up" by angel hands on his frontier kitchen table, or in his vivid use of gaming imagery for his sins, seems to present a challenge to the reader. To some, this whole question is merely the result of modern misreading: Alan B. Howard, for instance, has argued that Taylor's metaphors seem grotesque only to modern readers who are unaccustomed to the allegorical "decorum" of the emblem tradition, and are therefore too literal-minded in their reading. Building on this, William J. Scheick has argued for an underlying coherence in Taylor's use of his theological and Biblical sources, arguing that the "nearly chaotic proliferation of Bablic meanings" was a superficial decoy, concealing a deeper and harmonious "divine art" in Taylor's Scriptural and typological elaborations. But even Scheick's interpretation acknowledges the tension, and Grabo, Gatta, and others have persistently emphasized that "the effect of whimsical surprise cannot be explained away" by genetic source study, and that, within Taylor's poems the incongruity of the imagery plays an important role in acting "to stimulate a wonder of recognition."[22]

While it must be acknowledged that Taylor's poetry is unrepresentative of American Puritan literature in general in stimulating this particular critical debate, it does present an example of verse that seems to incorporate some kind of aesthetic challenge into its design. One touchstone of aesthetic decorum for many modern readers, and perhaps even for Taylor himself, is the poetry of George Herbert, with which Taylor seems to have had some familiarity, though this cannot be established for certain. Taylor worked as a schoolmaster in England, had evidently had "at least some kind of nonconformist education beyond the basic schools," possibly even at Oxford or Cambridge, and did not emigrate until he was about twenty-six.[23] Together with his averred appreciation for "the Muses Copses," and the fact that he knew the poetry-loving Elnathan Chauncy, these facts make it quite likely that he was well-versed in English poetry.[24] If then, as Lewalski has suggested, Taylor borrowed his oft-used phrase "Crumb of dust" from George Herbert, it is hard to accept that no significant aesthetic distortion was intended in his elaboration of this tender image into the grotesque vision of "Clods of Dust" attempting to "toote" praises to God, which Taylor presents to the reader in *Gods Determinations*.[25]

While Kenneth Silverman's view that certain Puritan writers

seemed "to strive in their verse for a deliberate awkwardness" is probably an exaggeration, it does highlight the fact that even by the standards of the time New England writers sometimes took a rather challenging approach to poetry and elegance.[26] Silverman's comment exaggerates because it attributes a destructive literary intention to the Puritan authors which risks turning them into the Philistine spoilsports H. L. Mencken later caricatured, and for this we have no evidence.[27] But to deny or overlook the presence of poetic awkwardness or other kinds of resistance (such as the unexpected restrictiveness of Anne Bradstreet's later verse) would be to take empathy too far and ignore literary and aesthetic qualities in the poetry that the Puritans themselves were aware of. Scheick champions the aesthetic quality of Taylor's and Bradstreet's poems, but his argument that the poems have a strong "aesthetic order" in the form of emblematic designs "concealed" beneath their "awkward artistry" highlights too that the texts have a certain aesthetic resistance. Through powerful, elucidatory readings of Bradstreet and Taylor, Scheick shows how a contextualized formalist approach can, in some cases, unlock this resistance. Yet his turn to the preacher's motto "*Artis est celare Artem*," to help explain why the poets concealed the artistry that his analysis reveals, is not fully satisfying.[28] As I argue in chapter 1, although according to Puritan sermon theory studious learning was to be concealed, this was because the theory prioritized immediacy of communication, and values such as transparency, directness, and popular accessibility of language. In different ways, Scheick's and Hammond's work both highlight the aesthetic conundrum in the "design" of Puritan poetry. While my research builds on Hammond's and Hambrick-Stowe's in its aim to trace a relationship between Puritan poetry, devotional experience, and ecclesiastical practice, it is also influenced by Scheick's commitment to exploring Puritan literary aesthetics. Trying to combine elements of each approach, I want to address the design of more popular verse than just that of Bradstreet and Taylor, but without allowing aesthetic concerns to be resolved too easily into the contextually problematic category of performative ritualism.

New England Literary Culture

Recent interest in the "history of the book" has given us the timely reminder that intellectual culture, including literary aesthetics, is inevitably informed by the conditions of material culture. For earlier twentieth-century critics, the small size of the population, and the provincial circumstances of the New England settlement, were enough to account for the apparent aesthetic limitations and predominantly popular style of much colonial Puritan verse.[29] Yet Edward Taylor was self-consciously intellectual enough to feel keenly the cultural limitations of Westfield. In a now well-known letter to Samuel Sewall, who wanted to spar intellectually on an eschatological subject with his old schoolfellow, Taylor responded very wittily, but also reminded Sewall that he was now "far off from the Muses Copses: and the Foggy damps assaulting my Lodgen in these remotest Swamps from the Heliconan quarters, where little Save Clonian Rusticity is Al-A-Mode, will plead my apology." Ironically, in this brief allusion Taylor resists the provincial loss of his classical Muses by a tongue-in-cheek recasting of his frontier surroundings as pastoral retreat.[30] Anne Bradstreet also resisted the cultural deprivations of her New World environment, and in her "Quaternions" and elegies on Queen Elizabeth and Sir Philip Sidney demonstrated a strong allegiance to the elite, classical, and courtly tradition within British Protestant poetry. Taylor and Bradstreet were not the only ones to have a sense of poetic tradition: Jonathan Mitchel alluded to Herbert, as did other New England writers including Philip Pain, John Danforth, Joshua Scottow, and Cotton Mather.[31] Even Wigglesworth owned a copy of Horace, and had evidently read some of the "Christian poets," whose invocations of pagan muses he "abominate[d]" in his "Prayer to Christ" which prefaced *The Day of Doom*.[32] One must conclude that the styles of these New England writers were shaped by challenging choices that were made not in isolation but in relation to a wider and transatlantic poetic tradition.

Although the availability and variety of literary texts was much more restricted in Boston and its surroundings than in London, strong evidence of relatively wide circulation of books in the colonies has been found in the inventories of private libraries, correspondence, commonplace books, and the import records of booksellers. The widespread borrowing, buying, and giving of books afforded verse-writers the opportunity of self-comparison. Interesting examples from private collections include, for instance, Thomas Dudley's owning a copy of *Piers Plowman*, and Increase Mather's owning two different editions during his lifetime of George Herbert's poems, which may suggest that he gave one copy away.[33] Although poetic texts are not specifically mentioned, colonists' letters indicate a considerable amount of informal book circulation, both within the colony and across the ocean.[34]

Since poetry did not feature much in the Harvard College library, informal circulation probably accounts for the availability of the range of poetic texts from which Elnathan Chauncy (A.B. 1661) was able to copy extracts into his commonplace book. Among the poems he copied were verses by Spenser, Herrick, and Cleveland, and a recent elegy on Cromwell. In terms of vernacular poetry, the 1723 Harvard Library catalogue lists a Chaucer folio, the works of Abraham Cowley, a six-volume Shakespeare (1709), and Milton's "Poetical Works" (1720), but no verse, for instance, by Spenser, Donne, or Herbert. Seaborn Cotton (A.B. 1651) also kept a commonplace book while at Harvard, and copied into it extracts from several popular ballads, showing that (the library notwithstanding) reading was available in Cambridge, Massachusetts, to satisfy a range of tastes.[35]

Although the colonial presses were under close ministerial and magisterial control in the seventeenth century, there was a more liberal standard for imported books.[36] Import records from the 1680s indicate that there was a market for light reading in Boston, including, for example, collections of popular ballads, traditionally called "garlands." John Usher, who succeeded his father, Hezekiah, as one of Boston's principal book traders, received in a package from the London bookseller Robert Boulter, in 1683, twelve copies of a "Joviall garland," twelve of "Crown garland," and six "Garland of delight," as compared (in the same package) with two biographies of Cromwell, twelve stories of Dr. Faustus, and one Sidney's *Arcadia*. Usher's orders also suggest that he was selling modest numbers of *Paradise Lost* in the 1680s.[37] Travelers like Samuel Sewall and Increase Mather "feasted" on the London book market and took back many texts, illustrating that New England literary appetites were not being met; but Wright concludes, nevertheless, that "the colonists were under no greater handicap than if they had been living in some remote place in the north or west of England."[38]

So, if popular verse forms such as couplets and ballad meters prevailed even in the colonial verse written by the highly educated, it is only fair to assume that it was within a context of informed choice.[39] Similarly, even after allowance is made for the limits of individual talent and the influence of a certain cultural impoverishment, the knotty styles of Edward Taylor and John Fiske should still be read as demonstrating literary options being taken, rather than compositions made in a cultural vacuum. As the colonists' rather ambivalent comments about poetry have suggested, "the Puritan experience of poetry" owed much of its angst and inconsistency to the problem of negotiating the connotations of the genre in British Protestant culture—for instance, its pagan classical inheritance, and its associations with pleasure, idleness, and venery.

For this reason I have tried in my research to shun the "bogey of exceptionalism" and to trace where relevant the transatlantic dimension to early New England literary development.[40] As Lawrence Buell has observed, the relevance of examining American literature in a transatlantic perspective has been, if anything, underlined by recent trends encouraging the comparative study of multiethnic, multilingual literatures within the United States. And the rapidly developing field of "hemispheric" studies, in which the literature and culture of "the Americas" are placed in a comparative perspective, further encourages careful consideration of the local factors that shaped the development of such distinct colonial cultures, addressing both the influence of the Old World imperial centers and the circumstances encountered or constructed in the New.[41] The perspective of my study is perhaps best summed up by William Spengemann's remark that "the extension of British culture into the New World" provides as a subject of research "the resulting impact of this extension of that culture."[42] While my work is indirectly influenced by other approaches to early American studies, I have taken as my primary task to analyze qualities that became distinctive in the religious and poetic culture of seventeenth-century colonial New England.

I shall be focusing on how the development of a kind of aesthetic resistance may have arisen as a means of warding off some of the associations of poetry that their theological context would have made particularly unwelcome to colonial New England readers, and, more importantly, how poetry contributed to the goal of communicating a religious message in an American Puritan context. While Hammond is surely correct that "unlike the post-Romantic poem, which exists as an expressive end in itself, the Puritan poem was written to further spiritual processes, both pre- and post-conversion, mandated by [Puritan] theology," his excellent studies still leave more to be said about the precise way in which literary design provided room for the contribution of the "spiritual" component in such "processes."[43]

POETRY AND RELIGIOUS PRACTICE IN NEW ENGLAND

The literary implications of New England theology were sounded in Kenneth Murdock's classic study *Literature and Theology in Colonial New England,* in which he distinguished between "Puritan" and "Anglican" literary tempers.[44] Since Murdock, contextual studies of New England poetry have become narrower but more sophisticated, as specific threads within colonial Puritan theology and religious practice have been isolated and their literary implications explored. In this vein, Robert Daly has analyzed the theology governing the Puritan use of figures and imagery, a topic Karen Rowe has narrowed further in her exploration of the influence of typology on Edward Taylor; Hammond has traced the role of devotional reading and listening in the formation of New England poetics; Ivy Schweitzer has examined the impact of Puritan soteriology on the lyric from a feminist and psychoanalytical perspective; and Scheick and Craig have focused on the poetics of Biblical intertextuality.[45]

Building on Barbara Lewalski's seminal work on the centrality of the Scriptural Word to the self-conscious verbal patterning of Protestant poetry, Craig has shown how Edward Taylor made "new songs" by recasting "biblical allusions to create intertextual patterning." According to Craig, "what is poetic about Puritan poetry" is its Biblical allusiveness, its "broidering" of the wedding garment of the saved soul with the "Word and words of poetry."[46] This argument dovetails with Hammond's in suggesting that, for Puritan readers, beauty is found in the binding in of the individual poem into the metatext of Scripture, a textual process analogous to the soteriological assimilation of the individual soul (potentially including the reader's soul) into the holy pattern of the "saintly self." But Craig (like Rowe) in focusing on Biblical intertextuality overlooks somewhat the formal considerations that were also a part of the literary aesthetics inherited and developed by the Puritan colonists. Yet Craig's helpful application of John Cotton's teaching on psalm-singing to Taylor's poetic methodology highlights the interrelation between colonial Puritan concerns about linguistic forms and ritual formality in the church service, and the development of poetic style.

Similarly, while Mason I. Lowance's work on the development of typology in New England has helped to clarify our understanding of this key method of Scriptural interpretation and its influence on American Puritan literature, particularly historiography and poetry, Lowance's findings indirectly suggest other complementary avenues of research. By tracing developments in the way typology was used in New England, Lowance has illustrated how subtle the distinction between appropriate and inappropriate ecclesiastical continuities could be. Showing typology being invoked on the one hand to justify the rejection of Medieval *allegoria* and Old Testament or Roman Catholic ceremonies, Lowance shows typology being applied, on the other hand, in a quasi-allegorical way itself—in personal salvation stories, in providential readings of New England history, and later in Jonathan Edwards's interpretations of the book of nature. The idea suggested by Lowance's and other typological studies, that Puritan writers found creative ways of producing a nonidolatrous figurative language by closely linking their creativity to methods of Biblical exegesis, has now been pursued in some depth.[47] My study seeks to complement this line of investigation by suggesting that there was also a need for New England Puritan poets to negotiate for themselves a nonidolatrous use of poetic *form*. Lowance's findings imply that in getting rid of one kind of linguistic or literary "help," Puritan theologians inadvertently opened the door to other kinds. Out of such exploration of the potentially paradoxical application of New England theology to literary practice arises the current interest in the question of compensatory "ritualism" within Puritan literary culture which I would like to examine more critically.

While New England saw distinctive theological developments in soteriology and typological interpretation, highly distinctive developments also occurred in the realm of ecclesiology and church order. Given this, it seems time that this important religious thread was given some focused attention. Indeed, when the church teaching and practice concerning forms and formality and the role of language in the church service are examined, it is surprising that the resonances for poetic form and language have been overlooked for so long. The church order that was first established at Salem, Dorchester, and Boston, and then hammered out by successive Massachusetts synods, exerted a formative influence on the life of all the faithful, and beyond. It is true that Congregational church order developed slightly differently in the different New England colonies. But the Massachusetts Bay Colony was the most populous and dominant settlement and the economic, intellectual, and political hub of New England in the seventeenth century. For this reason, for the sake of simplicity, and since the principal literary texts I will be addressing were all published in the Bay Colony, I will be focusing on Massachusetts church order.[48]

If the centrality of the Bible encouraged many Protestant poets to envisage their own creative work in dignified, even sacred terms, the use of the Psalms as the divinely inspired model and justification for early modern vernacular poetry is particularly well attested.[49] Especially since a new metrical Psalter was the colony's first native book of verse, the Psalmic model was readily available to early New England poets, and indeed, their verse seems to have emulated the Psalter's role as "poetry with a purpose."[50] But what precise view of the rela-

tionship between language and the Holy Spirit did such Scriptural
and ecclesiastical models imply for the Puritan colonist? The post-Ro-
mantic poem may offer the reader the spirituality of Frost's "momentary clarification of life," and for postmodern critics like Jerome
McGann poetry might be the source of spiritual truth, because
"'God' . . . has died and been reborn as language."[51] But such ideas
about the relationship between language and spirit are scarcely com-
patible with the processes of conversion and salvation envisaged by
New England churchgoers. Yet, ironically, in insisting upon the efficacious power of Scriptural intertextuality or of devotional reading
and listening in Puritan culture, the contextualizing critic can risk
verging close to such post-Romantic even postmodern views of the
spiritual life of the text. It is true that Biblical allusion and devotional
reading and listening practices played a central role in the spiritual
lives of the New England Puritans, as conversion relations testify, but
claims such as "Puritan faith in the Word constituted a near-deifica-
tion of the symbolic and the verbal" need careful nuancing, as I hope
my study will show.[52]

Despite the great spiritual power accorded to the Scriptures, words
in general were not considered divine by Puritans. Even in Craig's
bibliocentric model of "biblical allusions creating intertextual patterning," the position of the Bible as the ultimate metatext remains
unique: Puritan poetry may have been a "porch" to Scripture, as
Hammond has argued, but the de-centeredness of such a position was
crucially significant.[53] The words of the Bible were regarded as being
exceptionally empowered by the Holy Spirit, and it was this empowerment that all the other formulations celebrated and upon which they
depended. As illustrated in *Grace Abounding*, where Bunyan's narra-
tor-persona gets almost physically attacked by the Biblical texts he re-
members, a Puritan view of Scripture usually distinguished between
the spiritual force of direct Biblical quotations and the more moderate power of language in general.[54] This is clear, too, for instance, in
the way New Englanders referred to the sermon as the "opening" of
the Biblical text, as if the sermon itself had no significant verbal presence relative to the words of Holy Writ.

Moreover, according to New England ecclesiology, a further hierarchical distinction was made between words that were officially "ordained" of God for the purpose of worship and teaching in the
church service, and other words. John Cotton, for instance, reminded
his readers of one reason liturgy was not permitted in New England
churches: "Wee conceive it also to be unlawful to bring in ordinarily
any other Bookes into the publique worship of God, in the Church,

besides the Book of God."[55] For this reason, metrical psalms could be sung in church, but not hymns. It is not likely, therefore, that it would have been permissible to read religious poetry like Taylor's or Herbert's in the strict churches of Cotton's generation. Sermons and prayers in church had to be delivered from memory rather than recited from a script. This method was also approved because it seemed to make the final wording more available than liturgical or scripted forms to spontaneous alteration at the bidding of the Holy Spirit, during the act of delivery. Thus, there were hierarchies of language, and the words of the Bible, and then those of the church "ordinances," were expected to exert a relatively stronger spiritual power than other kinds of language.

It is for this reason that the Cambridge minister, Jonathan Mitchel, encountered some difficulty when attempting to commend *The Day of Doom* to Puritan readers. Whereas John Bunyan proffered the allegory of *The Pilgrim's Progress* in free and easy terms, arguing "let Truth be free / To make her Salleys upon Thee, and Me, / Which way it pleases God," Mitchel evidently felt it best (or perhaps necessary) to present *The Day of Doom* as a sermon *manqué*.[56] The ambiguity this caused was inherent in his opening quotation, which both allied and distanced his colleague's poem from the ordained language of the sermon:

> A Verse may find him who a Sermon flies,
> Saith *Herbert* well. Great Truths to dress in Meeter;
> Becomes a Preacher; who mens Souls doth prize,
> That Truth in Sugar roll'd may taste the sweeter.
>   No Cost too great, no Care too curious is
>   To set forth Truth, and win mens Souls to bliss.[57]

Mitchel's stance is emphatically apologetic, even defensive. With diction like "Cost" and "Care," and in the next stanza, "Costly Verse" and "laborious Rymes," Mitchel carefully qualified his references to the poem with language designed to associate its composition as far as possible with the studious and godly efforts of sermon preparation. The trouble was that Wigglesworth's "serious strains" were self-evidently in verse, not sermon form. Indeed, the poem had come into being because Wigglesworth was ill and unable to do his primary task of preaching. As both Wigglesworth and Mitchel recognized, preaching was unquestionably the preferable and ordained means of communicating the gospel. "The Sins of Hearers, Preacher Lips do close," lamented Mitchel, accusingly, "But from this Eater comes some Meat." Thus, Mitchel commended the poem with the enthusiasm normally reserved for a consolation prize.

Partly as a result of his efforts to underline the sermonic features, Mitchel also equivocated about the alluring "taste" of the poem. His hesitancy about how to play the potential value of this common (originally Horatian) defense of poetic form as a sweetener, illustrates a fundamental ambiguity in the position of verse in New England piety. In the first stanza, Mitchel equated "Meeter" with a "sugar" coating that would helpfully render the presumably bitter pill of doctrine more attractive. This linking corresponds phonically and allusively to the "Meat" that came from the "Eater," which was the honey Samson found inside the dead lion in Judges 14. Yet in Mitchel's second stanza, the most pleasurable associations seem to cluster instead around the "Poets wonted Crimes" of "Toyes" and "Fables":

> In Costly Verse, and most laborious Rymes,
> Are dish't up here Truths worthy most regard:
> No Toyes, nor Fables (Poets wonted Crimes)
> Here be; but things of worth with Wit prepar'd.
> > Reader, fall too; and if thy tast be good,
> > Thou'lt praise the Cook, & say, 'Tis choicest Food.

The food is "choice," but, instead of sweet or tasty morsels, the Truths as "dish't up" are now "worthy most regard." Instead of appealing to the reader who did not like sermons, Mitchel now described Wigglesworth's poem in terms that promoted it implicitly as an aesthetic test of the reader's spiritual state. Untangling this doublethink, it seems that Mitchel initially needed to use the idea of poetic allure ("sugar") in order to justify the existence of the poem in the first place, but then, in order to validate it as religious reading, he had to turn around and confute the associations of poetry with literary redundancy and mere entertainment ("Toyes"). Thus, on closer examination, that a riddle lies at the heart of Mitchel's commendation—Samson's "Meat from the Eater"—is symptomatic of the overall complexity of his task. The role of poetic form in communicating a spiritual message does seem to have presented this New England writer with a "honeyed knot."[58]

Mitchel's difficulty in establishing the "worth" of *The Day of Doom* as a religious poem illustrates not only the potential literary effects of distinguishing ecclesiastical from other uses of language, but also the problem caused by the Puritan dislike of any language that appeared to be redundant, or an end in itself. Both linguistic pitfalls amounted to much the same thing in that they both betrayed the fundamental purpose of religious communication, which was to guide the soul to Christ. As Michael Clark has shown, this was to be done through the kind of language that can be described as based on the "sign" as opposed to the "image": "signs" being representatives of a truth beyond the world, and "images" claiming to reveal God in the material world.[59] The opposition to liturgy shows that even within the official church ordinances, the role of words was carefully qualified, in such a way as the leaders believed would best maintain this position of means, rather than end, or a misleading amalgamation of both.

The rules and customs regulating the New England church service and covenant suggest that language, particularly in the form of any only indirectly Scriptural text, was felt to be potentially dangerous as a distraction from the true spiritual *telos* of all worship. For instance, in words that resemble Cotton Mather's later warning about poetry, Mather's grandfather, John Cotton, warned of the danger of church liturgy, because it sent one's "eyes . . . a whoring after the imaginations and inventions of men."[60] One could argue that such comments merely show that language was seen to be immensely powerful, and for that reason needed to be carefully harnessed to a benign cause. While this is true to some extent, the Puritans were Calvinist, not Manichean: the power with which they believed language was able to distract the soul from its Maker could not have been equal to the power with which it drew the soul to salvation—salvific force had to be greater and more irresistible. Language was therefore something that could channel grace, though it could not claim or contain it intrinsically, and this view seems to underlie the church rules and customs, as I show in more detail in chapter 1.

As Hambrick-Stowe has put it, "Puritanism was as affective as it was rational," and the many private journals and funeral elegies written by the colonists strongly attest to this.[61] Yet while a belief in the power of verse to "stir the affections" contributed to John Cotton's strong endorsement of psalm-singing in church, elsewhere the minister noted this kind of stirring was a secondary one. Cotton implied that the "affections" that really mattered were "gracious affections" and by this he meant ones with which God "blessed" his worshippers in reward for their obedience.[62] Cotton was doubtless more concerned than more preparationist ministers (such as Thomas Shepard) to underline the ineffectiveness of "affect" in leading to salvation unless accompanied by God's grace, but the theology of predestination and emphasis on God's sovereignty shared by the first-generation New England Puritan ministers meant that they all ascribed the ultimate control over human responsiveness to God. And the distinction between natural and spiritual responses to language resurfaced in later writing, for instance, in a section of the autobiographical account that Michael Wigglesworth's son, Edward, wrote, some time after his father's death in 1705. All the "instructions, cautions, counsels, & admonitions" of his father and the "earnest exhortations & tears" of his mother were in themselves insufficient in procuring his salvation, he explained. For,

> though these things in the time of them have moved my affections greatly, (insomuch that I have been terrified & astonished . . . & that I have even melted into tears at my mothers affectionate charges & entreaties; Notwithstanding I say that these things thus touched my affections, yet they never reached my heart, so as to leave any abiding impressions there.[63]

Words may have been a necessary and powerful tool in the communication of the gospel, and alternatively a dangerous weapon in the armory of the Devil, but in New England Puritan piety, rhetorical power that could stir the affections was not quite synonymous with the spiritual power that (in Edward Wigglesworth's terminology) reached the heart.

The subtlety of the distinction—whether between "affections" and "heart" or "affections" and "gracious affections"—suggests a complex and potentially capricious intersection between the humanistic and pietistic impulses of New England Puritanism on this issue. As Perry Miller demonstrated, rhetoric (of which poetry was considered a "heightened form") was a matter of humanistic mechanics, of persuading the intellect and stirring the affections, and seventeenth-century Puritan ministers learned this art at school and university.[64] Salvation, on the other hand, was believed to be a matter of God's sovereign will and timing, and while ministers encouraged individuals to "prepare" for grace by cultivating their piety, they also accepted the principle that God's will was arbitrary. Though he situated the comments within an overtly persuasive and evangelistic poem, Michael Wigglesworth, for example, gave Christ the following speech, asserting the divine prerogative of election:

> If upon one what's due to none
> I frankly shall bestow,
> And on the rest shall not think best,
> compassions skirts to throw,
> Whom injure I?[65]

Without God's assistance, no amount of rhetorical or poetic skill could construct the divine encounter necessary for salvation, and this fundamental contingency ensured that language in New England Puritan culture could not really acquire Godlike qualities. Although revisionist critics have called Miller's emphasis on the rationalism of New England piety into question, Miller's bias in according such a central role in New England faith experience to a fundamentally humanist view of rhetoric and persuasion has not yet been sufficiently reversed. Perhaps because of what they share of Miller's own humanistic outlook, Hammond and other critics have insufficiently highlighted the fact that despite the great respect Puritan ministers had for the functioning of rhetoric and the affective potential of verse, they still viewed such means as spiritually inadequate, in and of themselves. Cotton and Shepard, for instance, though each wrote sermons that were very artful in their own way, still maintained that the redeemed would be able to understand the Scriptural message they were presenting in a way that the unredeemed would not, that is, the prime factor determining response was not the minister's rhetorical strategy, but something beyond their control.[66]

Although the Puritan churchgoer was expected to meet God through diligent attendance at the ordinances, and "wholsome" church attendance laws were therefore in place, the encounter with God was not quite envisaged as a rhetorical, literary, or even verbal experience.[67] It was something other, that words were expected to prompt, inspire, and then express, but it was not contained in the words. For Thomas Shepard, a nearer analogy was that of vision: in his diary, he frequently wrote of his spiritual lessons with the words "I saw. . . ."[68] Spiritual realization and revelation were perceived as something that no scripted text (even the Bible) could inherently or predictably control, and this mystery deeply influenced the way in which New England religious poets wrote. Such poets, including the Bay Psalm Book compilers, Wigglesworth and Taylor, did not use poetic form directly to body forth spiritual meaning through its rhetorical and affective power. Instead their verse seems crafted, in various different ways, to serve as a "foil" to spiritual experience.

In the first chapter I present in more detail some of the aspects of church order that appear to have exerted a particularly significant influence on New England verse and the aesthetics that underlay it. These include ideas about liturgy, the ordinances, sermon rhetoric, and the conversion relation. I suggest that the "halfway" position of the vow of "owning the covenant" offers, in certain respects, a useful ecclesiastical analogy for the "set form" of poetry, and epitomizes the ambivalence surrounding language in New England church order. Having illustrated some of the problems and issues facing New England religious poets, I proceed, in chapters 2, 3 and 4, to examine how they were tackled in the texts of the 1640 Bay Psalm Book, Wigglesworth's 1662 *The Day of Doom*, and Taylor's *Gods Determinations*, written circa 1680. The chronological sweep represented by these texts, all of which bear a particularly strong relation to church order, allows me to show how the poetry reflected ecclesiastical and cultural developments in the colony.

Whereas most book-length studies of New England verse crystallize around readings of Bradstreet and Taylor, the most literary of the early New England poets, two of my main texts are popular bestsellers that have not received much critical attention. By shifting the critical focus in this way, I am responding to Gura's call for scholars to address not only canonical literature, but also "other kinds of discourse hitherto neglected or prejudged."[69] Through the efforts of Hammond and Ronald A. Bosco, Wigglesworth's poetry is beginning to be given serious consideration, and Daly's verdict that it was "wrecked" by the minister's beliefs is beginning to lose ground.[70] The role of the Bay Psalm Book, however, as the first and most influential book of verse in the colony, has received little literary critical attention, despite the fact that popular texts in general are becoming more acceptable and even fashionable subjects of literary research, as illustrated by Hall's *Worlds of Wonder, Days of Judgment,* and by the inclusion of essays on "promotion tracts and undergraduate doggerel" in a tribute volume for Harrison T. Meserole.[71] However, as the term "doggerel" implies, awkward questions remain about the identity and value of so-called popular literature, and the role of the literary critic in assessing it.

One of the perspectives my research offers on such questions is in suggesting that the use of "plain" or popular styles of verse involved a sophisticated artistic collusion (though not necessarily an intentional one) between poetic design and the goals of New England theology. Critics have long been aware that "the Puritan plain style . . . was a highly conscious art in which the supreme virtue was to conceal the art," and the ministers themselves admitted as much.[72] Ann Kibbey has suggested how this artfulness might be explored, stressing the importance of orality and of rhetoric as gesture in the construction of plain-style preaching.[73] But the questions of mechanics and mystification, raised peripherally in Kibbey's research, invite closer examination, particularly in the relationship between poetry and the ideal of the plain style. As Michael Clark has argued, Puritan literary aesthetics, like Puritan theology, involved a certain replacement of "sensation" by "intention."[74] Popular and didactic verse, therefore, could be plain (in the sense of formally, linguistically, and intellectually accessible) and yet not make the corresponding affective connection, thereby highlighting a kind of dissociation of sensibility. Clarity and access are different from spiritual realization and conversion: the halfway position of the poetic text in this regard can be interpreted as protecting the mystery of conversion and the exclusiveness of the church covenant, while simultaneously sharpening desire for inner spiritual clarification. To rephrase Walter Benjamin, if it could not incarnate spiritual power, early New England poetry could at least "reflect the great longing for *spiritual* complementation."[75]

1

The Meaning of Forms

Jeffrey Hammond and William J. Scheick have observed that the fashion for historically based explication has permitted modern critics of New England Puritan poetry to circumvent some of the aesthetic questions raised by the verse.[1] Yet Karen Rowe, Raymond Craig, Hammond, and others have used the reconstruction of context to demonstrate ways in which the poetry could have been understood and appreciated by the Puritan reader. In this way, their critical approaches have broken down the larger question of aesthetics into focused studies on the function of particular aspects of poetic style. Craig has explored the idea of "elegance" in Puritan texts, and shown how Taylor's poetry corresponded to an ideal of Biblical intertextuality in the generation of "new songs" from old. In a similar vein, Hammond has argued that the "seemingly flat images" of poems such as Bradstreet's "As Weary Pilgrim," when read "as *biblical* images . . . suggested a nearly inexhaustible network of interpretive associations, strategies and responses." For Rowe, it is figuralism and Biblical typology that provide the "artistry" of Taylor's poetry, and that give it imaginative and contemplative resonance: "Neither in metrical form nor lyrical variety does Taylor venture so bravely as he does in creating typological conceits, scriptural metaphors and his own tropes."[2]

Such research has proved extremely fruitful, but Rowe's dismissal of Taylor's use of "form" is telling. While it is undeniable that New England poets in general did not show much interest in the kind of broad metrical variety found, for example, in Herbert's and Vaughan's poems, their verse would not have been verse without its fundamental form, shaped by rhyme and meter. The question of the "formality" of Puritan verse, and its associated aesthetic functioning, does seem to have been neglected in the effort to explore the imagery and Biblical allusiveness of the texts. Other approaches, such as structural comparison to meditation or homiletics, and analysis of certain theological themes, have similarly disregarded the verse form.

Scheick has criticized Rowe's work for "mak[ing] no case for the poetry," despite being very well informed about Taylor's typology, but the gap between aesthetic and archival criticism becomes even broader in studies of Wigglesworth's poetry. In this field, Wigglesworth's brand of Puritan theology is invariably explored at the expense of considering his literary style and his use of verse form.[3]

I aim in this study to contribute further to the mending of this critical divide between literary and historical approaches. By historicizing American Puritan verse in the context of the uses of verbal forms in New England church order, I show how New England's early colonial poets were faced with specific aesthetic and literary problems, owing to the connotations of visibly formalized and fixed language in their religious culture. Whereas earlier studies have addressed the theological and Biblical contexts of Puritan verse, my contribution involves special consideration of the influence of ecclesiastical practice as well as theory on Puritan poetics. It will open into an exploration of how certain poets variously created literary opportunities out of the problematic connotations of forms, conformity, and formality with which they were faced.

New England Church Order During the Seventeenth Century

The tenuousness of religious orthodoxy in seventeenth-century Massachusetts has been highlighted through the research of (among others) Philip Gura, Janice Knight, and Michael Winship into the theological controversies and doctrinal heterogeneity in the first decades of the colony. Yet these investigations also suggest that a measure of control, or unifying compromise, was successfully enforced over the fissiparous theologies and fractious tempers within Massachusetts' Congregationalist communities. As well as by force of law, this was done through teaching and synods, and through debates and treatise defenses by the leading ministers. The Cambridge Platform of 1648 enshrined the basic tenets of church order that Congregationalist ministers such as Thomas Shepard, John Cotton, and Thomas Hooker had brought with them from their nonconformist days in England and Holland, along with some practices they had learned from their neighbors in Plymouth. Published shortly after the Westminster Confession of 1644, the Cambridge Platform was a similar attempt to make an orthodox model out of religious practices that had originally thrived in rebellion against the official forms.[4]

But during the 1640s and 1650s, the English "Independents" (a group that included Congregationalists similar to those in New England) developed a pragmatic toleration of radical sectarianism through the experience of having to join forces as a coalition of different sects, first against high church Anglicans and then against the advocates of Presbyterian forms of ecclesiastical liturgy and hierarchy. The leading New England Puritans, by contrast, sought to establish conformity to their own official forms in the relatively autonomous isolation of their colonial outpost. As Michael Winship has noted, by releasing the Puritan believers from the tightening control of an increasingly hostile Anglican hierarchy and by empowering a ministerial and magisterial elite who could determine and enforce orthodoxy in ways not available to them in England, colonial circumstances made the potential for a "clash between destabilizing radical heterodoxy and destabilizing radical orthodoxy" particularly severe. This clash occurred in 1637–38, in what became known as the Antinomian Controversy. Even if, as revisionist accounts suggest, the crisis ended in compromise rather than a victory for the enforcers, a strong emphasis on unity and (at least outward) harmony ensued.[5] The resulting banishment of Anne Hutchinson, John Wheelwright, and their followers demonstrated that severe punishment could be faced by those who refused to compromise with the leading clergy and the General Court, or who (like Hutchinson) were willing to claim an "immediate revelation" from God that crossed the will of the male elders and defied the prophetic ministry of the clergy.[6] That overt, subversive forms of antinomianism continued to be suppressed in the Bay Colony is instanced in the expulsion and eventual executions of Quaker missionaries in the 1650s. Roger Williams, one of the early New England dissidents who spoke in favor of toleration, was expelled from Massachusetts in 1635 for his extreme separatist views. During the subsequent two decades, Williams's protoleration stance was repeatedly dissected and rejected by Boston minister John Cotton in a treatise debate published in England.[7]

The fascinating fact remained, however, that despite this enforcement of at least outward conformity to the New England Way (which for most people consisted in compulsory attendance at their local Congregational church), early New England Puritanism was a religion focused on personal conversion: while it allowed that an "outward" or "federal" holiness could be passed from parent to child, such external good behavior and acceptance of God's covenant with the New England church as a whole could only be a mere starting point for the adult believer, who had to progress to a more personal and inward belief. Hartford minister Thomas Hooker, for instance, reminded his readers not to be satisfied with this "relative holinesse" because "there be many persons that enjoy federall holinesse, that shall not have glory."[8] New England ministers generally held as fundamental the requirement that spiritually regenerate adults must be able to examine their consciences and discern, to the best of their knowledge, the marks of salvation in themselves. Without being able thus to attest to some kind of conversion experience, whether long and gradual or short and sharp, no individual could be admitted to the inner covenanted group of members, at the core of every local church, who were qualified to receive communion. By 1640 it was established practice in New England churches that this conversion had to be attested through a relation of the experience, given by the candidate (usually orally) and approved by the minister and church members.[9]

As a result of this contrast between enforced conformity to the colonial church on the one hand, and awaited inspiration on the other, the position of a "federally holy" baptized churchgoer who was not yet able to take communion was ambiguous. As the century wore on and many of the children of communicant church members grew up and did not proceed as expected to this fullest form of adult membership, their ambiguous status presented an increasingly pressing difficulty, especially since ministers disagreed over whether or not such people could have their children baptized: Thomas Hooker probably spoke for many of the first generation ministers when he reluctantly but firmly asserted that they could not. His view was opposed, however, by Richard Mather, who outlived many of his fellow first generation ministers, and indeed by the posthumous voice of Thomas Shepard in a letter published by his son, Thomas Shepard, Jr.[10] In 1662 the Massachusetts synod, consisting largely of a second generation of New England ministers, began to enforce regulations designed to address the question of baptism for the children of non-communicant members of the federal covenant. These reforms, laid down in the 1662 *Propositions Concerning the Subject of Baptism and Consociation of Churches,* later became known as the "Halfway Covenant."[11] In order that the children of baptized but non-communicant members could be baptized themselves, a rite of "owning the covenant" was devised whereby the non-communicant members could formally affirm their intent to live under church discipline in the hope of receiving further light and grace. In the definition of the Roxbury church, it meant for an individual "personally, publickly and solemnly to avouch the Lord in an ecclesiasticall way to be their

God according to the Covenant of Grace, and to submit themselves to the power and government of Christ in his church." It involved formally assenting to a prescribed form of words, and conferred upon the candidate the status of patiently and obediently awaiting a conversion experience.[12] Although the Halfway Covenant met lay resistance in some quarters (including the Boston church), and some important leaders opposed it, including John Davenport of New Haven, Charles Chauncy, President of Harvard, and (initially) Increase Mather, by 1680 most of the Massachusetts churches had implemented the Halfway Covenant, spurred on in many cases by the external pressure of King Philip's War (1675–76). Indeed, many churches continued to liberalize their baptismal policy further than its terms required, and by the late seventeenth century, the extension of baptism was no longer the major focus of ecclesiological controversy.[13]

What increasingly took its place was debate about what demonstrated visible sainthood in adults and thereby entitled them to communion, and whether the New England church covenants, and the membership procedures designed to protect them, had Scriptural validity. The Halfway Covenant did not solve the problem of growing numbers of adult churchgoers who were non-communicant: although it was intended as a step towards communicant membership, and some used it as such, others owned the covenant and then proceeded no further. Many did not even progress so far. In the aftermath of King Philip's War, in addition to individuals "owning the covenant," mass "covenant renewals" also became popular and were incorporated into official fast days. A covenant renewal ceremony consisted of solemn vows taken collectively by congregations "to enforce them unto an outward Reformation."[14] They were championed by Increase Mather and officially recommended by the Reforming synod of 1679. Through the rest of the century many preachers used mass covenant renewals as a focus for a period of revival preaching. As the careful phrasing "outward Reformation" suggests, covenant renewals weren't seen by most ministers as "engines of conversion" (to quote Harry Stout) but rather as "recruiting devices" to draw local inhabitants into church participation.[15] Although covenant renewals were not integral to the Halfway covenant, they were clearly related, and confirmed participants in a spiritually comparable status to that of individuals who had personally "owned the covenant," that is, as outwardly conforming but not yet inwardly converted. One telling difference, between the earlier rite and the mass rite that developed out of it, was that covenant renewals increasingly tended to involve townspeople who had no church connection, and thus became more civic and less voluntaristic.[16]

So with increasing numbers of people associated with the church and pledging their commitment and outward conformity to its religious teaching, did it still make sense to regard such members as unconverted and exclude them from communion? What status of membership did these pre-scripted and therefore rather "liturgical" pledges confer upon the participants? In 1691 Increase Mather negotiated and signed *The Heads of Agreement* with English Presbyterian and Congregationalist leaders, a document marking the rapprochement that had been taking place between Congregationalists and Presbyterians since the Restoration of Charles II. It included a broad definition of what qualified people for church membership: such people live nonscandalous lives, have sound knowledge of doctrine, and "to a Judgment regulated by the Word of God, are persons of visible Godliness and Honesty; credibly professing cordial subjection to Jesus Christ."[17] While Increase Mather remained completely committed to the requirement of conversion relations in New England churches, he was at least prepared to create an alliance with Presbyterians who required prospective members to recite a pre-scripted profession of faith. Twelve years earlier, at the Reforming synod, there had been a debate about the wording of a similar definition: the synod determined that it was "requisite that persons be not admitted unto Communion in the Lords Supper without making a personal and publick profession of their Faith and Repentance, either orally, or in some other way, so as shall be to the just satisfaction of the church." While this statement seems relatively clear in its endorsement of the established practice of requiring conversion relations, in 1709 Solomon Stoddard was able to support his own counterarguments by revealing that the synod had in fact chosen this wording over Increase Mather's more explicit proposal, "that persons should make a Relation of the work of Gods Spirit upon their hearts."[18]

From about 1677 Stoddard had begun to argue for what could be described as a more Presbyterian approach to church membership in New England, including the replacement of voluntaristic conversion relations with scripted professions of faith. By 1690 he had begun to institute a more open policy towards communion in his Northampton church.[19] By the start of the eighteenth century, Stoddard was not alone in overtly dropping the requirement of the conversion relation. In 1699 the newly formed Brattle Street Church in Boston issued a manifesto that included making conversion relations an optional part of the membership procedure. In *The Doctrine of Instituted Churches* (1700), Stoddard radically proposed the abandonment of the New England church covenants, which he considered theologically unsound, in favor of a hierarchical and parochial church polity. In subsequent publications, Stoddard also argued that communion should be more open because it helped bring about conversion.

Increase Mather and many of his colleagues (including Edward Taylor) were forthright in their initial response: they claimed that the church covenant, with its "fenced" communion table, and the conversion relation that had been the main means of protecting it, were fundamental to the New England Way.[20] But the formation of the Brattle Street Church marked a growing dissatisfaction with the older model. By the time John Leverett became President of Harvard in 1707 and the Connecticut churches had produced their own *Saybrook Platform* in 1710, Increase Mather's views, his passionate commitment to the conversion relation and to the closed communion table, had lost their authority. Many churches gradually liberalized their admissions procedures, and "Anglicized" by adopting a more inclusive parochial model. At Benjamin Colman's Brattle Street Church this Anglicization included reintroducing the recitation of the Lord's prayer, which was once a symbol of the ritualistic liturgy rejected by New England Puritans. Some churches, like that of Timothy Edwards (Jonathan's father) in Windsor, Connecticut, retained the conversion relation requirement, but had to accept the changes in neighboring churches.[21] The issue subsided, only to return with divisive vigor during the Great Awakening, when Jonathan Edwards announced in 1748 that he would no longer give communion to those who could not testify to an experience of conversion.

Through all these debates about church membership, questions of forms and conformity were constantly at issue. How could one demonstrate visible sainthood, that is, a state of conversion that went beyond mere conformity to local religious practice and thereby qualified someone for communion? Conversion, as a spiritual event, was largely defined against outward conformity, which was a human willed act. This crucial difference in quality was reflected in the form of language most commonly used in seventeenth-century Massachusetts churches to attest to conversion, that is, an unscripted, semi-spontaneous form of expression. From 1662, the Halfway Covenant created an official position for those who had not progressed this far, but the prescribed wording of the rite of owning the covenant signaled its relative inadequacy as a spiritual position, in the framework of Massachusetts Congregationalism, as established before a more Stoddardean or Anglicized ecclesiology took hold. Outward conformity of language and behavior was enforced as a *sine qua non* by the churches, but it was also simultaneously the foil against which the same churches ultimately defined true, spiritual faith and salvation. In this chapter, I will provide a more detailed examination of some of the key attitudes to language within Massachusetts ecclesiology and church practice, particularly those that seem to form the basis of later developments, namely, the attitude towards written liturgy, and the language of the ordinances, particularly the sermon.

POETRY AND THE REJECTION OF LITURGICAL SET FORMS

As Walter Ong has pointed out about the plain style, the linguistic ideal for the Puritan preacher or writer often found its closest analogy in visual terms, such as plainness or perspicuity.[22] In Massachusetts churches, formal or scripted language was ascribed an objectionable kind of materiality, which contrasted with the more fluid and transient qualities of approved language. Such a paradigm had significant implicit consequences for poetry, which was a scripted text whose formality was self-evident, self-conscious, and particularly insistent. In his strident defense of the New England poet's theological and ecclesiastical mandate for creative composition, Raymond Craig has cited John Cotton, the influential first-generation minister of the Boston church, as allowing that "any private Christian, who hath a gift to frame a spirituall Song, may both frame it, and sing it privately, for his own private comfort."[23] In his treatise *Singing of Psalmes, a Gospel Ordinance* (London, 1647) Cotton argued that the Psalms were "a kind of holy Poetry" and that therefore literary skill was necessary to translate them into verse. Since not all ministers had that skill, and since God ordained the Psalms for congregational singing, a standardized translation was necessary, he argued. However, Cotton's granting of permission to private individuals to exercise their own poetic skill at home was in the wider context of a ban on all such language in church: as a divinely ordained "set form," the metrical Psalter was presented by Cotton to be an unique exception. Indeed, when reflecting on the use of prescribed forms of prayer or meditation, even in private, Cotton leaned in the opposite direction.

In his reply to a Presbyterian argument in favor of liturgy, Cotton allowed that someone may "compile to himselfe a set forme of Prayer, and may use the same for his Prayer," but Cotton's sense of the dangers of set forms made him extremely wary even of this. An individual using such a prayer should not "limit himselfe to those words," he warned, "seeing he knoweth not what farther occasion may be given him of inlarging his Petitions." For Cotton, the danger was that such

a prayer would "turne into a customarie, and empty forme." Later
on, he gave the example of someone discovering a skull by "God's
Providence" and being spontaneously put in mind of his mortality, as
opposed to someone who kept a skull beside him as a meditative aid.
Such fixed, material aids, according to Cotton, were like set prayers,
and would "instead of a crutch" "prove a cudgell to break the bones
of the spirit in prayer."[24] Cotton's suspicion of set forms as spiritually
dangerous for their readers was not therefore wholly containable
within the context of church order. Though his ecclesiological objection was carefully based on the Puritan principle that all things in
church worship "ought evidently to be prescribed by the word, or
else ought not to be done," it nevertheless had wider literary implications.[25]

One of the practical implications of the rejection of liturgy by New
England churches was the loss of the Book of Common Prayer as a
poetic resource and resort. The option of poetic elaboration on the
words and form of the Anglican liturgy was not open to the New England poet. This not only ruled out explicitly liturgically based designs, as in Donne's "A Litanie," which follows the structure of the
prayer-book litany, but also limited the allusive use of liturgical cadences, which had formed a strong tradition within English devotional verse by the mid-seventeenth century.[26] Tracing the origins of
the self-consciously liturgical style and presentation of George Herbert's *The Temple* (1633) and the subsequent tributes and imitations it
inspired, Ramie Targoff has shown that by the early seventeenth century the association between poetry and liturgy, which had temporar-
ily loosened when the prayer book was translated out of Latin verse
into English prose, had returned stronger than ever. There was now
a new emphasis on the role of eloquent vernacular prayers as a
"means . . . of quickening & stirring up of the spirit of him that pray-
eth." Correspondingly, poets and clerics began to lament the poor
poetic quality of the Anglican Psalter, seeing its verse through new
eyes as not simply a mnemonic aid or a pious tradition but a potential
literary means of stirring the believers' affections.[27]

Donne noted potential objections to a private layman's taking
"such divine and publique names, to his own little thoughts" in composing his "A Litanie," but his adaptation of liturgical and hymn
forms in this and other religious poems highlights the fairly close relationship he perceived between ecclesiastic and poetic forms.[28] Similarly, Thomas Nashe's "Adieu, farewell earths bliss," in *Summers Last
Will and Testament* (1600) uses prayer-book cadences in a song about
death and mortality. As a critic of sectarian preachers and of the Puri-

tan influence at Cambridge University, and probable author of at least one anti-Marprelate tract, Nashe's adaptation of liturgy into a poetic song within a play was fully in line with his religious politics.[29] The final line of each stanza of his "Litany" echoes the *Kyrie* in a repetitive format alluding to that of the prayer-book Litany, providing a note that could gently join earthly despair to a hint of theological hope:

> Beauty is but a flower
> Which wrinkles will devour;
> Brightness fall from the air,
> Queens have died young and fair,
> Dust hath closed Helen's eye.
> I am sick, I must die,
>   Lord, have mercy on us![30]

At the end of each stanza, hope enters the poem through this understated liturgical allusion that turns a lament into a prayer. The "absolute preference for formalized over spontaneous voice" that, according to Targoff, characterizes religious verse inspired by the prayer book, may not have found its culmination until *The Temple*, but Nashe's and Donne's lyrics and the Sidney-Pembroke Psalter demonstrate that the crossover between liturgy and poetry was well established by the time New England was founded.[31] The prayer book provided a model for combining poetic and religious instincts, and for embodying this combination in incantatory, formalized, and repetitive language. As P. G. Stanwood has argued, "*liturgy* should inevitably suggest shape, form, repetition, order, the regulation of private feelings into normalized, public expression."[32] The rejection of the Book of Common Prayer in New England therefore entailed not only the loss of the specific text and forms of prayer, but also the loss of a key model for the religious use of scripted and ritualized forms of language.

As John Cotton's enumeration of the dangers of the "empty form" and of scripted words that "limit" the Holy Spirit suggests, his rejection of the prayer book was not simply a quibble on its content but a rebuttal of the whole idea. In this his response was broadly representative of Congregationalist as opposed to Presbyterian attacks on the prayer book. Though the Antinomian Controversy highlighted some of the differences between Cotton's teaching and that of his New England colleagues (some of which will be considered in the next chapter), there was unity on the matter of liturgy. Thomas Shepard

complained that the prayer book had "stunk above ground twice 40
yeeres, in the nostrills of many godly, who breathed in the pure ayre
of the holy Scriptures," and Harvard-trained Samuel Mather also
published a treatise against it, while he was working in Dublin at the
time of the Restoration.[33] Echoing Cotton's "Tennisse Plaie" to condemn the liturgical practice of antiphon, Mather ridiculed the "ab-
surd broken responds, and shreds of Prayer," "whereby they toss
their Prayers, like Tennis balls between the Priest and People."[34] Alluding to the litany, Mather condemned its "Tautologies—*O Lord deliver us,* eight times; *We beseech thee to hear us good Lord,* twenty times;
etc. etc."[35] In contrast, it became Cotton Mather's boast that "New-
England can show, even young ministers, who never did in all things
repeat *one prayer* twice over."[36]

If liturgical antiphon and repetition were portrayed as a meaning-
less horizontal "play" of words, making no connection with the divine, then this went hand in hand with the perception that the words
involved were too artifact-like, almost objects in themselves, vain
"toyes," instead of communicating signs. The fact that so many English people showed great loyalty to the Book of Common Prayer in
the suppressions of the 1640s would only have confirmed to its theological opponents, that it was indeed "abused to idolatry," and that
it distracted attention from the divine focus of prayer.[37] The English
Bishop Richard Hooker had feared, however, that the alternative to
liturgical prayer would be "endless and senseless effusions of indi-
gested Prayers."[38] Though a rare example of an extemporary prayer
remembered and written down by Increase Mather suggests that the
university-trained ministers of New England maintained a certain decorum of speech, Bishop Hooker's image of "effusion" was significant.[39]

Whereas fixed liturgical forms objectified language and limited
spontaneous variation, true prayer, as defined by Cotton, was "a lifting up (or pouring out) of the desires of the heart unto God." The
gerunds "lifting" and "pouring" convey Cotton's sense of the dynamic and rather formless spiritual core of prayer: its verbal nature is
significantly obscured by the metaphorical emphasis on movement
and flow.[40] Edward Taylor used the same language, a generation later,
in his poem "The Experience," to describe how his prayer was
"Pour'de out to God over last Sacrament":

> Oh! that I always breath'd in Such an aire,
>   As I Suckt in, feeding on Sweet Content!
> Disht up unto my soul ev'n in that pray're

Pour'de out to God over last Sacrament.
What Beam of Light wrapt up my sight to finde
Me nearer God than ere Came in my minde?

Most Strange it was! But yet more strange that shine
    Which filld my soul then to the brim to spy
My Nature with thy Nature all Divine
    Together joynd in Him that's Thou, and I.
    Flesh of my Flesh, Bone of my Bone. There's run
    Thy Godhead, and my Manhood in thy Son.[41]

What in the official Anglican service was a formally scripted prayer of consecration was for Cotton and Taylor a spontaneously composed prayer of thanksgiving that created an openness to God's communication which could result in such unexpected moments of soul-filling refreshment. Though always offered at the same point in the service, one of the prayer's key features was that it did not congeal into any particular fixed language. Even in the fixed form of Taylor's poem, the special moment of spiritual communion that accompanied this particular instance of prayer (the "experience" of the title) is conveyed indirectly, and as an experience that is recollected, not reenacted in the words of the poem.

Poetry in an Antiliturgical Context: Ballad Meters

As a fixed piece of language, a religious poem could not evade all similarity to the set forms that Cotton and his colleagues so vehemently rejected. New England religious poems were liturgical, like many of their English counterparts, insofar as they were carefully crafted and presented as a means to encourage spiritual development in the reader. But there were stylistic ways of demonstrating awareness of the danger, and of strongly promoting the impression that the poem and its verbal elegance were not ends in themselves. Although a large proportion of published New England poems were written by well-educated ministers, their Puritan values led them to choose the most accessible forms, so early New England verse was dominated by the simple meters of rhyming pentameter couplets and common ballad quatrains. While being popularly accessible, these forms were also unostentatious as poetry and implicitly made few artistic claims. Taylor's private use of slightly more complex stanza forms stands out as unusual in this context, but it's worth noting that Taylor also used ballad meter for his metrical versions of Job, fragments of which only found their way into the volume he labeled his "Poetical Works" by being used as stuffing for the binding. Taylor used the rest of his complete metrical Job in the bindings of two other hand-made books, his "Dispensatory" and his "Christographia" sermons, the latter's binding also containing some metrical Psalm versions.[42] That Taylor considered such popular forms potentially more transparent is implied by his use of them for Biblical translation. But by the same token, Taylor apparently did not regard these metrical translations as part of his "poetical works," nor considered them so worthy of preservation as his other verses. If plainness in poetry and sermon style aimed at a kind of stylistic invisibility that ran the least possible risk of drawing the reader's attention idolatrously to the manner rather than the matter, then the commonplace verse forms of couplets and ballad meters seemed best able to provide this.

Such meters have the added value of being potentially endless, and therefore better able to give the impression of spiritual flow and "effusion" than other more sophisticated forms. While New England poems were of course, in a sense, set or fixed forms of language, the impression of "limitation" could be minimized. Thus, although *The Day of Doom* was written about the cataclysmic culmination of time in the Second Coming, its lolloping ballad stanza conveyed better an impression of time's flow than of its finitude. In the first stanza this flow helps represent the illusion of the endlessness of the temporal world, but in "A Short Discourse on Eternity," appended to *The Day of Doom*, the ballad form is used to suggest eternity. The verse form's potential for indefinite extension reinforced the metaphors of multiplication and projection, as in Stanza 21 on the fate of damned souls:

> To lye in wo, and undergo
>   the direful pains of Hell,
> And know withall, that there they shall
>   for aye, and ever dwell;
> and that they are from rest as far
>   when fifty thousand year,
> Twice told, are spent in punishment,
>   as when they first came there.[43]

Significantly, too, images of time and multiplication are confessed as inadequate representations of eternity within the same poem, "A Cockle-shell may serve as well / to lade the Ocean dry, / As finite things and Reckonings / to bound Eternity."[44] In this way, even the

potentially endless form of the poem was undermined as a still too
limited suggestion of the spiritual concept of eternity.

The final poem appended to *The Day of Doom* takes a slightly different approach to meet similar ends. Entitled "A Song of Emptiness, to
fill up the Empty Pages following," and subtitled "Vanity of Vanities,"
it highlights the self-conscious materiality of its own text by claiming
to be determined by the size of the book. At the same time, the title
also hollows out the text, suggesting that the poem "fills" the pages
only with a verbal kind of vacuity, thereby deliberately underlining
the song's participation in a vain, fallen world and a fallen language.
According to the words of the poem, the human ability to imagine
infinity is connected to our spiritual cravings, which are never sated
by the worldly stuff we use to feed them:

> All Earthly things, man's Cravings answer not,
> Whose little heart would all the World contain,
> (If all the World should fall to one man's Lot)
> And notwithstanding empty still remain.[45]

In these ballad meter poems, the limitations inherent in the verses,
even the suggestion of their ultimate worthlessness, are fore-
grounded. Wigglesworth's argument benefits from the verse form's
potential reiterative endlessness, which enables it to serve as a foil for
eternal truth, and from the nonostentatious, relatively self-effacing
quality of ballad meter: to the extent that the verse risks idolatrously
distracting the reader from its message to itself, Wigglesworth explicitly makes this part of his point, reminding "Vain Man" in his "Song
of Emptiness" that "Thy best enjoyments are but Trash and Toyes."[46]

A very different effect was created by George Herbert in his shape
poems, like "Easter Wings," and "The Altar."[47] In these works, the
visually emphatic "set forms" of the verses illustrated in their design
a fundamental unity of word, symbol, and meaning, as a counterbal-
ance to the divisive polemic between Puritans and ritualists in the
early seventeenth-century British church. By portraying an altar and
at the same time describing his heart, Herbert affirmed a middle way:
that the Holy Spirit could reconcile and focus inward meaning
through the use of external ritual objects, and indeed through very
artifact-like poetic forms: "A broken ALTAR, Lord, thy servant
rears, / Made of a heart, and cemented with tears." In "Easter Wings
(1)," Herbert uses the shape of angelic wings to convey the results of
Man's Fall, the Resurrection of Christ, and the hope of human redemption:

           Lord, who createdst man in wealth and store,
               Though foolishly he lost the same,
                 Decaying more and more,
                     Till he became
                       Most poor:
                        With thee
                       O let me rise
                   As larks, harmoniously,
               And sing this day thy victories:
           Then shall the fall further the flight in me.

Herbert's shape poems offer finite and carefully self-reflexive forms as worshipful aids, not distractions, but it is a style that implicitly approves carefully crafted, liturgical as opposed to spontaneous or effusive prayer. As such it is not a style that early New England theology and church practice would have encouraged colonial poets to emulate.

ANAGRAM ELEGIES AND THE QUESTION OF RITUAL

New England anagram poems probably provide the closest American Puritan analogy to Herbert's shape poems. American Puritan funeral elegies, of which anagram poems were mostly a subset, have been identified as bringing an unacknowledged compensatory ritualism back into the iconoclastic culture. Their use of conventional images and patterns, and their related tendency to compose a collective, communal "self" have led critics like Scheick and Hammond to present New England funeral elegies as fulfilling a broadly liturgical function. Hammond suggests that such elegies have "the special virtue of liturgy" in that they are able to provide "the comfort that comes from an expected message, the predictable rhythms of belief reconfirmed through language," and even "scripts for what one could become."[48] It is certainly true that the growth in popularity and production of elegies accompanied the increasing elaboration of funerary rites in New England during the seventeenth century. Ceremonies that were initially brief, civil, and austere developed to involve religious processions, souvenirs, funeral sermons, and printed elegies.[49] But funeral elegies, though undeniably formulaic, are also clearly distinct from church liturgy in their individual reformulations of the conventional models for each occasion. The use of puns and anagrams reinforces this personalized aspect: there are elegies on Samuel Hooker, John Cotton, and Samuel Stone, for instance, which meditate on the usefulness of the objects embedded within their names: "Shall angling cease? & no more fish be took / That thou callst home thy Hooker with his Hook?" asked Edward Taylor.[50] As with conversion relations it is easy to emphasize the formulaic aspect of elegies without recognizing their complementary stress on the continual need to reformulate the model using new words.

According to Larzer Ziff, the use of puns and anagrams in colonial Puritan elegies illustrated an underlying "folk belief in the animism of language," by suggesting that "the meaning of words . . . was not arbitrary but organically connected with the essence of the things signified by the word."[51] This interpretation is in line with Scheick's understanding of Puritan poetry as seeking to explore the hidden design imposed by God upon His creation, but it underplays the awareness Scheick highlights of the fallenness of language and its potential to betray—a potential that I argue was particularly associated with formally fixed language.[52] Hammond's view that funereal wordplay was part of the "rage for order" and the "Puritan determination to apply wit to the regulating of emotion" underlines the importance of process in the elegies. Although in Hammond's terms this process meant that elegies performed a liturgical, ritualistic function that he goes so far as to compare with the Catholic Mass, he also highlights the way in which a clear functionality prevents the iconization of the verbal forms themselves: "despite their militant logocentrism, Puritans saw language as a temporary expedient," so each elegy, rather than proclaiming itself a static verbal monument, "dissolved as an artifact in its own redemptive use."[53]

Similar qualities could of course be ascribed to liturgy but not as Puritans envisaged it, which makes the stylistic ways in which their elegies were designed to avoid some of the ostensible pitfalls of ecclesiastical set forms particularly significant. In *The Temple*, Herbert exploited the materiality of printed language as providing a locus for verbal and spiritual harmony, analogous to that offered by the prayer book, but a similar potential was left unfulfilled in Puritan anagram elegies. For example, many New England anagram elegies involved more than the usual latitude in the spelling of the name of the deceased, such as "O honie knott" for John Cotton, "lo, now I am past ill" for William Tompson, and "o i am blest on top" for Elisabeth Tompson.[54] The sense of strain, albeit fairly slight, brings in a dissonant note and a reminder of the fallibility as much as the animistic power of human language. Puritan authors were aware of the strain and misspelling, and were even willing to joke about it. In an elegy on John Wilson, a renowned anagrammatist himself, he is welcomed into heaven by angels speaking "his anagram," which is "I Pray Come in, Heartily Welcome; Sir."[55] This "anagram," though affectionately reflecting his virtue of hospitality, comically bears little relation to Wilson's name and is far too long.

Contrary to Scheick's assessment, anagrams were frequently used in popular funeral poetry in both Old and New England, but, judging by the sample of broadside elegies in Draper's *Century*, there were some interesting differences in their usage that bear on the issue of liturgical poetics.[56] In Draper's collection, anagrams are most commonly found in epigrammatic couplets that accompany separate elegies, in a similar format to Herbert's "Mary/Army" couplet: "How well her name an *Army* doth present, / In whom the *Lord of hosts* did pitch his tent."[57] In New England, by contrast, anagrams were more commonly used as the starting point of a whole elegy. In John Wilson's elegy "most holy paule mine" (on William Tompson), for example, the anagram provides the first four words that set off a twenty-quatrain elegy: "Most holy paule, mine answer was, / In my temptacions all, / When as the deuill tempted me, / As much or more then paul."[58] In John Fiske's elegies "o, honie knott" and "in fanne: rig," the text weaves around these images, relating them in numerous different ways to the subjects, John Cotton and Ann Griffin. Rather than providing the tidy summation of a neat couplet, the anagram in both New England models operated as a verbal/visual spark for a poetic unraveling of meaning that was less finished and artifact-like than a couplet epigram, and more akin instead to the kind of spontaneous, evolving meditation that John Cotton recommended. Fiske's elegy on Ann Griffin has two false endings, as if he went back to the subject again to pick up where he left off. Fiske's central images are a threshing fan and a ship rigged and prepared to sail, and he comes to an apparent moral conclusion:

> When once Afflictions doe thee seaze, thinke then
> Death will ere long approach, to thy long home
> Thee hence to fetch: to Rest prepar'd who ben
> Who Tyrant-like to unprepared come.
> J. F.[59]

But after signing off here, Fiske returns and picks up the theme again for two new stanzas, signaling his awareness of the false conclusion with an apparently spontaneous, "But more" to introduce stanzas, which then rephrase the same message:

But more, in Fanne of tryalls seest a saint
Yea one whose aged yeers the Deeps might know
Think't time for us to Rig, for us acquaint
Will God with Tryalls such, And lay us Low

Yea lay us Low, and humble us Hee will
Or first or Last ere that he us will rayse
And follow us with waves and billowes still
Ere that for aye him we in Glory prayse.
                                                    J. F.[60]

After these two stanzas Fiske signed off again, and then added one more concluding stanza. That Fiske's elegy is preserved in manuscript rather than print is obviously an important determining factor, but it would have been quite possible for him to preserve his poem in a more smoothly finished version. Instead, his form and language has an unpredictable, unrevised, oral flavor, and avoids seeming conclusive, fixed, or "finished." Nathaniel Ward could have been discussing such elegies when he joked that, "We have a strong weaknesse in N. E. that when wee are speaking, we know not how to conclude: wee make many ends, before we make an end: the fault is in the Climate."[61]

So, while New England poetry could not stave off all association with liturgy, and indeed even accrued certain ritualistic roles, the authors' stylistic choices suggest an awareness of the dangers outlined by the ministers in their opposition to set forms, and a desire to remind readers that the poem is not a linguistic resting point but a spur for further spiritual progress. Edward Taylor, whose opposition to liturgy contributed to his decision to emigrate in 1668, wrote in perhaps the most ritualized style of all New England poets, but his sense of the inadequacy of verbal expression seems to be sharpened rather than lessened in his poetic writing. In his poem series, *Gods Determinations* (as I discuss in chapter 4), Taylor echoed some liturgical forms, despite expressing a contemptuous opposition to them in an early poem, "The Laymans Lamentation."[62] Yet by drawing on forms that were at that time exiled from his church, Taylor turned his verses into an effective foil for the form that he most wanted his poem series to inspire in the reader, namely, the conversion relation, by which his reader could formally and officially enter into church membership.

COLONIAL MIGRATION AND THE SACRIFICE OF LITURGY

A much earlier immigrant, Thomas Tillam, also evoked liturgical forms only to turn away from them, in his poem "Upon the First Sight of New-England / June 29, 1638." In addition to its interesting parodic use of liturgy, this poem illustrates the way in which antiliturgical teaching drew on a broader sense of how losing certain "helps" and "means" actually brought the believer closer to God. This idea, when applied to language, had important implications for New England verse. Tillam's poem evokes with pathos the sense of sacrifice experienced by migrants who left behind "Country, dearest friends, and goods" in pursuit of ecclesiastical purity, and yet his verses incorporate into this cultural, social, and economic sacrifice the loss of a formal or liturgical comfort. The recasting of the *Ave Maria* in his opening lines may reflect Tillam's Roman Catholic background. His threefold repetition "holy" in the first couplet is reminiscent of the *Sanctus:*

> Hayle holy-land wherin our holy lord
> Hath planted his most true and holy word
> Hayle happye people who have dispossest
> Your selves of friends, and meanes, to find some rest
> For your poore wearied soules . . .

Needless to say, Tillam's kind of "rest" was to be found in the enjoyment of "ordinances in their puritye," which would patently not include any of the old liturgical forms. The remainder of his poem left these liturgical allusions behind entirely.[63]

Tillam's immediate association of the settlers with people who have "dispossest" themselves, and his coupling of "dispossest" and "rest," implied a definition of purity that involved the stripping away of such false "friends, and meanes" as New England ministers identified in the liturgical practices of the Church of England. While to its defenders liturgy was a useful "meanes," to Cotton it was a "crutch" and a "help" that was idolatrously relied upon instead of "such affections . . . but also such matter and words as [God's] spirit helpeth us unto."[64] This discourse of rejecting established religious practices because instead of "helping" they in fact hindered the achievement of salvation and true piety was a key thread in Reformation and Dissenting polemic. It was applied to many areas beyond liturgy, including the Medieval exegetical tradition of *allegoria*, and, as Mason I. Lowance has shown, the discourse produced many ironies, since interpretive strategies rejected as idolatrous (e.g., *allegoria*) often resurfaced in another guise (e.g., typological readings of New England history).[65] Yet it is significant that in rejecting these exegetical practices and the Old Testament and Roman Catholic ceremonies with which he grouped them, William Ames (like John Cotton later) recognized their original role as aids to faith: they "taught our mynds and so helped and stirred our hearts to grace or duty."[66] Thus, the loss of such "helps" for a greater and more purely spiritual obedience was portrayed as a kind of necessary sacrifice, a rejection of lesser means of assistance in the expectation of better, more numinous ones. Tillam's poem resonates with the language of such a sacrificial loss: a dispossession experienced in the pursuit of a more spiritual and organic religious faith. The need to abandon forms that could give a false kind of security or rest, coupled with the hope of finding spiritual growth and empowerment through that loss, was later summed up by the British dissenting minister, John Owen, who compared the situation of believers relying on liturgical "helps" to swimmers who would "never enter the water but with flags or bladders under them" and therefore would "scarce ever learn to swim."[67]

As Tillam's poem progressed, the "rest" he was hailing became increasingly qualified: the immigrants had been "opprest of late . . . with Envye, spight, and hate," their reward was one which they would "receve in heaven" rather than now, and having "hazarded [their] lives o'th raginge floods" to come to a place that was allegedly "free from all anoye," they were warned that Satan was lurking "Cunningly" among them, waiting to catch them with his "wylye baites." Finally, the place to which they had come for "rest" was, at the same time, one in which they were commanded by Christ to "live not then secure." This dispossessing kind of rest involved not resting in the kinds of false and spiritually "empty" helps that liturgy offered, but also not resting in outward forms in general, that is, in mere conformity. When Thomas Hooker complained about the supposedly Reformed Dutch congregations he had lived among before emigrating to New England, his comment reflected the way in which antiliturgical teaching associated the "forms" of the liturgy with deceptive outward conformity, concealing an absence of inner spiritual depth, and even of salvation: "For the better part [with respect to] heart religion they content themselves with very forms though much blemished; but the power of godliness, for aught I can see or hear, they know not."[68] The liturgical forms were not portrayed as a "help" that language could offer in bridging the gap between outward conformity and inner faith, but rather as an empty cover.

This language of a complacent "resting" in "forms" and conformity, instead of seeking to go beyond the limited level associated with them, recurred in early New England teaching on church ordinances. Once the immediate suffering of migration was over and colonists' material lives grew easier, ministers were faced with the task of trying to keep their flocks from religious complacency.[69] Even though the New England Congregational churches were stripped of prayer-book liturgy, the ordained forms they did have were described in such a way as to clarify that they were never ends in themselves. The singing of metrical psalms, the prayers and preaching of the minister, were all construed as means that were obligatory but still insufficient. John Cotton urged his hearers to "feele after [God], grope after him . . . labour to finde him in his Ordinances," rather than to "rest in any good means of grace wee do enjoy."[70] Thomas Shepard commented that some people (and judging by the anxiety expressed in his diary he was probably including himself) found their spiritual desires increased rather than satisfied by living under purified ordinances in New England.[71] The ordinances of the church were supposed to inspire people to quest spiritually beyond the level of "outward forms." This was the way in which the dual emphases on conversion and conformity were held in tension in the seventeenth-century New England churches, and suggests one way in which poetry may have found a valid role as a formalized foil.

Ordinances, including psalm-singing, were all compulsory for non–church members as well as members. This raised the obvious question of hypocritical conformity—a question that was settled in the early years of the colony by John Cotton's rebuttal of Roger Williams's arguments for a radical separation of church and state: Williams was hauled before the governor in 1635 for having "taught publicly that a magistrate ought not to tender an oath to an unregenerate man, for that we thereby have communion with a wicked man in the worship of God, and cause him to take the name of God in vain."[72] Williams's purist principles underlay his ensuing attacks on the religious intolerance of the civil authority in New England, and Cotton's response to them implied that he thought a certain conforming hypocrisy far better than out-and-out atheism. The unconverted who nonetheless "profess the truth of the doctrine and worship of Christ, they live a kind of spiritual life, though not such as accompanies salvation," Cotton argued, and "if the religion of the nation be good, it is not imprisonment" but instead offers spiritual protection to save even spiritually "dead" people from being "made worse by corrupt teachers."[73] Nevertheless, Cotton also directed many a sermon against the dangerous state of hypocritical or complacent conformity to Puritan religious practice. He acknowledged that obliging all people to sing psalms would force some into hypocrisy and "empty out-side-performances," but concluded that they would receive some blessing through their obedience, though not such as led to salvation.[74] Thus, the Bay Psalm Book, as the only communal liturgy of the New England churches, did not completely evade the danger of spiritual emptiness by being a pure and ordained form. Despite its inspired Biblical language, part of the Bay Psalm Book's explicit role as an ordinance was as an outward form, through which the singers were to "grope" (as if in darkness) for a more truly spiritual encounter with God. Its verse style, as I show in chapter 2, captured the ambiguity of the position: it evoked conformity and accessibility, but stopped short of the distraction of admirable elegance, and also of tightly controlling the reader/singer's affective response. As the only model of devotional verse ecclesiastically ordained by the New England clergy, the Bay Psalm Book occupied an influential position, particularly in the absence of all other liturgy.

THE INFLUENCE OF PLAIN-STYLE PREACHING

The increased element of didacticism in one major work influenced by the Bay Psalm Book is significant in suggesting a trend that was already incipient in the metrical Psalter, and which can also be attributed to the New England theology of ordinances. Wigglesworth's *The Day of Doom* succeeded the Bay Psalm Book as the best selling book in seventeenth-century New England. According to remarks by Edward Taylor and Cotton Mather, by the end of the century it was not uncommon for women and children to memorize and recite *The Day of Doom*, even though the poem was written in a sermonic style and not an expressive creed- or psalm-like style.[75] As the early ecclesiastical emphasis on establishing some kind of colonial Puritan orthodoxy suggests, didacticism was a major part of New England church experience from the start. This was all the more the case in the absence of communal liturgy. Apart from the psalms and the occasional vow or conversion relation, all the ordinances were administered through the minister's voice. In each service, the congregation would listen to a sermon of about two hours and then one hour of the minister's spontaneous prayers, to which they would add their assenting "Amen."[76] Even the psalm-singing would have sometimes been a didactic rather than expressive experience, because the style of the metrication tended to turn Hebraic parallelism into verse that gave the impression of catechistic rote-learning, as in the opening of Psalm 121, for example:

> I to the hills lift up mine eyes,
>   from whence shall come mine aid
> Mine help doth from Iehovah come,
>   which heav'n & earth hath made.

In such instances, the propositional meaning is apparent, but it is not phrased in a way that would organically and emotionally assist the singers to (as Augustine put it) "form [their] spirit by the affection of the Psalm"; the phrasing is flatly didactic, operating with catechistic discipline as a rote-learned question and answer.[77]

APPROPRIATION OF THE DIDACTIC VOICE IN RELIGIOUS VERSE

In the absence of liturgical set forms, it is easy to see how appropriation of the familiar didactic voice was more likely to become itself a valid form of expression. The seeds of this development are present in Tillam's 1638 poem. Tillam's initial couplet hailing the "holy land" was implicitly participatory and could have been spoken by all the immigrants. Yet it gave way immediately and for the rest of the poem, to a didactic address, "hayle holy people."[78] Thus, an apostrophe borrowed from communal prayer was adapted into a sermon: the individual voice took over from the collective voice, and, in the process, a monitory and didactic relationship between speaker and listeners was established.

Much of the poetry written in New England was written by ministers. The verse of Anne Bradstreet is an obvious exception, but the next most well known Massachusetts poets of their day were probably the ministers John Wilson and Michael Wigglesworth, both of whose poetic endeavors feature in Cotton Mather's memorials of them. Among Wilson's many funeral elegies are several in which he ventriloquized the voice of the deceased. In one of these, his elegy on Abigail Tompson, Wilson speaks in the voice of Mrs. Tompson who is announcing her own death to her husband. (William Tompson was away on a preaching trip to Virginia at the time his wife died.) Speaking of the joys of heaven which she was now experiencing, Wilson's Mrs. Tompson remembered her husband's sermons and reflected:

> Thou little thinkst, or Canst at all Conceiue,
> What is the bliss that i do now receiue.
> When oft i herd thee preach & pray & sing
> I thought that heauen was a glorious thing,

And i belieud, if any knew, twas thou
That knewest what a thing it was; but now
I se thou sawest but a glimps, and hast
No more of heauen but a little tast,
Compared with that which hear we see & haue,
Nor Canst haue more till thou are past the graue.
Thou neuer touldst me of the Tyth, nor yet
The hundred thousand thousand part of it.[79]

Hammond has argued that the "frank artifice" of the dead speaker enhanced the credibility in such poems as this, since the words of the dead and dying carried great weight in the community.[80] This suggests Puritan readers trained themselves simply to turn a blind eye to the artificiality of the mode, but in Wilson's poem the frankness of artifice is part of a broader theological point made in the poem about representing heavenly things. Wilson's elegy underlined the idea that there were levels of spiritual realization: the living Mrs. Tompson's, Mr. Tompson's, and the dead Mrs. Tompson's. It emphasized that the fullness of spiritual knowledge was beyond the scope of the sermon, and therefore even beyond the power of the poem to convey: "Thou little thinkst, or Canst at all Conceiue." By highlighting these levels, the poem appeared to turn the tables on the authority of the ministerial voice, but at the same time it fundamentally endorsed it, despite its limitations: if Abigail Tompson had been given only the description of someone else's taste or glimpse, she had nonetheless managed to find its fullness later. One rationale for encouraging such popular appropriation of a ministerial voice was that it was a verbal version of outward conformity, and therefore a useful starting point for a believer, since as Cotton argued, "God never calleth any unto fellowship with himself in a Covenant of Grace, but ordinarily he first bringeth them into a Covenant of Works."[81] That any earthly representation of the spiritual message would be relatively inadequate was, however, simply to be expected, this poem implied.

Wilson's Abigail Tompson says that her faith was shaped not by her own prayers or meditations, but by listening to her minister-husband in church. Since receiving teaching was evidently so central, and the ministerial voice so dominant in New England verse, the sermon was an influential ecclesiastical and rhetorical form, whose role and portrayal had an important bearing on poetic development. If the sermon replaced the liturgy, by and large, as the verbal crux of the service in all the early New England churches, it did so in a way that reinforced some of the stylistic preferences implied in the rejection of "set forms." These included, of course, a preference for didactic rather than liturgical or inductive kinds of communication; but also important were the potential variability of language as opposed to scripting, the ideal of an almost invisible style of communication, and, as hinted at in Wilson's elegy, the mystery of the different levels of spiritual understanding that a sermon could evoke in its listeners.

SERMON RHETORIC, ORALITY, AND DIVINE INSPIRATION

Most literary studies of New England sermons have focused (with good reason) on the rhetorical strategies, the structure, language, and imagery of the sermons. Some have also highlighted the different styles of the ministers. But, as Stout has pointed out, studying sermons as published texts results in some significant distortions: for instance, most sermons were not published, and among those that were, an unrepresentatively large proportion were election sermons and therefore more political than ordinary Sunday preaching. Another distorting factor is that the textual version of a sermon comes stripped of its church context, and yet it was the sermon's oral delivery by a minister preaching before his congregation that made a sermon a divine ordinance, and gave it its converting power.[82] The scholarly analysis of the rhetoric of printed sermons can therefore lead to an exaggeration of the intellectual humanism of Puritan preachers, at the expense of their more mystical sense of what they believed happened when someone preached successfully. For the New England ministers, the two dimensions were held in tension; as Hammond puts it, "Puritan [literary] art embodied the practical pursuit of what can only be called mystical ends."[83] It is undoubtedly true that Puritan sermon theory was strongly informed by traditional faculty psychology, so that "the Puritan sermon was designed to address, in order, the memory, the understanding, and finally, the will and affections."[84] Yet, as William Perkins implied in his brief outline of the ideal sermon structure, that final crucial connection to the will and the affections was not a purely mechanical step. According to Perkins, the preacher had to "apply (if he have the gift) the doctrines rightly collected, to the life and manners of men, in a simple and plaine speech."[85] The parenthesis, a qualificatory statement of dependence on some kind of divine assistance, was vital. Indeed, such qualifications recurred frequently in New England writing on sermons, and injected an element of unpredictability, a limit on human control that scholarship has largely ignored.

The published extracts of Michael Wigglesworth's college orations on eloquence, for example, have all excluded the section, just before the conclusion, in which Wigglesworth subordinated everything he had said in celebration of eloquence, to the sovereign power of God. While Wigglesworth did claim that "Eloquence overturn's, overturn's all things that stand in its way, & carrys them down with the irresistible stream of its all controuling power," he also denied that he was making "a goddess of Eloquence" or arguing that "any man can bestow such inlargement of faculty, as I spake of in the understanding, or stir up affection at his pleasure." "No, I know assuredly that an orator can effect nothing of all this by his owne power," Wigglesworth conceded.[86] At first glance, Wigglesworth's youthful confidence in the Holy Spirit's usually choosing to work through the efforts of skilled rhetoricians appears to justify the modern critic's not making too much of this concession. However, in later years Wigglesworth became the author of comparatively low-brow poetry which he sought to defend using the Pauline inversions of foolishness and wisdom, "If this my foolishness / Help thee to be more wise."[87]

This later development makes Wigglesworth's early awareness more important in retrospect: he explicitly recognized the potential conflict between a humanistic, mechanized view of rhetorical power, and the pietistic view of the preacher's complete dependence on God for the spiritual impact of his sermon. This recognition is also apparent from Wigglesworth's apologetic comment to his listeners after describing the amazing effects of the speeches of the classical orators: "you hear something about an orator speaking, but you do not now hear an orator speak, you do not now see an orator act, if you did you would feel the verity of what I affirm."[88] Wigglesworth knew that the secret of all-powerful rhetoric was not entirely available to him at this point in his life, and later on he turned even further away from his supposedly ideal models of oratory, to poetry, which was (compared to the sermon) a second-rate, nonordained verbal form. Thus, the Harvard classical education had its limits: rhetorical devices were, like the liturgy, human devices. Though they were, in the form of the sermon, ordained of God, they were also, like the Bay Psalm Book, not immune from the qualifications imposed by the pietistic view that set forms existed to be dynamically surpassed.

Hence, even in the sermon, the centerpiece of the weekly New England service, the role of language was at times highly ambiguous. Because of the dangers associated with set forms and a kind of language that had too much presence in itself, New England ministers promoted the value of the sermon in terms that minimized its textuality and fixity. As the common use of popular ballad meters suggests, New England poems were probably conceived of as a more oral genre than poetry today; nevertheless, they could not match up to the almost spontaneous orality of the New England sermon. Like the nonliturgical prayers, whose spontaneous flow was extolled by John Cotton and Cotton Mather, the sermons of New England ministers were supposedly rendered more open to the Holy Spirit by not being read from a script. Although ministers studied, prepared, and very possibly memorized them, their final wording was not definitively fixed until the moment of delivery.[89] Apart from being an obvious reaction against the use of the Book of Homilies to patch over the problem of uneducated clergy in the Anglican church, this New England church convention was based partly on the idea, voiced by John Cotton, that the Bible should be the only text present in the service, and also on the understanding of the church ordinances as live channels of grace. According to this latter point, the sermon's most spiritual power was in its divinely ordained ecclesiastical performance, compared to which its mere text was a dead letter.

The Dean of St. Paul's, John Donne, by contrast, had argued that by composing his sermons word for word in advance, he could deliver "God['s] messages, with consideration, with meditation, with preparation; and not barbarously, not suddenly, not occasionally, not extemporarily, which might derogate from the dignity of so great a service."[90] It is easy to see how the same attitude influenced his tightly written poems. However, for the majority of first-generation New England ministers and many later ones, there was more dignity and less quenching of the Spirit if less concern was shown for the exact verbal formulation of the sermon; and this distanced yet another possible model for the New England poet. That the ministers did not believe spiritual power intrinsic to the precise verbal arrangement of a sermon is illustrated in the common practice of allowing sermons to be written up from notes, either their own or those of a listener. Ideally the minister would then correct and authorize such an edition. Ministers' time was limited, and they generally chose to prioritize regular preaching above writing sermons out for publication.[91] Illustrating another phenomenon, Thomas Hooker never seems to have considered his sermons in final form. His life's work was a series about the stages of the regenerative process, the last version of which was entitled *The Application of Redemption*. According to Goodwin and Nye, Hooker's English editors, "[Hooker] *Preach'd* more briefly of this Subject *first*, whilst he was *Fellow* and Chatechist in *Emanuel Colledg* in *Cambridg*. . . . And then again, a *Second time*, many yeers after, more largely at *Great Chelmsford* in *Essex*, . . . And *Last* of all; now in *New-England.*"[92] Hooker wrote and rewrote his sermon treatise on this topic, and indeed left it unfinished when he died.

The influence of the ministers' emphasis on performative aspects of the sermon can be detected in the preoccupation with process (as opposed to completion) that critics, including Karl Keller, have identified in New England poetry. As Stout has pointed out, most Puritan colonists learned their theology in an oral/aural rather than literary context, which informed their ministers' sermon style: "what seems like endless repetition and tedious word splitting to modern readers was, to colonials, a necessary means of storing systematic doctrines in their memories." More than this, repetition, Biblical intertextuality, and collation in early New England sermons were designed to give the hearers a sense of "intimacy with the divine," in other words, to "open" Scripture more fully to the comprehension of the hearers. Such habits of form and sermon construction influenced Edward Taylor as he wrote his Meditations, and writers of anagram elegies like Wilson and Fiske.[93]

THE SERMON AS A DIVINE ORDINANCE

Yet the fact that a sermon was special because it was, precisely, a sermon, makes direct applications to poetry more problematic than has generally been acknowledged. Daniel Patterson, for example, has suggested that poetry could emulate the New England sermon by similarly depending on the text of the Bible, and Hammond has cited Jonathan Mitchel's implicit equation of the goals of poem and sermon as being "To set forth Truth and win men's Souls to bliss."[94] Yet, while true to some extent, this view of the ministerial poem as a kind of sermon is problematic insofar as the sermon was an ordinance and the poem was not, a fact of which Jonathan Mitchel and Michael Wigglesworth show themselves to be painfully aware in their apologetic prefatory verses to *The Day of Doom.* Whereas Donne's interest in fashioning elegant and meaningful combinations of words in his sermons was clearly analogous to his poetic style, the careful way in which New England preachers tended to obscure the verbal nature of their sermons seems designed precisely to imply that their most valuable potential was not contained within their rhetoric and therefore was not simply translatable to another literary context.

The intimate, unique, and divinely ordained interdependence of sermon and Bible is apparent, for example, in Thomas Hooker's domesticated elaboration on the image of the Scriptures as a sword, in Hebrews 4:12: "The Word is like the Ax, that must be lifted by a skilful and strong arm of a cunning Minister, who like a Spiritual Artificer must hew and square, and take off the knotty untowardness in the Soul before we can come to couch close and settle upon the Lord Christ as the Cornerstone."[95]

The preaching manuals of William Perkins and Richard Bernard, with their practical advice on constructing and delivering a sermon, presented the sermon as a kind of neutral tool. Their methodology, which could be equivalently applied to the task of "opening" any Bible text, paradoxically minimized the sermon as a rhetorical genre in itself.[96] Similarly, Stout has found a noticeable absence of the word "I" from manuscript sermon notes, which he judges to be "less a reflection of the minister's distance from his discourse than of his intent to create the impression that God himself was speaking."[97] The preacher's identity and his personal contribution to the construction of the verbal medium of the sermon were carefully minimized. Notably, Hooker's comment depicts the sermon not even as the tool, but as the action of the arm wielding the tool. Though a vivid image of its effectiveness, Hooker's picture completely obscures the fact of a sermon's wordiness. It underlines instead that the unique and spiritually ordained role of the sermon was to give the Bible a performative life. If the sermon was therefore "authority incarnate," it was so in the etymological sense, even more than the colloquial sense: the preacher, as God's modern-day prophet, was portrayed as almost literally giving his own "alive-ness" to the Scriptural text.[98]

Clearly, a poem could strive to imitate this kind of dynamic action, and poems, like sermons, cultivated Biblical intertextuality as a means of generating meaning and authority. Yet however dependent a poem was on the Biblical metatext, it was not the divinely ordained form for "opening" Scripture. Moreover, poetry's demand that the poet focus on the verbal detail of rhyme could not but reinforce its theologically secondary position in relation to the ordained and more verbally fluid sermon form. A printed poem also remained more of a textual than a personal encounter, and as Hooker's image of a live meeting suggested, a textual encounter was believed to be less spiritually powerful than hearing a sermon. Stout has reminded us that "recognition of high literacy rates" should not obscure the fact that the Puritan colonists occupied an "aural" world in which "most communications traveled by word of mouth in face-to-face social settings."[99] New England Puritans probably even "conceived of the

Bible more as oral performance than as written text," since "much,
if not most, Bible reading was done aloud—as befitted the texts that
were believed to represent God's *spoken* Word."[100] And, despite David
D. Hall's claim that "people in New England perceived speech and
writing as continuous and interchangeable," there does seem to have
been a hierarchy between aural and written forms in the context of
the sermon: "*faith comes* not by reading, but by *hearing*," remarked
John Cotton, elaborating on Romans 10:17.[101] The printed sermons
of New England ministers were widely read in the colony, and were
referred to in conversion relations as spiritually helpful, as Hall has
noted. Nevertheless, the face-to-face encounter was stressed as the
more spiritually powerful experience: "Mr. Mathers Ministry was like
daggers in my heart," declared John Ingerson of Westfield. Indeed,
in the six relations recorded by Edward Taylor in his "Church Records," there are references to hearing sermons by Richard and Increase Mather, Mr. Stone of Hartford, Mr. Eliot of Gilford, Mr.
Newton and Mr. Hooker of Farmington, and Mr. Wareham; but the
candidates only mention one book of sermons between them, "a
book of Mr. Jeremiah Burroughs."[102] According to Wigglesworth's
transcript, John Collins of Cambridge recalled in his conversion relation how the benefit of reading Thomas Hooker's sermons had been
completely overshadowed by a later experience of hearing him
preach. Collins described his reaction in terms that turned the public
context of listening to a sermon into a personal and intimate meeting: "I thought he certainly knew what a sinner I had been[,] what
covenants I had broke and seeing I had held the truth in unrighteous-
ness I thought I was as good as in hell already . . ."[103] Poetry could be
read aloud, and publicly, as was certainly the case with funeral elegies;
and manuscript poetry, like Taylor's, may have been able to capture
something of the feel of a live encounter, or at least to present a "halfway" experience. All the same, the issues of spontaneity and the inspired presence of the minister were as irresolvable for the poet as
the simple fact of writing verse instead of delivering a sermon.

The disappearing language of the sermon was linked particularly
to the sermon's special role as an ordinance, and as an agent of spiritual change when performed in the correct context. By de-emphasiz-
ing its precise wording, other and ostensibly more spiritual aspects
could be brought to the fore. However, sixteenth- and seventeenth-
century writers (never mind modern critics) realized that the idea of
an invisible kind of rhetoric was paradoxical: it implied stylistic features as well as a particular conceptual view of the sermon. William

Perkins' advice to ministers to conceal even their efforts at rhetoric suggests that the paradoxical "art" of preaching involved an almost sinister sleight of hand:

> *Humane wisdome* must be concealed, whether it be in the matter of the sermon, or in the setting forth of the words *1.Cor.2.1.* . . . because the hearers ought not to ascribe their faith to the gifts of men, but to the power of God's word. . . . the Minister may, yea and must privately use at his libertie the arts, Philosophy, and a variety of reading, whilest he is in framing his sermon: but he ought in publicke to conceale all these from the people, and not to make the least ostentation. *Artis etiam est celare artem.*[104]

Could Perkins possibly have been suggesting that the minister should deceive his flock into ascribing to the Holy Spirit feelings that his own human rhetoric had self-sufficiently aroused? Not exactly. Perkins himself believed that the hearers' faith was rightly ascribed "to the power of God's word," and it is for that reason that he advocated a style that was as self-effacing as possible.

SOME PARADOXES OF PLAIN-STYLE PREACHING

Perkins's Latin motto, "Artis est celare artem," was also quoted by Increase Mather in his biography of his father, and Scheick has argued for its influence on Puritan poetics, as inspiring the artistic concealment of elaborate emblematic designs in the poetry of Bradstreet and Taylor, which the reader is invited to uncover as a religious exercise. But this seems unlikely, since the motto, invariably applied to preaching, seems to prioritize the goals of transparency, accessibility, and condescension to the level of the listeners' understanding, rather than encouraging writers to seal a puzzlelike complexity into their texts. Increase Mather, for example, associated it with his father's gift of "making abstruse things plain." But of course, as Scheick's interpretation highlights, there was an implicit tension in the task ascribed to Puritan preachers of mediating complex divine mysteries through plain, everyday forms of speech.[105]

A glance at the different preaching styles of New England ministers, as reflected in their books of sermons, shows that Perkins's advice and the tradition of plain preaching resulted in no small variety of approaches. John Cotton had a relatively abstract, monosyllabic, verbally repetitive style; Thomas Hooker's was visual and vivid, full of imagery as in the "axe" example cited above. Though maintaining the tradition of praising the plain style, Cotton Mather wrote in a very convoluted and allusive way (Miller called it "hysterical"), and Edward Taylor, with an irrepressible relish for language, exhibited a highly metaphorical style in his sermons.[106] Indeed, though Miller singled out the plain style as a key part of New England's literary legacy, he acknowledged many apparent exceptions, such as treatises by Nathaniel Ward and Edward Johnson.[107] However, in terms of the weekly sermon, the plain style commonly manifested itself in a regularity and clarity of structure. The preacher moved steadily from defining the doctrine, to expounding the reasoning of it, and thence to its "uses" or "application" to the lives of the congregation. He used a direct tone of address, and presented the message in a generally accessible way. The variety of expression possible within this rubric made plainness more of a flexible conceptual ideal than a precise stylistic directive. In this context it is not surprising that New England religious verse was not all written in the very straightforward styles of the Bay Psalm Book and *The Day of Doom:* the "plainness" of Fiske's anagrams, Cotton Mather's Psalms, and Taylor's occasional verses, were of different kinds.

From another point of view, however, plainness as an ideal could be far more demanding than plainness as a mere combination of stylistic prescriptions. In denigrating any preaching that used "that pompous gaudiness, and elegancy of Speech, which after an unsuspected manner steals away the mind and affection from the truth and stayes it with it self," Thomas Hooker used the words "frothy tinkling."[108] Hooker's account is strongly reminiscent of Cotton on the temptations of liturgy. If it is stretching things too far to suggest that Wigglesworth's jaunty ballad meter could have been construed as "frothy" in some sense, it certainly is not hard to imagine his rhyme risking being viewed as "a jingling and a tinkling, nothing but a sound of words"; Cotton Mather implied as much when he criticized the "Clink" of rhyme, in the preface to his defiantly unrhymed metrical Psalter.[109] Similarly, John Cotton's onomatopoeic epithet for a nonplain style, "a blubber-lipt ministry," could be applied to the sound properties of certain of Taylor's lines.[110] As Emory Elliott has suggested, some of Taylor's language twists the tongue to such an extent that one wonders if he was trying to reinforce the reader's sense of spiritual weakness. "In Jasper Cask, when tapt, doth briskly vaper," is one such line.[111] Ann Kibbey has argued that the aim of Puritan iconoclasm as applied to the "material" of language was to prevent violation of "the holistic character of the sign as figure," by dividing

"the manner and matter of speech."[112] The vague stylistic criticisms
of the ministers, however, fall short of specifying this end, and instead
leave poetry in an awkward and ill-defined position. It would have
been hard in writing poetry to avoid fully the impact of such linguistic
criticism, since the medium obliged the writer to pay particular attention to the sound of words, and even to their visual appearance in the
case of the many anagrams and acrostic poems. If it was detrimental
to the ideals of plainness and clarity for words to draw attention to
their physical or textual form, then writers of poetry faced some difficulty.

Edward Taylor, like Wigglesworth, wrote in his youth about eloquence, in a piece that was similarly overblown in its collegiate rhetoric. Reading this early poem through the lens of his later verse, it is
noticeable how willing the young Taylor was to push the paradoxical
potential of the plain-style ideal as far as it could go. He began with
the image of language as a vehicle, which, like Jonathan Mitchel's
image of the sugarcoating, had the potential to neutralize "form"
and suggest that it was separable from (and therefore not in danger
of contaminating) the sacred "matter" or content. Yet, like Hester
Prynne embroidering her scarlet letter, Taylor began his playful verse
declamation on the English language with an image that ambiguously
evoked a dazzling and bejeweled kind of clarity: "Speech is the Crys-
tall Chariot where the minde / In progress rides." He went on to describe language as a satin cloth, gorgeously (if tastefully) decorated,
"With rare embroderings, & laid with lace / Set out with Silver
Chits & Ribbons grace," and "Tasled with Rhetorick."[113] Taylor seems
to have developed his own unique approach to the need for a plain
style. By cultivating a poetic style that at times would have served the
young Wigglesworth well as a vernacular example of the "overweening" style he associated with poetry, Taylor gave his expressions of poetic humility a subversive "Puritan" resonance.[114] "My Quaintest
Metaphors are ragged Stuff," he later complained in Meditation 1.22,
"Making the Sun Seem like a Mullipuff."[115] Whatever a mullipuff was,
it may have been ragged but it was not plain. It is a frothy, fluffy pom-
pom of a word, and its distorted representation of the sun highlighted the limitations of the human perspective. Taylor's verse shows
that a method of inversion was one of the ways open to the poet facing the ideal of the plain style.

Taylor's image also highlights another poetic application of the
plain-style sermon, namely, the evocative potential of conveying the
impact of a plain sermon's idealized, formless clarity and God-given
force upon its listeners. According to Cotton Mather, John Wilson

said of his co-minister: "Mr. Cotton preaches with such authority, demonstration, and life, that, methinks, when he preaches out of any prophet or apostle, I hear not him; I hear that very prophet and apostle; yea, I hear the Lord Jesus Christ speaking in my heart."[116] Cotton's ability to erase his own style and speak as if he were merely opening a window on the Bible text was further commemorated in one elegy that described him as:

> A living breathing Bible: Tables where
> Both Covenants at large engraven were;
> *Gospel* and *Law* in's Heart had each its Colume
> His Head an Index to the Sacred Volume.
> His very Name a *Title Page*, and next,
> His Life a *Commentary* on the Text.

Although Hammond has found this poem to be "a striking example of the Puritan tendency to equate an experience of the faith with reading," its portrayal of Cotton as a selfless apparatus through which the Bible can be accessed seems specifically related to his ability to "open" the Scriptures in his role as preacher, in such a way as to enable the words of the text to take on a more lively quality.[117] Indeed, the metaphor of the textualized Cotton is immediately followed in the elegy by a section that eulogized his preaching, thereby continuing the theme of Cotton's bringing the Bible to life. In his preaching, the poet claims, Cotton spoke a "Heavenly Eloquence,"

> To fix the Ear, and charm the Conscience;
> As if *Apollos* were reviv'd in him,
> Or he had learned of a *Seraphim.*
> Spake many Tongues in one: one Voice and Sense
> Wrought Joy and Sorrow, Fear and Confidence.
> Rocks rent before him, Blinde receiv'd their sight;
> Souls levell'd to the dunghil, stood upright.
> Infernal Furies burst with rage to see
> Their Pris'ners captiv'd into Libertie.[118]

As the author, Benjamin Woodbridge, probably knew, the word "charm" is derived from the Latin "Carmen," so there was a suggestion of poetic power in his description of Cotton's eloquence. Yet the "heavenly" rather than humanistic emphasis quickly took over, as the effects of Cotton's preaching were elided with those of the Christic and Scriptural Word of God, through the weaving in of references to Messianic prophecies.[119] Moreover, the elegy itself did not attempt any such similar effect, but rather elicited a sense of awe at the spiritual force unleashed when Cotton preached in person. Typical of many New England elegies, it suggested that the significance of the deceased minister was as an agent of spiritual power now forever lost.[120]

Such poems that portrayed the impact of idealized preaching, without themselves being sermons or wielding such idealized spiritual power, entailed a certain amount of distancing; but the suggestion at least was there, that God could use language very powerfully on occasion. The dialogue between Christ and the damned in Wigglesworth's *Day of Doom* presents another example of the portrayal, rather than enactment, of empowered spiritual utterance. One of the aspects that made *The Day of Doom* more exciting than Wigglesworth's later advice verses in *Meat Out of the Eater* was that the reader witnessed not only the content and the argument but also the effect of Christ's answers on the audience within the poem. For instance, the group of damned souls who protest they have been helplessly predestined to go to hell respond in the following way to Christ's reply:

> These words appall and daunt them all;
> dismai'd, and all amort,
> Like stocks they stand at Christ's left-hand,
> and dare no more retort.[121]

That Wigglesworth described such responses suggests he may not have expected his readers to be feeling quite so affected themselves. His portrayal of Christ's eloquence was idealized beyond the scope of his own poetic form, and as a result, the verse seems slightly hesitant about its own poetic effect. By representing rather than assuming Christ's powerful utterance, the poem gained something by association, but also pointed up its own comparative limitation.

THE SPIRITUAL MULTIVALENCY OF SERMONS

In such ways, powerful Christic utterance was portrayed as numinous rather than as rhetorically embodied in the limited form of the text. One effect of this was that the relationship between the precise words chosen by the minister (or poet) and the formative impact upon the audience was left ambiguous and undefined. The elegist's description of the spiritual multivalency of the sermon particularly disrupted a mechanistic view of rhetorical cause and effect: John Cotton "Spake many Tongues in one: one Voice and Sense / Wrought Joy and Sor-row, Fear and Confidence," according to Woodbridge. Ministers commonly addressed different sections of the congregation in their sermons. When preaching on hypocrisy, for example, Cotton de-scribed and addressed the needs of two different kinds of hypocrites, the swine, who recognized their own carnality, and the goats, who thought they were holy because even to themselves they looked very like sheep.[122] Edward Taylor, too, carefully divided up his sermons so as to highlight the application most relevant to each group of people, addressing those "that are not of this Mysticall Bodie," and those "who by Grace are members of this fulness." Nevertheless, Taylor also confirmed the implications in the elegy on Cotton that, through the divine sovereignty of God, the power of the sermon was not limited to (nor even ultimately controlled by) the rhetorical efforts of the minister:

> For at the Same time in the Same Seate or House by the Same individuall Word or Sentence in a Sermon one is not observant at all, another hears it, and may be never heeds it more, another is inlightened, another Con-victed, another is inraged, another is humbled, another is reformed, an-other is regenerated, another is Edified and brought up higher in Grace by it: and everyone hath So much from it as exactly answers the Decree of God touching everyone there. Now what wisdom is this that mannages this Word, and fills it full of Light, and Grace, and sends it forth equally as Spoken, unto all that heare it, and unto one persons eare it enters and leaves no light, nor grace; into another it leaves a little Light, but no grace; into another it enters, and its light Discovers, and greatly provokes to madness; and entring into another it leaves a Convincing, or hum-bling touch; to another, it's a Sanctifying influence in its Light unto the Soule, either regenerating, or Edifying of it to Eternall Life? 2 Cor. 2. 16. To one its Savour of Life unto Life, and to another the Savour of Death unto Death, and to everyone its proportion according to the Decree.[123]

Taylor's comment reinforced Cotton's provocative statement, made two generations earlier, that "if there were no revelation but the word, there would be no spiritual grace revealed to the soul; for it is more then the Letter of the Word that is required to it: . . . there is need of greater light, then the *word* is of it self able to give."[124] So even the Scriptures required this greater light in order to be activated. The light was given, Cotton affirmed, by the Holy Spirit, which miracu-lously enabled the Bible, through the medium of the sermon, to in-spire faith in the hearers.

While a sermon, as I have highlighted, had a special and spiritually more elevated significance than a poem, the idea of its multivalency implied a dislocation of spiritual affect from rhetorical control. Besides hinting (paradoxically) that the plain style was almost a mystical form in the way it operated through divine grace, this dislocation, applied more widely to religious rhetoric, had poetic implications. It made the project of literary composition similar to the paradox of working towards one's salvation, as summed up by Edward Taylor's Saint, in *Gods Determinations:*

> Do all Good Works, work all good things you know
> As if you should be sav'd for doing so.
> Then undo all you've done, and it deny
> And on a naked Christ alone rely.[125]

At first sight this paradox seems to cancel out the need to worry about the ultimate dislocation of affect and rhetorical control, but on closer consideration it lays a strong emphasis on making explicit an awareness of the ultimate spiritual weakness, indeed powerlessness, of one's efforts. One stylistic implication of this was that the New England poet was encouraged to look for literary ways of visibly accentuating his or her work's dependence on spiritual grace. This could involve, for example, acknowledging the relative superficiality of poetic effect compared to a genuine spiritual encounter, as exemplified in Mitchel's use of the ambiguous "sugarcoating" image for poetic form. It could also involve, as in Taylor's *Gods Determinations*, using the poem to urge the reader to realize a nonliterary form of spiritual progress, by entering into the processes of church membership. In the case of the Bay Psalm Book, which was both the Word of God, and an official ordinance, the potential for multivalency and the channeling of spiritual power seems to have been usefully highlighted by the relative failure of the poetry of the version to incarnate in its verbal form the legendary powers attributed to the Psalms. For, as Taylor noted, the dislocation of rhetorical control and spiritual effectiveness in the sermon meant that sometimes the words could have no effect whatsoever on a listener, and this was not the fault of the minister, but rather an indication of the listener's current spiritual state.

It was a paradox of the plain-style sermon, with its Ramist emphasis on persuasion by clarity, that it made the spiritual nature of the battle to communicate yet more apparent, and heightened the mysteriousness of conversion.[126] The limits of what was being achieved by preaching were clear if the main goal was established as a direct aim to communicate the Biblical call to repentance, rather than attempting to satisfy what John Norton called "an *Athenian* Itch after some new thing, as to the Ornaments of Rhetoric and abstruser notions of Philosophy." This reference comes from Norton's account of the conversion of John Cotton, in which he describes how Cotton and then John Preston were converted through and to the means of plain preaching: "But [Cotton's] Spirit now savouring of the Cross of Christ more than of Humane literature, and being taught of God to distinguish between the word of wisdom, and the wisdom of words, his speech and preaching was not with the enticing words of man's wisdom, but in the demonstration of the spirit and of power." Yet, as Norton described it, Preston's was the sole positive response to Cotton's first plain-style sermon, and it came in the context of the "nonacceptance" of the rest of the audience: "the discouragement of this non-acceptance returned [Cotton] unto his chamber not without some sadder thoughts of heart."[127]

THE "DECREE OF GOD": RESPONSIVITY AS A SPIRITUAL TEST

Plain preaching made all the more apparent the arbitrariness of an individual's acceptance or "nonacceptance" of the message, and highlighted the blank spiritual intransigence of those minds that refused to understand or respond. New England preachers hammered week after week at the impenetrability of their listeners: "When thou considerest but thy Course," asked Thomas Hooker, "dost thou not wonder that the great and Terrible God doth not pash such a poor insolent worm to pouder, and send thee packing to the pitt every moment."[128] Behind the spitting plosives of Hooker's strategic incredulity was an understanding (reflected in his alliteration) that the message had to be repeatedly enforced, since his hearers would respond at different times, or possibly not at all, according to "the Decree of God touching everyone there."[129]

The synod's decision to enforce the Halfway Covenant reforms in Massachusetts in 1662 confirmed to some extent the potential arbitrariness of spiritual response: not all baptized children of communicant members were proceeding directly on to full adult membership, despite the purified state of the New England ordinances. Hence, the turn from the (albeit limited) lyricism of the Bay Psalm Book to the sermonic voice of Wigglesworth's *Day of Doom* reflected the ministerial response to the church membership crisis. Yet curiously this change in focus was accompanied by an increased awareness of the potential futility of rhetorical assaults on the faculties of a listener or reader. In this context, there was a metaphorically halfway quality to *The Day of Doom*, because it used poetic form to be more accessible, appealing, and inclusive, but at the same time insisted on the straitness of the way to salvation, and the exclusive nature of the true conversion experience.

Public funeral elegies of this period also captured the ambivalence in the relationship between spiritual and rhetorical power: they appeared to rebound from an impenetrable façade. Urian Oakes's elegy on the death of Thomas Shepard Jr., in 1677, for example, blamed the unrepentance of the people for the death of their leader:

> See what our sins have done! what Ruines wrought
> And how they have slain our *Shepard!* we have bought,
> And dearly paid for, our Enormities.
>   Ah Cursed sins! that strike at God, and kill
>   His *Servants*, and the Blood of *Prophets* spill.[130]

This message, that the deaths of preachers (and other sufferings) were God's punishment for the people's sins, has been interpreted by modern scholars as designed to inspire hope as well as fear, in that it reassured the faithful that, although New England needed reforming, it still had the Almighty's full attention.[131] However, the recurrence of the trope in elegies, funeral sermons, and jeremiads enforces the impression that the people did not learn, however clearly the lesson was put to them. Indeed, their deafness in this respect was often in part the subject of the poem. Hence, although such elegies technically presented opportunities for repentance and reform, they also inherited a strong element of fatalism. Such is certainly the impression a modern reader receives from the gradual degeneration of Nathaniel Morton's 1669 history of New England into a series of elegies lamenting the ominous passing of all the great "gap-men" ("And I sought for a man among them, that should make up the hedge, and stand in the gap before me for the land, that I should not destroy it," Ezekiel 22:30).[132] Thus, in Puritan poetry and preaching, ideas of plainness, coupled with the limitations of human rhetorical power, could be used paradoxically to suggest how predestination or God's sovereign control intersected with human rejection of God, in the hardened unresponsiveness of people's hearts.

Viewed from this perspective, it is more evident how the reader's response to a given sermon or indeed poem could become an index to his or her spiritual condition. The combination of rhetorical persuasion and spiritual test in verse like the Bay Psalm Book and *The Day of Doom* is awkward, but the presence of these two contrasting aspects enabled both spiritual exclusivity and an evangelistic drive to coexist within the poetry. The fact that the words and verse form of a poem were not perceived to be prime agents of spiritual change made the combination all the more feasible. However, the important qualification of a poem's spiritual power had paradoxical consequences for the role of aesthetics. If gracious affections came via more mystical means than simply the design of the author, then the beauty of a poem was likely to depend on whether or not the reader was spiritually enlightened. Jonathan Mitchel conveyed this inversion when he exhorted the readers of *The Day of Doom*, "fall too; and if thy tast be good, / Thou'lt . . . say, 'Tis choicest Food."[133]

Edward Taylor grappled with the issue more fully in a poem near the beginning of *Gods Determinations*, which established the framing predestinarian design of the world, and therefore of Taylor's verse. In the poem, "Gods Selecting Love in the Decree," Taylor depicted the church as a beautiful coach, coming to earth to collect those whom God had predestined for heaven. Its "Silver Pillars fair," its "Golden bottom," and the "Purple Canopy" of "the Spirits sumptuous building cleare" evoked the exquisite craftsmanship of the royal chariot in Canticles 3:9–10, and indirectly thereby, Solomon's magnificent temple.[134] Yet in Taylor's portrayal, all this beauty was lost on the reprobate: when they discovered Whose the building was, "Their Stomachs rise: these graces will not down. / They think them Slobber Sawces: therefore frown."[135] The sudden shift from décor to food imagery underlines the inappropriateness of the response, and the insensitivity of the reprobate to what Taylor emphasized was a spiritual rather than a worldly aesthetic.

The idea of this spiritual aesthetic involving a semivisible, nonmaterial kind of beauty sat well with the mistrust of any language that had an objectified and self-conscious beauty, after which the eyes may be tempted to go "a whoring."[136] And it would have been reinforced by the aesthetics of the purified New England ordinances, which, as the Bay Psalm Book preface acknowledged, were lacking in formal "elegance." In his defense of the New England practice of psalm-singing without musical accompaniment in church, John Cotton argued that although the "melody" of Old Testament-style worship, "might be more beautiful and glorious to the outward appearance": "[Y]et seeing the Spirit of Grace is more abundantly poured out in the *New Testament*, then in the old, if the holy Singers sing with more life and grace of the Spirit, our melody is the more beautifull and glorious before the Lord, and his spirituall Saints, though theirs was more beautifull, and glorious in the outward sence."[137]

Thomas Lechford complained about the "uncomely singing" in the churches in his 1641 account of his visit to New England; but, as the debate about liturgy made clear, the New England ministers were uncompromising in their prioritizing of Scriptural obedience over the intuitive human preference for attractive and comforting forms.[138] Moreover, the paradox of the invisibility of this ideal spiritual "beauty" confirmed the equally important New England Puritan tenet that mere conformity, or a religiosity that valued outward appearances, was hypocritical and spiritually inadequate.

THE LANGUAGE OF CONVERSION RELATIONS

It seems likely, too, that this aesthetic paradox helped sustain the rise to prominence of the conversion relation in the New England church system, as the means by which a candidate was admitted into full membership. That the conversion relation came to be considered the most authentic form of personal spiritual expression suggests the development of a preference for kinds of language that deliberately inverted the formalized, crafted aesthetic of the liturgy. There was, as Edmund Morgan pointed out, a common "pattern" to conversion relations, which gave them even "the appearance of a stereotype," and this tendency is further illustrated in Thomas Shepard's provision of an exemplary formula.[139] However, Shepard's advice equally shows that within this outline there was a great deal of latitude: it formed "a rubric within which individual expression [could] occur."[140] Criticizing "extravagant enlarged discourses," Shepard asked to hear from a candidate: "[S]uch things as tend to shew, Thus I was humbled, then thus I was called, then thus I have walked, though with many weaknesses since, and such special providences of God I have seen, temptations gone through, and thus the Lord hath delivered me, blessed be his Name, &c.[141]

In contrast with the Presbyterian use of a formal "profession" of faith, which involved using a prescribed form of words, the conversion relation required a certain descent into the prosaic particulars of an individual's experience. Though they may have all been structurally formulaic and full of Biblical allusions, every relation was nonetheless uniquely personalized from a verbal point of view. Apart from drawing on the importance of presence and orality (as in New

England sermon theory) in their power as testimonies, these relations also relied on certain flaws in their "outward" aesthetic.

As Morgan has noted, the candidate was expected to be humbled and aware of his or her shortcomings, and these spiritual imperfections were reflected in the humble and often rather hesitant style of the relations.[142] When becoming a founding member of the covenant of the Westfield church, Isaak Phelps ended his relation on the following qualified note: "Yet I confess to my griefe that I finde a body of Death working in me, that the good I would do I do not & what I would not, that do I. But if my heart deceive me not I finde Sin a bitter thing & dare not allow myselfe in any known Sin: But do desire to injoy Christ in all his ordinances & to have Fellowship with Gods people therein."[143] Like the other New England ecclesiastical forms, the conversion relation was strongly influenced by the Pauline inversions of strength and weakness, insofar as consciousness of one's shortcomings and failures could be an encouraging sign if it caused one to turn to depend on God's grace. In fact, it was by further extending the principle of inversion, and the belief in the ultimate unreliability of even this kind of verbal "form," that Solomon Stoddard and his supporters eventually abolished the use of the relation altogether.[144] But, until the views of Stoddard and Brattle prevailed, New England ecclesiology was driven by the effort to create and use special verbal forms that could defy empty formalism.

As a verbal form almost diametrically opposite to church liturgy, the conversion relation embodied the ultimate promotion of those ideals and stylistic values of New England church practice that most posed a challenge to the poet: spontaneity, lack of refinement, incompletion, personalization, and an awareness of the uniqueness and spiritual exclusivity of the feeling described. New England poets created poetry that in some ways shared, and in other ways served as a foil to, these values. In chapter 4 I discuss Edward Taylor's verse in the context of the conversion relation, but Wilson's elegy on Abigail Tompson (a section of which I cited earlier) demonstrates some straightforward ways in which the conversion relation could influence poetic design. As I have noted, Wilson highlighted the different levels of realization an individual could experience in religious belief. His poem drew on the relation in its style of first-person testimony, and in its sense of coming "after the fact" of a dramatic spiritual transformation. However, like the speaker of a conversion relation, Abigail Tompson could only express her own marveling at this spiritual revelation. Part of the value of the experience lay in its spiritual exclusivity: she could not offer a linguistic form that would be able to induce the revelation in someone else. Indeed, the fact that her voice was fictionally recreated for the purpose of the poem undermined the benefit of her testimony. This illustrates yet another way in which poetry remained at a remove from the most powerful forms of utterance, even (or perhaps especially) when it was most influenced by them.

This suggestion of an incomplete affective connection, reflecting the sermonic emphasis on personal and spiritual encounter instead of textual meeting, was further accentuated by Wilson's stark language. The challenge to faith to be literal, even when most stretched by grief, made this poem severely in need of "spiritual complementation":

> It was a blessed, a th[r]ice blessed, snow
> Which to the meeting i then waded through,
> When piercd i was upon my naked skinn
> Up to the middle, the deep snow within.
> There neuer was more happie way i trodd,
> That brought me home so soone unto my god
> Instead of Braintry Church;[145]

For this imagined woman, faith was quite literally a pedestrian experience. The rhyme of "god" and "trodd" had both a gritty and a casual quality, marking a determined continuity between spiritual and material dimensions that also characterized conversion relations. Yet the dreadfulness of the woman's experience of dying in the snow threatened the easy neatness of the verse. The awful difference in scale between "god" and "Braintry Church" (even if attenuated by decapitalization) seems designed to challenge rather than to induce faith in the reader. The stark, confronting plainness, epitomized in the "god"/"trodd" rhyme, is another example of the spiritually challenging clarity that was available to New England poets through ecclesiastical models. As Thomas Shepard's diary and Anne Bradstreet's poems show, a death within the family was immensely painful, even for those with the strong faith in the afterlife that Wilson's Abigail described. When his second wife died, Shepard was overcome by grief, despite knowing that this was not what his religious ideals ought to lead him to: "He did teach me to prize a little grace gained by a cross as a sufficient recompense for all outward losses. But this loss was very great. She was a woman of incomparable meekness of spirit, toward myself especially, and very loving . . ." Shepard's statement of the positive lesson of this experience of bereavement is followed by a lengthier confession of his love and loss, suggesting that the emotional toll posed a heavy counterweight to the spiritual gain.[146] Anne Bradstreet, as well as feeling keenly the loss of her grandchildren, occasionally was driven to doubts about which was the true religion.[147] In this context, the stark, apparently confessional plain-speaking in Wilson's elegy turns the poem into a challenge to the reader's faith.

THE "HALFWAY" AESTHETIC OF PURITAN POETRY

The New England church promoted distinctive literary and linguistic values through its ecclesiastical practices and teaching. In this context, the task of the poet involved negotiating the rejection of the kind of linguistic formality that characterized his or her medium. As I have begun to show, this did not result in a lack of art, but rather in an unconventional artfulness. To some extent, poets borrowed or aped some of the characteristics of the approved ecclesiastical forms. They also exploited the possibility of the Pauline inversions that were promoted in church practice, to help redeem the weaker nature of their chosen nonordained genre. Because all this left poetry in a halfway position, with regard to its limited potential as a channel for spiritual power, its status is analogous in some ways to that of the halfway church membership that was officially recognized in 1662.

Both poetry and halfway membership were culturally approved, though paradoxically so. The rite of owning the covenant involved the candidate's promising to "walke according to the holy Order & Rule of the Gospel according to [his or her] best light." In return, the church would perform "her duty of Church Inspection & care And also to be ready to owne [him or her] afterward to further privileges in the church, as the Lord shall qualify [him or her] thereunto."[148] The wording was prescribed, and the candidate's position was clearly spiritually insufficient. But there was a recognition that by conforming in this deliberate way, and by confessing his or her helplessness to advance any further without further spiritual revelation, the candidate could express an openness to receiving that greater "light." Rather like the paradoxical development of religious poetry within an antiliturgical context which promoted a spiritualized, nonmaterial aesthetic, the halfway rite of "owning the covenant" was positioned as a set form to be used in the battle against "the formality and deadness" that Jonathan Mitchel (for one) felt had "overgrown many churches."[149]

In a culture where "formality" and "deadness" were yoke-fellows, poetry found itself in a curious position, dwelling in contradiction. In the ensuing chapters, I show how these contradictions, arising from New England church order, were tackled, developed, and, to some extent, enforced in the Bay Psalm Book, *The Day of Doom*, and *Gods Determinations*. Building on poetic genres and styles brought over from the British tradition, New England writers developed creative ways of serving their spiritual goals in their colonial context through the medium of verse. The first and probably most influential verse work published in the Bay Colony was the Bay Psalm Book, and it is to this text that we will now turn.

2

The Bay Psalm Book
and the "Halfway" Poetics of Worship

In a farewell sermon to Winthrop's party in 1630, John Cotton commended and defended a list of reasons for migration, one of which was to secure the freedom to establish what he believed to be the right forms of church worship. Thomas Tillam's poem echoed this aim in 1638: for his narrator, the enjoyment of "ordinances in their puritye" was the object of the believers' search for "rest." The author of an anonymous 1643 promotional pamphlet summing up the early accomplishments of the Bay Colony listed as "above all our other blessings," the establishment of God's ordinances "in their native simplicity without any humane dressings."[1] As the preface to the 1640 Bay Psalm Book declared, the Psalms were the exceptional "set formes prescribed by God," and as such, were to be sung, in the purified form offered by the Bay Psalm Book, as "an holy Duty of God's Worship," so that "wee might inioye this ordinance also in its native purity."[2]

The language of nakedness and unadorned "native purity" certainly fitted the rather pared down style and plain-text appearance of the Bay Psalm Book verses. At the time, it also reinforced the New Englanders' theological distinction between psalm-singing and other "human" "set forms," which invited false and idolatrous security. However, as Milton's allusion to Shakespeare's "native Wood-notes wilde" shows, even such apparently anti-aesthetic terms could not escape the notion of a certain literary artfulness.[3] The Bay Psalm Book embodied an ecclesiastical rejection of an aesthetic approach that mystified and elevated verbal "elegance," and that thereby conflated poetic and spiritual power. Yet in rejecting one approach, the New England compilers inevitably fashioned an alternative aesthetic and promoted a different kind of poetic effect. As I will go on to show, the poetics of the Bay Psalm Book were influenced by more than the literal "fidelity" proclaimed in the preface. The verse form strongly evoked accessibility, and encouraged a kind of conformity to local church orthodoxy, which was of course paradoxical given the Nonconformist identity of Congregationalists in England. In addition to reinforcing the centrality of these qualities of accessibility and Nonconformist conformity in New England ecclesiology, this use of verse form offered a model for future poetic endeavors, notably the work of Michael Wigglesworth, but also the later verse of Anne Bradstreet.

The verses were written in plain language and were metrically strict, but, as with the plain style of preaching, the accessibility of the verse was paradoxical: owing to the poetic awkwardness of some of the lines, the Psalms acquired a certain emotional disengagement. While the verse was "formal," it did not offer a distracting literary satisfaction that could "content" the singers with its own mere "outward form"; nor was its poetic design such that could promise liturgically to "inform" the religious affections of the singer. Like *The Day of Doom*, the demystified poetry of the Bay Psalm Book generated a paradoxical kind of aesthetic, allowing the role of the verse to oscillate between a means and a test of grace. While the musical aspect and the appeal of meter amplified the verses' role as a means, in the New England context the tradition of the Psalms' superlative qualities (as divinely inspired poetry) paradoxically highlighted their role as test.

Cotton Mather urged readers of the Psalms to "Endeavour to get the like pious Frame Excited and Exercised in you . . . till you find your souls *Mount up* as with the Wings of Eagles, and get up to the World of Rest, and Peace, and Joy"; but he also confessed that an "*Unregenerate Mind* [was] poorly qualified for such an Exercise as this."[4] Evidence that the Bay Psalm Book, with its lack of verbal elegance and its limited affective design, did indeed take on the role of test for some of its singers is found in Joseph Tompson's spiritual journal. Tompson listed psalm-singing as one of the sabbath duties through which he examined his inner spiritual state and need of grace. On 12 December 1669 he wrote: "[B]eing saboth day I took notis of mine hart to be exeding dead in duty & exeding indisposed for the saboth[,] dead in hearing and praying & singing both publick & privat[.] the Lord was pleased to with draw from me almost the sent of all good in me and I saw my hart filed with all evill[;] the Lord was plesed to bring my spirit low in the sent of it.[5]

Saint Augustine envisaged the recitation of psalms as the sealing of "a covenant" between the singer and God: "when thou recitest those words, *Like as the hart desireth the water-brooks, so longeth my soule after thee, O God*, thou hast sealed a covenant, betrothed and ingaged thy soule to God, and must never have a coldnesse or indifferency to him thereafter.[6] Given the rather stiff verse of the Bay Psalm Book, and the developing tension between conformity and conversion in New England ecclesiology, the covenant mediated by the verse of the Bay Psalm Book was of a distinctly "halfway" variety.

Like modern historians of hymnody since, in 1702 Cotton Mather traced the origins of the Bay Psalm Book back to the Reformation.[7] In 1560, the future Bishop of Salisbury, John Jewell, had celebrated the popular religious music of the vernacular metrical psalms, because they were the "means" by which "the sacred discourses sink more deeply into the minds of men."[8] For the compilers of the Bay Psalm Book, although they could "blesse God in many respects for the religious indeavours of the translaters of the psalmes into meetre usually annexed to [their] Bibles," this old Church of England version was now understood to be too periphrastic, and to include many needless "addition[s]" to and "detractions" from the literal sense of the original.[9] On this pretext, a committee of New England divines compiled a new purified version. As Theodore Dwight Bozeman has highlighted, New England Puritanism was a fascinating combination of radical and conservative impulses: the primitivist pursuit of Scriptural purity and the traditions of the early church meant looking backwards to older ideals, and yet the foundation of a newly organized church and society in Massachusetts Bay brought an exciting sense of opportunity and of being at the vanguard of religious developments.[10] So, while it aspired to an older purity, the literary style of the Bay Psalm Book was informed by the contemporary circumstances and concerns of the New England churches, and, as the strong aesthetic statement in its preface suggests, the verse text established standards that influenced not only the expectations of churchgoers, but also those of future writers and readers of religious poetry in Massachusetts.

READING THE BAY PSALM BOOK AS POETRY

Among modern scholars, the significance of the Bay Psalm Book has tended to be placed either in the development of American hymnody or print culture. As Hugh Amory has pointed out, the current emphasis upon the Bay Psalm Book as the first book printed in North America has turned it into an artifact that "in some real sense, we are forbidden to read."[11] That Steven Day was awarded 300 acres of land by the Massachusetts General Court in 1641 for "being the first that set upon printing" suggests the early colonists had more of a sense of "firsts" than Amory allowed.[12] But Amory was right in claiming that, since the enthusiastic reviewers of Zoltán Haraszti's facsimile edition and monograph in 1956 announced that "the work of the literary and textual critics has just begun," relatively little literary critical work has been done on the text.[13] This dearth is probably the result of the enduring successfulness of the 1640 preface in averting attempts to scrutinize the text from a literary point of view.

The committee of translators declared that they had "attended Conscience rather then Elegance, fidelity rather then poetry, in translating the hebrew words into english language, and Davids poetry into english meetre," a statement that has resulted in literary comments such as: the compilers of the Bay Psalm Book "knew they were not writing poetry and said so," and, "[the Bay Psalm Book's] verse has been mistaken for poetry, which it never claimed to be." Yet as Raymond Craig has noted, the original statement "presupposes a literary sensibility" that anticipated the "literary expectations" of the audience.[14] By so doing, it conveyed the force of the tension that the compilers felt, between certain values conventionally associated with poetry and the aims of their psalm translation; it did not imply that they believed themselves to be writing outside the parameters of poetry. Being an accurate Scriptural text and an official church ordinance certainly put the Bay Psalm Book in a privileged and unique position, and theoretically above the level of literary criticism. Yet it also made the verse, with the literary choices that informed its style, into a highly visible model. It was because the compilers were aware of this that they defended their text so carefully.

In his historical description of the creation of the Bay Psalm Book, Cotton Mather stressed the ecclesiastical and Scriptural dimension, but also weaved in the literary aspect. Even the humorous rhyme that he cited illustrates the awareness of poetic art and form amongst the participating ministers:

> Resolving then upon a new translation, the chief divines in the country, took each of them a portion to be translated; among whom were Mr. Welds and Mr. Eliot of Roxbury, and Mr. Mather of Dorchester. These, like the rest, were of so different a *genius* for their poetry, that Mr. Shepard, of Cambridge, on the Occasion addressed them to this purpose:

> > You Roxb'ry Poets, keep clear of the crime,
> > Of missing to give us very good rhime.
> > And you of Dorchester, your verses lengthen,
> > But with the text's own words, you will them strengthen.[15]

Mather's use of the word "Poetry" and Shepard's "Roxb'ry Poets" confirms that the compilers expected the verse of the New England Psalter to be a kind of poetry. In John Cotton's words, only a verse translation was able to "expresse the holy Art of the Originall Hebrew Poetry, which the Prose doth not attend unto."[16] In this context, it is clearly wrong to deduce an entire repudiation of poetry from the privileging of "fidelity" above "poetry," and from the preface-writer's rejection of "poeticall licence to depart from the true and proper sence of Davids words."[17] Indeed, the recognition that the Psalms were written in poetic form gave the genre divine sanction, and obliged the New England translators to use it. Moreover, although the preface strongly defended this translation, and set it apart (in its spiritual and literal fidelity) from versions with other less laudable priorities, this self-distancing was polemical, and came in the context of the ongoing British debate about metrical psalm translation.

Metrical psalms were an important genre in sixteenth- and seventeenth-century British culture: many poets from Wyatt, and Mary and Philip Sidney, to James I, George Wither, Richard Crashaw, John Milton, and even Edward Taylor, composed versions of the Psalms, often as exercises for spiritual and poetic development. As Rivkah Zim and Philipp von Rohr-Sauer have shown, the translations all had different political and poetic implications, and, according to Ramie Targoff, concern about the poetic quality of metrical versions grew at the end of the sixteenth century, contributing to a reconsideration of the 1562 Sternhold and Hopkins Psalter used in Anglican worship.[18] The political implications of English Psalm versions ranged from the personal and courtly, such as in Wyatt's penitential psalms which can be read confessionally in the context of his fall from grace at court, to the public and governmental, as in the pointed emphasis on the theological significance of kingship in James I's/William Alexander's psalms.[19] But the prime area in which metrical psalmody became politicized in the seventeenth century was the question of selecting a Psalter to be officially recommended for congregational singing in the Anglican liturgy.

When, during the early seventeenth century, dissatisfaction with the 1562 Sternhold and Hopkins version led to a movement to replace it, agreement could not be reached on a substitute. This was partly because the dissatisfaction came from different quarters. Some found the poetry of the Old Version inadequate—"I behold these Psalmes are become / So well attyr'd abroad, so ill at home" wrote John Donne—while others, like the Bay Psalm Book compilers, found the version too periphrastic.[20] George Wither, in his *Psalms Translated into Lyric Verse,* tried at least to reconcile poetic ideals with the demands of metrical simplicity imposed by church use, but his concerted efforts to have his Psalter adopted by the Anglican Church were thwarted, as were James I's. During the Civil War, the Lords and the Commons wrangled over whether to accept versions by William Barton or Francis Rous, making the eventual acceptance of Rous's by the Westminster Assembly in 1644 (which also formally abolished the Book of Common Prayer) highly controversial.[21] In such a context, the compilation, acceptance, and widespread popular use of the 1640 Bay Psalm Book in colonial New England was an achievement of stark political and ecclesiastical significance.

Given the breadth of the poetic genre of metrical psalmody at the time, however, the verse of the Bay Psalm Book also had a vivid poetic significance. The 1646 Psalm versions by the Catholic poet Richard Crashaw illustrate the concern for poetic elegance at one extreme of the spectrum:

> On the proud bankes of great Euphrates flood,
>   There we sate, and there we wept:
> Our Harpes that now no Musicke understood,
>   Nodding on the Willowes slept,
>   While unhappy, captiv'd wee,
>   Lovely Sion, thought on thee.
>
> They, they that snatched us from our Countries brest
>   Would have a song carv'd to their Eares
> In Hebrew numbers, then (ô cruel jest!)
>   When Harpes and hearts were drownd in Teares:
>   Come, they cry'd, come sing and play
>   One of Sion's songs to day.[22]

Not intended for congregational singing, and influenced by Herbert's liturgical accommodation of poetic and spiritual beauty, Crashaw's versions have an elevated grandeur of language, a dramatic quality, and a self-consciousness of their own "carved" "numbers." With its sensuous and dignified elaboration of the words and sentiments of the Psalm, Crashaw's rich baroque style applied what had become by the 1640s a characteristically Roman Catholic or high Anglican interpretation of the conventional theory that the Psalms were the supreme, divine model for poetry.

The view that the Psalms were theoretically the epitome of poetic excellence had been inherited from such fathers as Saint Augustine, had influenced the patristic poet Sedulius, and was reasserted in the

Reformation writings of Luther and Calvin.[23] By the late sixteenth century the idea of the Psalms as "heavenly poesy" was well-established as a literary and theological commonplace, so that Philip Sidney was able to argue: "And may I not . . . say that the holy David's Psalms are a divine poem? If I do, I shall not do it without the testimony of great learned men, both ancient and modern." His sentiments were echoed by Ben Jonson who affirmed that the art of poetry "had her original from heaven," and was first "received thence from the Hebrews." In their manuscript Psalter, Sidney and his sister, the Countess of Pembroke, used such a large variety of meters and verse forms that their project seems to have melded devotional meditation and poetic apprenticeship, and a similar convergence is found in Milton's early metrical Psalm translations, which suggest a poet trying to absorb Biblical poesis in order to develop his own style.[24] As Targoff has argued, Sidney's use of the Psalms to affirm the value of Protestant poetry in general seems to have marked a new development in the perceived relationship between poetry and religious devotion, and a new sensitivity to how the notion of the poetic supremacy of the Psalms might be applied in metrical translations. In the ensuing debate about the potential affective power and devotional usefulness of poetry, increasing concern arose about the poetic style and quality of metrical Psalters.

Although for the New England Puritans in the late 1630s the demand for Scriptural accuracy, and the strong reaction against the elaborate ceremonialism championed by Archbishop Laud, tended to overshadow these aesthetic and affective concerns, the idea of the Psalms as supreme poetry did accompany the migrants to New England. So much is clear from the comment in the Bay Psalm Book preface that "the Lord seemeth to stoppe all mens mouths and mindes ordinarily to compile or sing any other psalmes . . . for the publick use of the Church, seing, let our condition be what it will, the Lord himselfe hath supplyed us with farre better."[25] Also, in 1662, Jonathan Mitchel reminded readers of the "Soul felt Notes" of King David, "that Singer sweet," in his commendatory verses to Wigglesworth's *Day of Doom.*[26] Hence, although the Bay Psalm Book compilers distanced themselves from the "poeticall licence" that characterized the more periphrastic poetic tradition of Wyatt, the Sidneys, and Crashaw, they were writing within a tradition in which the spiritual authority and the poetic power of the Psalms were often regarded as mutually validating.

In some of the more elegant versions, the conflation of spiritual and poetic power led to "poetical licence" being considered necessary in order to be true to the divine beauty of the original: "Poesy resolves with poesy," wrote George Sandys, in his poetic dedication "To the King," at the beginning of his 1636 version. While the Bay Psalm Book compilers agreed with this to the extent that they strongly defended a translation into a poetic form, their explicit prioritizing of "fidelity" over "poetry" demonstrated their sense of the need to judge boldly between what ultimately became conflicting interests. And yet how could the Psalms reflect what John Cotton described as "every elegancy of the Holy Ghost" in the literary design of the original, if they were translated in such a way as to prioritize their version's being literal and singable?[27] Offering more of a challenge than a resolution on this issue, the Bay Psalm Book preface emphasizes Scriptural obedience as the fundamental rule.

The preface notes that in the unique case of the Psalter, obedience required a metrical version, since God ordained the text to be performed: "if in our english tongue wee are to sing them, then as all our english songs (according to the course of our english poetry) do run in metre, soe ought Davids psalmes to be translated into meeter."[28] Although John Cotton elaborated in his subsequent prose treatise, *Singing of Psalms*, that "[t]he translating of the *Psalmes* into verse, in number, measure, and meeter, and suiting the Ditty with apt Tunes, doe helpe to stirre up the affection," his stress remained on the use of a metrical translation as an act of obedience: "And the singing of *Psalmes* being appointed to God, they tend to make a gracious melody to the Praise of God and edification of his People." In *Singing of Psalms* and his earlier *Modest and Cleare Answer*, Cotton presented a number of *ad hominem* reasons in defense of metrical psalmody, including the benefit of stirring up the affections, but such points are always subordinated to, if not deduced from, a statement of divine diktat, "If God commands the people to join together as well in voice as in heart, to sing *Psalms*, and to sing them with understanding . . . even as Grammar will be a necessary help to translate the *Psalms* into *English*; So Poetry will be requisite to translate the *English* into verse."[29] Because Cotton was defending the Psalms as a unique form of "holy Poetry," and the only kind of liturgy permissible in purified worship, he could not soften his ultimate appeal to Scriptural obedience, and had to keep firmly secondary all the more subjective and practical considerations that might equally be used in defense of the prayer book, such as the affective and edifying potential of verbal "elegance."

As many have observed, the verse of the Bay Psalm Book illustrates this sacrifice of other concerns to obedience and "fidelity" through its comparative awkwardness:

> The rivers on of Babilon
>   there when wee did sit downe:
> yea even then wee mourned, when
>   wee remembred Sion.
> Our Harps we did hang it amid,
>   upon the willow tree.
> Because there they that us away
>   led in captivitee,
> Requir'd of us a song, & thus
>   askt mirth: us waste who laid;
> sing us among a Sions song,
>   unto us then they said.
>
> (Psalm 137:1–3)

This particular psalm is slightly more metrically sophisticated than most in the Bay Psalm Book, with the internal rhyming later used by Wigglesworth in *The Day of Doom*. Even so, its awkwardness illustrates how the priorities of "fidelity" and singability led the compilers to "procrusteaniz[e] their Muse," to quote Norman Grabo. Grabo argued that better poets (including Herbert, Wither, and Sandys) were no more successful when constrained by the demands of producing psalms appropriate for church use; and indeed the Rous Psalter shared many of the stylistic problems of the Bay Psalm Book.[30] Willis Barnstone has found the verse of the Bay Psalm Book relatively appealing within its sub-genre, and has argued, therefore, that the poetic disclaimers in the preface were compensatory rather than apologetic.[31] But the defiant tone of the Bay Psalm Book preface seems to undermine such friendly and attenuating literary criticism. Given the limitations inherent in the task of producing a church Psalter, it is striking how the Bay Psalm compilers boldly turned the self-evident weaknesses of their chosen style and form to religious and even poetic effect.

The theoretical position that allowed the Bay Psalm compilers to affirm a loyalty to the Psalms as divine poetry, and yet to promote a translation that was visibly lacking in poetry's most winning qualities, was incipient in George Wither's 1619 treatise, *A Preparation to the Psalter*. In his exposition of the rhetorical functioning of the Psalms, Wither expressed some similar anxieties to those that later emerged in New England teaching on church forms concerning the interplay of rhetorical and spiritual effect. Like Donne who claimed that "there are not so eloquent books in the world as the Scriptures," Wither praised unreservedly the literary qualities of the Bible, freely extolling the merits of the Psalms as poetry, and listing the different rhetorical devices that could be found in them. At the same time, however, he also seemed to recognize the implication that if the Psalms were simply the sum of all these parts, then their power would be entirely imitable, and their spiritual effect coterminous with their poetic effect. To counter this implication, he reminded the reader of the "test" aspect, arguing that the Psalms were "expressions of spirituall passions: and therefore it is impossible, they should please or move carnal men." [32]

In addition, Wither affirmed that, above all the flowers of rhetoric that could be isolated and analyzed, there was an ineffable and insuperable quality in the spiritual poetry of the Psalms:

> Nay, I could show you Straines of *Poesie*, and such flowers of Rhetoricke, as among [the classics] could never yet be found. But some there be that are not expressible, and I may resemble them to the purest sort of Lightning. For, as that passeth through a purse, which is a *porouse* body, and there melts the Coyne, without leaving any impression or signe upon the leather: So, there be certaine Rhetoricall passages in these *Psalmes*, so pure from sensibilitie that they can and do convey things through the sense, unperceived; and yet melt the heart, and worke strange operations in the soule, such as no man can imagine, but he that hath felt them.[33]

Through such a paradox, involving invisible rhetoric, Wither was able to hold in tension both the idea that the effect of the Psalms was in some sense supernatural, and the concept that they illustrated the supreme potential of crafted rhetoric. For Wither, a professional poet, this exaltation of the Psalms' poetry did lead at times to a rather heady exaltation of the powers of his own medium; but the Bay Psalm compilers developed the idea of the Psalms' mysterious power in a different direction, towards John Cotton's aesthetic of worship.

THE AESTHETICS OF OBEDIENCE

As I showed in chapter 1, Cotton argued that the purified and Scripturally obedient worship of the New England churches was better than worship that was "beautiful and glorious to the outward appearance" because it had instead the "life and grace of the Spirit." Puritan worship was to have an invisible spiritual beauty, as opposed to that formal or "outward" ceremonial beauty cultivated by Laudian Anglicans in their pursuit of "the beauty of holiness" in England in the 1630s.[34] When the verse was so evidently lacking in poetic elegance as in the case of the Bay Psalm Book, the amazing, affecting power of the Psalms had to be more fully identified with the action of the Holy Spirit rather than with any humanly crafted aesthetic "helps." And if (as Cotton taught) the obedience of the people was the key, then the Holy Spirit would choose to work through those forms of worship that were more obviously purified, rather than relying upon the aesthetically pleasing quality of the verse. Hence, although nonbelievers could sing psalms, according to Cotton, it was only believers who could "performe the same in the faith of Christ, and in the obedience of God's command," and would therefore be able to find in them the full benefit of "a gracious blessing of God."[35]

N. H. Keeble has linked the "spiritist" sympathies of later Dissenting writers with the development of a Romantic notion of poetic inspiration, and this seems incipiently true of Wither; but an overemphasis on potentially subversive personal revelation, such as contributed to the crisis in the Boston church in 1637, was the last thing the authorities in New England wanted to encourage in 1640.[36] As Louise Russell Stallings has highlighted, the Bay Psalm Book verses and preface were prepared for publication during the period immediately following the banishment of Anne Hutchinson, John Wheelwright, and their followers for their role in the bitter debate over free grace that split the Boston church. While banishing these scapegoats on the one hand, the Massachusetts clergy were trying hard on the other to minimize the damage and heal the divisions that the debate had opened up amongst themselves and their congregations. Echoing the emphasis on unity in John Davenport's sermons to the conciliatory synod of August 1637 and other postcontroversy texts, the preface to the Bay Psalm Book stressed the need for "holy harmony" in place of "crotchets of division," on the matter of metrical psalmody, thereby making a punning connection between spiritual and musical unity in congregational psalm-singing.[37] The Psalter text itself stood as a reminder of the importance of seeking God communally through the forms officially recommended, and in this special case pre-scripted, by a consensus of the Massachusetts church leaders. Amory has pointed out that no law was passed to compel congregations to accept this new Psalter. But one reason for a large translation committee, which Thomas Prince later claimed to include "near *thirty* pious and learned *Ministers*," could well have been to ensure widespread acceptance of the text.[38] That this was both intended and achieved is suggested by the fact that its first printing ran to seventeen hundred copies, and the revised version which was produced in 1651 became the standard New England Psalter for the rest of the century.[39]

Significantly, John Cotton, the leading minister whose career had been most severely tainted (but not quite toppled) by the Antinomian Controversy, became the principal defender of the Bay Psalm Book. Cotton drafted an early version of the preface, and was the recipient of some unidentified psalm versions from Frances Quarles, passed on by John Josselyn, a visitor to Boston in 1638.[40] Cotton also published an anonymous treatise defense of congregational psalm-singing, *Singing of Psalmes, A Gospel Ordinance* in 1647 to coincide with the Psalter's printing in England. As Anne Hutchinson's pastor and initial defender in 1637, Cotton had been suspected by his fellow ministers, including John Wilson and Thomas Shepard, of inciting the spiritual restlessness within the Boston church, and of indirectly encouraging the rebellious faction's lack of respect for church authorities through such exhortations as urging listeners "not to rest in any such changes or graces, or Deutyes, or ordinances (as church-fellowship &c.) as may leave them short of saveing fellow-ship with Jesus christ." In many ways, the teaching of the other ministers was equally responsible: Shepard, for instance, displayed a fairly mystical sense of Scriptural "revelation" in his sermons, and all the ministers encouraged congregants to discuss theology and engage with Scripture at home.[41] But despite this complicity, and despite the fact that Thomas Shepard was also to blame for the crisis, in that it was sustained by his aggressive efforts to root out heterodoxy, Shepard had retained the moral high ground while Cotton's position had grown perilous, to the extent that in 1637 he had considered leaving the colony.[42] It is interesting, therefore, that Thomas Shepard, Jr., later reported hearsay that Cotton attributed the "chief hand" in *Singing of Psalms* to Shepard, Sr.[43] While the attribution is unconvincing, both the gesture and the report confirm the collaborative, conciliatory image that the Psalter project acquired.

Central involvement in the Bay Psalm Book project marked a significant step of reintegration for Cotton and gave him the opportunity to restore his credibility and strained relationships with fellow ministers. By committing himself to organizing and writing about matters of church order (he also published *The Way of the Congregational Churches Cleared* in 1648), Cotton could avoid the kind of doctrinal debates over free grace that would inevitably reveal continuing differences between himself and ministers like Hooker and Shepard who gave greater emphasis to outward efforts of preparation and signs of sanctification. Yet Cotton's involvement in the Bay Psalm Book project also makes it appropriate to read the text as a literary out-working of some characteristically Cottonian emphases, such as the spiritualized aesthetic and the individual's need to reach *through* verbal forms and not to rest *in* them.

The explicit rejection of "sweetnes," "smooth[ness]," and "pollishings" in the final paragraph of the preface provides the most profound illustration of the extent to which Cotton's vision of the stripped-down and dissatisfying New England "altar" differed in its poetic implications from the kind represented by George Herbert's neatly formed and polished poem of that name:

> If therefore the verses are not always so
> smooth and elegant as some may desire or
> expect; let them consider that Gods Altar
> needs not our pollishings: Ex. 20. for wee
> have respected rather a plaine translation,
> then to smooth our verse with the sweetnes
> of any paraphrase, and soe have attended
> Conscience rather then Elegance, fidelity
> rather then poetry, in translating the
> hebrew words into english language, and
> Davids poetry into english meetre; that
> soe wee may sing in Sion the Lords
> songs of prayse according to his owne
> will; untill hee take us from hence,
> and wipe away all our teares, &
> bid us enter into our masters
> joye to sing eternall
> Halleluiahs.[44]

Despite the virtually ironic formal elegance of this paragraph, its implications for poetry were severe: the scornful rejection of the misleading "sweetnes" of paraphrase, for example, simply reinforced the mistrust of poetic appeal that Mitchel and Wigglesworth had to tackle twenty years later.

Moreover, while a certain amount of literary self-deprecation was the norm in the presentation of seventeenth-century poetic texts, the reference to Exodus 20 indicated that on this occasion it went much further than courtesy. In Exodus 20, Jehovah laid down the Ten Commandments and then the basic rules for worship. The reference highlighted the seriousness of the ordinance of psalm-singing for the New England leaders, and also suggested the privileges and responsibilities of a chosen people, echoing John Winthrop's similar use of Deuteronomy throughout his sermon on the Arbella in 1630.[45] Through the Biblical allusion, the safeguarding of the right forms of worship was conveyed as a major responsibility, and in this mode, the Bay Psalm Book was presented not simply as an adequate form, but as precisely the form God required. On that basis, it posed a challenge not merely to the idolatrous refinement of the Book of Common Prayer, but also to contemporary poetic taste. Like Cotton's and Shepard's writings against liturgy, the use of the Exodus 20 passage associated true obedience with what was potentially a stylistic preference: "An altar of earth thou shalt make unto me, and shalt sacrifice thereon thy burnt offerings, and thy peace offerings, thy sheep, and thine oxen: in all places where I record my name I will come unto thee, and I will bless thee. And if thou wilt make me an altar of stone, thou shalt not build it of hewn stone: for if thou lift up thy tool upon it, thou hast polluted it."[46]

In keeping with the antiliturgy treatises, the reference to the earthen or rock altar implied the elemental rightness of New England church order, and this belief was still to inspire Edward Taylor at the end of the century. Yet over and above its earthy religious primitivism, the allusion had an almost sardonic thrust. Because the true altar was so roughly made, polishing was not merely unnecessary, it was impossible. Thus, the final paragraph of the preface did more than apologize for the verse style of the Bay Psalm Book, it portrayed it as the only style appropriate if worship was to be truly godly.

THE SHAPING OF FORM TO SENSE

The defiant allusion to the unpolished altar shows that the Bay Psalm compilers were willing to spurn the periphrastic approach to psalm translation in full recognition of the aesthetic and affective losses this would incur. According to their challenging presentation of true spiritual aesthetics, these losses could even be construed as welcome. Such losses included not only the baroque elegance of Crashaw's version, but also the advantages of a more careful tailoring of form to sense, as illustrated in George Sandys' simpler but still elegant versions. In Sandys' Psalm 51, for example, the freedom of periphrasis allowed artistic manipulation that rhetorically enforced certain aspects of the meaning, and thereby enhanced the affective potential of the poem:

> With Hysope purge from blemish cleare;
> O wash, then falling Snow more white!

> Lord, let me thy remission heare!
>   The bones, which thou hast broke, unite.
> Blot out my crimes: o separate
>   My trembling guilt far from thy view!
> A cleane heart in my breast create;
>   A mind, to thee confirm'd, renew.

Through the use of a double caesura, Sandys made the last line of the first quatrain syntactically, visually, and orally mimetic of brokenness. The deferral of the verb "unite" conveyed the speaker's longing for and dependence upon the healing power of God. The effects of this line are then echoed in the last line of the second quatrain, thereby reinforcing the parallel between the healing of the body and the healing of the mind and will.

Faukland commended Sandys' version to those who would not "be led by Solecismes to Heaven."[47] Besides sounding snobbish, Faukland's praise underlines the belief that to be spiritually elevating, Psalms had to be expressed in language that was grammatically faultless, and by implication, elegant according to the conventions of English rhetoric and poetry. In line with the suspicion of humanly crafted set forms that was registered in the antiliturgical writings of Cotton, Shepard, and Samuel Mather, the text of the Bay Psalm Book embodied a rebuttal of this stance. In fact, the use of versification in the Bay Psalm Book presented an opposing perspective to the elision of divine influence and human literary effort, represented in lines such as, "A mind, to thee confirm'd, renew." Through his rhetorical composition of this line, Sandys contributed to the generation of the grace that he was simultaneously requesting: the postponement of "renew" to the end of the line expresses a resolution of mind analogous to that which the Psalmist was asking to obtain from God. This apparent coincidence of literary and spiritual effect, similar to that found in Herbert's verse, underlined the basic theological difference between Sandys and the Bay Psalm compilers, which led in the first place to Sandys' choice to create a paraphrase version: "since no narrow Verse such Mysteries, / Deep Sense, and high Expressions could comprise."[48]

The Bay Psalm Book compilers, however, appeared to believe precisely the opposite, namely, that "narrow Verse" was what was divinely ordained. Correspondingly, their preface implied, divine grace would not meld with the verse, but would work through it in a more invisible way, through the obedience of the singers to the ordained Scriptural form. Hence, whereas Sandys' simple elegance served to enforce his meaning, the lack of comparable polish in the Bay Psalm verses fore-grounded another kind of fidelity. In the two versions of Psalm 51 provided in the 1640 Bay Psalm Book, the versifiers' "laborious Rymes" (as Jonathan Mitchel might have called them) conveyed a tangible, sacrificial kind of faithfulness: the effort to fulfil the obliga-tion of holding to the chosen verse form, while not straying from a word-for-word translation.[49] Verses 7 and 8 of the first version are as follows:

> With hysope doe me purify,
>   I shall be cleansed so:
> doe thou mee wash, & then I shall
>   be whiter then the snow.
> Of joy & of gladnes doe thou
>   make me to heare the voyce:
> That so the bones which thou hast broke
>   may cheerfully rejoyce.

The use of verse form in this extract is representative of one of the dominant poetic styles in the Bay Psalm Book. With its grammatically unnecessary additions of "so" and "doe" and "to," this version re-sembles a child's mnemonic verse or nursery rhyme. The rhyme and rhythm maintains a momentum that would have contributed to mem-orization, and to the enjoyment of singing, by ensuring a good fit of word to note. However, the emotion sketched out by the matter is not aptly communicated by the manner, since the reassuring sing-song quality of the verse style is unlikely to evoke a tearing sense of an-guish. One cannot, for instance, imagine a Hamlet soliloquy given in such a form, and yet the intensity of emotion in Psalm 51 is poten-tially very great. The redundant little words give the Bay Psalm verses an inappropriate lightness and superficiality that jars with the acute-ness of the prayer.

The poetic potential of using a jolly verse form for a very serious subject was later developed further in Wigglesworth's *Day of Doom*, and, though avoiding any direct reference, Anne Bradstreet also adopted simple meters in her later poems which suggest the influ-ence of the Bay Psalm Book. While Bradstreet's language is spare and rarely redundant, her tetrameter meters exert a force that appears to have helped her maintain theological conformity and a measure of cheerfulness in the face of painful adversity, as exemplified in her "Upon the Burning of our House" in 1666:

> I, starting up, the light did spy,
> And to my God my heart did cry

To strengthen me in my distress
And not to leave me succorless.
Then, coming out, beheld a space
The flame consume my dwelling place.
And when I could no longer look,
I blest his name that gave and took,
That laid my goods now in the dust.
Yea, so it was, and so 'twas just.[50]

The simplicity of Bradstreet's submission was in unsentimental conformity to the literal facts of the matter. She deployed the sing-song verse form more skillfully than the versifier of the Bay Psalm Book's first Psalm 51, but the effect of the childlike rhythmical momentum and starkness of message is comparable: the simplicity of acceptance suggested by the blessing at the end of the cited extract could imply either an incomplete emotional realization of what has happened, an icy, repressive submission, or an inspiration of grace and resilience.

This poetic ambiguity, which occurs particularly in Bradstreet's late poems and elegies, has led to critical arguments over their precise tone. Hammond is surely right in suggesting that it is the modern preference for expressive poetry that has directed the critical spotlight onto such of Bradstreet's verses as suggest rebelliousness or doubt. Nevertheless, the verses in which Bradstreet's poetic language lays itself open to ironic readings, for instance, "Let's say He's merciful as well as just" in her elegy on her grandchild Simon Bradstreet, are not unrepresentative of the prevailing didactic mode of Bradstreet's later poetry. On the contrary, it is precisely the didactic, slightly self-distancing quality of these lines that produces the potential ambiguity.[51] Commenting on Bradstreet's late lyrics, Ray Craig has noted how "borrowing the model of the Psalms allows the poet to develop open-ended poems, poems that describe the process of resolving doubt." This effect of ambiguity is still more explicable given the style of the Bay Psalm Book, which accentuated the possibility of emotional disengagement, making the words of the Psalms available as a spiritual crux, an opportunity for willed resolution on the part of the Puritan singer. As Hammond put it, referring specifically to Scriptural poetry, "Whether or not the reader could achieve inward 'unison' with the biblical poem provided a telling index of his or her spiritual condition."[52] Therefore, where both Bradstreet's and the Bay Psalm Book's verses seem flatly didactic, awkward, or impersonal, they could be read as enacting a restraint of rhetorical power, such that would allow for a range of reader responses, from emptiness and deadness to more "gracious affections."

A Poetics of Sacrificial Fidelity
and Nonconformist Conformity

The Bay Psalm Book's second version of Psalm 51 illustrates some other characteristic qualities of the book's verses. Prosaic and syntactically tortured, every line is broken-backed in some way. The cramped feeling, typical of many Bay Psalm verses, poetically highlighted the translator's godly efforts to keep the total number of words closer to that of the compact Hebrew original:

> Purge me with hyssope, & I cleare
> shall be; mee wash, & then the snow
> I shall be whiter. Make me heare
> Ioye & gladnes, the bones which so
> Thou broken hast joy cheerly shall.

Although there is a certain felicity in the way the enjambment captures the Psalmist's confessional yearning, the verse of this extract exemplifies the "sentences wrenched about end for end" that Moses Coit Tyler lamented, and the lines condemned by Mather Byles in 1730 as "Rough horrid Verse" whose "jarring Discords tore the tortur'd Air."[53]

It would be simplistic to accuse the translator of writing willfully unharmonious verse, since errata and the 1651 revisions show that efforts were made to reduce syntactic inversions.[54] Nevertheless, the degree of inversion that resulted from the compilers' other priorities is so pressing in the Bay Psalm Book as a whole, as to be a major stylistic feature in itself. In the cited example, the twisted final part of the sentence, which overflows into the beginning of the next quatrain, provides a particularly appalling anticlimax: "the bones which so / Thou broken hast joy cheerly shall," especially if compared to Sandys', "The bones, which thou hast broke, unite." However normal syncope, clipped words, and syntactical inversion all were in the context of a seventeenth-century church Psalter, their insistence in the Bay Psalm Book versions contributes significantly to the overall feel of the verse.[55] In the context of New England worship, such a use of verse enforced the fundamental importance of a certain conformity in (albeit Nonconformist) worship, and the idea that true fidelity inevitably involved sacrifice.

Remembering Cotton's antiliturgy argument that the only valid "help" was the Holy Spirit, not human "inventions," it seems that another altar may have been lurking behind the one from Exodus 20 in the Bay Psalm Book preface, namely, the earthen altar that Elijah erected to humiliate the prophets of Baal (1 Kings 18). The Bay Psalm Book translators claimed to be following the directions of Jehovah to the letter, and this led them, like Elijah, to do things that flew in the face of conventional (and in this case, literary) wisdom. The preface declared that the Psalms were made by the Holy Spirit "to suit all the conditions, necessityes, temptations, affections, &c. of men in all ages; (as most of all our interpreters on the psalmes have fully and perticularly cleared)."[56] They thus had the multifarious powers of ordained language like the sermon, and being Scripture, they also surpassed all other songs that could be devised. Yet in the version promoted by the compilers, these great qualities were not visible in a humanistic or literary sense. Acting in faith, therefore, the compilers apparently decided to dowse their altar with water, metaphorically-speaking, and to wait for God to send down the fire from heaven. By this mysterious and ostensibly unliterary means, their verse Psalter would receive its full spiritual power in performance.

As I have suggested, however, this aspect of the Bay Psalm Book was not really "unliterary," since the design produced its own poetic effect. This effect reinforced New England teaching on the ordinances. By foregrounding the sacrificial fidelity of the verses, the Bay Psalm Book compilers created a sense of expectation—a desire to reach God through obedience, instead of through admirable, self-reflexive forms in which the participant might be tempted to "rest." In addition to the element of sacrifice, the verse of the Bay Psalm Book highlighted fidelity, in the sense of strict conformity, both to the Hebraic text, and to the chosen "popular" stanza forms. This was in line with the New England ministers' concern to avoid encouraging further antinomian individualism, but it also reflected a further political motive: the efforts of the New England leaders to resist accusations of Separatism. As J. H. Dorenkamp has argued, the preface-writers' rejection of Henry Ainsworth's Psalter, as a possible replacement for the old Sternhold and Hopkins version, was almost certainly owing in part to its Separatist connotations.[57] Though the preface accounted for the rejection on the grounds of the "difficulty" of Ainsworth's tunes, his Psalter was nevertheless sung preferentially by the brethren in Plymouth and in the Bay Colony's Salem church for at least another twenty-five years after the publication of the Bay Psalm Book.[58]

Paradoxical though it may be, since the Bay Psalm Book was produced by a group of Nonconformists, its text emphasized conformity. Not only did its preface explicitly stress conformity to a literal version of the text, and its verse, conformity to accessible forms for singing, but its presentation overtly suggested a conformity to a purified version of the Church of England. The two New Testament epigraphs on the title page of the Bay Psalm Book (Colossians 3:16 and James 5:13) were both lifted straight from the front of the Anglican Sternhold and Hopkins Psalter, with alternatives such as Ephesians 5:18–19, for example, which featured on Ainsworth's title page, silently rejected. This borrowing of epigraphs was matched by the strong resemblance of the two official titles: Sternhold and Hopkins was often entitled "The Whole Booke of Psalms," with the continuation: "collected into English metre by Thomas Sternhold, John Hopkins, and others" and the Bay Psalm Book was, "The Whole Booke of Psalmes *Faithfully* Translated *into* English *Metre*."[59] Moreover, in the Bay Psalm Book's final "admonition to the Reader" concerning the tunes for singing, the compilers referred the congregation back to Thomas Ravenscroft's settings for the Sternhold and Hopkins Psalms. Finally, as Irving Lowens has noted, all of the Bay Psalms were written in meters already represented in the older Psalter. In fact, the New England compilers reduced the metrical variety from seventeen different verse forms in Sternhold and Hopkins—there were similarly sixteen in Ainsworth—to a mere six in the Bay Psalm Book, picking the easiest and most familiar forms and tunes.[60]

Such deliberate imitation formed part of the political designs of the colonial leaders to combat the damaging rumors of Separatism that were circulating in London, while also trying to set a "pure" example for the British church. Yet the similarities had a soteriological dimension, too, which chimed with the spiritualized poetics of the Bay Psalm Book and the New England ordinances. When John Winthrop's party urged the Church of England in 1630 to "consider us as your brethren," and Francis Higginson exhorted his Salem party not to say on leaving England, "Farewel, Babylon!", "farewel, Rome!", but rather, "farewel, the Church of God in England," they were stressing the need that they perceived for a colonial church that was "no innovation, but a renovation, and the doctrine not new, but renued" (to borrow a phrase from Thomas Cartwright).[61] "We do not go to New-England as separatists from the Church of England, though we cannot but separate from the corruptions in it," explained Higginson, "but we go to practise the positive part of church reformation, and propagate the gospel in America."[62]

"Whatsoever wee did or ought to have done when wee lived in England, the same must wee doe, and more allsoe, where we goe," urged John Winthrop to his followers, "That which the most in theire Churches mainetaine as truthe in profession onely, wee must bring

into familiar and constant practise."[63] Winthrop subtly set the superlative faithfulness that he anticipated from his followers against the
mere outward form of verbal "profession." In a similar way to how
the individual believers were urged both to conform and then to surpass the mere formalities of their faith, the New England church was
envisaged as having to surpass and outgrow the forms upon which it
was based, in order to be redeemed. Of course, in the case of the
church, this involved altering or "purifying" the forms themselves;
but the recognizable presentation of the Bay Psalm Book meaningfully captured this vital tension between conformity and renewal.

For the individual participants, this tension in the text of the new
Psalter encouraged the psychological internalizing of the need to
seek renewal. "Oh! that I ever felt what I profess. / 'T would make
me then the happi'st man alive," exclaimed Edward Taylor in Meditation 1.35, voicing a frustration that also leaps from the journals of Michael Wigglesworth, Joseph Tompson, and Thomas Shepard.[64] Yet as
Taylor's lyrics show, the halfway position of striving to believe one's
beliefs was a potentially fruitful, and at least noncomplacent position.
In his advice on using the Psalms as "lesson" as well as "prayer," John
Cotton admitted almost as much. He argued in his draft of the 1640
preface that "where the matter of the Psalmes doeth not suite with
our estates," they should be sung self-didactically, since "Davids example Instructeth us what wee ought to do."[65] Thus, if the familiar
presentation and the reassuring aspect of continuity in the Bay Psalm
Book did not erase the affective resistance that the clarity of the plain
style tended to point up, then this distance between the heart and
mind of the singer had its spiritually didactic uses.

A "PLAINE AND FAMILIAR TRANSLATION"

In fact, when the aspect of "familiarity" is examined in this "plaine
and familiar translation," the design seems more likely, if anything,
to have compounded the singers' difficulty in moving through the
verse to a level of heart-belief.[66] The familiarity of the music, and the
allied, ostensibly folklike qualities of the verse style are a case in point.
Notably missing from the title page of the Bay Psalm Book, given its
similarity to that of the Sternhold and Hopkins version, are the words
often found on the latter expressing the hope that this new Psalter
would replace "ungodly songs and ballads which may tend onely to
the nourishing of vice and corrupting of youth."[67] Although the original English Psalter tunes were drawn from sixteenth-century popular

song, partly via Calvin's and Luther's versions, the work of the English composers Allison, Tallis, Damon, Este and then Ravenscroft progressively reshaped the Reformers' tunes "into tunes totally foreign to the native song of the New England congregations."[68] According to Waldo S. Pratt the "first stage" of youthful vitality in Protestant song persisted into the mid-seventeenth century; it had certainly become transitional by 1640.[69] The tune that has come to be known as the "Old Hundredth," which was originally borrowed for the Geneva Psalter from a French folk song, would have had ecclesiastical rather than popular connotations in 1640 New England, and the compilers of the Bay Psalm Book did not exploit the occasion of their new version as an opportunity for initiating any musical renewal.[70] The Reformation idea of using popular tunes as a means of helping to bridge the gap between the ecclesiastical and the personal level was not part of the rather unadventurous "familiarity" in the design of the Bay Psalm Book.

More than this, however, the Bay Psalm Book appears to have begun a deliberate and progressive simplification of the Psalms in New England, from a metrical and musical perspective. Its emphasis on accessibility and continuity went hand in hand with a narrowing of musical scope and, thereby, a reduction in the expressive potential of the songs. The 1640 "admonition" announced that "almost this whole book of psalmes" could be sung to only three tunes, "being tunes most familiar to us."[71] These three tunes probably covered common meter, long meter, and short meter psalms, which together made up 147 out of the 156 psalm versions in the book.[72] This emphasis on easy musical access dovetailed with the criticism in the preface of the "difficulty" of Ainsworth's tunes.[73] Pratt's study of Ainsworth has suggested that this "difficulty" may have been related to Ainsworth's use of decasyllabic lines and long stanza forms, which required a longer melody.[74]

The trend away from such "difficulty" was continued in the 1651 revision of the Bay Psalm Book, which involved a further diminishment of variety in the verse forms (and therefore tunes) represented.[75] Indeed, by the early eighteenth century, judging by Samuel Sewall's diary, it appears that usually only a handful of melodies were used. Sewall only mentions seven psalm tunes in the diary he kept between 1674 and 1729 (Windsor, York, Martyrs, St. David's, Low Dutch, Oxford, and Lichfield), though he frequently records his psalm-setting in church and other gatherings. His comments also suggest it was not uncommon for a congregation, singing unaccompanied of course, to veer out of a less familiar tune into one that everybody knew well (though Sewall blamed his own lack of ability as setter): "In the Morning I set York Tune," he noted on 2 February 1718, "and in the second going over the Gallery carried it irresistibly to St. David's, which discouraged me very much. I spake earnestly to Mr. White to set it in the Afternoon, but he declines it. p.m. The Tune went well."[76]

The singing reforms of the early eighteenth century strongly suggest that church singing had become noticeably dull and that the population had grown in need of musical education.[77] Although this does not seem to have been the case in the early days of the Bay Psalm Book, the compilers' original decision to stick to the most familiar tunes for the 1640 edition, and to limit the tunes even further for the 1651 edition, played its role in the ultimate trend. The limitation to familiar verse forms and tunes increased the accessibility of the Psalms in one way, but it also made them less varied and potentially less enlivening in another. Like the rejection of elegance, the text's insistence on the most common forms and tunes increased the Psalter's simplicity at the expense of affective flexibility and aesthetic expressiveness.

In addition, while the familiarity of the Bay Psalm Book, in the sense of its popular accessibility, was increased by the safer homogeneity of its forms and tunes, the resulting risk of blandness in this kind of availability was not counterbalanced by the choice of diction within the psalm versions. The Bay Psalm Book text noticeably lacked some of the language that had made the original Sternhold and Hopkins version familiar in another sense of the word, that of being intimately engaging. Compared with the Bay Psalm Book, for example, the Sternhold and Hopkins verses made much more use of colloquial idiom. Scattered through the text are alliterative couplings like "time and tide" and "by and by." Such phrases chime with the swing of the verse form, and give the poetry a more authentic folkloric tone than the more formal language preferred by the Bay Psalm Book translators.[78] Whereas the typical voice of the Sternhold and Hopkins Psalter was sanguine—dramatized, but still homely—the diction of the Bay Psalm Book came from a more formal register, and was at a greater remove from colloquial speech. For instance, Bay Psalm Book Psalm 10:13 reads:

> Wherefore doth the ungodly man
> contemne th'almighty one?
> he in his heart saith, thou wilt not
> make inquisition.[79]

In the Sternhold and Hopkins Psalter, the equivalent verse was translated:

> What blasphemy is this to thee,
>   Lord, dost thou not abhor it,
> To hear the wicked in their heart
>   say, Tush thou car'st not for it.

With words like "tush" and without words like "inquisition," the verse of the Sternhold and Hopkins Psalter was evocative of proverbial and familiar speech. Because the verses create this more popular-sounding "voice," they seem more suited to their sing-song stanza forms than do those of the Bay Psalm Book. The more elevated register of the Bay Psalm Book versions further compounded the tension within the text, between the ready accessibility of the verse and its risk of affective detachment. Through the institutionalization of the tunes, the "popularity" of the ballad meters had become a rather theoretical means of spiritually stirring the populace, compared to how earlier Reformers like John Jewel had envisaged it. The relatively impersonal register of the language in this context of popular song simply distanced the Bay Psalm Book further from its Reformation folk roots.

There were thus key aspects in the style of the Bay Psalm Book that worked against the kind of familiarity that favored the use of this ordinance as an intimate dialogue. In this regard, the New England compilers rejected not only elegance but also a kind of homely charm, both of which losses contributed to limiting the affective power of the poetry. The lack even of a winning, homely charm to the unpolished "altar" of the Bay Psalm Book's verse undermined significantly the populism of the gesture of translation into ballad meter. However, as I explore in more detail in the next chapter, the qualified inclusiveness represented by this metrical aspect of the verse was heightened still further in later works, such as *The Day of Doom*, written at the time of the Halfway Covenant. The 1662 ecclesiastical reforms gave greater emphasis to the tension between the impulse for outreach and inclusiveness, and the desire to protect the exclusivity of the church covenant and the spiritual mystery of conversion. Through his use of religious parody of the secular ballad, Wigglesworth played on the poetic paradoxes inherent in de-familiarizing the familiar in this way, and making an inclusive form serve subtly exclusive ends. Yet as the use of verse form in the Bay Psalm Book demonstrates, this tension was already building up in Massachusetts church order and its verbal forms, even in the colony's earliest years.

Relation to the King James Bible

Apart from the features I have already explored, there was another highly significant way in which the Bay Psalm Book was crafted so as to embody a rather plain, and ecclesiastically conformist kind of familiarity. This was in its use of the 1611 King James Bible. The extensive reliance of the New England compilers on the 1611 translation was the immediate reason behind the formal and prosy language of the Bay Psalm Book, when compared with the verse of the 1562 Sternhold and Hopkins Psalter. Haraszti was the first to point out the extent of the Bay Psalm Book's indebtedness, and he used it to support his defense of its verse style.[80] Curiously following the position taken by the seventeenth-century Bay Psalm Book compilers, Haraszti's argument ignored the question of whether good prose could simply become good poetry by versification. Comparison of the Bay Psalm Book verses with verse by Crashaw and Sandys and verse from the Old Psalter has shown that verse form and poetic style were not merely neutral or superficial additives, they had inevitable aesthetic and affective consequences. Yet by strongly resembling the text of the 1611 Bible, the Bay Psalm Book evoked something of the religious authority of the Authorized Version, without the full complement of its magisterial style; and such a combination turned out to be highly appropriate to the New England emphasis on obedience, and to John Cotton's spiritualized aesthetic.

The 1611 Bible and its precursor, the Geneva Bible, were logical sources for the Bay Psalm Book, since they were the most commonly used Bibles in early New England. Moreover, although the minister-translators probably learned Hebrew at university—it was certainly an important part of the curriculum established at Harvard—translation requires a special facility in both languages, and reference to other versions would have been invaluable.[81] All the same, the compilers of the Bay Psalm Book preface insisted "it hath been one part of our religious care and faithfull indeavour, to keepe close to the originall text."[82] There is a hint in the preface of a certain indulgence that the compilers allowed themselves with regard to using other English versions, in their explanation that they had followed the method of "our english Bibles (to which next to the Originall wee have had respect)" in avoiding "Hebraisms, lest they may seeme english barbarismes."[83] This parenthetical reference in fact covered a multitude of borrowings. Taking the example of Psalm 6, verses 5 to 8 read as follows in the 1640 Bay Psalm Book and then in the Authorized Version:

> In death no mem'ry is of thee
> and who shall prayse thee in the grave?
> I faint with groanes, all night my bed
> swims, I with tears my couch washt have.
> mine eye with grief is dimme and old:
> because of all mine enimies.
> But now depart away f[r]om me,
> all yee that work iniquities:
> for Iehovah ev'n now hath heard
> the voyce of these my weeping teares.

For in death *there is* no remembrance of thee: in the grave who shall give thee thanks? I am weary with my groaning; all the night make I my bed to swim; I water my couch with my tears. Mine eye is consumed because of grief; it waxeth old because of all mine enemies. Depart from me, all ye workers of iniquity; for the LORD hath heard the voice of my weeping.

Although the level of similarity varies from psalm to psalm, the trend suggested by this example proves constant throughout the Bay Psalm Book. During her detailed analysis of Psalm 23, for example, Stallings compared it to the 1611 Bible text and concluded that "[t]he two versions are almost identical"; she later gave the same verdict on Psalm 58.[84] Like Haraszti, Stallings goes on from this point to highlight in particular the moments when the compilers opted for words that were not in the English Bible text, nor in any of the numerous metrical versions she consulted. These examples illustrated, she argued, the innovative concern that the Bay Psalm compilers showed, to find the most literally accurate translation.[85] However, the evidence of Stallings's own analyses shows that such innovations were deviations from the norm for the New England divines who were working on the project.

A further finding that emerges from Stallings's work is that, where the compilers strayed from the main text, they often drew words from the verbal gloss of the Authorized Version, as if they preferred to remain where possible within the textual circumference of the English Bible. Of course, a proportion of words and phrases were also brought in from other sources, including Ainsworth, as in the example of the image of "grassy folds" for the grass in Psalm 23:2: "Hee in the folds of tender-grasse, doth cause me downe to lie."[86] But, in the same example, the epithet "tender" is found in the 1611 Bible gloss (and in Sternhold and Hopkins). In Psalm 58:4, as Stallings noted, the word "Aspe" in the phrase, "like deafe Aspe, her eare / that stops," is borrowed from the 1611 gloss, and substituted for the

bi-syllabic word "adder" found in the main text.[87] Closer examination reveals quite a trend, since later in the same psalm (verse 11) the
Bay Psalm translator again took the option offered by the gloss and
used "fruit" where the Bible main text has "reward": the 1611 text,
"So that a man shall say, Verily, *there is* a reward for the righteous," is
adapted for the Bay Psalm Book, "So that a man shall say, surely / for
righteous there is fruit."[88] Similar examples can be found scattered
throughout, for example, in Psalms 35:25, 100:1, and 142:2.

Thus, while the Bay Psalm Book was a relatively literal version, it
had its own style and bias, and a key factor in this bias was its remaining fairly close to the well-known text of the Authorized Version, or
occasionally (as in Psalms 99 and 119) to the text of the Geneva
Bible.[89] Owing to the similarity between the two Bible texts it is often
difficult to ascertain the main text for each psalm, but the apparent
overall preference for the King James confirms the shift in Biblical
allegiance that scholars have noted among seventeenth-century Puritans in general, and the New England colonists in particular. While
the Geneva Bible with its copious notes was often more expensive, as
a text associated with the religious radicalism of an embattled minor-
ity it was also arguably less suitable than the King James Bible for the
purpose of serving a newly founded semiautonomous community,
and significance has been attached to the fact that Anne Hutchinson
and John Wheelwright both referred to the Geneva Bible. Whereas
the Geneva Bible notes placed the focus on personal salvation, the
King James Bible, which did not have interpretive notes, left the ministers free to develop interpretations specifically concerning the colony (such as the "federal covenant"). The King James was also "an
establishment Bible of impeccable social and intellectual creden-
tials," the use of which could help support the legitimacy of the colonial social order and help affirm the rather tenuous claim of
solidarity between the Puritan settlers and their brethren in the Anglican church in Britain.[90]

If this closeness of the Bay Psalm Book to the King James and Geneva Bibles gives another nuance to the preface's phrase "a plaine
and familiar translation," it also underlines the paradox of purity and
conformity, as represented in the text of the Bay Psalm Book. The
church ordinance was designed to be spiritually faithful, but from a
literary point of view, this impression was achieved by some strategic
choices on the part of the compilers. A sense of sacrificial fidelity and
obedient conformity was produced by the strain necessary in fitting
the words into the chosen verse forms; but this was not (as the compilers would have it) simply a result of their direct following of the He-

brew source. Henry Wilder Foote and Willis Barnstone have noted that the Hebrew lines are indeed difficult to compact into short te- trameter, trimeter, and dimeter lines; but the most immediate cause of the crampedness of the Bay Psalm Book's verses was the chopping up of the King James Bible's expansive prose.[91]

Furthermore, by maintaining such a close textual allegiance to the official English Bible, the compilers created an impression of literal fidelity that emphasized textual conformity and familiarity more than was strictly necessary from a linguistic point of view, especially given the fact that they were translating into a different form and genre. Yet because of the Bay Psalm Book's textual allegiance to the King James prose, its text would appear to the New England congregations as far more faithful than either the Sternhold and Hopkins metrical Psalter, or the Coverdale prose version included in the Book of Com- mon Prayer. Because these versions were mainly based upon earlier versions (the Coverdale and Great Bibles of the 1530s) and because they were produced under different theological and philological con- ditions, they bore much less verbal resemblance to the Geneva Bible and the Authorized Version. And although the Sternhold and Hop- kins Psalter, by being based on the Coverdale Psalms in the Book of Common Prayer, resonated with the language of the prayer book, this reassuring verbal similarity would have been lost on congregations who used only the Bible in church.[92] So it is easy to imagine how, to the average New England churchgoer who would not know Hebrew, the alleged corruption of the older metrical Psalm translations would have manifested itself in their verbal difference from the more re- cently translated and official prose text. Such a reader would have been impressed by the closeness of the Bay Psalm Book to this text; but the emphasis on translation from the original in the Bay Psalm Book preface implies possible artfulness on the part of the compilers, which casts in a rather new light the preface's explicit concern for what readers "may think": "Neither let any think, that for the meetre sake wee have taken liberty or poeticall licence to depart from the true and proper sence of Davids words in the hebrew verses, noe; but it hath beene one part of our religious care and faithfull indeavour, to keepe close to the originall text."[93]

If, with respect to the issue of literalism, the New England ministers seem to have preferred to make their efforts coincide with the per- ception of the less erudite, this kind of concealment of complexity was, after all, part of their training in the "art of prophecying." Later endeavors at poetic outreach, such as Wigglesworth's *Day of Doom* and *Meat Out of the Eater,* also gave importance to a ministerially conde-

scending kind of popular appeal. In view of the variability of other
literal Psalm translations, however, the foregrounding of the appearance of faithfulness in the Bay Psalm Book seems to have been yet
another means of forming the text according to a spiritualized aesthetic: the similarity of the verse to the prose version suggested that
God had to be sought through spiritual, as opposed to linguistic or
literary, exploration. Not only was the poetic form demystified in itself by being so comparable to the prose, but the impression was reinforced that the role of language was simply to repeat and reiterate the
same propositional truth. Once this truth had been set down in various (linguistically collated) media, the question of how God would
actually make it come alive in the soul of each individual was implicitly a separate one.

COMPARISON WITH AINSWORTH'S PSALTER

Comparison with some verses from Henry Ainsworth's Psalter suggests how different an impression could be given by an alternative
literal and metrical version. Ainsworth's Psalter was the preferred
Psalter of English Puritan Separatist congregations in Holland. It was
first published in 1612, which means that Ainsworth was working on it
while in exile in Amsterdam, at about the same time that King James's
scholars were preparing the 1611 Bible. Ainsworth's versions were
therefore in a roughly contemporaneous English to the 1611 Bible
but were verbally distinct from it.[94] In the 1612 and 1644 editions,
Ainsworth's verses were printed side by side with his own prose translation. A reputed Hebrew scholar, Ainsworth published detailed philological commentaries on the Pentateuch, Psalms and Song of Songs,
and he chose to incorporate some linguistic observation and discussion into his metrical Psalter, in the annotations at the bottom of each
page.[95] The following quotation highlights the distinctness of Ainsworth's approach from that of the Bay Psalm Book compilers. Most
notably, he allowed some of the unsettling implications of the quest
for literalism to seep through and into the religious experience of the
ordinary reader. These verses correspond to those quoted earlier to
compare the Bay Psalm Book with the Authorized Version:

> For record none of thee in death *appears*:
>   who shall confess to thee, in deadly-lake?
> I faynt with sighes; my bed to swim I make,
>   each night: I bath my bed-sted, with my tears.

Gnawn is with indignation mine eye:
    it is waxt-old, for all that me distress.
Away from me, all that work wretchedness,
    for heard hath Iah, voice of my weeping-cry.

                                     (Psalm 6:6–9)

Ainsworth made liberal use of hyphens, indicating either that his metrical version was amplifying a single word from his prose version ("weeping-cry" for "weeping"), or that the original Hebrew word had no single word equivalent in English ("waxt-old," and in Ps6:1 "angry-heat"). He also sometimes refrained from translating into English metaphor. He put "Gnawn," for example, where the Bay Psalm Book and Authorized Version have "dimme" and "consumed." "Dimme" and "consumed" are tamer and less disturbing words that "gnawn," largely because they are more easily read metaphorically. In his commentary, Ainsworth enforced the literal meaning of "gnawn" by citing a cognate word: "*moth-worm, Psal.39.12.* that fretteth garments."[96] He put "deadly-lake" in his verse and "hell" in his prose version where the Bay Psalm Book and Authorized Version have "grave," and explained in his annotations the difficulty of finding an equivalent for the Hebrew "sheol." Through such reminders of the intralingual aspects of translation, together with the verbal alternatives offered by the parallel text and gloss, Ainsworth forcibly involved the reader in the dilemmas of the translator. One overall effect of this approach was to highlight the ultimate provisionality even of a literal translation of Scripture.[97]

    The difference in the presentation of Ainsworth's and the Bay Psalm Book versions reflected Ainsworth's greater willingness to expose the nuts and bolts of the translator's task. By comparison, although the Bay Psalm Book compilers presented a number of Psalms in two versions, their presentation of the text suggested a general preference to avoid drawing particular attention to the verbal material of their text. Reading the Bay Psalm Book preface side by side with Nathaniel Holmes's defense of psalm-singing only reinforces this impression of evasiveness on the part of the Bay Psalm compilers. Holmes's *Gospel Musick*, a defense of psalm-singing published in London in 1644 (the year of the Westminster Assembly), appended approvingly a long extract from the Bay Psalm Book preface, but the two texts contrast dramatically in style. Like Ainsworth, Holmes forefronted the complexity of translation by referring frequently to Hebrew and Greek words. Holmes even went a step further (understandably given the need for some ecclesiastical compromise in England at that time) and explicitly stressed the need to tolerate a level of error and impurity in translations.

By contrast, the emphasis on literal fidelity cultivated in the Bay Psalm Book preface and text seems to have been more designed to respond to popular, aspirational notions of purity than to involve readers in the unsettling complexities of translation. Linguistically, the Bay Psalm Book is strongly related to the King James version which would have generated a mutually validating relationship between them. Thus, in accordance with Cotton's teaching on the ordinances, the Bay Psalm Book's text seems carefully designed to be a "set forme" that was materially as self-effacing as possible, and this impression of purity and transparency was enhanced by its being printed without accompanying apparatus or parallel text. This plaintext presentation gave its literalism a sacrificial kind of fidelity and an artificial cleanness and simplicity. Despite the accidental inkblots, wobbly lines, and show-through which betrayed the amateurism of the 1640 printing, the Bay Psalm Book seemed to claim for itself visually the achievement of a textual purity that Ainsworth missed by encumbering his text with apparatus.

The lack of an accompanying gloss was accentuated in the first edition of the Bay Psalm Book by its publication in quarto format, unusual for a Psalter. Later editions were in the more conventional duodecimo (or smaller), and there were probably practical reasons why quarto was chosen for the first one.[98] Still, the resulting appearance emphasized the narrowness of the text, which was printed as a single column in the center of each page. Apart from enforcing the aspect of constraint in the literally "narrow" ballad form, the broad blank borders also reflected the pared-down purity of this text and of the ordinance of psalm-singing in New England. Also, like the blank borders of the special edition of the Psalter that Martin Luther had once had printed for his students, the empty space was an invitation for the individual singers to make their own personal application of this text, unmediated by any gloss. The eye has nowhere to rest on the page except on the words of the text itself, enforcing a direct confrontation with Scripture, and the space surrounding the text presents what Certeau has called "an autonomous surface." Although Certeau envisaged the blankness of a page for writing on, his terminology can be adapted to the New England context, where the faithful reader and singer of psalms was placed, spiritually, in "the position of having to manage a space that is his own and distinct from all others."[99] This kind of creative potential and responsibility was given to members of the congregation by the Bay Psalm Book, not so that they would write (although some did write journals) but so that they would seek a spiritual encounter that invisibly complemented the formal words of the text. By presenting a definitive translated text, with blank borders instead of any commentary or gloss, the 1640 Bay Psalm Book reflected the balance struck in much New England church life between acceptance of the authority of the learned and ordained ministers, and the responsibility of the people to judge, interpret, and use the Scriptural text to develop their own inner lives.[100]

Further, the use of the first person plural in the Bay Psalm Book preface reminded readers of the committee of experts behind it. In contrast with Ainsworth's unilaterally produced Psalter, this put the Bay Psalm Book more on a par with the 1611 Bible and suggested its definitive status as a translation. Indeed, although New England's Psalter maintained the tradition of Sternhold and Hopkins in its lack of annotations, it nonetheless broke from tradition by not printing the initials of the translator after every psalm. It was, as published, completely anonymous. All signs of the ministerial intervention that produced it, save the divisions and verse numbering derived from the prose Bible, were removed from the main text of the Bay Psalm Book. In this way, the anonymous and stripped down presentation of the text reinforced the impression given by the preface and the poetic style of the verse, that this version was faithful, definitive, and pure.

THE BAY PSALM BOOK AND THE NEW ENGLAND ORDINANCES

The poetry of the Bay Psalm Book expressed its own "fidelity" through its relationship to the literary alternatives available, and through its deviation from conventions of elegance and affective engagement. By definition, its deviation was based upon the compilers' awareness of continuity and of the presence of the traditions and preferences they chose to repudiate. On the one hand, this paradoxical literary relationship mirrored to some extent the ecclesiastical relationship of the New England churches to the Church of England; on the other, it established a New England stylistic model to which all later New England poets had to respond, and which they henceforward could choose to adapt, develop, or else reject. As the preface suggested, this model was intimately connected to the contemporaneous teaching on the ordinances, and the poetry of the Bay Psalm Book was bound up with its role in church order. In this context, obedience rather than charm was valued, as was a sense of the slight disconnection of the forms of the ordinances from the inner spiritual renewal they were designed to frame. For Cotton, Shepard, and Winthrop (and countless others amongst the first-generation settlers), their preconversion experience involved living many years under the ordinances of the church. All three men had been faithful churchgoers and Shepard and Cotton were already training for ordination at the time they had retrospectively pinpointed as their conversion. When they settled in New England and established the purified ordinances, such men retained the sense that the forms of church worship, even if pure and plain, could be (like the words of Scripture) insufficient in and of themselves to transform the individual. It has been argued, too, that the move to New England, away from the cultural and religious institutions that had in practice nourished the faith of the first generation, caused the early colonists to develop a nostalgic sense of the absence of Christ and the need to recover spiritual desire, and resulted in the religious declension among the young in later generations.[101] Whether from such nostalgia or based on their own experience, first generation leaders, especially Cotton, urged congregants not to rest in outward profession and not to view the ordinances as an end in themselves, but rather to see such conformity as the basis for the subsequent reception of "greater light."

The increased awkwardness and detachment of the Bay Psalm Book compared with Sternhold and Hopkins shows that one consequence of the purification of the ordinances was that it made their humanistic rhetorical and affective limits more evident. The Bay Psalm Book, as the text supplying the ordinance of psalm-singing, had an aspect of poetic dissatisfactoriness that could in practice be beneficial. In the early twentieth century, Walter Benjamin articulated how literal "fidelity" in translations could be used as a sort of rhetorical lever: "the significance of fidelity as ensured by literalness is that the work reflects the great longing for linguistic complementation."[102] In the case of the Bay Psalm Book, the "longing for linguistic complementation," conveyed by the impression of sacrificial fidelity embodied in its verse translation, provided an apt literary representation of a longing for spiritual complementation. By projecting spiritual fulfilment beyond the scope of the presented text, the poetic limitations of the translation contributed to its function as an ordinance, and helped avert some of the dangers of its similarity to liturgy.

Cotton's image of a certain quality of emptiness in the ordinances, through which individuals were to "feele after [God], grope after him," resonated with the poetic style of the Bay Psalm Book: the text's blank borders, which suggestively implied that the verbal mediation of a gloss was to be replaced with something more silent and numinous; the self-effacing quality of its poetry, which threatened to dissolve it conveniently away into the language of the prose Bible; the detachment and awkwardness of the diction, syntax, and form, which lacked the affective and popular connection they nonetheless gestured towards; the vaunted lack of literary elegance and of great poetic allure, in the face of the theological and poetic convention of the Psalms' supremacy.[103] Shepard's balancing of the alternative ways in which people responded to the purified ordinances in New England also seems to reflect some of these stylistic qualities. Shepard observed that whereas some individuals were like spiritual vessels which God kept refilling, others had the special glory reserved for them that, "though the Lord is not filling of them, he is a widening of them: there is such a vertue that the Lord do's enlarge the heart with secret desires and longings after more of God's grace and Christ's." This trope of aesthetic dissatisfaction becoming a spur for spiritual desire is echoed in one of Bradstreet's prose meditations: the "spacious room" of the soul is described as not satisfied with what eyes and ears can provide, but "like the daughters of the horseleach, cries, 'Give, give'; and which is most strange, the more it receives, the more empty it finds itself and sees an impossibility ever to be filled but by Him in whom all fullness dwells."[104] Ministers like Cotton and Shepard who preached and wrote on the ordinances also shared the experience of worship in their congregations. If the clergy "were dynamic, interacting components with the laity in a single protean movement," it is likely that the literary qualities of this New England Psalter contributed to, or at least reinforced, the formation of the ministers' views on the operation of purified ordinances and the consequent way in which they guided their congregants' personal piety. [105]

Twenty years before the Halfway Covenant, the idea that outward forms and conformity were a foil against which true inner piety could emerge had become a part of the functioning of the ordinances in New England. In the verse of the Bay Psalm Book, this idea was given a literary vehicle that would reach and influence all churchgoers. Although the aesthetics of the verse and the accompanying preface were profoundly shaped by the demands of being a translation and a Scriptural ordinance, the challenge they posed had ramifications for literary forms beyond the realm of ecclesiology. Precisely because the Bay Psalm Book text contributed to poetic issues through the medium of a central church ordinance, it had implications for all New England poets who sought to write in such a way as to develop piety in themselves and their readers. Cotton Mather's 1702 account of the production of the Bay Psalm Book was strongly influenced by the 1640 preface: he even cited the "fidelity not poetry" section. Mather Byles' use of the phrase "inelegantly good" in 1730 also suggests that Byles may have read or at least known about the first preface.[106] Thus, although the 1640 preface has not been found in any of the extant later New England editions, it nevertheless remained in circulation or at least in renown.[107]

INFLUENCE ON BRADSTREET AND WIGGLESWORTH

The influence of the Bay Psalm Book can also be felt in the later verse of Anne Bradstreet (as I have already suggested) and in the poetry of Michael Wigglesworth. Referring to British writings, N. H. Keeble has remarked: "Nonconformist texts were very rarely thought of as having intrinsic merit; their virtue resided in their potential to transform lives."[108] Yet constructing a form to live up to such a self-effacing standard was no mean feat. In the New England context it probably influenced the turn to more popular verse forms in the later work of Anne Bradstreet, and the use of ballad meters throughout Wigglesworth's oeuvre. By picking verse forms that were not conventionally recognized for their literary merit, these poets indicated their willingness to foreground devotional function by presenting their efforts on visibly unpolished altars.

Having written much poetry in the courtly Protestant tradition of Sidney and Sylvester, in later life Anne Bradstreet wrote in increasingly simple poetic forms: columns of rhyming couplets and of ballad meter quatrains. Her ballad stanzas simplified progressively from the *abab* rhymes of poems like "What God is like to him I serve," written in 1656, to the *abcb* rhymes of the seven ballad verse poems she wrote in 1661–1662, including, "My thankful heart with glorying tongue / Shall celebrate Thy name," and the verses, "In thankful remembrance for my dear husband's safe arrival. Sept 3, 1662."[109] Though it seems that Bradstreet did not herself make verse psalm translations, some of her late occasional poems are strongly reminiscent of the metrical psalter not just because of the emotional ambiguity I have already discussed, but also because of their verse forms and syntax. Kenneth Silverman has suggested that the Bay Psalm Book's influence was reflected in Bradstreet's increased use of syntactical inversion in her later poetry, and Hambrick-Stowe has found the "hymn or psalter form" so insistent that he judged it "likely that she sang them to God in her secret devotions."[110]

Further, like Edward Taylor's Meditations a generation later, some
of Bradstreet's poems ended with the request that God grace the
speaker with a deeper heart-faith and the ability to praise and serve
more sincerely. In two of the poems this was expressed in the idea of
paying vows, as if the linguistic commitment in these poems were a
formal pledge of praise and love:

> O help me pay my vows, O Lord,
> That ever I may thankful be
> And may put him in mind of what
> Thou'st done for him, and so for me.[111]

In another similar poem, Bradstreet described her desire to praise as
"weak," and as the verse enacted a formal turning to God, the
speaker confesses her need of spiritual strengthening to consolidate
and complete her attitude, to enable her to assume what Hammond
would describe as her "saintly self." Bradstreet's speaker offers her
fidelity, and promises to render praises for prayers answered: but
even to achieve this she depends upon divine help:

> I owe so much, so little can
>   Return unto Thy name,
> Confusion seizes on my soul,
>   And I am filled with shame.
>
> .   .   .   .
>
> What did I ask for but Thou gav'st?
>   What could I more desire?
> But thankfulness even all my days
>   I humbly this require.[112]

In this use of formal language to instruct the soul while in the act of
expressing feeling, Bradstreet was drawing on the complexities inherent in the simple language of the Bay Psalm Book. The discipline of
praise and yet the sense of weakness, the circularity of the request for
a thankful heart and the pledge to praise, the tension of the popular
ballad form being also an ecclesiastical form, all reflect the Bay Psalm
Book's construction of a valid but carefully limited literary form.
Whereas Hammond argued that, for the New England Puritans,
"True poetry . . . was defined by affect rather than form," the example of the Bay Psalm Book underlines how, according to New England
ecclesiology, poetic affect could sometimes be expected to work best
when it was self-denying.[113] Although Bradstreet's comparatively well

developed poetic sensitivity led to her verses generating far fewer moments of strain and inelegance, her simple style and her turning to God for affective and spiritual assistance in the act of praise, were nevertheless evocative of the Bay Psalm Book's "altar." Indeed, Bradstreet's simpler verses are easier to appreciate according to the understanding that the best altar was a poem that was self-consciously incomplete and that invited the aid of God to activate its poetic power.

This perspective seems even more true of Wigglesworth's verse. His reliance on the ballad meter verse forms represented in the Bay Psalm Book demonstrates the text's literary influence on his own endeavors as a writer of popular verse. But Wigglesworth's indebtedness went beyond stylistic borrowings: he even incorporated Bay Psalm Book verses verbatim into his work. Twenty lines of "Light in Darkness: Song IX," in *Meat Out of the Eater*, are copied from the 1651 Bay Psalm Book versions of Psalms 49 and 130.[114] Wigglesworth's willingness to transfer the verses directly into his poem testifies to the cultural value of the Bay Psalm Book as poetry and not simply a church ordinance. The title of Wigglesworth's 1689 collection of religious verse, *Meat Out of the Eater*, refers to the illness that Wigglesworth suffered during the years when he was unable to perform his parish duties and turned to writing poetry instead. Like Mitchel's evocation of the same image in his commendatory verses to *The Day of Doom*, however, the title *Meat Out of the Eater* was also suggestive of the paradoxical role of poetry in New England religion. As a genre that was theoretically secondary to preaching, which was the officially ordained means of converting people, poetry was in a halfway position. Even in the Bay Psalm Book, the question of the verse form remained a source of some anxiety, and as the preface and text both implied, the verse was ultimately measured against the prose text of the Bible, to which it bore a strong resemblance.[115] Most of Wigglesworth's poetry was versified preaching, as in the latter half of the poem referred to above, "Light in Darkness: Song IX." The "song" that is borrowed from the Psalter at the start of this poem culminates in a series of psalmic interrogations, including "My soul, O wherefore dost thou bow / Thy self down heavily?" These are responded to by an extended didactic address to the souls of the readers: "Upon the Lord for evermore / See that your selves you stay."[116] Out of the lyric of the Psalter developed a ministerial poetic voice; and this trend was encouraged by the absence of other communal liturgy and by the Bay Psalm Book's emphasis on obedience.

Where verse was used for preaching rather than for congregational praise, its form became even more of a curiosity, and difficult to defend. Wigglesworth's verses in *Meat Out of the Eater* trod the line between private hymn and sermon, as the titles of "Meditation" and "Riddles Unriddled" suggest: their combination of poetic simplicity and humility with prosy didacticism followed in the tradition of the Bay Psalm Book. *The Day of Doom*, on the other hand, was a more radical work, building as it did on the secular and sensational connotations of its ballad verse form. In the sense that it, too, was a work that looked "New Englandly" at European poetic traditions, *The Day of Doom* contributed significantly to the literary foundations laid by the Bay Psalm Book. Focusing directly on the question of who was "in" and who was "out," it reflected the progressive development in church order. This progression was away from an internal focus on the godly, represented in the production of the Bay Psalm Book, to a more outward-looking perspective.

If the Bay Psalm Book mirrored the teaching on the ordinances given by first-generation ministers including Cotton and Shepard, *The Day of Doom* reflected the movement that produced the Halfway Covenant reforms. The book's concern with inclusion and exclusion, in both an ecclesiastical and a poetic sense, built on certain characteristic traits of the Bay Psalm Book. These included its didacticism, and also the awareness it showed of its own poetic and affective limitations, and its implicit recognition of the potential hypocrisy that accompanied an emphasis on conformity. Both poetic works placed spiritual and poetic power in an uneasy relationship, with the set form of verse maintaining an insufficient, "halfway" position. Verse was useful as a frame, but the Bay Psalm compilers and Wigglesworth refused to promote its formality as able to capture or reenact an encounter between a reader or singer and God. Although *The Day of Doom* was more sermonic than lyrical, its rather self-undermining use of the plain style in a poetic form suggests a significant indebtedness to the challenging aesthetic established in the text and preface of the Bay Psalm Book. In the next chapter I show precisely how Wigglesworth exploited the aspect of challenge in the Bay Psalm Book's aesthetics in *The Day of Doom*, in order to reflect the paradoxes of covenant extension and of the role of set forms, in the later context of the 1662 reforms.

3

The Halfway Covenant and
The Day of Doom

"The *unseen things* of the world to come are the only *great* things," wrote Jonathan Mitchel and John Wilson, in their preface to Samuel Whiting's 1664 *Discourse of the Last Judgment*. "But such is the natural dulness of sinfull men, and so much do we hang upon present sense," they continued, "that all sorts of means prove too little to realize to us these future unseen things, and to get our Hearts affected with them."[1] One of the available "means" at this time in New England for helping people "to realize to [themselves]" the "*unseen things* of the world to come" was Michael Wigglesworth's book-length poem, *The Day of Doom*. This 224-stanza poem, with accompanying verses, was published at the author's expense in Cambridge, Massachusetts, in 1662, and then reprinted in 1666 and 1701.[2] In a notebook entry, written in an unusually careful hand as if for posterity, Wigglesworth announced: "It pleased the Lord to carry me through the difficulty of the aforementioned work . . . & to give vent for my books & greater acceptance then I could have expected, that of 1800 there were scarce any unsold (or but few) at the yeers end; so that I was a gainer by them, & not a loser." "About 4 yeers after," he later added, "they were reprinted with my consent & I gave them the proofs & Margin. notes to affix."[3]

As Hugh Amory has commented, it could well have taken the full four years between editions for the 1,800 copies to be sold by the retailers after leaving Wigglesworth's hands, but an average rate of 450 copies per year for four years was "an astonishing record" in the colonial market.[4] Although the Bay Psalm Book sold more copies over time, the instant success of *The Day of Doom* was particularly dramatic because it was optional rather than required reading for the colonists. It was closer to our modern concept of a bestseller. While the Bay Psalm Book held its position as the most common book of verse in seventeenth-century New England, and continued to exert an influ-

114

ence on later writers, its poetic centrality was eclipsed by *The Day of Doom*. After 1662, the Bay Psalm Book was no longer the colony's only book of verse written wholly for the benefit of popular piety.

Whereas *The Day of Doom*'s more outward-looking perspective and preachy tone reflected trends in ecclesiastical development since 1640, its ballad meter form, and its rather challenging aesthetic, built on the literary statement made by the Bay Psalm Book. In terms of its defiant poetic stance, *The Day of Doom* was directly descended from the Bay Psalm Book: Wigglesworth implicitly rejected other possible literary approaches to the topic of Judgment Day, both the more elegant and the more sanguine. Like the preface to the Bay Psalm Book, the prefatory verses to *The Day of Doom* took a self-consciously polemical tone, carefully explaining the extenuating circumstances that had resulted in a preacher's producing a poem rather than a sermon on the subject. Unlike the Psalter, *The Day of Doom* had no divine precedent that required a metrical version, and the fact that Wigglesworth was writing in verse about a matter of such great importance as divine judgment apparently required a defense in the New England context.

In addition to presenting his choice of medium as rather brazen, Wigglesworth also situated himself within poetic tradition with further defiance. This helped justify his use of verse, and also developed the Bay Psalm Book trope of bold, spiritual fidelity. In his prefatory "Prayer unto Christ / The Judge of the World," Wigglesworth condemned other supposedly Christian poets, who invoked the pagan Muses.[5] By distancing himself from the likes of Sylvester, Sidney, and even Anne Bradstreet, who invoked a "foolish, broken, blemished Muse" in her "Prologue" in *The Tenth Muse* (1650), Wigglesworth also distanced himself from the more élite and erudite styles associated with such courtly and classical verse.[6] Even more than the compilers of the Bay Psalm Book, Wigglesworth was self-consciously daring in espousing a popular style and colloquial diction: his choice of verse form for the book's main poem was a particularly swinging ballad meter.

However, as with the Bay Psalm Book, popular accessibility and poetic appeal were in an uneasy relationship with the theology underlying the endeavor. Although *The Day of Doom* was less implicated than the Bay Psalm Book in debates about liturgy, Wigglesworth's poem lacked the unquestionable authority that the Biblical text itself had, and the status of being a church ordinance, both of which supported the effectiveness of the Bay Psalm Book in performance. The kind of accessibility to spiritual encounter that could be offered by *The Day of Doom* was more clearly secondary and limited. This was all the more so because of the ambiguity of its gratuitous popular appeal, which risked attracting and pleasing readers for superficial reasons: Jonathan Mitchel distanced the poem from the "Toyes" that poets were known for creating; but the explicit act of distancing, in his commendatory verses, paradoxically reinforced the association.[7] In Wigglesworth's "A Postscript unto the Reader," "vain Toyes" fall in the category of "Creature-comforts" which, because they are absorbingly delightful, make you forget "How near thou art unto the burning Lake."[8] As with the Bay Psalm Book, the verse form of *The Day of Doom* had to steer a course between accessibility and distraction, and the poetry had to aim constantly to drive the reader to seek God, rather than allow him or her to relax into enjoyment of the poem. Mitchel's image of the "Truth in sugar roll'd" illustrates the almost oppositional relationship of pleasure and teaching that Wigglesworth had to work with in the poetic design of *The Day of Doom*.[9]

As Mitchel's verses also highlighted, one way to steer this difficult course was through the use of a paradoxical, spiritualized aesthetic, according to which *The Day of Doom* was offered as both sweetener and test. That the poem was portrayed as aesthetically challenging in this way, despite its not being shaped by the demands of literal translation, goes some way to confirm that more had indeed been at issue in the case of the Bay Psalm Book's compilation. Though none of Wigglesworth's own sermons survives, *The Day of Doom*'s stylistic links with New England homiletics suggest that the poem's dual role of attraction and test was partly grounded in churchgoers' experience of having the gospel message clearly and regularly explained to them, while a key part of this message was that they would be led by God to repent in their own individual time, or not at all, according to His will. Hence, like the ordinance of psalm-singing (based as it was on the Bay Psalm Book), the plainness of the style in *The Day of Doom* was not matched by a sense of the poetry as fully informing, much less controlling the reader's spiritual response. There is a certain reticence in the poem as to the relationship between the power of the verse and the spiritual response of the readers, even though it is an overtly didactic text and, in its way, designed to touch the affections.

The potentially self-undermining aspect to the poetics of *The Day of Doom* was exacerbated by Wigglesworth's keen emphasis on predestination, and on the narrowness of the way to salvation as he portrayed it. Thomas Shepard had suggested that one in a thousand people would be saved, and the large proportion of Wigglesworth's poem given over to the experience of condemned souls enforces a similar sense of difficulty.[10] In this context, the overtly popular and inclusive ballad form of Wigglesworth's sermonic poem appears all the more paradoxical. But since he was using a poetic kind of "set form" in the battle against "formality and deadness," Wigglesworth needed to develop a style that could operate within such rhetorical paradoxes and ironies. The result was a poem that is much more subtle and poetically artful than critics have thus far allowed. Like the Bay Psalm Book, *The Day of Doom* exploits the felt need for "spiritual complementation" in its poetic attempt to "affect" the "Hearts" of its readers with "unseen things."

THE QUESTION OF JUDGMENT AND NEW ENGLAND ECCLESIOLOGY

While the poetic design of the Bay Psalm Book can be directly linked to the aesthetics of the New England ordinances, the need for "complementation" in *The Day of Doom* reflects later ecclesiastical developments. Wigglesworth's twin commitments to maintaining the churches' core exclusivity and to making the covenant more accessible echo the concerns expressed in the 1662 Halfway Covenant reforms. In the years between 1640 and 1662, the controversy over Antinomianism had widened into the political and ecclesiastical issue of toleration, and Wigglesworth's text, with its theme of the discernment of true believers, reflected the controversy which existed on several levels. On the political and administrative level, the conservatism of the Massachusetts magistrates set them against their former Congregational allies in the Commonwealth government who had come to accept some civil religious toleration as necessary in order to maintain political power in Britain. On the ecclesiastical level, there was ongoing debate about whom purified churches should include and exclude. Was the conversion relation still the appropriate test for communicant membership? What was the position of children who were born into the federal covenant but grew up without proceeding to communicant membership? Which ordinances could someone participate in without belief, and which were too sacred and would be corrupted? The Halfway Covenant reforms were an attempt to make the churches more inclusive, without diluting the doctrine of conversion.[11]

The 1648 *Platform of Church Discipline* had stressed the need to maintain the purity of the church covenant and to exclude those who conformed outwardly to the Puritan religion without being able to attest to conversion. The 1662 *Propositions Concerning the Subject of Baptism and Consociation of Churches,* by contrast, gave greater emphasis to the churches' responsibility towards the young and the need to extend the promises of the covenant to as many of the next generation as possible.[12] Language was given a special role in this, in the form of the new rite of owning the covenant, which allowed unconverted but baptized parents to have their own children baptized. But ministers insisted that the spiritual value of this ecclesiastical set form was limited.[13] In contrast with the conversion relation, the rite of owning the covenant was scripted. It was designed to make a degree of church fellowship more accessible, without demanding much in terms of the candidate's inner spiritual progress. In accordance with the earlier teaching on the church ordinances, the form of owning the covenant set in place a right framework of belief, in the hope that true faith would at some point be kindled within it.

At such a time when the churches were considering how to judge who should be considered in and who out, Wigglesworth's poem staged an appeal to the ultimate authority and example of Christ. In the final Assize, Christ would not shrink from separating the sheep and the goats. This ultimate judgment was what all church forms and regulations concerning "visible" sainthood and covenant membership were supposed to foreshadow:

> His winged Hosts flie through all Coasts,
>   together gathering
> Both good and bad, both quick and dead,
>   and all to Judgment bring.
> Out of their holes those creeping Moles,
>   that hid themselves for fear,
> By force they take, and quickly make
>   before the Judge appear.
>
> Thus every one before the Throne
>   of Christ the Judge is brought,
> Both righteous and impious
>   that good or ill had wrought.
> A separation, and diff'ring station
>   by Christ appointed is
> (To sinners sad) 'twixt good and bad,
>   'twixt Heirs of woe and bliss.[14]

As the emphasis on "all" and "every" in this extract suggests, *The Day of Doom* was in one sense a very inclusive poem, which addressed and portrayed "all flesh," and its common meter form reinforced this inclusivity. At the same time, the basic premise of the poem was the exclusivity of salvation, and the deep spiritual separation between people, which would be fully realized at the Second Coming.

As Wigglesworth made apparent in the long central section of the poem, the "diff'ring station[s]" of people were not as straightforwardly recognizable as one might expect: even ministers and church members were to be among the condemned. However, in categorizing the damned sinners into these various groups, Wigglesworth implicitly endorsed the use of such distinctions in the New England churches. The ministers and then the communicant church members came forward first to put their cases, and they were immediately followed by the supposedly diligent church-attenders, and then the good citizens (stanzas 69–106). In the initial overview of the array of sinners, moreover, the church members are situated nearest to Christ:

> At Christ's left hand the Goats do stand,
>   all whining hypocrites,
> Who for self-ends did seem Christ's friends,
>   but foster'd guileful sprites:
> Who Sheep resembled, but they dissembled
>   (their hearts were non sincere)[15]

After these came the "Apostates and Run-awayes," then "a num'rous band, / that no Profession made," and then "vile" sinful people of various sorts. A definite hierarchy of shame was established, with those who appeared outwardly more advanced in standing coming first in line for divine rebuke and eternal condemnation. Wigglesworth's unpublished poem, beginning "Whenas the ways of Jesus Christ," confirms that he was a keen supporter of the church covenant and its regulations. His strict adherence to the form of the ballad stanza in both poems, emphasized in *The Day of Doom* by the use of internal rhyme, reinforced the message: the verse form conveyed an impression of firm regulation that mirrored Wigglesworth's own unbending allegiance to church order and discipline. The poet's ominous tone in *The Day of Doom* and "Whenas the ways" puts the popular connotations of the ballad meter form to use paradoxically as a vehicle for communicating in simple terms the need to keep the churches "unpopular," in the sense of not allowing them to be overrun by an "unruly rout." Whereas Milton disdained the "populo inerti" in the élite safety of a Latin poem ("Ad Patrem"), Wigglesworth expressed his belief in the exclusive church covenant in strikingly vernacular poetic form.[16]

WIGGLESWORTH AND THE HALFWAY COVENANT

Such is the sternness of "Whenas the ways" that it has been used as evidence to show Wigglesworth's opposition to the covenant extension mandated by the 1662 reforms, and has been dated accordingly circa 1665. The following stanza is perhaps the most explicit:

> When some within, and some without,
>   Kick down the Churches wall
> Because the doore is found to be
>   Too strait to let in all:
> The best can then nought else expect
>   But to be turned out,
> Or to be trampled under foot
>   By the unruly rout.[17]

Unfortunately, the official records of Wigglesworth's Malden church prior to 1770 have been lost, so it is unknown whether Wigglesworth applied the Halfway Covenant.[18] The circumstantial evidence is ambiguous. By 1662, Wigglesworth's friend and mentor in Cambridge, Jonathan Mitchel, had become the chief advocate of the reforms, though, according to Cotton Mather, he was still undecided in 1653, the year Wigglesworth left Harvard for Malden. Mitchel wrote the official report of the synod's decision and authored various subsequent defenses.[19] On the other hand, Wigglesworth's old pastor at his parents' church in New Haven, John Davenport, was one of the reforms' most influential and vociferous opponents and joined Charles Chauncy in campaigning against them.[20] Shorthand evidence from one of Wigglesworth's notebooks shows that he was attending and making notes from Davenport's sermons during the months before he took up his position at Malden.[21]

While Wigglesworth's precise view on the Halfway Covenant is unknown, it is recorded that he experienced difficulties at Malden with an influential church member, Joseph Hills. Wigglesworth eventually prosecuted Hills for his liberal views. According to the indictment recorded in the Middlesex County Court files for December 1659, the false beliefs of Hills, as described by Wigglesworth, included the view that "the Declaration, or Relation of the worke of Grace (as is required of them, that desire Admission) is not requisite," and that "Baptized persons, as who are vnder the badge of the covenant doe clayme there right in church priviledges. (or to this effect)."[22] Hills was leading a faction demanding far more concessions than the Halfway Covenant would allow, including an opening up of the communion table to the potentially unconverted. For this reason, it is possible and even likely that Wigglesworth was referring to this situation in "Whenas the ways," rather than making (as Bosco suggested) a "sarcastic allusion to the Half-Way Covenant."[23] In my view the handwriting supports an earlier date of 1657–58.[24] As he made clear in his rather defensive poetic address, "To the Christian Reader," prefatory to *The Day of Doom*, Wigglesworth knew that his "unruly rout" at Malden were all too ready to be suspicious of "their Shepheards faithfulness," and to "slight & undervalue" the minister, as he phrased it in "Whenas the ways." "Who can tell but this work may be my last: for the world seem now to account me a burden," wrote Wigglesworth in his notebook, referring to his poor relationship with his congregation at the time he was working on *The Day of Doom*.[25] In return, while Wigglesworth was evidently keen on reaching out and appealing to the simple reader in *The Day of Doom*, his verse also showed that he was uncompromising in his defense of the exclusiveness of salvation, and of the church covenant that represented this exclusiveness on earth.

Yet far from putting him at odds with the principal defenders of the Halfway Covenant, Wigglesworth's protectionism regarding the sanctity of the communion table linked him all the more closely with ministers like Jonathan Mitchel, and (after his eventual change of heart to support the reforms) Increase Mather. For although, on the one hand, defenders of the 1662 reforms were more outward-looking in their approach than the conservative John Davenport, they were also keen to resist the liberal drift exemplified by Hills and his faction in Malden. Moreover, as supporters of the "halfway" set form of "owning the covenant," these ministers held strongly to the idea that such mere forms were there to be outgrown, and ought to function therefore as spurs to conversion and heart-piety. Like earlier teaching on liturgy and the ordinances, such views had ramifications for literary as well as ecclesiastical forms. "The power of godliness will soon be lost," warned Mitchel,

if only doctrinal knowledge and outward blamelessness be accounted sufficient for all church-privileges, and practical confessions (or examinations of men's spiritual estate) be laid aside. For that which people see to be publickly required, and held in reputation, *that* will they look after, and usually *no more*, but content themselves with that. Consider if this hath not been a reason of the formality and deadness that hath overgrown many churches.[26]

Mitchel was implicitly underlining the fact that the new rite of owning the covenant was not like the creedal professions of Presbyterian or other more liturgical churches. It was a form that existed in a context where "formality" implied "deadness." The pre-scripted nature of the rite, and its basis in doctrinal knowledge and outward conformity, exposed it, in the New England church context, as intrinsically spiritually insufficient. It marked a prior stage to that of true conversion, and therefore, according to Mitchel, could not be used to confer the privilege of communion.

Although in *The Day of Doom* and "Whenas the ways" Wigglesworth generally endorsed the established forms of the Massachusetts Congregational churches, his verses also show that he shared Mitchel's abiding concern that people should be directed not to rest in set forms or in outward conformity. Both poems are noncommittal about the specific issues of halfway membership and the conversion relation: in "Whenas the ways" each stanza begins with rather vague, timeless warnings, "Whenas the ways of Jesus Christ / Are counted too precise," or "When Godly men cannot agree . . ." *The Day of Doom* took some distance, too, from the reforms being debated at the time of writing. The judgment portrayed in the poem was Christ's and therefore infallible, which overtly contrasted with the judgment of the congregations and their leaders on earth, who had let in numerous hypocrites. However, in both instances, by rising above the practical matter of the official church forms, Wigglesworth's intention was not to overrule them.

On the contrary, his leap to a more general or cosmic perspective suggested that divine authorization would ultimately be revealed behind New England church order. Edward Taylor later developed this idea further in *Gods Determinations*, through which poem series he elevated specific aspects of local church order to cosmic status. Wigglesworth was more concerned to emphasize the churchgoers' responsibility to perform their outward observances with spiritual sincerity, to the best of their ability. In his verse "Postscript" to *The Day of Doom*, his language melds the rites of church attendance with inward seeking: "O wait upon him with true diligence, / And trembling fear in every Ordinance."[27] Moreover, the danger of resting in outward forms and conformity was one of the principal themes in the main text of *The Day of Doom*. It was particularly highlighted by the many stanzas (69–187) relating to the condemnation of groups of souls who were either outwardly religious or at least self-confident in their theological positions.

THE USE OF NEGATIVE EXAMPLES IN *THE DAY OF DOOM*

By giving these complacent souls a voice, Wigglesworth's poem created concrete examples of the effects of a piety that was based, according to Mitchel's fears, on dead, outward forms, and the pursuit of what was "publickly required." The first three groups who present their cases before the Judge in the poem are ministers, communicant church members, and keen churchgoers well-versed in theology:

> We thought our sin had pard'ned been;
> that our Estate was good,
> Our debts all paid, our peace well made,
> our Souls wash'd with thy Blood.[28]

Turning the idea of the conversion relation upside down, Wigglesworth depicted these groups of souls as giving spiritually insufficient accounts of themselves before Christ. Though they had what was "publickly required" in terms of outward holiness, and even in terms of plausible rational arguments, the narrator stresses at the start that, "Amongst the many there come not any, / before the Judge's face, / That able are themselves to clear, / of all this cursed race."[29] Before they even begin to justify themselves, the arguments of the condemned souls are portrayed as empty words, their arguments as hollow as their outwardly pious life.

Though in practice it became the end point of many people's ecclesiastical journey, the status of halfway membership, or going "under the watch of the church" was supposed to point the individual towards the greater step of becoming a communicant member. In this respect, a significant part of its theological meaning was negatively defined: it was an individual's official and public declaration that he or she was in "need of greater light"—that further "revelation" which was more than the word's dead letter alone was "of it self able to give."[30] The negative approach to evangelism found in *The Day of Doom* therefore related the poem still more closely to the Halfway Covenant. Whereas Edward Taylor's approach in *Gods Determinations* was more constructive, Wigglesworth's worked on the principle

of awakening the complacent reader to the possibility of spiritual failure, including the deadness of formality. As in the rite of owning the
covenant, Wigglesworth's poem combined a form that had a popular
appeal, with a message that communicated exclusivity, even the possible spiritual exclusion of the participating reader. So, analogously to
the church form, the much-observed negativity of Wigglesworth's
poem exploited the limitations of its own formal nature to poetic and
theological effect.

Critics have long noted a contradiction between Wigglesworth's
Calvinist defense of predestination and limited atonement in stanzas
40–47 and 148–49, and the overtly evangelistic and persuasive intent
of the poem. Wigglesworth's Christ "May this Man chuse, and that
refuse, / redeeming whom he will," and yet in "To the Christian
Reader" the poet explicitly declared the literary and religious aim to
"Advantage" people with his pen, through this popular medium. The
work was in one respect (as Wigglesworth styled it in his "Postscript")
a poetic version of the knock on the door by a friend who saw that
the house was on fire.[31] In another respect, it was a limited means
of spiritual communication predestined to awaken only certain of its
readers. Moses Coit Tyler considered Wigglesworth's poetic oeuvre a
"chant of Christian fatalism," and Hyatt H. Waggoner judged that
the author's predestinarianism gave the poetry of *The Day of Doom* its
fatal flaw: "The more Wigglesworth succeeds in making clear and
vivid to us the details of the [predestinarian] beliefs he hoped to in-
culcate, the more he fails as a poet who can speak to us."[32] However,
when seen in the context of the ecclesiastical reforms, the predestinarianism of Wigglesworth's poem appears less an aesthetic flaw than
an interlocking part of an overall rhetorical design. In reinforcing his
predestinarian beliefs in the context of an innovative evangelistic effort, Wigglesworth was mirroring the spiritualized aesthetics that underlay the concept of the poem as test, and that made its superficially
appealing nature more theologically acceptable. As with the Halfway
Covenant, the poem showed a concern for extending membership,
but the superficial accessibility of its popular form was combined with
a reinforcement of exclusivity on a deeper and more spiritual level.

Waggoner was correct in a way, though, to balk at the literary implications of Wigglesworth's predestinarian and exclusivist emphasis,
because this emphasis was undermining to the kind of poetics exemplified in the verses of Sandys, Crashaw, and Herbert, cited in chapters 1 and 2. However, when in his Harvard oration Wigglesworth
claimed not to be an orator but only a describer of oratory, he
showed that he knew how to use his own words as a foil to evoke a

greater power; and this is one of the qualities that he developed in the poetic style of *The Day of Doom*.[33] In its portrayal of the spiritual failure of the various groups of souls, the poem necessarily suggests that its own rhetorical and poetic persuasion is ultimately limited and not quite the point. Perhaps the strongest instance of this is the depiction of the hypocrites and failed Christians whom Wigglesworth's Christ condemned as having blindly rejected his offers of grace:

> I often stood tend'ring my Blood
> to wash away your guilt:
> And eke my Spright to frame you right,
> lest your Souls should be spilt.
> But you vile Race, rejected Grace,
> when Grace was freely proffer'd:
> No changed heart, no heav'nly part
> would you, when it was offer'd.[34]

On the one hand, such arguments construct a present opportunity for the reader to realize his or her complacency or hypocrisy or plain need of salvation. On the other, the harnessing of the depiction of this future event to the purpose of present persuasion has an ironic self-reflexivity.

Whereas Wigglesworth's message contained the same warning as Whiting's treatise, which urged people "[t]o beware we be not found wicked ones at that day," and "[t]o beware of hypocritical justifying our selves here," Wigglesworth's use of a fictionalized narrative instead of a sermon format is more rhetorically problematic. His extended condemnation of hypocrites challenged his readers, but it also had a more prophetic aspect than Whiting's warning. Because it narrates a future event, the poem suggests more strongly that on the Last Day many will still be unaware of their unregenerate state, and will only realize retrospectively that they have not accepted grace. In answer to the protest of one of the outwardly holy groups, Wigglesworth's Christ reprimands them as follows:

> How oft did I Hypocrisie
> and Hearts deceit unmask
> Before your sight, giving you light
> to know a Christians task?
> But you held fast unto the last
> your own Conceits so vain:
> No warning could prevail, you would
> your own Deceits retain.[35]

There is an aspect of *mise en abîme* in such a statement, which conveys a dual message: at the same time as it unmasks hypocrisy before the eyes of the reader, it also affirms the potential blindness of the reader. In the fight against "formality and deadness," *The Day of Doom* could not circumvent its own limitations. Though on the one hand its form was designed to be popular and accessible like the rite of owning the covenant, on the other, this very design made it also more formalized. As a poem, *The Day of Doom* was therefore less capable of doing the spiritual "unmasking" than the ordained form of the sermon.

THE RHETORICAL DISTANCING OF SPIRITUAL POWER

Whiting's was a written treatise, and therefore a step closer than Wigglesworth's poem to the more auspicious form of the sermon. However, because his chosen medium was less prestigious, and because poetry permitted a slightly greater measure of fictional distance, Wigglesworth, in fact, had a freer hand with which to portray eschatological dialogues. As John Cotton explicitly acknowledged, and supporters of the Bay Psalm Book implicitly accepted, the singing of metrical psalms could be a didactic as much as an expressive exercise. Though their psalms were "empty outside-performances," the unregenerate were still encouraged, even obliged to participate. Sometimes, even for the saved, David's words of praise, commitment, and (especially) self-justification became a portrayal of the right attitude rather than a liturgical enactment of it.[36] I have argued, too, that the awkwardness of the Bay Psalm Book's verse style contributed to this effect, and highlighted the faithful singer's need to seek spiritual complementation. The Christic dialogue that constitutes the major part of *The Day of Doom* has similar properties. Like the descriptions in funeral elegies of the seraphic eloquence of deceased preachers, Wigglesworth's representation of Christ's authoritative answers to the souls' protests paradoxically distanced any suggestion of performativity through its exalted accounts of the spiritual effect of Christ's words on the fictional listeners.

A seventeenth-century reader could be expected to find the arguments of Wigglesworth's Christ cogent and possibly convincing. It seems unlikely, however, that Wigglesworth anticipated quite the same response to his representation of Christic utterance as that which he depicted in the condemned souls. A group of the "impudenter sort," who claim that "Gods Decree" excused them from responsibility for their actions, all listen to Christ's rebuke and then find themselves "dismai'd, and all amort, / Like stocks they stand at Christ's left-hand, / and dare no more retort."[37] Similarly, near the end of the poem, Wigglesworth described how, after hearing all of Christ's confutations, every soul fell into silent assent:

> Thus all mens Pleas the Judge with ease
>   doth answer and confute,
> Until that all, both great and small,
>   are silenced and mute.
> Vain hopes are cropt, all mouths are stopt,
>   sinners have nought to say,
> But that 'tis just, and equal most
>   they should be damn'd for ay.[38]

This response of universal acceptance and heart-belief after the verbal communication of a spiritual message was unheard of, a New England preacher's dream. Wigglesworth was portraying a form of spiritual utterance that he could not hope to enact, especially in the lolloping ballad form he chose as his medium. The folksy connotations and the narrative distancing of this form, however, were also what allowed Wigglesworth to represent such a supernatural interaction. Thus, his own limited representation acted as a foil to the power of the genuine encounter depicted.

Therefore, it is not the sign of unqualified poetic failure that the modern critic may suppose, if Christ's actual speeches within the dialogue appear "platitudinous," as Matthiessen put it.[39] Such an effect was almost inevitable given the verse form, which Douglas Robinson has aptly labeled "incongruously bouncy."[40] But within the poem, Wigglesworth also highlighted the impossibility of communicating a satisfactory answer to readers with an unredeemed understanding:

> Christ readily makes this Reply,
>   I damn you not because
> You are rejected, or not elected,
>   but you have broke my Laws:
> It is but vain your wits to strain,
>   the end and means to sever:
> Men fondly seek to part or break
>   what God hath link'd together.[41]

As Wigglesworth emphasized in his sermonic verse "Postscript unto the Reader," part of the poem's message was that readers should become aware of the limitations of their human faculties damaged by sin: "Thine Understanding dismally benighted, / And Reason's eye in Sp'ritual things dim-sighted, / Or else stark blind . . . All thine Affections are disordered."[42] If the popular medium of bouncy verse had rhetorical limitations in the shaping of form to sense, this failure aptly reflected the limitations inherent in fallen human understanding.

Moreover, the lack of rhetorical strength in these speeches also heightened the emphasis on the spiritual contingency of their power. As I have shown, spiritual and poetic forces were perceived by New England ministers as potentially in unholy competition, not least of all in the case of the Bay Psalm Book. By making Christ plain-speaking, and by using a humble form of verse, rather than the "overweening" style he cited in his second college oration, Wigglesworth emphasized the spiritual rather than verbal source of his authority.[43] But whereas Alan H. Pope has argued that the truth and reliability of Christ's speech was made manifest in the perfect logic and rhetoric given Him by Wigglesworth, the antihumanistic strain within the poem supports a different interpretation.[44] Although Christ's speeches constitute serious rhetorical and logical responses to the hypocrites, their power, within the context of the poem, was not conveyed as manifest primarily in Christ's use of language, so much as in his supernatural perceptiveness. As Sargent Bush, Jr., has argued concerning the importance of the Scriptural Word of God in New England culture, the emphasis was not on its "rationality" but on its "*truth.*"[45]

In Wigglesworth's representation, Christ's omniscience gave him a unique power to judge rightly, and this was implicitly contrasted with the fallible approximations made by ministers and church members, through whose erroneous permission hypocrites had been allowed to rise into positions of responsibility. Thus, the real power was located in a Christic ability to use language infallibly, which Wigglesworth could therefore only represent, not emulate, within the limited form of his poem. Only an omniscient God had the authority to address a group of ministers in the following way:

> You that the dead have quickened,
>   and rescu'd from the grave,
> Your selves were dead, yet never ned,
>   a Christ your Souls to save.[46]

It was Christ's inimitable power to "detect" insincerity and the motive of "self-love" that gave him the right and ability to expose and condemn hypocrites. Christ's "shewing" overcame all outward "shows":

> Thus Christ detects their vain projects,
>   and close Impiety,
> And plainly shews that all their shows
>   were but Hypocrisy.[47]

This sure knowledge of the true state of a soul is what made Christ's arguments powerful and beyond reply, because when personally accused, the consciences of the damned, even those who were more brazen than hypocritical, "must needs confess / his Reasons are the stronger."[48] In this way, by leaning in his portrayal on the supernatural perceptiveness of Christ, and by detailing not only Christ's arguments but also their effects on the hearers, Wigglesworth distanced the rhetorical authority of his own verse from the spiritual authority of the real Christ. Wigglesworth's language thus had a "halfway" quality insofar as it refused to "give" the spiritual encounter between Christ and the soul that it so carefully portrayed.

"A Postscript unto the Reader," written in heroic couplets, comes after the end of the main poem. This is a much more direct address to the reader, but it is marginalized by its very title. Moreover, by returning to a voice more nearly his own in the "Postscript," Wigglesworth made his address more sermonic at the cost of losing the Christic voice. Christ, or more commonly in the "Postscript," God the Father, is not embodied but is a third person with whom the speaker constantly urges the reader to go and make peace. Instead of God's authority, the speaker has a pleading tone which underlines his peer status. His "Awake, awake, O Sinner, and repent," is immediately followed by an anticipatory, "And quarrel not, because I thus alarm / Thy Soul, to save it from eternal harm."[49] True to its title, the "Postscript" implies there was much left to be done after perusing the main poem, but it is itself confined to being yet another outward form, an "after-script" caught within the loop of being a prescribed form that urges readers, in a rhyming and repeatable way, to "awaken" from their lulled state of complacency.

The subtle awareness of the limited spiritual power of the rhetoric, conveyed through these various structural features of *The Day of Doom*, helps preserve a tense harmony between the conservative predestinarian theology and the evident vocation to evangelism felt by the poet. In the context of the Halfway Covenant's combination of conservative exclusivity with a bias towards extending the promise of the covenant, the poetics of *The Day of Doom* entailed a development of some of the spiritual qualifications of rhetorical power emphasized by John Cotton. Wigglesworth's concession, in one Harvard oration, that "an orator can effect nothing . . . by his owne power" shows how, faced with a dilemma similar to that of George Wither in *A Preparation to the Psalter*, the young scholar patched together the conflicting implications of a classical humanist education and the radically spiritualized aesthetics of New England Protestantism.[50] At this early stage in his life, Wigglesworth could posit "the frequent concurrence of a devine power going along with Eloquence," though he distanced it coyly from his own speech.[51] By the time he wrote *The Day of Doom*, Wigglesworth's ministerial career was marred by persistent illness, and popular verse was his only means of preaching. As a result, the idea latent in his orations of using rhetoric as a kind of foil rather than a powerful enactment, suddenly became much more pertinent to his writerly situation.

The development of a self-consciously rather limited poetic style was congruent with key aspects of the Halfway Covenant. It was also an extension of the idea, present in the sermon theories of John Cotton and (later) Edward Taylor, that it was the prerogative of God, beyond even that of the ordained preacher, to control the hearers' responses. Wigglesworth's adaptation of this idea of forms of words presented to listeners/readers as a special framed "space" through which God had to do all the work, is particularly illustrated by the poem's condemnation of motives that resulted in an untrue hypocritical faith. In stanzas 84–106, Christ exposes and condemns the motives of false, self-interested believers; first the overtly pious and second the good citizens. His criticism of the earlier group includes the following:

> As for your care to get a share
>   in bliss; the fear of Hell,
> And of a part in endless smart,
>   did thereunto compel.
> Your holiness and ways redress,
>   such as it was, did spring
> From no true love to things above,
>   but from some other thing.
>
> .   .   .   .
>
> Your Penitence, your diligence
>   to Read, to Pray to Hear,

> Were but to drown'd the clamorous sound
>   of Conscience in your ear.
> If light you lov'd, vain glory mov'd
>   your selves therewith to store,
> That seeming wise, men might you prize,
>   and honour you the more.[52]

These stanzas condemn fear, efforts at penitence, and even keen attendance at the ordinances as thoroughly inadequate motives for
conversion. However, all such motives and actions were plausible responses to *The Day of Doom*, written as it was in the *Dies Irae* monitory
tradition. But because they do not break the circuit of human self-
interest, or "wheels of self-love," such responses are all carefully dis-
counted as unspiritual by Wigglesworth's Christ.

The "wheels of self-love" are inadequate because of their selfish
circularity, but also because of the humanly mechanistic approach
they suggest. The unreliability of such approaches to the spiritual
matter of salvation is further reinforced in the condemnation of the
"Civil honest Men" who emphasize their obedience to God's laws:
"Our way was fair, our dealing square, / we were no wastful spenders, /
No lewd toss-pots, no drunken sots, / no scandalous offenders."[53] According to Wigglesworth's Christ, such good behavior was irrelevant,
because "God looks upon th'affection / and temper of the heart;"
which meant that, however hard people tried, all their works would
prove "empty" if they were devoid of faith and love:

> Nor from true faith, which quencheth wrath,
>   hath your obedience flown:
> Nor from true love, which wont to move
>   Believers, hath it grown.
> Your argument shews your intent,
>   in all that you have done:
> You thought to scale Heav'ns lofty Wall
>   by Ladders of your own.[54]

Thus, no efforts made by the souls without the spiritual gifting of God
were valid. This stanza even implies that the effort to argue in one's
own defense is a sign of unspiritual self-reliance. Humanly built ladders are depicted by Wigglesworth as absurdly incapable of bridging
the distance between earth and heaven; and these ladders implicitly
include rhetoric and self-interested responses to rhetoric.

Hence, although Wigglesworth did not explicitly apply any of this
reasoning to poetics, *The Day of Doom* conveyed a perspective on the
use of "human devices" which nevertheless had implications for its

own functioning. Like the rite of owning the covenant, the poem embodied in its own language the absolute need for an encounter that its own form and words could not provide—for a conversion into a spiritual meaningfulness that would completely overshadow the merely mechanical power of poetic rhetoric. However, as in the case of the rite of owning the covenant, or the preaching of a sermon, it was nevertheless through words that this ineffable "interruption" of rhetorical cause and effect had to be promoted.

THE DAY OF DOOM AND THE NEW ENGLAND SERMON

The fact that *The Day of Doom* was a book of verse, and therefore unconventional as a vehicle and officially nonecclesiastical, gave it a particularly de-centralized status in the context of New England religious life. In terms of the tension between exclusivity and extension, predestination and evangelism, this "halfway" status was key to its poetic design. In many respects, *The Day of Doom* was strongly related to the sermon: Jonathan Mitchel made a suggestive link in his introductory poem, in the quotation, "A Verse may find him who a Sermon flies." Moreover, in contrast to the bare Scriptural text of the Bay Psalm Book, *The Day of Doom* was sermonlike in its combination of Scriptural allusion and elaborated re-telling. A sense of wordiness, even orality, was increased by the fact that, despite the sensational possibilities suggested by the title, much of the poem's action is verbal and dialogic rather than visual and narrative—stanzas 38–181 out of 224 consist of dialogue. In addition, the logical format of the dialogues has been observed to follow the conventional structure of New England sermons. This method involved (after the reading of the text) a statement of doctrine, followed by the "reasons" for that doctrine. Following, or integrated into this section was a list of "objections" to that interpretation, each of which was refuted in turn.[55] The sermons concluded with an application section, or "uses," the place of which was supplied in *The Day of Doom* by Wigglesworth's "A Postscript unto the Reader." The "Postscript" drew from Thomas Hooker's *Application of Redemption* and anticipated Jonathan Edwards's preaching, not only in its imagery but in its direct and earnest tone of address:

> Thou hangest over the Infernal Pit
> By one small threed, and car'st thou not a whit?
> There's but a step between thy Soul and Death,
> Nothing remains but stopping of thy breath,

(Which may be done to morrow, or before)
And then thou art undone for evermore.
Let this awaken thy Security,
And make thee look about thee speedily . . . [56]

The colloquial and plain language of Wigglesworth's poems, "car'st thou not a whit?", "look about thee," and elsewhere, "But all too late, grief's out of date" also reflected the well-known commitment of New England preachers to discourse in "homely dresse" in order to convey their message to the simplest among their congregations.[57]

Thus, in some important ways, as Hammond has noted, "the devices of the puritan sermon pulse . . . strongly" in *The Day of Doom*.[58] Indeed, much recent research on Wigglesworth seems to treat his famous poem as if it were indistinguishable from a sermon. Except for his citations, Gary Sloan's 1998 explication of *The Day of Doom* in terms of Calvinist versus Covenant theology, for example, could just as easily have been about a sermon as about a work of poetry. Analysis of the poem in terms of its Ramean logical structure by Alan H. Pope and John C. Adams, and treatment of it by Harsharan Singh Ahluwalia as embodying New England patterns of soteriology have also cemented its association with the sermon in recent critical perspectives.[59] Probably the greatest value of such approaches to the poem is that they get around the problem raised by much of the earlier literary scholarship, namely, that Wigglesworth's verse suffers when judged from a formal poetic point of view. Adjectives used over the years to condemn the verse of *The Day of Doom* on aesthetic grounds include: "rude," "feeble," "rough," "crude," "rugged," "halting," "cheap," "shrill," and "grotesque." In 1978, Robert Daly summed up years of this line of inquiry in his simple evaluation of the poem as a "failure."[60]

However, despite all the obvious advantages of approaching the *Day of Doom* as a kind of sermon, the work was clearly, to Wigglesworth and to his readers, a book of poems, as well as a kind of theological treatise; and it was this that made all the difference. In a reference to *The Day of Doom* in Mitchel's and Wilson's preface to Whiting's 1664 treatise, it was suggestively half-referred to as one of "two or three *Treatises*" on Judgment Day. These were listed in the margin as "Mr. *Shepard* on the *Parable of the Virgins*. Mr. *Wigglesworths* Poem. And now this present Treatise."[61] Clearly, the only one that could be in any doubt as a treatise is the "Poem." This ambiguity perhaps reflected an anxiety that was more directly conveyed in the prefatory poems to *The Day of Doom*, including the verses by Mitchel that I examined in my Introduction. These paratextual poems exhibited, and sought to manipulate, awareness of the fact that the poetic form of *The Day of Doom* made the work tangibly different from a conventional sermon or treatise.

The impression conveyed in these paratexts is significant, since such poems provide what Gérard Genette has termed the "seuils" or "thresholds" that guide the reader "by explaining why and how he should read the text."[62] In the case of *The Day of Doom*, the presentation of the text through the prefatory verses, by Mitchel and by Wigglesworth himself, colored it with the idea that it was in some way disadvantaged by being in verse. Mitchel's commendation is only partially successful in its attempt to defend Wigglesworth's turn to popular verse, since it enforces seventeenth-century Puritan prejudices against poetry in the act of apparently trying to combat them. Wigglesworth dealt with the more personal aspects of his choice in "To the Christian Reader." By relying in this poem on the Pauline inversions of strength and weakness and by emphasizing his illness and rejection by his congregation, Wigglesworth compounded the sense of his having produced a text that was indeed second-rate according to conventional religious and literary standards. Far from negligible, therefore, his chosen verse form apparently had connotations that were all too obvious to the pious seventeenth-century New England reader.

Wigglesworth's presentation of verse as a second-rate form, in "To the Christian Reader," paralleled Mitchel's. Like Mitchel, Wigglesworth also grappled with the awkward relationship between poetry and the genre of the sermon. Although his opening, "Reader I am a fool," evokes the literary convention of the self-deprecating proem with its "paradoxically value-enhancing function" (as in Anne Bradstreet's "Prologue," for example), Wigglesworth added a sharply literal and theological dimension to this traditional device:

> Reader I am a fool,
> And have adventured
> To play the fool this once for Christ,
> The more his fame to spread.
> If this my foolishness
> Help thee to be more wise,
> I have attained what I seek,
> And what I only prize.[63]

Wigglesworth's "foolishness" alludes to 1 Corinthians 1:18–29, and hence identifies the poet with the Apostle Paul (and via him, Christ) in his "foolish" sufferings for the gospel. "Hath not God made foolishness the wisdom of this world?" whispers the Apostle to the Puritan reader's inner ear.[64] Such Pauline echoes also cleverly associate the apparent foolishness of preaching in verse with the basic simplicity of the plain style to which many New England ministers aspired, and which was commonly contrasted with a more ornamental style that involved Latin tags and rhetorical flourishes. As I suggested in chapter 1, styles that could claim the virtue of plainness could evoke for well-trained Puritan readers a reassuring sense of clarity and an almost mystical feeling of dependence on the Holy Spirit. Yet although there is a clear allusion, too, in "To the Christian Reader" to the trope of strength in weakness in 2 Corinthians 12, by focusing on Wigglesworth's actual experience of illness and suffering the poem also endorses the impression given by Mitchel that poetry was a genre born of weakness:

> Weak heads, and hands, and states,
> Great things cannot produce:
> And therefore I this little Piece
> Have publish'd for thine use.[65]

Like St Paul, Wigglesworth claimed to have "gloried" in his "infirmities" as Christ's opportunities to strengthen him: "In God I have been strong, / When wearied and worn out." These spiritual strengths, however, were admittedly not manifest, and his failure to preach was evidently a source of friction between Wigglesworth and the small community who were supposed to be financially supporting him: "Some for, because they see not / My chearfulness to fail . . . Do think I nothing ail." Thus, what he called elsewhere his "poor piece of service" was the best he could muster under the circumstances; it was not a form that Wigglesworth could extol quite to the level of Paul's plain and faithful preaching.[66] Like Mitchel, Wigglesworth portrayed his poetry as the sign of his falling short of a better calling, "Who had he strength would not refuse, / More pains for thee to take." He took up his pen only because he was left "wanting other means," or as Cotton Mather put it, "when he could not *Preach* he *Wrote* several Composures."[67] Mitchel may have styled him in the bardic tradition, as a "Christian Poet" singing in "these Vast woods" whose affliction gave him a foothold into the spiritual world, but as soon as Wigglesworth was recovered enough to resume his preaching ministry, he appears to have more or less abandoned poetry. Thus, although the success of *The Day of Doom* led him to write in more positive terms about his "great work" (referring to the poems he was working on for *Meat Out of the Eater*), Wigglesworth never endorsed the poetic medium above the more traditional preaching medium of the sermon.[68] For him, as for Mitchel, the verse form of *The Day of Doom* remained and even vaunted itself as *ersatz*.

As Jeffrey Hammond and Raymond Craig among others, have highlighted, the Pauline inversions of strength in weakness and wisdom in foolishness were often exploited in New England religious aesthetics.[69] The important role of the conversion relation, a relatively humble and colloquial form, is an example of this. In his later verses in *Meat Out of the Eater*, Wigglesworth wrote much on the theme of such reversals in value: "I have endeavoured / The Cross for to adorn, / By setting forth its comeliness, / Although the world it scorn."[70] For Wigglesworth, however, the inversions were not just abstract but tangible because of his debilitating illness, which exerted a formative influence on his poetic writing. Not only did his illness prompt him to write in verse but there are suggestions that it shaped the kind of verse he wrote. In a diary entry from May 1657, Wigglesworth lamented "the return of my nightly distemper occasioned by study about church Government & my want of insight thereinto, or of strength to attain it."[71] Under the stress occasioned by his controversy with Hills, and possible doubts over the reforms already being discussed by ministers, Wigglesworth's turn to the less serious medium of verse, and the less controversial topic of Judgment, probably provided a helpful distraction.

The link with illness also gave the text and the "pains" Wigglesworth took an extrinsic costliness. Notably, Samuel Whiting, author of the 1664 prose treatise on Judgment, was also mentioned as suffering from a "painfull infirmity of body." The words of the dying were accorded a special weight by New England Puritans because the dying were believed to be closer to God, and more directly facing their own mortality. Cotton Mather's treatise entitled *Thoughts of a Dying Man*, for example, illustrates the spiritual authority that such an awareness of death was believed to give to a writer.[72] Wigglesworth was not dying, but Mitchel gave his illness a special sacrificial meaning, not least by blaming it on the sinfulness of society, "The Sins of Hearers, Preachers Lips do close."[73] However, in this suggestion of a deeper spiritual meaning being represented through the choice of a weaker medium, the inversion of value still did not remove the aspect of weakness by mystically exalting it: instead, the verse became a fallible, material embodiment of the poet's weakness for which he was still expected to apologize.

In one of Wigglesworth's numerous lists of complaints in his note-book, he expressed frustration that he could only think or pray in "short ejaculation[s]":

> I cannot think a few serious thoughts, scarce once in a whole day many times, except it be now and then a short ejaculation, which doth not so effectually take off the heart from things below and carry it into heaven as set and solemn meditation was wont to do.[74]

Given that Wigglesworth's illness involved a serious nervous anxiety about frequent nocturnal emissions, there is an obvious Freudian irony in such a comment; and Cherniavsky has recently linked the aspects of flow and repetition in Wigglesworth's poetry and journal-ing with his sexual anxiety.[75] But Wigglesworth's comment is sugges-tive, too, from the point of view of metrical form. If Wigglesworth was looking for ways of "composing" his religious thoughts, the verse form of *The Day of Doom* was well-fitted to such a purpose: the rhyme scheme would have provided an absorbing mental puzzle and the meter a strong momentum. The rigid verse form had a stability that would have made it a useful external structure for controlling unruly thoughts. George Herbert's poetic "ejaculations" could only be so called in the tradition of exaggerated flippancy, whereby a poet's work was trivialized in terms of effort, in order to magnify it in terms of achievement. Wigglesworth's verse, on the other hand, really does seem rough-edged and if not spontaneous then at least unpolished.[76] His journal shows that he wrote quickly and considered himself par-ticularly blessed if he wrote a large number of stanzas in one day. Hence, similar to the constraints of translation in the case of the Bay Psalm Book, Wigglesworth's illness contributed materially to the de-velopment of a poetic form that could spiritually exploit its literary weakness.

In view of the emphatic reversals of value in the prefatory verses, it seems, in fact, fitting that *The Day of Doom* was not imbued with the evocative force of more ambitious poetry. Although many critics have lamented the use of a popular or doggerel verse form to treat so "large" and "dignified" a theme, the choice of ballad meter and its limitations, in terms of elegance and poetic sensitivity, were appro-priate to the spiritualized aesthetics of the poem. When Kenneth Murdock commented that "the trotting verses seem sadly unsuited to the subject," he may have been making a mental comparison with the more "spacious and solemn form" of Milton's "On the Morning of Christ's Nativity," with its striking use of hexameter lines at the end of each stanza.[77] Indeed, when compared to such verses, Wigglesworth's poetry does appear rather trivializing: "Yet first to those ychain'd in sleep, / The wakefull trump of doom must thunder through the deep," wrote Milton, and in the next stanza:

> The aged Earth agast
> With terrour of that blast,
>   Shall from the surface to the center shake;
> When at the worlds last session,
> The dreadful Judge in middle Air shall spread his throne.[78]

When Christ arrived, in Wigglesworth's poem, by contrast:

> His brightness damps heav'ns glorious lamps
>   and makes them hide their heads,
> As if afraid and quite dismay'd,
>   they quit their wonted steads.[79]

There is a touch of the homely and paradoxically reductive in Wigglesworth's verse, foreshadowing Emily Dickinson's toying with such themes in lines like, "I went to Heaven— / 'Twas a small town–."[80] But devoid of any Dickinsonian irony, Wigglesworth's lines are relatively weak and diminishing. They evoke panic and confusion, but not quite the kind of terror on a grand scale that would shake the "aged Earth" to its core.

The difference suggests that *The Day of Doom* was neither written to compete with the rhetorical command of more culturally ambitious poetry, nor designed in an effort to redeem the genre of verse per se in New England. Rather, its form was to seem an empty vehicle, a kind of "sugar" coating on the pill of doctrine, which could not therefore be construed as contaminating to the message. In this sense, and because poetry was a potentially self-aggrandizing form, the rhetorical weaknesses of *The Day of Doom* formed a necessary part of its style. As in the Bay Psalm Book, a certain amount of aesthetic jarring of message against form acted to "expose" the verse as a mere formal vehicle and defuse what was evidently feared by some to be a potentially insidious power. The foolishness of St. Paul, to which Wigglesworth alluded, was also related to the Apostle's construction of a rhetorical dichotomy that opposed the wisdom of Man's words to the power of the Holy Spirit, similar in some ways to the "fidelity, not poetry" dichotomy of the Bay Psalm Book: "And my speech and my preaching was not with enticing words of man's wisdom, but in demonstration of the Spirit and of power: That your faith should not stand in the wisdom of men, but in the power of God."[81]

By suggesting that the limited power of poetry lay in its relatively superficial appeal as a pleasant vehicle, Wigglesworth and Mitchel ensured that, as William Perkins had advised, the readers would ascribe any spiritual effects to God and not to human skill. Also, the restriction of Wigglesworth's verse to only the most common and repetitive verse forms, namely, fourteeners (and heroic couplets for the "Postscript"), meant that the potential for poetic exaltation was minimized. Despite their shared Protestant heritage, Sidney's image of the divine frenzy of classical poets, Wither's sense of the poet's superior powers, and Milton's idealized view of the melding of mystical and prophetic inspiration—as in the image of Holy Spirit/Urania bringing him the words of *Paradise Lost* in the night—have very little in common with Wigglesworth's pragmatic attitude and pedestrian verse style. His approach was much closer to that of Bunyan who also emphasized the possibility of inversion, in his prefatory verses to *The Pilgrim's Progress*: "a Pearl may in a Toads-head dwell, / And may be found too in a Oister-shell." But neither Wigglesworth nor Mitchel resorted to such blatant images of predatory deviousness as the fowler's "Gun, his Nets, his Lime-twigs" in describing Wigglesworth's chosen medium.[82] Wigglesworth encouraged rather than challenged the idea that he was stooping to the genre of verse, and in this respect he diverged considerably from Herbert, Sidney, and Milton. Curiously, however, Wigglesworth and Mitchel expressed a greater sense of weakness and loss than Bunyan in the turn to a popular medium. This was perhaps because, as highly educated and influential men, the New England ministers were all the more sensitive to the fact that Wigglesworth had condescended to write in a style that was particularly unrefined, even within the genre of poetry. Wigglesworth's choice of a low-brow verse form within the supposedly second-rate genre of verse thereby further reinforced the aspect of conscious "weakness" in his words, and contributed to making *The Day of Doom* a defiantly demystified and demystifying poem.

POPULAR BALLADS AND *THE DAY OF DOOM*

The particular low-brow form Wigglesworth chose was an adaptation of ballad meter, and in view of the ambivalence concerning inclusiveness and exclusiveness in his poem and in the Halfway Covenant measures, his style of adaptation was especially apt. Although presented in book form, Wigglesworth's poem had strong links with the popular ballad. Of course, popular broadside ballads were never as long, and even when collected in book form in "garlands" were never so textually arrayed with invocations, epilogues, and commendatory verses as *The Day of Doom*. Unlike *The Day of Doom*, ballads were also conventionally printed in black-letter type and usually included the name of a tune to which they could be sung. But Wigglesworth's use of a jaunty kind of common meter as the verse form for the centerpiece poem was nevertheless a strong allusion to and borrowing from the popular ballad tradition. This borrowing, couched within such a self-consciously literary frame of paratexts, demonstrated Wigglesworth's application of the kind of aesthetic defiance he learned from New England church order and the Bay Psalm Book. In choosing ballad meter, Wigglesworth was working within a long Christian tradition of adapting popular poetic forms to a didactic purpose. But the techniques of "appropriation, imitation, and correction" associated with religious parody nevertheless placed *The Day of Doom* in a complex relationship with the ballad genre.[83]

The ballad form borrowed for this popular-style narrative poem suggested a broad level of inclusiveness that was rather duplicitous, given the ecclesiastical system of the exclusive inner church covenant. Although, as I noted in the previous chapter, the common meter verse form with an extra internal rhyme was found in Psalm 137 in the Bay Psalm Book, it was also commonly used in British broadside ballads, both secular and godly. In the broadsides, as in *The Day of Doom*, the form usually conveyed slightly more narrative and dialogic content than that of the Psalms. Seventeenth-century ballads in the same meter included, for example, "Walking alone not long agone," a ballad that retold the story of Job, and "A merry ballad of a rich maid that had 18. severall suitors of severall countries: otherwise called the scornefull maid." The latter was written to be sung to the presumably lively tune of, "hoop do me no harme good man."[84] To the modern reader, the meter of *The Day of Doom* is probably most familiar as that of "The Nut Brown Maid," a ballad known to have been reprinted many times during the sixteenth and early seventeenth centuries, and that may have been current orally in Wigglesworth's time.[85] Such ballads were lively, popular, and inclusive, but on closer inspection, the adaptation of the genre to religious purposes was not without its complications, and these were increased rather than diminished in *The Day of Doom*.

According to the Stationers' Register and booksellers' stock-lists, there were a few religious broadsides that were frequently reprinted and evidently well-loved in early modern England; these included "St. Bernard's Vision" and "The Clarke of Bodnam," two ballads on the topic of Judgment. In general, however, secular ballads proved the most enduring.[86] The "Nut Brown Maid," for example, was parodied circa 1535 in a version entitled "The New Notbrowne Mayd upon the Passion of Cryste."[87] This version borrowed the form and the dialogue structure from the original, but substituted Christ for the maid's lover. Although the original "Nut Brown Maid" was reprinted many times, the religious version was quickly forgotten. Even in the heyday of the broadside ballad, the late sixteenth century, religious ballads made up a maximum of about one third of registered copy, and by the time Wigglesworth took up his pen in the Restoration period, new religious broadside ballads had become a rarity in Britain.[88] To take two popular ballad collections that made their way to New England in the 1680s as a further illustration, in Richard Johnson's *Crown Garland* there are no godly ballads, and in Thomas Deloney's *Garland of Delight* there is only one: "A Godly *Ditty* exhorting to Repentance." This godly song is placed at the very end of the book, following a long series of love laments and "wooing" ballads, as if repentance must put an end to such profane singing.[89]

Partly because of the disproportion in the circulation of secular to godly ballads, the popular British ballad thus retained a secular and even scurrilous profile, and connotations of petty immorality, as evoked by Shakespeare in his characterization of the balladmonger Autolycus in *A Winter's Tale* as a singing pickpocket and con artist.[90] As I mentioned in chapter 2, throughout the seventeenth century, reissues of the Sternhold and Hopkins Psalter continued to sport on their title page the epigraph instruction: "Set forth and allowed to be sung in all Churches, of all the people together . . . and moreover in private houses for their godly solace and comfort: laying apart all ungodly songs and ballades which tend onely to the nourishing of vice, and corrupting of youth." And while in his 1642 treatise on liturgy John Cotton had allowed that people could compose and sing their own spiritual songs in private, he emphasized that only Psalms were "fit to be sung in the public holy Assemblies of the Saints," and he supported his argument with a lateral analogy of "the carnal and profane Sonnets of drunken Poets" which were not fit for civil assemblies but only "Taverns and Alehouses."[91] By allowing that original religious compositions could be sung privately, Cotton endorsed a compromise position; but the terms of his argument reinforced the traditional dichotomization of sacred and profane song and in particular the scurrilous reputation of the secular ballad.

If the poor reputation of the ballad was partly a result of the high proportion of secular ballads in circulation, the emphasis in strict Calvinist churches on singing psalms only (as remained the practice in seventeenth-century Massachusetts churches) also contributed. Because of the negative characterization of the ballad in religious circles, the efforts of popular poets like Wigglesworth and the writers of the godly ballads were often imbued with a careful condescension. The "New Not-browne Mayd" was unusual in its close reference to a single original ballad, but an element of self-conscious parody was a common feature of the godly ballad. Most godly writers were not whole-heartedly adopting and offering to redeem the ballad as a literary and religious genre. Instead, they were self-consciously using it for didactic purposes, as the "sugar" of form, in the sense that Mitchel suggested regarding *The Day of Doom*. Since the form was borrowed, if it seemed a little ill-fitting as in the case of *The Day of Doom,* then this would help to safeguard the distinction between the sugar and the truth that was rolled in it. Wigglesworth introduced the idea that this kind of borrowing was indeed part of the design of *The Day of Doom* in the first stanza of the main poem, in which his narrator both alluded to and condemned the secular ballad:

> Still was the night, Serene and Bright,
>   when all Men sleeping lay;
> Calm was the season, and carnal reason
>   thought so 'twould last for ay.
> Soul, take thine ease, let sorrow cease,
>   much good thou hast in store:
> This was their Song, their Cups among,
>   the Evening before.[92]

The fact that lines from an apparently fictional but representative tavern ballad could be seamlessly incorporated into the poem illustrates that its familiar form and jaunty swing were indeed borrowed from folk tradition. However, Wigglesworth evoked the convivial and comforting associations of his ballad meter in order to confront them four stanzas later with the dramatic arrival of Christ. Such a significant limitation to the jovial appeal and inclusiveness of *The Day of Doom* made its poetic form as qualified and ambivalent a "popular measure" as the Halfway Covenant itself.

Wigglesworth's allusion to tavern singing in this first stanza attests to the presence of secular ballads in the colony, and reinforces the traditional clerical condemnation of them. *The Day of Doom* implicitly offers itself as a more morally improving albeit less carnally appealing substitute. Although no printed broadside ballads like those collected by Pepys in London are known to have survived from mid-seventeenth-century New England, there is evidence (over and above Wigglesworth's own reference) that they were sung in Massachusetts and therefore that the genre Wigglesworth was parodying was current. A satirical ballad detailing "New England's Annoyances" was composed in about 1643, although only eighteenth-century printings of it survive.[93] It satirized the promotional literature of the colony with long complaints about the weather, living conditions, and staple diet of pumpkin. In addition, Seaborn Cotton, one of Wigglesworth's classmates at Harvard, copied three complete ballads and many fragments into a commonplace book that he began at college. Samuel Eliot Morison compared Cotton's versions of "The Love-sick Maid," "The Last Lamentation of the Languishing Squire," and "The Two Faithful Lovers" with British broadsides and decided that the variants indicate oral transmission.[94] Perhaps this kind of oral transmission sometimes accompanied the idle music-making among Harvard students that Wigglesworth noted with distaste in his diary when he was tutoring there in 1653.[95]

By criticizing a genre the form of which it shared, the first stanza of *The Day of Doom* established a firm opposition between its spiritualized perspective, which prioritized "unseen," but valuable, things, and the indulgent, materialistic worldview represented in secular drinking songs. In so doing, the poem sets limits from the very start to its association with the broadly human, inclusive, and accessible features that made popular songs the chosen vehicle for the project. The element of inclusivity, for example, is deftly and theologically reconfigured. Although *The Day of Doom* actually outdoes the worldly ballad in inclusiveness, because it depicts the Judgment of "all flesh," the ultimate purpose of the Judgment is, as I have already noted, discrimination, resulting in the exclusion of the Reprobate from Heaven. As implied by Mitchel's warning to the reader to "judge right" and to exercise spiritually "good" taste, *The Day of Doom* quickly develops into the kind of poem that jars with the open and affable connotations of its ballad measure. Although this is not an uncommon aspect of godly parody, it is intensified in *The Day of Doom.*

Wigglesworth depicted final judgment at work not simply through the deliberations of Christ but through the rousing of everybody's secret conscience. Their conscience "judgeth them, and doth condemn, / though all the world say nay," and thereby divides "each Man's self against himself."[96] In this way, the poem ultimately gives precisely the opposite message to "Soul, take thine ease, let sorrow cease." But it turns this worldly message around by allowing superficially religious versions of it to be refuted in the extended dialogues between Christ and the condemned souls. The dialogues that constitute the large central section of the poem, build on the sharing of the form between secular and godly established in the opening stanza. The same ballad form and colloquial diction serve both Christ and the damned souls.[97] While the structure of objection and answer was common in the New England sermon, in the context of the ballad tradition this format also reflected the duality of secular ballad and godly parody. First the Puritan reader was allowed to be taken in by the reassuring but false arguments, each of which represented some kind of spiritual complacency. Then, Christ's reply, like the godly parody itself, condescended to the level of the speaker or reader and exerted a forceful corrective influence. One group asserted, for example, that "Natures Light shin'd not so bright / to teach us the right way," and Christ's response picked up the metaphor and even echoed the rhyme:

> How came your mind to be so blind?
>   I once you knowledge gave,
> Clearness of sight, and judgment right;
>   who did the same deprave?[98]

Thus, Wigglesworth's use of dialogue subtly exploited the duality inherent in the tradition of the godly ballad.

A counterside of parody is, of course, the danger of reversion to type, but in *The Day of Doom* this weakness also seemed well fitted to the theological purpose of a tensely limited kind of covenant extension. Like Mitchel's mentioning of the distracting "toy"-like potential of poetry, Wigglesworth's initial association of his verse with the spiritually lulling qualities of the secular ballad was potentially subversive, and cemented the connection in the act of seeking to generate distance. The lulling qualities of the cited first stanza may be read as a demonstration of the deceptions of "carnal reason." Indeed, in an inverted but typologically accurate fashion, Wigglesworth foreshadowed the terrifying event of the Second Coming with hints of the Nativity: "Still was the night, Serene and Bright, / when all Men sleeping lay." Nevertheless, the explicit association with a popular form portrayed in the first stanza as distinctly nonawakening was already suggestive of the limits of Wigglesworth's chosen verse form. This undercurrent reinforced the predestinarian irony that underlay the efforts of evangelism and covenant extension associated with the Halfway Covenant. Subjected later to the memorization and childlike repetition that the verse form invited, the images of sudden awakening and spiritual recognition would be undermined still further by a performative context that was based on reiteratability. Despite the poem's relatively complex theological dialogues, its prefatory addresses, and its opening allusion to tavern ballads, all of which strongly imply that the poem was intended for a broad adult audience, by the early eighteenth century it seems to have been associated with children and regarded as a catechistic poem.[99] In this way, the unsophisticated connotations of its verse form could be said to have undermined to some extent the poem's theological aims. As a fixed and highly reiteratable form of words, *The Day of Doom*, like the new rite of owning the covenant, had the potential to revert to the kind of empty form or spiritually complacent use of language against which it had originally been written.

The verse form, which showed itself in the opening stanza to be well fitted to the comfortable message and rhythmic swing of the secular ballad, thus imbued *The Day of Doom* with a subversive potential, and enforced the message of the difficulty of realizing those "unseen things." As the poem progressed, the combination of the theological subtlety of Wigglesworth's message and a common, simple ballad meter only enhanced the tension between poetic accessibility and challenge. Although many ballads promoted the pleasures of life— love, sex, drinking, escapades—the monitory and didactic tone was also very common. While religion featured prominently in this ballad wisdom, it was generally reduced to a basic sense of goodness and wickedness. In very few ballads was the fullness of Reformation theology represented with its emphasis on salvation through faith and forgiveness, rather than good works. "In slumbring sleep I lay," in which the sinner managed to trust in "the blood of Christ" when Satan came to claim his soul, and the story of the distinctly Reformed "Clark of Bodnam" are rare examples; but because of their brevity, even these ballads had nothing of the degree of theological debate found in *The Day of Doom*.[100]

The ballad measure contributed to the design of covenant extension by giving the poem accessibility to a wide audience; on the other hand, however, it played a kind of deception, in that the difficulty of achieving a right and spiritual response, emphasized throughout the poem, contrasted with the simple language and easy swing of the verse: "The Mystery of Pietie / God unto Babes reveals," asserted Wigglesworth's Christ in response to one group of damned souls:

> If to fulfil Gods holy will
>   had seemed good to you,
> You would have sought light as you ought,
>   and done the good you knew.[101]

Although, as in the tradition of religious parodies of ballads, the sense of the form as a superficial disguise acted ostensibly to safeguard the integrity of the religious message, the tension caused by the accentuated disparity of form and content contributed to the self-limiting aspect of Wigglesworth's poetic style. Like the rite of owning the covenant and the extension of baptism under the Halfway Covenant, the kind of admission offered by the attractive verse form of the poem was a lure that appeared in the final count woefully insufficient, and only a tiny stepping stone in the difficult task of finding salvation. The gulf between "sugar" and heavenly "bliss" remained, and Wigglesworth's poetic style only served to make it more apparent.

Moreover, with its role as vehicle explicitly emphasized, the verse form became a less forceful medium for conveying the full impact of the subtle and challenging theological message to the kind of people who relished a good ballad. The poem's aspect of covenant extension or popularization was thereby reinforced as "halfway," reflecting both the use and mistrust of popular appeal and the "set form" of verse. If in Wigglesworth's adaptation he had accentuated some of the innate tensions in the conventions of the godly ballad, then similar literary complications resulted from the way in which he adapted the sensational *Dies Irae* tropes evoked by the title. David D. Hall mentioned *The Day of Doom* as an example of the folk cult of the "sensational."[102] This is true to the extent that Wigglesworth turned to a popular and sensational theme in his choice of setting and title in an effort to reach "him who a sermon flies." Yet the sensational aspects, too, were strongly and defiantly adapted by Wigglesworth, in such a way as to modify their folk appeal and to harness the genre securely to the spiritualized and challenging New England ecclesiastical aesthetic.

DIES IRAE SENSATIONALISM AND THE DAY OF DOOM

As its title suggests, *The Day of Doom* was written in the tradition of *Dies Irae*, the "day of wrath," a theme named after the opening of a thirteenth-century liturgical lament: "Dies irae, dies illa, / Solvet saeclum in favilla: / Teste David cum Sibylla."[103] The message of this song was reflected in the paintings and carvings that decorated cathedrals and churches in pre-Reformation England. With all its potential for drama, and evocative description, it is easy to see how by the seventeenth century this kind of writing had become particularly associated with popular sensationalism. Although found in many literary genres, including of course the poetry of Dante, the genre of *Dies Irae* seems to have an enduring popular appeal: in the American tabloid press features about the Second Coming still sell newspapers today. In Britain in the 1660s and 1670s, similarly sensational broadside news ballads were hawked around the streets, with titles evoking the religious supernatural, including "The World's Wonder, or the Prophetical Fish" (1666) and "Strange News from Staffordshire, or a Dreadful Example of Divine *Justice*" (1677).[104] One very popular British broadside specifically on a *Dies Irae* theme was "St. Bernard's Vision," a ballad reprinted throughout the seventeenth century and beyond. As its vivid accompanying woodcuts suggest, it drew on all the conventions of dramatizing the devastating consequences of Divine Judgment, and the pain and punishment of Hell.[105]

Hall has argued from strong evidence in diaries and prose treatises that despite there not being an extant tradition of such broadsides in New England, the settlers shared the contemporaneous British obsession with prodigies and wonders. While Hall's citation of *The Day of Doom* as an example of this is slightly misplaced, his observation does highlight the curious disparity between the sensational connotations of the title Wigglesworth chose and the kind of portrayal he actually gave. Writing on this theme, and using a kind of meter associated with broadside ballads, Wigglesworth would probably have been aware of the literary alternatives open to him. Yet *The Day of Doom* does not, for instance, fit the pattern Hall identified with sensational literature, namely, that "though God (or good) prevails, evildoing is described in rich detail."[106] Instead (as in his use of the form and connotations of the secular ballad), Wigglesworth played the appeal and accessibility associated with *Dies Irae* tropes against the stark resistance of the poem's challenging theological message. This message included the idea that the poem required divine "complementation" if it was to have a real spiritual impact on its readers.

For instance, opportunities for visually and viscerally evocative description of intense joy and hellish suffering (never mind earthly evildoing) were left relatively unexploited in the poem. Laying the emphasis upon the procedure of judgment, Wigglesworth gave proportionally little space to the gruesome details of damnation, though these form a central part of other *Dies Irae* writings. He portrayed the panic caused by Christ's arrival at the beginning of the poem, and touched, at the end, on the experiences of damnation and bliss that awaited the judged. But these experiences Wigglesworth described in terms that tended towards the theological and abstract. He described Heaven, for instance, as follows:

> O glorious Place! where face to face
> Jehovah may be seen,
> By such as were sinners whilere
> and no dark vail between.[107]

Hell is portrated as a place of pain where sinners cannot die even though they want to:

> They live to ly in misery,
> and bear eternal wo;
> And live they must whilst God is just,
> that he may plague them so.[108]

The damned do experience "pois'ned darts" in their hearts, but even these seem metaphorical, since it is "[t]he pain of loss" that "their Souls doth toss, . . . to think what they have cast away."[109]

A particularly noticeable omission is that of salacious details of the particular physical torments and personally tailored punishments that the damned could expect to find in Hell. Wigglesworth resorted to ineffability and to hyperbolic abstractions that merely hint at hellish suffering: "But who can tell the plagues of Hell, / and torments exquisite?", "The least degree of miserie / there felt's incomparable."[110] By contrast, in one popular British ballad, "The deadmans song," the very aspects for which Wigglesworth struggled to find words provide the central focus. In this ballad, Hell is depicted in a way characteristic of the genre, that is, with what one editor called "a prodigal use of frightful and loathsome imagery" inherited from the apocryphal Apocalypse of St. Peter, church paintings, and Dante.[111] It is a place where the gluttonous are fed with "dishes full of crawling Toades" while having their flesh plucked off with red hot pincers, and liars and swearers are "hung up by the tongue / over a flaming fire." The printer, of course, found a suitable woodcut to enforce the imagery.[112]

Such imagery was not restricted to broadside ballads. It was found, too, for example, in *Dekker His Dreame*, another popular work, similar in length to *The Day of Doom* and published in London in 1620. Although both Dekker's and Wigglesworth's extant doomsday works were published without gruesome illustrations, Dekker's literary style was very graphic and pageantlike. He used, for example, the allegorical figures of "Vengeance, Horror, Incest, Rape, / Famine and Death."[113] By, as he put it, "Picturing forth" the Apocalypse and the suffering in Hell, Dekker worked hard to make the moral and religious dangers sensuously apprehensible. Hell's darkness, for instance, is described as "glutinously-thick" (like Dekker's word-painting in general).[114] There is no way of knowing whether or not Wigglesworth had read *Dekker His Dreame*, though the brief incident near the end of Dekker's text in which a damned soul protests and is answered by Christ raises the tantalizing possibility.[115] Either way, Wigglesworth would have been familiar with the *Dies Irae* tradition by cultural osmosis. His implicit repudiation of the conventional and popular tropes represented in *Dekker His Dreame*, was a literary choice that reflected an alternative approach to religious didacticism, an approach that was influenced by spiritualized aesthetics and the suspicion of forms in New England ecclesiastical practices.

Through personification, Dekker gave abstract wrongs an emotive force, like "Religion" who wore in the Last Days "a Garment" "Stayn'd like a painter's Apron."[116] By interspersing his rich and figurative verse with prose notes that interpreted the "vision," Dekker implied that he considered poetry a particularly concentrated medium, and one that created a certain impact that could then be applied through prose explanations. By comparison, Wigglesworth's dramatization seems thin, propositional, understated, even mundane. But the conclusion drawn by critics like Daly and Murdock that Wigglesworth simply lacked the poetic instinct for imagery is inadequate. Believing that Wigglesworth "might conceivably have created an emotionally moving picture of Doomsday, full of color and compact of poetry," Murdock attributed his failure to do so to a concern not to shoot "above his readers' heads."[117] *Dekker His Dreame* and the broadside ballads show that there was nothing intrinsically élitist about colorful and emotive portrayals of Judgment.

Daly, on the other hand, attributed Wigglesworth's lack of imagery to his rather "Gnostic" view of life, and this is probably nearer the truth.[118] However, Wigglesworth still chose to write in ballad meter and to give his work a sensational title, thereby packaging it, superficially at least, for a sanguine popular readership. Moreover, the orations upon eloquence that he prepared for his Harvard examinations show that Wigglesworth knew about rich and evocative language. By setting up certain expectations for the contemporary reader, and then distorting and undermining them, Wigglesworth further developed the tension between accessibility and exclusivity that epitomized the piety of the Halfway Covenant. Avoiding colorful portrayals of individual retribution, and using a simple rather than intensely evocative language, Wigglesworth emphasized the spiritual rather than fleshly dimension of the task of realizing "unseen things." Though he wanted his readers' hearts to be affected, his message also conveyed the deceptiveness of outward forms and appearances.

In *The Day of Doom*, conceptual debates that situated themselves in the individual reader's conscience replaced the conventional poetic emblems and tableaux that guided the reader's response in works like Dekker's. Wigglesworth concentrated on the trial scene, rather than on the punishment that bodied forth people's sins and made their wickedness self-evident. At this prior stage, appearances were portrayed as often misleading. Each group of sinners found grounds for its defense, and although Wigglesworth raised the objections in order to answer them, he composed some very strong objections, doubtless drawing from his pastoral experience in teaching and counseling. As Richard Bernard advised would-be ministers: "If [people are] exhorted to good things, they have their excuses; all which must be taken away."[119] The contemporary New England reader, therefore, was likely to have found some of the objections relatively convincing before hearing Christ's reply. Enforced by repetition, this structure gave the impression that hypocrisy was easily fallen into, and that one's own error could easily pass undetected in this life.

The protests of the damned included apparently plausible and religious claims: "But we have in thy presence been, / say some, and eaten there" or "Thou knowest us / that we were blameless livers;" or "We were misled . . . By their Example, that had more ample / abilities than we," or "We had thy Word, . . . but wiser men than we / Could never yet interpret it." This latter group, for example, argued with apparent reason:

> How could we fools be led by Rules,
>   so far beyond our ken,
> Which to explain did so much pain,
>   and puzzle wisest men?[120]

Yet Christ exposed and refuted them forcefully: "Was all my word abstruse and hard? . . . It did contain much truth so plain"

> But what was hard you never car'd
>   to know nor studied,

> And things that were most plain and clear
> you never practised.[121]

In Whiting's *Discourse*, the objections of similarly self-deceiving souls are described in the analogy of the drowning man who "will catch hold of sticks and straws that can no way help" and this is Wigglesworth's ultimate point, too.[122] Yet in Wigglesworth's dramatized presentation, the debate shifts much more dynamically to and fro, inviting the reader's sympathy for the wrong side before Christ addresses and confutes each protest until, "never a man, or dare, or can / a further Answer make."[123]

In this way, although "the reader's potential resistance to the doctrine" was "linked solidly with the strident arguments of the damned" (to quote Hammond), true spiritual righteousness was also portrayed by Wigglesworth as far harder to identify than in the self-explanatory emblematic tableaux of other doomsday literature.[124] In line with the ethos of the New England covenanted churches, Wigglesworth conveyed regeneration as something that had to be ascertained. Moreover, in each encounter between the protester and Christ, the potential for reader sympathy formed a test or trap that could expose the readers' false and "carnal reason" and by extension highlight their need for salvation. In this way, the poetry was designed less to guide readers liturgically into faith, so much as throw them onto the mercy of Christ, exhorting them, like Whiting, always "To fear lest we should fall short of [Eternal Life]."[125]

Further, whereas in more sensational depictions of Hell and Judgment the vivid depiction of punishments unveiled the true and ugly nature of the damned soul, Wigglesworth's verse rejected such powerful literary symmetries. Dante's images of violent souls, condemned to wade in boiling blood and be ruled over by centaurs (half-beasts), and heretics, who were forced to lay in burning tombs, were emblematic punishments that revealed spiritual truths about those sinners' inward dispositions.[126] In *Dekker His Dreame*, frivolous fine women were transformed into ugly "hagges" whose characteristics exposed their sin of being temptresses, in addition to entailing the destruction of their former beauty: "Their Painted cheekes, turn'd into Witches looks, / Bright Haire to Snakes, long Fingers into hooks."[127] In such examples, Hell represented a spiritual inversion of temporal life, in which obvious wrongs were justly righted, and, like in the portrait of Dorian Gray, moral evil was made to appear in its true colors. In the rhetorical strategy of *The Day of Doom*, however, such efforts to evoke assent from the contemporary reader's intuitive sense of balance and natural justice would have been out of place.

Wigglesworth did not convey spiritual revelation and divine justice to be truths towards which the reader was expected to feel full emotional assent. On the contrary, while the judgments in Dekker's poem were given weight and meaning through their resonance with his reader's intuition, in *The Day of Doom* it was rather the reader's conscience that was judged by Christ's decrees. That it was Wigglesworth's intent to confront rather than exploit natural sympathies and folk wisdom is confirmed by his strong emphasis on the hardest cases: featuring prominently are religious hypocrites, the unevangelized, and the Reprobate among the Innocents. The fact that these Innocents were condemned to "the easiest room in Hell" shows that Wigglesworth found the doctrine emotionally difficult to accept, but also that he was keen to enforce it, all the same.[128]

The concession to the Innocents was small, and Wigglesworth continued to emphasize the unappealing nature of the doctrines he believed to be orthodox by describing in explicit detail some of the most counter-intuitive moments of the Judgment. In stanzas 195–200, for instance, he underlined the complete lack of sympathy of the saints towards their former friends and companions who were about to be thrown over the brink of Hell:

> The tender Mother will own no other
>   of all her numerous brood,
> But such as stand at Christ's right hand
>   acquitted through his Blood.
> The pious father had now much rather
>   his graceless Son should ly
> In Hell with Devils, for all his evils
>   burning eternally,
>
> Then God most high should injury,
>   by sparing him sustain;
> And doth rejoyce to hear Christ's voice
>   adjudging him to pain;[129]

Wigglesworth's son, Edward, recalled his father threatening him with this idea: "I have been terrified & astonished when my father hath been setting life & Death before me & then telling me if I chose death rather than life he would appear as a witness against me in the great & terrible day of the Lord."[130] This reference implies that Wigglesworth used the image as a deliberate shock tactic, and directly intended to cause pain and astonishment. The enjambment across stanzas, rare in the rest of the poem, confirms that this was a moment of particular tension; the momentum and the easy swing of the ballad meter, unsuited to the awkwardness of the situation described, only accentuates this tension.

Popular verse form was thus used to convey the defeat of human instinct by a superior power of justice, but by the same token this superior justice was almost incomprehensible in emotional terms. The effect, similar to that in the elegy on Abigail Tompson and Bradstreet's late elegies, was to underline the distance between the natural response of the reader and the kind of total acceptance of the doctrine that would make one content with such a blasé description. In Dekker's and other similar representations of divine justice, the concept of evil drew heavily upon a predictable echo in the reader's breast. The provocativeness in Wigglesworth's poem demonstrated, however, a greater concern to show that God's thoughts are not our thoughts, nor our ways His ways: "The Mystery of Pieties / God unto Babes reveals, / When to the wise he it denies, / and from the world conceals."[131]

Lack of "Dream Vision" Liminality

A further way in which Wigglesworth's aesthetic gave his style a "halfway" quality was in his total resistance to the spiritual mystification of poetry in *The Day of Doom*. The almost exaggerated clarity and mundane tone of his presentation of doomsday contrasted with the use of prophetic conventions in the verse genre, conventions that were used to give creative portrayals a kind of mystical religious authority. Dekker, for example, used the common device of the dream vision, which was emphasized in his book by the insertion of a frontispiece woodcut of the author asleep in bed.[132] The broadside ballad "A prophesie of the judgment day" used an even more elaborate framing device by claiming that the verses were "lately found in Saint Denis Church in France, and wrapped in Leade in the forme of an heart."[133] Wigglesworth, on the other hand, consistent with his repudiation of muses and the classical exaltation of poetry, entirely rejected any such separation of his verse from everyday life. The realm in which his poem operated placed the human and the divine in a raw and would-be factual conjunction, as in the face-to-face and occasionally conversational dialogue of Christ with the damned souls.

Dekker's seven-year "dream" corresponded to an actual period of imprisonment.[134] The poet transformed this experience, for the purpose of this piece of writing, into a "dream" in which, "beeing rapt with a Poeticall Enthusiasme, the great Volumes of Heaven and Hell to Him were opened, in which he read many Wonderful Things."[135] These images in the subtitle of the work illustrate how Dekker used metaphor and even the implication of the textuality of Biblical "Revelation" in order to build a satisfying literary bridge across the distance between this world and the next. However, although Wigglesworth's diary records that while at Harvard he did actually experience a dream of judgment "and was thereby exceedingly awakened in spirit," he made no allusion to this in the poem.[136] Wigglesworth hence avoided suggesting that there existed any mutually validating relationship between prophecy or vision and poetry, and kept his poetry free from all hint of Antinomianism.[137] Indeed, it appears to have been part of his main design to separate "Enthusiasme" from poetry, and to demonstrate that poetry could, in fact, present a reassuringly plain explanation of the faith.

Probably the most striking example of Wigglesworth's poetic plainness is the collision between the domestic and divine dimensions at the moment of the Second Coming, without any dream or other device to create a mysterious "poeticall" perspective. Instead, the realms overtly collide, with the moment of conjunction being framed in an almost absurdly literal way, by an ordinary window:

> They rush from Beds with giddy heads,
>   and to their windows run,
> Viewing this light, which shines more bright
>   then doth the Noon-day Sun.
> Straightway appears (they see't with tears)
>   the Son of God most dread;
> Who with his Train comes on amain
> To Judge both Quick and Dead.[138]

In the context of a literary genre in which more sophisticated framing devices were common, particularly the dream, this unmediated, present-tense contact seems almost comic. As in elegies like Wilson's on Abigail Tompson, this stark portrayal challenged the reader's religious belief to be equally demystified: Wigglesworth's verse communicates very plainly, yet refuses to provide any helpful mediation that would make the experience more acceptable by at least acknowledging its difficulty and mysteriousness. The power of *Dies Irae* writing, and of visionary poems like Milton's "Methought I saw my late espoused saint," often relied on a mediating element of poetic mystery. Wigglesworth's theological and stylistic approach, on the other hand, favored the starkness and challenging clarity of the "Noon-day Sun." This decision to associate his poetry with the plain-style sermon, rather than either more literary or more sensational works, allowed Wigglesworth to convey the idea that the force was in his message, not his medium. But the aesthetic challenge it posed to the reader, like that of the plain-style sermon, had its own inverted kind of mysticism in its apparent self-sacrificial reliance on spiritual complementation.

The kind of popularization Wigglesworth espoused was, like the Halfway Covenant, all the more justifiable because it did not dilute the tough theology of predestination and salvation by grace through a personal inner faith. His verse style, though superficially popular, nevertheless enforced the difficulty of achieving salvation. Specifically, it highlighted the pitfalls of self-deception, hypocrisy, and relying on dead outward forms. The chafing between the ballad form and the theological content, and the allusion to and divergence from the *Dies Irae* tradition, contributed to a poetic effect that, though perhaps aesthetically and affectively limited, was on the other hand suggestively evocative of the limits of "carnal reason" and unenlightened worldly sympathies.

With its stylistic awkwardness and stubborn resistance to aesthetic analysis, *The Day of Doom* was written in the tradition of the Bay Psalm Book. Moreover, like this earlier work, Wigglesworth's best-selling poem manipulated British literary and cultural conventions in its production of a different and challenging style. Wigglesworth's poetic style was adapted to the needs of the New England church in the 1660s. It highlighted the ambivalence of the attempt to propagate and popularize a religion that was based on intense personal experiences through measures like the Halfway Covenant. As Calvinist predestinarian theology implied, these experiences usually occurred only in the lives of a chosen few. *The Day of Doom* was written with the purpose of contributing to the extension of the church covenant, yet its self-limiting poetics safeguarded the central mystery of conversion and helped maintain the exclusive core of the church covenant.

As the seventeenth century wore on, the pressure on the covenant increased. Leaders like Solomon Stoddard and William Brattle inched away from the compromise of the Halfway Covenant towards promoting open communion. The immense popularity of *The Day of Doom* and the more moderate success of Wigglesworth's 1670 verse collection, *Meat Out of the Eater*, seemed to open the doors to the publication of more, and more varied, religious verse in the colonies.[139] But the republication of John Wilson's 1626 poem *Song of Deliverance* in Boston in 1680 marked a cultural shift towards a less pietistic view of the New England mission. The intense focus on inner salvation and on the fascinating tension between human effort and spiritual grace which had shaped the aesthetics of the Bay Psalm Book and *The Day of Doom*, progressively dissipated under the pressure of King Philip's War and the societal bonding it inspired. At a time when other poetic works were interweaving the religious story of New England with political history and current affairs, Edward Taylor's unpublished manuscript, *Gods Determinations*, stands out in its dogged adherence to an exclusively religious emphasis, as in *The Day of Doom*.

Faced with the increasing opposition of Stoddard, Taylor combined the aims of religious persuasion and encouragement with a defense of traditional New England church order. One of the key aspects Taylor sought to defend was the established procedure for church membership which involved the delivery of a conversion relation by the candidate. This rather antiformal ecclesiastical form was, in some ways, the embodiment of the ecclesiastical aesthetics that produced the Bay Psalm Book and *The Day of Doom*. Taylor's attempt in *Gods Determinations* to use poetic forms to defend this distinctly unpoetic church form represented a later and quite different poetic application of the paradoxes of the Massachusetts Halfway Covenant, as the next chapter will show.

4

Gods Determinations and
the Conversion Relation

Whereas *The Day of Doom* appears to have opened up the field in New England to the publication of more forms of pious popular verse than just the elegy, the poetic work that best followed up on Wigglesworth's attempt to draw more people into the church was not even published. Edward Taylor's *Gods Determinations* is a series of poems, written in various lengths, meters, and voices, that depicts the gradual progress of several groups of elect souls through conversion and into church fellowship. It is bound into Taylor's 400-page hand-bound manuscript volume, entitled "Poetical Works," but it is a self-contained piece with its own title page.[1] Taylor probably wrote it in about 1680, shortly after his Westfield church was officially gathered; but, as with most of his poetic works, he never published it.[2] Although the tone of *Gods Determinations* is far more positive and encouraging than that of *The Day of Doom*, the series shares with Wigglesworth's poem a soteriological focus. Like the Bay Psalm Book, *Gods Determinations* prioritizes spiritual fidelity and identifies this with the structures and teaching of New England Congregationalism. While the design of Taylor's poetry differs in certain obvious ways from that of the earlier poetic works I have addressed, these differences reflect not only Taylor's undoubtedly greater poetic ability, but also the effect of the changing times.

Since the publication of the Bay Psalm Book in 1640, Massachusetts Congregationalism had seen many changes. *The Day of Doom* was written at a transitional moment, when concerns about the purity of the churches and hypocritical conformity were beginning to give way to concerns about declining membership. The Halfway Covenant, which had marked this change, was more or less universally enforced in Massachusetts churches by 1680, and there were signs that ministers like Solomon Stoddard were wanting to take the reforms even further.[3] In the late seventeenth century, Increase Mather began negotiating with Presbyterians in England, and his efforts culminated in the "Heads of Agreement" of 1691. To the lay person, the differences between Congregational and Presbyterian denominations perhaps no longer seemed quite as significant as they had in the 1640s and 1650s, and the advent of religious toleration by the 1680s implied to many that "Congregationalism represented Massachusetts's preference rather than God's holy commandment."[4]

While Increase Mather, in fact, strongly defended a covenant-based ecclesiology, he could not prevent the application of the 1662 reforms from allowing the New England churches to develop a more inclusive "parochial" role, hence undermining the exclusivity of the covenant. In 1679, the year in which Taylor's church was formally gathered, and possibly while Taylor was working on *Gods Determinations*, Increase Mather publicly disagreed with Stoddard during the Reforming synod over the wording of a document concerning requirements for admission to the church covenant. After agreement could not be reached on Mather's favored wording, requiring "a Relation of the work of Gods Spirit upon their hearts," ministers compromised with requiring "a personal and publick profession of their Faith and Repentance," which at this early stage allowed both sides to claim victory.[5]

In the early eighteenth century, however, Stoddard was to make an explicit call for the complete abandonment of the church covenant, which, he argued, was unworkable and theologically unsound. "God don't bind his Church to impossibilities," Stoddard remarked, in his argument for dropping the special membership requirements for communion: "if he had made any such Ordinance he would give gifts to his Church to distinguish Sincere men from Hypocrites, whereby the Ordinance might have been attended."[6] Staunch supporters of the church covenant were therefore placed in the curious position of having to defend what had become a Puritan ecclesiastical rite. They had to affirm that the verbal form of the conversion relation was a valid and reasonably accurate way of estimating a candidate's spiritual state and of qualifying him or her to participate in the Lord's Supper. Stoddard was not a liberal, insofar as he believed profoundly in the spiritual necessity of conversion. He was also a New England traditionalist in that he disliked liturgy in general and preferred preachers not to preach from scripts or notes.[7] However, from the Puritan tradition Stoddard drew a particularly acute awareness of the ultimate impossibility of using verbal forms to probe spiritual depths. For this reason he rejected the conversion relation on the one hand, and on the other, was eventually prepared to countenance the idea that the nonverbal ritual of the Lord's Supper could complement the sermon as a means of conversion.

Westfield was a neighboring settlement to Stoddard's Northampton, in the Connecticut River valley in western Massachusetts, so Taylor knew all too well about his colleague's developing ecclesiological views, and he profoundly opposed them. Taylor had been one of a large wave of immigrants from England, following the Restoration of Charles II in 1660 and the ensuing Clarendon Code legislation against dissenters. Like the earlier immigrant ministers, Taylor had a particularly intense aversion to high-church rituals and scripted liturgy, and his firsthand experience of persecution in England made him especially keen to protect what he believed to be the purified ordinances that he found in the Bay Colony. When formally establishing his church at Westfield, Taylor intended to use as his doctrinal basis, "the Doctrine laid down in the Catichisme of the Assemblies of Divin[es at West]menster so far as it goes, & where it is deficient[, to acknowledge the Platform of C[hurch disci]pline put forth by the Rev. Elders & Messengers in a Synode held at Cambridge."[8] By the time he finished his studies at Harvard in 1671, Taylor was fully committed to what he saw as New England's ecclesiological orthodoxy. As his long battle with Stoddard later showed, Taylor believed this orthodoxy to be founded on the church covenant, with all its membership privileges and procedures.[9]

GODS DETERMINATIONS AND NEW ENGLAND CHURCH ORDER

In this context, *Gods Determinations* is an important work, both poetically and in terms of New England theology and religious culture. It was written in a situation where the poet could not afford to take the rites and practices of the Congregational church for granted: while the mistrust of religious verbal set forms persisted in late-century New England, this mistrust now risked threatening the very ecclesiastical order and forms that had previously been designed with it in mind. By encouraging more people to find their way through the church forms to full membership, Taylor could help to justify the rightness of the practices as they existed, and at the same time, through a positive portrayal of the church covenant in action in his poem series, Taylor could defend and promote the covenant. In this respect, there was more contextual reason for a measured reassertion of the beauty and benefits of established forms, both ecclesiastical and poetical, in Taylor's verse than in that of his predecessors. If, as Gatta and others have noted, Taylor's verse style has ritualistic qualities and conveys a more liturgical sense of sacred time and space than that of his New England predecessors and contemporaries, it is probably more than coincidental that a key part of Taylor's theological engagement in his verse was to preserve certain established church forms and practices, albeit supposedly antiritualistic ones.[10]

In the series of lyrics at the very end of *Gods Determinations*, we see Taylor's poetry endowed with particularly ritualistic qualities, if such are taken to include (as Gatta has suggested) "repeatability, order, tension, festivity, and limitation of sacred space." Nathalia Wright called Taylor's concluding string of lyric poems, the "choral epilogue" of *Gods Determinations*, and while this label misleadingly de-centers these lyrics from the vital spiritual action they are confirming, it quite accurately underlines their celebratory, songlike, and quasi-ritual quality.[11] One of these poems, "The Glory of; and Grace in the Church set out" begins:

> Come now behold
> Within this Knot What Flowers do grow:
>   Spanglde like gold:
> Whence Wreaths of all Perfumes do flow.
> Most Curious Colours of all Sorts you shall
> With all Sweet Spirits sent. Yet that's not all.[12]

"Yet that's not all" becomes a refrain that culminates in "And that's but all" in the last verse, following the pattern of Herbert's "Virtue" and "Praise," and Donne's "Hymne to God the Father," all of which poems have strong liturgical associations.[13] Thus, whereas *The Day of Doom* ostensibly steered clear of ecclesiological debates with its topic of "Judgment Day," the more ritualistic verses of *Gods Determinations* sought to endow the established order of Taylor's Westfield church with a formalized and cosmological authority. As Gatta put it, Taylor wanted "to show how 'Church Fellowship rightly attended' [could] turn even the wilds of western New England into the 'suburbs here of bliss.'" Notably, the achievement of formal church membership, rather than heaven itself, was the artistic and theological culmination of *Gods Determinations:* the final poem depicts the souls safely enclosed in the "coach" of the church, "As they to Glory ride therein."[14]

Yet Taylor's poetically ritualistic defense of the forms and rules of church membership came at a time when the "deadness" of rigid ecclesiastical formality was more in question than ever in New England churches. Michael Wigglesworth's second collection of verse, *Meat*

Out of the Eater, concentrated on encouraging the weak in faith, with very little reference to the place of the church in this faith. While this developed a trend in *The Day of Doom*, it was also a significant nonresponse to the growing pressure on the established church order. But in other poetic texts published in late seventeenth-century New England, Wigglesworth's emphasis on pious individualism was replaced with a perspective that was more clearly anticovenantal, insofar as it was proto-national rather than ecclesiastically defined, as Jim Egan has noted. Harry Stout has warned against exaggerating the secularization of New England Puritanism in the late seventeenth century, pointing out that while occasional sermons (which account for a disproportionately large percentage of published sermons) tended to be very politically engaged, ordinary Sunday preaching continued to be pietistic and conversionist.[15] Nevertheless, Wilson's posthumously republished *Song of Deliverance* (1680) and Benjamin Tompson's newsy verse account of the Indian Wars, *New Englands Crisis* (1676), both portray a Protestant community that is based largely on shared political and military experience, not on ecclesiastical forms or rites of passage.

In Wilson's case, since the poem was originally published in 1626, this communal experience was of the English Protestants being liberated from the foreign Catholic menace. As the 1680 preface by John Wilson, Jr., implies, the subject had become topical again, not just because of his father's death and the desire to commemorate him, but because of recent events in England, the ripples of which had reached New England's shores. In his preface, John Wilson, Jr., glossed the 1588 Armada invasion as the "Spanish Popish Plot," and noted that the poem was now relevant again "Considering (as heretofore) the Devil with his Instruments have contrived to swallow up that famous Kingdome, and the Church of Christ in it."[16] Evidently, the fears aroused by the so-called Popish Plot, rumors of which began in England in 1678, were helping to galvanize the collective and patriotic kind of communal Protestantism that had emerged in New England through the period of the Indian Wars. While the community that Tompson's verses depicted was more local to the colonies, it was similarly embattled, sharply defined, and religiously united in the fight to conquer the Indian enemy.[17] In this way, Tompson's and Wilson's poems seem to reflect the "shift in emphasis" that Phyllis M. Jones has noted in the soteriology of later New England sermons, "from the individual to the community."[18] These published poems portrayed the white Protestant community as a unitary whole, completely neglecting the less visible, more inward distinctions between communicant and non-communicant—distinctions that were realized through the use of the church covenant and its associated rites.

During his time in England, Taylor had been involved in religious politics and had written several polemical verses against Catholicism and high Anglicanism. If, as Stanford suggests, Taylor was influenced by English Catholic–Protestant pamphlet debates in his composition of the dialogues between Satan and the souls in *Gods Determinations*, it is all the more significant that he avoided any topical allusion in this direction.[19] It is striking, also, that Taylor's poetic response to the pressures of the Indian Wars, and to the nationalizing trend in verse publications illustrated by Wilson's and Tompson's works, was to focus on pious and ecclesiastical issues.[20] The wars of 1675–76 did not lead to the destruction of Westfield but they certainly had a huge impact upon the lives of the congregation. Taylor noted the "preservation" of Westfield ("tho' we lay in the very rode of the Enemy") in his "Church Records," which also list three of the seven founding members of the church in 1679 as having military titles.[21] According to historian John H. Lockwood, the center of Westfield would almost certainly have been surrounded by a palisade in anticipation of Indian attack. Neighboring settlements such as Deerfield were razed, and Westfield saw some military action, notably in the autumn of 1675 and in March 1676.[22] Even after the end of hostilities, the effects of the war dragged on: one of Taylor's disciplinary cases in 1682 involved a land dispute arising from fortification.[23]

Given this context, however, Taylor seems to minimize the role of the wars in his "Church Records," mentioning the military situation as only a secondary reason for the delay in formally gathering the church, the "worst" problem being an unnamed "[tem]ptation . . . thrust in amo[n]gst us by the Adversary."[24] Similarly, Taylor's ecclesiastical focus in *Gods Determinations*, given the historical context of a recent major war, testifies to how great a significance he accorded to the internal spiritual struggle facing the New England church. John Gatta has observed, regarding Taylor's use of typology, that Taylor "pledged primary allegiance to his heavenly country and declined to invest belief in the rising secular nation." *Gods Determinations* confirms this when read alongside the patriotic and Protestant *Song of Deliverance*, for example, in that Taylor offers no overt interpretation of the war, either as satanic rebellion or as a heavenly scourge upon the New England people.[25] But the earthly expression of Taylor's allegiance to his heavenly country involved seeking to preserve the established forms and membership procedures of the New England Way, even when they seemed less visible and therefore less important to a growing number of his fellow settlers.

As a religious poet in the New England tradition, Taylor faced dilemmas similar to those of the Bay Psalm compilers and Michael Wigglesworth. As I argued in chapters 2 and 3, outward obedience in religion was perceived as both a basic requirement and a danger when it became a complacent resting point. In view of this, even the popular, easily accessible style of the Bay Psalm Book and *The Day of Doom* had a certain undertow. These verses used the superficial appeal of a popular style to invite and teach their readers, but the formal qualities themselves were portrayed as limited outward features, mere foils to the spiritual experience of personal conversion and redemption. The apparently popular "surface," therefore, still reinforced the relative exclusivity of the experience being promoted, and faced the reader with a difficult and demanding spiritual challenge: that of finding the true spiritual life beyond the deadness of the letter. Although the writers ostensibly treated the verse as a vehicle for the religious message, what this precisely meant was influenced (as I have shown) by the use of forms in the local ecclesiastical context. Religious verse presented a rigid verbal framework which, like the ordinance of psalm-singing or the rite of owning the covenant, could take the reader only halfway on his or her quest for spiritual experience. By highlighting the readers' need for a more numinous and wordless encounter, these verses performed the dual function of transmitting memorizable teaching, and communicating the imperative to seek to experience God firsthand. In *Gods Determinations*, Taylor had to do this while also finding a way of simultaneously emphasizing the established church forms. As I briefly suggested in chapter 1, Taylor achieved this through his further development of poetry's potential as a formal foil.

Though not a popular work in the same sense as *The Day of Doom* and the Bay Psalm Book, *Gods Determinations* also had unliturgical or even antiliturgical qualities, in that its verse was designed to promote an individual's spiritual seeking, rather than script a collective spiritual experience. As Daniel Patterson and others have highlighted, the "occasion" of *Gods Determinations* was "the central concern of New England Congregationalism," namely, recruiting new members.[26] As Taylor put it in his sermon on the official founding of his Westfield church, "the building [i.e., God's church] stands in need of those that are prepared for it."[27] The relative decrease in the proportion of communicant members in the Colony's churches was pressing enough to be considered by the "Reforming Synod" of 1679 as a serious sign of decline.[28] Whether or not Taylor specifically addressed *Gods Determinations* to halfway members, as Michael Colacurcio has argued, the poet's clear aim was to encourage his reader to proceed formally to enter into full membership of a Congregational church.[29]

Although the poem series described the New England morphology of conversion, it did so with the purpose of coaching and directing the reader towards the act of joining the covenant.[30] This act hung upon the candidate's being willing to take the initiative and to come forward to deliver an account of his or her conversion. This conversion relation was the relatively informal verbal and ecclesiastical form to which the formal verse of *Gods Determinations* offered to act as a foil and a spur. Much work has been done on Taylor's sacramentalism, as found in his *Treatise Concerning the Lord's Supper* and his poetical Meditations, but relatively little critical attention has been paid to Taylor's particular faith in the membership procedures and specifically the conversion relation, though Gatta has suggested their influence on the "anguish of inexpressible feelings" in Taylor's Meditations.[31] Yet even prior to his composition of the Meditations, Taylor's allegiance to the practice of holding conversion relations as prerequisite for membership was an influence on his verse, since this was the rite that made practicable the ecclesiological view that underlay *Gods Determinations* and his later sacramentalism and contention that "the visibly unclean are not to have the Lord's Supper administered unto."[32] In poetic terms, this faith in the relation was a faith in the possibility of language to have some measure of adequacy in the effort to express the inexpressible; but, given the rough-edged form of conversion relations, it was also faith in a curiously unpoetic and unpolished form of language.

STYLE AND THE QUESTION OF AUDIENCE IN *GODS DETERMINATIONS*

Like the verse of Wigglesworth and the Bay Psalm compilers, Taylor's poetry in *Gods Determinations* was at a certain remove from the locus of verbal and spiritual power by virtue of its metrical form. Unlike these earlier works, however, *Gods Determinations* had a relatively élite poetic style, with its metrical variety, avoidance of ballad meter, and its composition as a patterned series. These more ritualistic linguistic qualities placed *Gods Determinations* at an even further distance from the ordained prose forms of the sermon and the conversion relation, even though the poem series was strongly influenced by these plainer forms in other respects. The fact that *Gods Determinations* remained in manuscript compounded its élite connotations, though the manuscript context can also be viewed as a way in which Taylor maintained some of the tension of the "halfway" availability that characterized those earlier popular verse works. Taylor's beautiful account of creation in the "preface" to *Gods Determinations* shows that he was willing to invest far more in the evocative potential of poetry than were most of his New England predecessors:

> Who Lac'de and Fillitted the earth so fine,
> With Rivers like green Ribbons Smaragdine?
> Who made the Sea's its Selvedge, and it locks
> Like a Quilt Ball within a Silver Box?
> Who Spread its Canopy? or Curtains Spun?
> Who in this Bowling Alley bowld the Sun?[33]

Such self-consciously fine poetry, drawing on the hexameral tradition and preserved in manuscript, seems on the one hand to hark back to a courtly British tradition.[34] There are moments, too, where Taylor, in spite of his strong objections to church liturgy, borrowed hymnic and antiphonal forms that had unavoidably liturgical associations, especially given the religious subject matter. Yet on the other hand, the manuscript format and Taylor's homely and idiosyncratic imagery also underlined the strong element of personalization in his use of such forms. In the New England context, the aspect of personalization related the poem series more strongly to the culturally important genres of the sermon and the spiritual diary.

Formally, as the cited examples show, *Gods Determinations* could not be described as popular verse. Its figurative language and metrical variety contrast with the narrative ballad meter and couplets of Wilson's and Tompson's verses. Moreover, as I noted in chapter 1, although Taylor wrote metrical versions of the Psalms and Job in such simple forms, he regarded these more simple verses far less highly than his Meditations and other "Poetical Works" and his sermon collections. Although Taylor at one stage apparently bound his two series of psalms in small booklets, he unstitched them and used them to stuff the binding of his sermon collection, *Christographia*. Similarly, he seemed to treat his Job versions as exercises to be repeated and discarded: these were apparently never bound together, and were used as stuffing in several different volumes. The following example from Job 12:15 exists in two similar versions by Taylor:

> Behold he the waters doth restrain:
> They up do dry therefore

He also sends them out again,
And they the earth turn ore.[35]

In their syntactic inversion and closeness to the King James Bible
these verses resembled the Bay Psalm Book in style.[36] By contrast, Tay
lor's higher style poems, which he gave the dignity of preservation
in his book of "Poetical Works," have since earned him the critical
designations of an "American metaphysical" or New England "ba
roque" poet.[37] Though the extent of Taylor's actual familiarity with
English poets is unknown, his stylistic preferences and the discrimina
tion he showed regarding his own different kinds of verses associate
him with a tradition of more highly crafted poetry, rather than the
popular verse I have connected, for instance, with Wigglesworth's
work.[38]

However, as I have begun to suggest, Taylor's use of more élite and
finely crafted verse involved the generation of a dynamic tension be
tween such ostensibly more ritualized and polished forms, and the
personal and popular connotations of his message. *Gods Determina
tions* is strongly influenced by the New England homiletic tradition.[39]
It is also a work that rendered in a different and possibly more digest
ible form the message of religious self-help manuals like Thomas
Hooker's *Application of Redemption* and David Dickson's *Therapeutic
Sacra*. As if to underline this connection, the opening description of
creation in *Gods Determinations*, while on the one hand linking it to
the hexameral poetic tradition, also contains close echoes of the start
of Thomas Shepard's preparationist guide, *The Sincere Convert*.[40]
Though he grouped *Gods Determinations* with Taylor's more private
verse, Karl Keller argued that much more of Taylor's oeuvre was writ
ten for public use than is usually thought, instancing correspon
dence, and comments made by Lockwood in the early twentieth
century.[41] Recent years have brought a particularly marked develop
ment in views of *Gods Determinations* on this question. References to
the audience have developed from Sargent Bush, Jr.'s "imaginary
reader," to Donald Stanford's estimate that *Gods Determinations* "may
have been intended for publication," to at least two critics referring
to it as Taylor's "public" poem.[42]

Although *Gods Determinations* remained unpublished, it has, in Col
acurcio's opinion, a "sense of audience" that far exceeds that of Wig
glesworth's *Day of Doom*. Hambrick-Stowe has estimated that had it
been published it might have rivaled Wigglesworth's best-selling work
in popularity, and although this view overlooks the effect of changing
times on the Massachusetts readership, it underlines the quality of

public address that makes *Gods Determinations* far less consonant with its manuscript context than Taylor's more obviously private Meditations. "Here Taylor steps from his study into the pulpit" writes Hambrick-Stowe, "a door closes on the humble and searching soul as the poet becomes apologist for the New England way." While this comment slightly overstates the separation between Taylor's poetic modes, given the key role played in *Gods Determinations* by the "humble and searching soul," there is internal evidence in the poem series that suggests the author's more public and politicized intentions. Patterson, for instance, has inferred from the plain style of the verse of *Gods Determinations* relative to Taylor's Meditations, and from features such as its proverbial phrases and homiletic structure, that the poem series was specifically designed for circulation, and possibly beyond the limits of the poet's own congregation.[43] To give an example, the conclusion of "A Dialogue between Justice and Mercy," near the beginning of *Gods Determinations*, turns from the third person to the second person for the last five stanzas. Mercy speaks the final lines of this dual address to the reader:

> My Dove, come hither linger not, nor Stay.
>   Though thou among the pots hast lai'n, behold
> Thy Wings with Silver Colours I'le o're lay:
>   And lay thy feathers o're with yellow gold.
>   Justice in Justice must adjudge thee just:
>   If thou in Mercies Mercy put thy trust.[44]

Furthermore, despite the lack of concrete evidence, the critical inclination to posit an audience for *Gods Determinations* seems to have grown with the increasing awareness of how its message would have fitted into the popular religious context of late seventeenth-century New England, and how it relates to Taylor's own ecclesiastical preoccupations and frustrations. Although the pristine state of the manuscript version bound into Taylor's "Poetical Works" makes it unlikely that this copy was circulated, the fact that is relatively legibly written in comparison with the other poems in the volume makes it possible that it was written to be copied and circulated. No such copies survive, however, and nor do we have records from when the manuscript was disbound to show whether the text of *Gods Determinations* was ever bound separately or is a separate signature from the rest of the book.[45]

Francis Murphy's warnings in 1962 against making too much of the publication issue highlighted the dearth of any evidence that could substantiate speculations about Taylor's reasons for not publishing his work. However, as I have noted, there is a considerable amount of suggestive internal evidence in the poem, and, as John Gatta has reminded us, devotional poetry in seventeenth-century England was often circulated in manuscript rather than published in the author's lifetime. Indeed, recognition of the phenomenon of "scribal publication" and systems of manuscript circulation in England means that we can no longer assume that a text was "unpublished" simply because it remained in manuscript. Although there is no evidence of any circulated copy of *Gods Determinations*, the poem series does have "a polished public style," and employs a discourse that if not fully public, at least implies a private, pastoral colloquy.[46] For Jeffrey Hammond, the most plausible solution was that Taylor preferred the compromise of semipublication via manuscript circulation because of the additional authorial control it would permit. Hammond has argued that the poem's positive, encouraging tone would have made it particularly appropriate for such private circulation: "[Taylor] may have felt that the poem, if circulated beyond his pastoral charges, might prompt those who were not ready for its comforting message to embrace that message prematurely."[47] This kind of exclusivity of readership certainly would have been more in line with Taylor's use of a much more encouraging and inclusivist tone than Wigglesworth's, coupled with his initial emphasis on the underlying Calvinist premise of election based on the "Determinations" of God. The fact that the poem was only semi-available would have developed a similar tension between access and exclusion as was enforced in *The Day of Doom*, though by different means.

Like Wigglesworth, Taylor emphasized predestination before going on to portray the progress of elect souls and to engage the reader in persuasive dialogues, and this had aesthetic and poetic implications for the poem series as a whole.[48] The first poems in *Gods Determinations* describe the Fall, and, through the allegory of the dialogue between Justice and Mercy, the redemption offered by Christ. In the subsequent poems, apart from images of spiritual warfare, Taylor also developed the image of a heavenly coach coming to rescue the elect. As I noted in chapter 1, this image reemphasized the spiritualized aesthetics suggested in the writings of Cotton, Mitchel, and Wigglesworth. According to the spiritual aesthetic of Taylor's coach, the reprobates' "stomachs rise" and they vomit when they see "Graces Needlework and Huswifry" displayed in it:

> They loath the same, wamble keck, heave they do:
> Their Spleen thereat, out at their mouths they throw.

> Which while they do, the Coach away doth high
> Wheeling the Saints in't to eternall joy.[49]

This test of the senses echoed preachers' comments about the reception of their message. Thomas Shepard, Sr., for instance, had complained, "Are not men blockish, dull, senseless, heavy under all means! they taste not, smell not, whereas elsewhere, O how lively and spirited are they!"[50]

In Taylor's account, though, most people were impressed by the coach at first. Still, even in their initial response, the reprobate betrayed their poor spiritual "taste" and gave the poet a plausible reason for avoiding widespread publication:

> It is the Chariot of the King of Kings:
> That all who Glory gain, to glory brings.
> Whose Glory makes the rest, (when Spi'de) beg in.
> Some gaze and Stare. Some stranging at the thing.
> Some peep therein; Some rage thereat, but all,
> Like market people seing on a Stall,
> Some rare Commodity Clap hands thereon
> And Cheapen't hastily, but soon are gone.
> For hearing of the price, and wanting pay
> Do pish thereat, and Coily pass away.[51]

The conceptual pun of the "costliness" of entry held the ideas of humiliation and value neatly in conjunction. It captured the difficulty of entering the church and living a devout Christian life, and yet the hidden spiritual beauty and worth of doing so. However, as I suggested in chapter 1, this coach, with its "Purple Canopy" and gorgeous furnishings, also seems to have represented or paralleled Taylor's own poetic text. The threat of "cheapening," turning it into a commodity and lowering its price, is suggestive of a possible reason for keeping his manuscript unpublished; but, as the image also implies, such sermons and sermon-poems were nevertheless often and deliberately sent out to endure such a fate at the hands of the spiritually blockish.[52] Like Mitchel's "if thy tast be good, / Thou'lt . . . say, 'Tis choicest Food," Taylor's image of commodification anticipated some negative responses, and thereby challenged readers to confirm their election by responding positively.

If *Gods Determinations* was indeed circulated in manuscript, then the rarity of the author's handwritten text may have meaningfully complemented sermons and more widely available popular print works like *Meat Out of the Eater*, by presenting itself as a physical reminder to the reader not to mistreat the gospel message as a cheap commodity. Harold Love has shown that manuscript, like print, could have many different connotations, but that where manuscript verse was circulated among privileged groups in England, it had a certain cachet, as Donne put the case, "Parturiunt madido quae nixu praela, recepta, / Sed quae scripta manu, sunt veneranda magis." Another reason for limiting an audience through choosing manuscript circulation was seeking religious privacy, as with English Catholic texts, and in this case the manuscript format marked the solidarity of that community.[53] Connotations of religious privacy would have been apt for Taylor's poem series, written at a time when the invisible spiritual distinctions that underlay the religious poetics of the Bay Psalm Book, *The Day of Doom*, and the church covenant had apparently begun to seem less significant to a large proportion of the popular readership.

The costliness of Taylor's verse was of a different kind from Wigglesworth's "Costly Verse, and most laborious Rymes," but it still presented a New England spiritualization of literary aesthetics. This adaptation involved more than simple authorial defensiveness, because Taylor suggestively linked reader response to the all-important issues of predestination and election. The tension between its attractiveness and its flawed nature surfaces constantly in Taylor's verse, communicating the duality and changeable quality of a form that is both a test of and an appeal to the reader. As Thomas Davis has observed, even the poetic beauty of the opening "preface" has a subtly self-undermining quality: by moving "from substance to filigree, from centrality to decoration," Taylor generated a curious "countermovement."[54] Though Taylor's domestic imagery in "The Preface" presented useful analogies to aid comprehension, it was provocatively reductive to describe the universe as a "Bowling Alley."

It has been much debated whether or not Taylor wrote in a poetic style that was deliberately flawed and inconsistent in order to enforce his theological point: Mignon, Shucard and Junkins have argued this, and Scheick and Schuldiner have disagreed.[55] Asserting that Taylor developed a "flawed" style assumes that he had an ideal style in mind from which to deviate, and this is difficult to prove. However, it is less difficult to establish that Taylor borrowed certain poetic forms associated with more smoothly crafted poetry, and even liturgy, and adapted them to a purpose other than that of creating the kind of beautiful set form in which a reader may have been foolish enough to rest. The way in which Taylor's verse was both fine and flawed, the way it associated itself with a Herbertian kind of religious poetic and yet was nonetheless defiant of some key implications of liturgy illustrates a dialectical development of the spiritualized aesthetics of the earlier New England texts. Taylor's verse, like his coach image, was rather purple and fancy, but unlike Herbert's and Donne's, Taylor's imagery was in an inverse relationship to the appearance and aesthetics of the bare New England meeting-house and Puritan church service.[56] After all, Taylor copied (presumably with approval) a text by John Cotton on the need to avoid Popish theatricality in church, that is, the "sort of Ornaments, which through there garishness, & gaudiness, do corrupt the simplicity, & sometime the power, of Gods Ordinances."[57]

LITURGICAL PARODY IN *GODS DETERMINATIONS*

If Taylor's gorgeous imagery thus sometimes acted as a foil (or as Gatta put it a *via negativa*) to set off the less visible but more spiritual beauty of the New England church, his use of liturgical forms, including hymn, prayer, and antiphon, similarly turned them into foils and means of evoking the superior, spiritual emphasis of New England worship.[58] In line with his belief in election, Taylor's adaptation of such forms not only served to enhance the quality of his verse, but also helped emphasize that spiritual affect and response were governed in each individual by the spirit of God. Whereas high-church ceremonialism and scripted liturgy was designed to generate and stress unity of faith, Taylor's poem series emphasized a diversity of experiences amongst believers; and whereas pre-scripted liturgical forms were known to have permitted empty conformity, Taylor's verses encouraged language as a response to inner spiritual experience. In both respects, Taylor's verse endorsed the key features of the conversion relation.

As to the first point, unity, or more specifically "uniformity," was strongly associated with the universal enforcement of the Book of Common Prayer in the Anglican church. It was the 1662 Act of Uniformity that had begun the silencing of dissenting ministers that had led to Taylor's emigration in 1668. Taylor's strong feelings about this Act, and how it put an end to an era of powerful ministry in England, are expressed in his poem, "The Lay-mans Lamentation upon the Civill Death of the late Labour[ers] in the Lords vinyard . . . Silenced on Bartholomew day 1662."[59] Although in *Gods Determinations* the progress of the souls from sinfulness to full communion schematically reflected the progression within an Anglican prayer-book service, Taylor's verses highlighted the inadequacies of forcing everyone to use the same form of words. The soteriological stories presented in the poem series illustrated the need for verbal forms that would allow for greater individuation and flexibility in describing conversion, and for ecclesiastical forms that recognized the historic uniqueness of a once-for-all conversion for the individual believer. "What is . . . remarkable about the morphological gesture of *Gods Determinations*" wrote Colacurcio, "is its tolerance—indeed its frank endorsement—of styles of saintly psychology that had once seemed diametrically opposed."[60] Whether the specific divisions are to some degree "factitious" or conform to distinct soteriological models, the presence of division is meaningful in itself.[61]

An impression of diversity in religious experience is conveyed by the disunity of the time frames and the inward experiences of the souls as Taylor portrayed them. He divided them principally into three "ranks": the differences between the second and third are very slight, but allow for some antiphonal discussion between them. The ranks are all "elect," but are distinguished early in the series by their different spiritual responses, depicted in "The Frowardness of the Elect in the Work of Conversion." In this allegorical account, the first rank submits to Mercy and Grace. After this, the second and third ranks split apart: the souls of the second rank, when pursued by Justice, "face about, and have / Their spirits Queld, and therefore Quarter crave"; the souls of the third rank "Cast down their Weapons and for Quarter pray" when "spying Mercy stand with Justice." However, as if to illustrate that division and diversity proliferate in souls' experiences with God, Taylor also briefly divided the first group into three subgroups:

> Grace therefore calls them all, and Sweetly wooes.
> Some won come in, the rest as yet refuse,
> And run away: Mercy persues apace,
> Then Some Cast down their arms, Cry Quarter, Grace.
> Some Chased out of breath drop down with feare
> Perceiving the persuer drawing neer.
> The rest persude, divide into two rancks
> And this way one, and that the other prancks.[62]

Before the remaining pursued souls "divide into two rancks," we have already seen three responses: immediate submission, surrender with a plea for "Quarter," and surrender out of fear and exhaustion. In this way, although Taylor was no antinomian and the goal was united fellowship in the heaven-bound coach, his verses convey a more fragmentary impression of spiritual experience than could be recognized in formal, communal liturgy.

While he believed that the starting point of the sinful state was "the Same in one and in all," Taylor portrayed the first rank achieving assurance and salvation less than halfway through the series, as celebrated in "An Extasy of Joy let in by this Reply returnd in Admiration."[63] The second half of the poem series then traced out the very different experience of the second and third ranks. Like Colacurcio, Patterson has seen in this structure an important binary model of two possible experiences: he argued that the first rank represented the quick conversion experience that "the founding generation of Puritans had hoped would be the common experience of all the children of the Covenant" and that the second and third ranks represented the more hesitant, halfway believers of the late seventeenth century, who were beset with doubts about their election and had not proceeded to full membership.[64] While this account is convincing, Taylor's use of further minor subdivisions is suggestive of a yet more complex and dynamic proliferation of options within the "model" conversion experience, which the formal and metrical variety of the poems in *Gods Determinations* seems to reinforce.

In his comment on the different effects of a single sermon upon a group of listeners, Taylor described the diverse responses of the people present at any one service: "one is not observant at all . . . another is inraged, another is humbled, another is reformed, another is regenerated."[65] Through his experience as a pastor in New England, it seems that Taylor further developed the idea of a preacher's ability to speak "a word in season" into recognition of the still more mysterious spiritual multivalency of the sermon.[66] Taylor evidently believed everyone listening to the sermon to be at a different stage in their journey, and that some even had a different spiritual destiny. If it was divinely ordained that people would respond differently to the same words in a single sermon, then obliging the same group to recite communally an identical form of words—indeed, one that was appropriate only for the saved—would force many into insincerity, create a false appearance of unity, and blur the very real distinctions between people.

Thus, while the poems of *Gods Determinations* did invite the reader to share in the experiences described, they also critiqued the use of liturgy by affirming that personal spiritual experience was the only source of a genuine profession of faith. The verses of "An Extasy of Joy let in by this Reply returnd in Admiration," for example, despite being very hymnlike, are firmly contextualized by their title. This title ties the poem to the events of two previous poems: a prayer and its "Reply." The fact that the joy was "let in by" Christ's "Reply" and then the words were "returnd" underlines that a specific spiritual exchange has taken place in the experience of the particular group in whose voice this poem is written. Other poems that constitute written forms of prayer, including "The Souls Address to Christ against these Assaults" and "The Souls Groan to Christ for Succour," are similarly situated at precise moments in the story when one particular group of souls has a spiritual reason and desire to pray.[67] Antiphonal dialogues such as "A Threnodiall Dialogue between The Second and Third Ranks" and the four Saint/Soul dialogues convey inner questioning at specific moments in the journey when those souls are in a quandary.[68] Thus, although these poems reflect liturgical forms, they are each presented as emerging directly out of a particular experience.

Hence, though it can't really be described as fictional, *Gods Determinations* is representational insofar as it portrays spiritual experience through a dramatized narration of the salvific "tales" of several sorts of souls. Through such means, the poems maintained a "halfway" distance from the pious seventeenth-century reader, who remained a potential rather than actual participant. This combination of availability and distance in the hymns and prayers recurs throughout the series, making the poems appropriate for meditation like the kind of found prayers that John Cotton had permitted.[69] According to Cotton, if a reader happened to "meete with" a written prayer that seemed particularly apt, then the reader could say Amen to it; but it was wrong to "set a part" such a prayer and make it a "crutch" to one's meditations; for then, "this instead of a crutch, will prove a cudgell to break the bones of the spirit in prayer."[70] That this suspicion was still current in Taylor's time is shown by a reference in the conversion relation of John Root, a founding member of Taylor's church. Root recalled that when he was struggling to learn "how to pray" he asked a minister "to de[vise] [him] up a form of prayer"; he was rewarded with a flat rejection and a Bible.[71]

In *Gods Determinations*, Taylor manages in effect to create the impression of "occasional" lyrics occurring within what is a fairly formal literary structure. He thus maintains a quality of extemporization which obeys at least in spirit John Cotton's warnings against prescriptive meditational aids that could become idolatrous like church liturgy. Even in his Meditations, as Gatta has noted, there is a feeling of extemporization in the way in which the imagery unfolds, and elaborates on the text, which blurs the distinction between "occasional" and "deliberate" meditations.[72] The hymn-poem "An Extasy of Joy let in by this Reply returnd in Admiration" aptly illustrates two key ways in which the design of *Gods Determinations* discouraged the petrification of its poems into such mistrusted set forms. First, as I have explained, by being bound into the overall narrative of the poem series, this poem exemplifies a preference for after-the-fact or response-based spiritual utterance. Second, through its curious and rather undignified imagery, it expresses a high level of personal idiosyncrasy that makes its verse less conducive to mindless appropriation by the reader:

> Had I ten thousand times ten thousand hearts:
> And Every Heart ten thousand Tongues;
> To praise, I should but Stut odd parts
> Of what to thee belongs.

> If all the world did in Alimbeck ly,
> Bleeding its Spirits out in Sweat;
> It could not halfe enlife a Fly
> To Hum thy Praises greate.[73]

The lines have an ecstatic lyricism, accentuated by the use of a shapely stanza form that is reminiscent of Elizabethan song: Taylor employed such lyric measures in several of his occasional verses, including "Let By Rain" and "Huswifery."[74] By decreasing from pentameter in the first line of each quatrain to tetrameter in the second and third, and trimeter in the fourth, Taylor's chosen lyric form enacts the self-diminution suggested in the words. This literary feature is harnessed, however, to a voice and tone evocative of spontaneity: the song seems to overflow from a soul that is emotionally and spiritually overwhelmed by the experience of conversion, and which as a result, speaks in an odd and idiosyncratic manner. The oddity and homeliness of some of the imagery and language (e.g., "sweat," "fly," "hum") associates Taylor with the so-called metaphysical style of verse, and yet, on the other hand, underlines the sense of verbal and poetic inadequacy in the poem's means of expression.

The idea, suggested by Taylor's style in such poems, that language should be prompted by a personal spiritual experience, and that it is therefore more authentic if it involves some homely and individualized forms of expression, was strongly related to the rejection of liturgy, and to the role of the conversion relation in New England church order. Taylor's support of this ecclesiology and his interpretation of its linguistic implications is conveyed in his early poem, "The Lay-mans Lamentation." In this poem, Taylor endorsed spontaneous prayer and satirized the high church clerics' reliance upon the prayer book. Borrowing John Owen's language of pentecostal fire, Taylor contrasted the "priests" whom he ironically dubbed "men of reading," with the ministers: "Such was their praying that I'll boldly say / They'll pray the Common-Prayer-Booke, quite away."[75] Further, Taylor's description of the ministers' manner of prayer also suggests an acceptance that a good command of "the language of Canaan" was evidence of an individual's salvation:

> And when they pray'd, soe warm was their request
> That sure the Spirit of fire was in their breasts.
> Noe Prayer-booke us'd they, since in place invested
> Having within Gods word soe well digested.[76]

According to this portrayal, the ability of the ministers to reformulate the language and ideas of the Bible to compose their own prayers was a visible outworking of the presence of the Holy Spirit within them.

Thus, the peculiar imagery of "An Extasy of Joy" (and indeed much of Taylor's oeuvre) served a vital purpose, as a demonstration of, and spur to, similar active and spiritual acts of reformulation. The imagery, in the cited stanzas of "An Extasy of Joy," grotesquely parodied Christ's suffering and blood: the world's blood, being distilled into a sweaty liquor, fails to animate even a fly. Christ's sacrifice, by contrast, is truly sufficient, so the image makes a serious point, albeit negatively. But the ungainliness of the image makes it seem particularly personal and, though not exactly spontaneous, at least unrefined. The fly, later joined by an ant and crumbs and clods of dust, wanders over the page of verse and spoils its finish. Though scarcely as provocative as Donne's blasphemously transubstantiating flea, Taylor's ant and fly fleck his verse with poetically reductive and miniaturizing tendencies, and this results in a rather self-satirical piece. In one sense, this constituted an extreme development of the idea of the unpolished, earthen altar referred to in the preface of the Bay Psalm Book. At the same time, the idiosyncrasy of the images also added to the resistance of the verses to a role in communal recitation or the public sphere.

TAYLOR'S NONLITURGICAL POETRY AND THE GOAL OF SPIRITUAL FORMATION

In some ways, Taylor's idiosyncratic language reflected the unusual level of personalization demanded of conversion relations despite the ecclesiastical formality of their context. While many critics have noted how Taylor's verses "imaginatively animate and personalize" the "often flat rationalism" which dominated ministerial treatises, the connection between this personalization and Taylor's stake in the conversion relation and its role in Massachusetts church culture has not been sufficiently emphasized.[77] In his sociological study of American Puritanism, Darrett B. Rutman described conversion as "the taking hold of and making personal the religious 'ideology'" and the conversion relation was a verbal form designed to express this.[78] Gatta has argued that the "digressive" or "associative spontaneity" of the imagery in Taylor's Meditations gives an impression of a "lively roaming after truth" and is linked to the "Puritan resistance to set prayers and homilies."[79] This is also true of the style of *Gods Determinations*, especially given the implicit relationship between the poem and the conversion relation it is designed to encourage, and the threat that the relation as a church practice was under at the time. Although George Herbert also constructed in his verse a strong religious and poetic self-consciousness, his voice was much less peculiar than Taylor's, and his verses more dignified and more comfortable to share and recite. Indeed, Herbert's "Antiphon," which begins, "Let all the world in every corner sing, / My God and King," is still sung as a hymn today.

While many of Herbert's poems do have a personal "I" (including "The Invitation" and "Love"), the ideas and dialogues they body forth have a universality that contrasts with the specific and narrative trajectory behind the poems of *Gods Determinations*. And, as Targoff has shown, this is because Herbert's poetic voice was inspired by two key principles governing the Book of Common Prayer: "the absolute preference for formalized over spontaneous voice" and the belief that prayer should be "simultaneously personal and communal." In "The Invitation" and "Love," Herbert also engaged with a specific moment in the liturgy: the Eucharistic invitation, when the priest invites the communicants to "draw neare, and take this holy sacrament to your comfort." The Book of Common Prayer also includes two optional exhortations, one for "when the Curate shall see the people negligent to come to the holy Communion," which Herbert particularly seems to have had in mind in "Love," and one for the contrary scenario when people risk receiving the sacrament unworthily.[80] Herbert's ideas seem to ripple outwards from these liturgical moments and texts, as if his poems represent an inner meditation on or dialogue with the official forms. In both poems, the resolution involves returning to the liturgical invitation with a deepened assent. In "The

Invitation," the final stanza justifies both the repetition of the refrain
"Come ye hither all" which has threaded through the poem, and the
repetitiveness of liturgy as potentially highly meaningful: "Lord, I
have invited all, / And I shall / Still invite, still call to Thee:"

The consolidated return to the liturgical form is still clearer in
"Love," a poem that explores the problem of self-conscious reluc-
tance. The subject is hence very similar to that of *Gods Determinations*,
and yet Herbert's brief poem was placed at the very end of *The Temple*,
and the hesitation appears as only momentary. Love is "quick-eyed"
to spot the speaker's uncertainty and successfully persuades the guest
after a very short dialogue to "sit and eat." In this way, Herbert conveyed the inward experience as apparently occurring within the time
frame of a liturgical moment, and the prayer book's invitation to join
in the Eucharist seems both to have provoked, and a moment later,
to have settled the thought. In these poems, as in most of Herbert's
work, the imagery is relatively sparse and the tone gentle and dignified, reflecting in these respects the language of the prayer book.
There is a powerful personal element, but, unlike Taylor, Herbert ex-
trapolated rather than parodied the liturgy. His poems found their
resolution in a reflective *approfondissement* of the established form of
words. Through its eccentricity, Taylor's poetic language distanced itself from the liturgy which was a central resource and model for Herbert's verse, and conveyed instead a slightly unstable vitality. This
vitality was suggestive of a heart unexpectedly "warmed" into spiritual "effusions," in a way that resonated with the ecclesiastical convention of the conversion relation.

The strong personal flavor in Taylor's verse style was complemented by the fact that *Gods Determinations* existed only as a handwritten text. As such, Taylor's presentation of patterns of salvation was
necessarily conveyed via a very personal medium. Following Walter
Ong, Harold Love has argued that chirography is midway on a spectrum between orality and print, in that manuscript retains a greater
sense of the voice and presence of the author than a printed text, and
thereby invites the reader into a more intimate and dialogic relationship.[81] Given the privileging of the preaching voice in Puritan culture,
a manuscript format for this kind of pastoral document would seem
particularly appropriate. While the formal structure of the individual
poems and of the series as a whole elevated and schematized the
process of coming to faith and fellowship, the individual quirks and
the manuscript format are likely also to have created for a seventeenth-century New England reader a link with more personal kinds
of religious writing. Visually, the handwritten script of *Gods Determina-*

tions would have associated the text with spiritual (auto)biography, including letters, listeners' notes of conversion relations, and introspective religious journaling. And insofar as the poems focus on the individual's responsibility to relate properly to God, they encourage such associations.

Poetic dialogues played an important role in the series: between Souls and Christ, Souls and the Devil, Souls and each other, and Soul and Saint. Through these exchanges Taylor's poetry connected with a dialogic language of religious self-consciousness that was not only used in the pulpit and in pious verse like Wigglesworth's *Meat Out of the Eater* but was also frequently appropriated in private journals, even by lay-folk. David Hall has asserted that only the clergy used diaries to "explore . . . their relationship to God." "The great lay diaries are providential but not pietistic;" he claims, "most do not refer to spiritual experience."[82] However, although the diaries of Shepard, Wigglesworth and Cotton Mather do embody an extreme of solipsistic reflection, Anne Bradstreet's "Meditations Divine and Moral" and the notebook of Joseph Tompson demonstrate that some laypeople also cultivated a sensitive spiritual self-consciousness.[83] Moreover, the line between Hall's "providential" and "pietistic" is thinly drawn: Tompson kept his notebook specifically for recording religious experiences—for "observing and noting what god is speaking to [him] by word and providences"—but this involved his continually "looking inward" and asking himself "what have my returns been to god?"[84]

Such texts demonstrate how investigating, telling and retelling one's story in writing could form an important part of a New England settler's spiritual life even for a layman like Tompson, who "apparently had little formal or advanced education."[85] And notebooks like Tompson's also show the extent to which other people's words could become incorporated into an individual's private religious expression. In Tompson's notebook, diary entries, sermon-notes, extracts copied from religious books, family records and mementos are all stitched together into one private spiritual compendium. Published and semipublished text is woven into the fabric of the author's personal journey through the pages of the book, and the author's handwriting and idiosyncratic spelling set his seal on his appropriation of these texts. Given the different sources of the material, the resulting overall narrative is extremely polyphonous, which accentuates the dialogic element that is central to all Puritan self-examination.[86]

One of the passages Joseph Tompson incorporated into his private meditations involved him in a dramatization of his spiritual experience in terms that correlate strongly with the allegory in *Gods Determi-*

nations. Tompson appropriated a description of his sinfulness, for example, that was as cosmic in its proportion as Taylor's, as the following comparison of an extract from *Gods Determinations* with a passage from the notebook shows:

> Alas! my Soule, product of Breath Divine,
> For to illuminate a Lump of Slime.
>
> .   .   .   .
>
>   Woe's mee! my mouldring Heart! What must I do?
> When is my moulting time to shed my woe?
> Oh! Woefull fall! what fall from Heavenly bliss
> To th'bottom of the bottomless Abyss?[87]

> But what have my returns been to God? O how unanswerable: this I have to mourn for, how vile by nature, and vile by life.
> .   .   .   .
> I have faln from thee by mine iniquity, and am by nature a son of death and a thousandfold more the Child of hell by my wicked practise, but of thine infinite grace thou hast promised mercy to me in Christ, if I will but turn to thee with all my heart. therefore upon the call of thy gospel I am now come in, and throwing down my weapons, submit myself to thy mercy.[88]

Tompson's language, though in the second passage apparently borrowed from a sermon or published text, conveys a persistent awareness of what Taylor called the "Host of Mercies that abused were," and contains similar imagery of the soul at war with God. Like Taylor in "The Frowardness of the Elect in the Work of Conversion," Tompson cast mercy as a kind of military victor as well as a source of conciliation. The image in Tompson's notebook is very similar to that in Taylor's lines: "Mercy persues apace, / Then some Cast down their arms, Cry Quarter, Grace." In addition, the pivotal "but" in the notebook's "but of thine infinite grace" in the second passage, gives the writing a to-and-fro movement that resonates with Taylor's schematized presentation of verse dialogues between the Soul and Christ, the Devil, or Saint. Similarly, Tompson's adoption of the present tense, "therefore upon the call of thy gospel I am now come in," gives his words a dramatic immediacy which is comparable to tones and techniques developed by Taylor. Tompson was apparently copying his text (which ends up in a marriage contract between himself and Christ) from another source, since at the end of the passage this source instructs him to write this contract out and sign it. While this dimension requires us to adjust our reading of the "I" in the passage, it nevertheless enhances the drama of the piece by further highlighting the inward quest to appropriate the language. Though the words are literally addressed to God, such a rhetorical harangue is also very much directed at the speaking self, and designed to interrogate and challenge the "new" author and would-be signatory of the ensuing marriage covenant.[89]

Tompson's religious expression in this journal is as intriguing a combination of the personal and the formalized as Taylor's poem series. But what the particular verse formality of Taylor's text adds, compared with the textual patchwork of Tompson's notebook, is a stronger literary structure. Through the heightening and schematizing qualities of verse, Taylor's account of the journey of exemplary souls is given a clearer order and direction, and the whole series is informed by the *telos* of church membership. But by keying into the personal voice of the spiritual autobiographer in his verses, Taylor engaged his potential reader in the poetic dialogues. With this achieved, the poem series offered to clarify the reader's experience, for instance, by identifying which voice within the reader's conscience belonged to the Devil and which to Christ. As in Bunyan's *The Pilgrim's Progress*, the particular form of representation allowed an authoritative revelation of roles and identities through the naming of speakers, which thereby served to instruct the reader in interpreting his or her own religious experience.

Unlike Bunyan's Christian, however, as Colacurcio has noted, Taylor's pilgrims are taken up in a coach rather than left to travel on foot.[90] The New England church was not a house through which individuals passed like the Palace Beautiful, it was rather the means of travel by which they were caught up and propelled towards heaven:

> Sure Grace a progress in her Coach doth ride,
>   Lapt up in all Perfumes, whose Sent,
> Hath Suffocated Sin, and nullifi'de
>   Sad Griefe, as in our Souls it went.
> Sin sincks the Soul to Hell: but here is Love
> Sincks Sin to Hell; and Soars the Soul above.[91]

It is possible that Taylor had read or heard the story of *The Pilgrim's Progress*. Records show that an edition of *Pilgrim's Progress* was printed in Boston in 1681 and *Pilgrim's Progress Part II* was imported in 1684, its first year of publication, suggesting that Bunyan had a significant following in New England.[92] The comparison highlights how Taylor, while sympathizing with Bunyan's emphasis on the personal aspects of growing in faith in *Pilgrim's Progress*, gave a greater role to the forms and formality of the church (as, indeed, Bunyan was to do in *Part II*, in his emphasis on the familial journey and the role of the pastor). Further, Taylor's use of poetic form throughout contrasts with Bunyan's incidental use of verse within his prose text, as spontaneous hymn or memorial inscription. Taylor's more self-consciously literary use of poetic formality conveys a message relatively radical in the New England ecclesiastical context, namely, that formality and deadness were, in certain important instances, not necessarily allied. In his use of verse form, Taylor created an opportunity to connect with and valorize the reader's personal, spiritual musings, but also then to place them in a literary and ecclesiastical framework that would form, guide, and even redirect the reader, yet still without taking the kind of prescriptive control or idolatrous devotional attention associated with liturgy.

This use of verse is particularly apparent in the extended dialogue passages between Soul and Saint. The interaction they present suggests how Taylor would have wanted his poetry to interact didactically with a reader. Although structurally similar to the Christic dialogue of *The Day of Doom*, insofar as Saint counters all the objections of Soul, Taylor's dialogues worked in the opposite direction. Whereas Wigglesworth's Christ uses poetic imitation within the dialogue to recast the self-justifications of the damned as useless and false arguments, Taylor's Saint uses similar methods in a positive way to encourage Soul to realize its election. As Gatta put it, the poem is a "counterjeremiad."[93] In a typical interaction, Soul tells a negative story about itself to Saint, and Saint rereads the same signs in a positive way, picking up on Soul's language and form, and redirecting it:

> Soul.
> Alas! alas! this Still doth me benight.
> I've no desire, or no Desire aright:
> And this is Clear: my Hopes do witherd ly,
> Before their buds breake out, their blossoms dy.
>
> Saint.
> When fruits do thrive, the blossom falls off quite.
> No need of blossoms when the Seed is ripe.
> The Apple plainly prooves the blossom were.
> Thy withred Hopes hold out Desires as Cleare.[94]

Saint engages the tools of interpretation and verbalization that Tompson's diary shows to have been already in the hands of laypeople.

Saint rechannels them towards the end of spiritual progress, instead of the existential paralysis from which Soul seemed to be suffering, and that appears to have plagued Joseph Tompson, too, at times. According to Saint, the busy and symbolic period of the harvest has come, and this is the reason Soul's attempts to detect evidence of Spring are in vain. This leap of chronology suggests a change of pace is necessary in Soul's spiritual life, and, indeed, urges action, since the time has come to harvest the ripe soul into the ecclesiastical garner. Thus, Saint reinterprets the signs and suggests a different way of "telling" the story.[95]

Saint's education of Soul resonates with the kind of interaction between the minister and the young believer implied in a conversion relation like that of Joseph Tompson's daughter, Mary Dane. In the account preserved in her father's journal, Dane described how her inclinations had swung back and forth, before she resolved upon requesting membership.[96] For example, reading Proverbs 15:8 ("the sacrifice of the wicked is an abomination to the Lord"), she decided that she "had nothing to do to pray, or better not to pray, at all fearing it was abomination to the lord & that I had nothing to do to take his Covenant into my mouth." But then her minister taught her that "it was the duty of all to pray, & that it was a sin in the wicked to live with out prayer, which made me afraid to live with out prayer least god should power out his wrath upon me." Dane's greatest difficulty was interpreting the death of her mother: "I was ready to fear that all aflictions was in anger to me, & that my spott was not the spott of gods children[.] I thought no child of god ever had a hurt so hard as mine." But then she recalled Hebrews 12 that "[the Lord] chastneth every son whom he receiveth." Finally, she explained, "I was ready to question much whither the promises belonged to me, then I herd from mr whiting that no sin was so displeasing to god as unbelief." Through such moments of reeducation, and through Bible study and by listening to sermons, Dane was brought to the final resolution to seek membership: "I now desire [. . . God's] people wold make way for me so that I may enjoy him in all his ordinances."

Dane's account shows how closely related the reinterpretive dialogue that Taylor designed in *Gods Determinations* was to the experiences of laypeople, despite its relatively complex imagery and its use of poetic form. If Taylor had metaphorically ascended into his pulpit in this poem, as Hambrick-Stowe suggested, he had carefully left the door to his private closet open.[97] But like Dane's relation, Taylor's dialogues went beyond the often inconclusive spiritual wrangling of successive journal entries, and added a momentum and an ecclesiastical goal in their progression towards the act of membership. Of course, Dane's representation of her inner dialogue marked the subsequent stage, in which the previously unsure layperson had become resolved and was actively pursuing the goal of membership. Taylor did not directly represent the Soul's retelling of its conversion story in his verse, but, given the potentially frivolous or liturgical connotations of verse form, this absence helped to emphasize the relation's alternative linguistic nature and more personal quality compared with the fixed form of his poem series. However, Taylor did bring the Soul's progress to a crescendo after Saint faded into the background, having apparently persuaded Soul. Soul then sings for joy (the so-called choral epilogue) and proceeds into church fellowship. This climax confirms that *Gods Determinations* is a carefully orchestrated piece in which the various forms of dialogic and lyric verse and the language of religious introspection all combine to build up an effective teleological narrative.

The ultimate goal was obviously salvation, but in the scope of the poem series, the key moment of transition is entry to church membership. It is presented as both a spiritual and ecclesiastical transition, thereby obviating any threat of antinomianism. After their two poems of lyric praise, the Souls proceed in the subsequent two poems to "seek" and then "enter" into church fellowship once and for all. The Soul, instructed by "the Trinity" and "Grace," comes to understand its need to be part of the church and to benefit from "Each Ordinance and Instrument of Grace." Therefore, despite the forbidding appearances of the church walls, with the forbidding watchmen looking down from the towers, it seeks "fellowship" there:

> But yet this Curious Garden richly set,
>   The Soul accounts Christs Paradise
> Set with Choice Slips, and flowers: and longs to get
>   Itself Set here: and by advice
>   To grow herein and so rejoyce.[98]

The narrative and rhetorical goal of the poem was thus closely bound up with the poet's firm belief in the spiritual rightness of the Congregational church order based on a covenant. Although the poem presents patterns and models, persuasive arguments and schematic dramatizations, it also portrays the converted Soul going on actively to "seek" to "enter" the fellowship of the church, which meant (in Taylor's terms) the status of full communicant membership.

Language as a Fruit of Conversion

In the context of gradually increasing opposition to the use of the conversion relation as part of the membership test, Taylor's account of the soul's gradual growth in self-confidence, and his poetic portrayal of its language as arising from this, made a firm theological point. By portraying the elect soul as eventually able to proceed to membership, Taylor affirmed that grace would result in the necessary courage and desire to perform the membership requirements, including the conversion relation. Throughout *Gods Determinations*, Taylor conveyed moments of epiphany through the ecstatic lyrics to which occasion gave rise: "My Sweet Deare Lord, for thee I'le Live, Dy, Fight," pledged the first rank's collective soul at the beginning of "An Extasy of Joy let in by this Reply returnd in Admiration"; "Whence Come these Spicy Gales? . . . Whence Come these Cloudy Pillars of Perfume?" asked the second and third ranks to each other, after the conclusion of their dialogue with Saint. Caught up by these "Ravishing steams" the third rank concluded: "Oh! let us then Sing Praise: methinks I Soar / Above the Stars, and Stand at Heavens Doore."[99] This pattern of language as a response to grace culminates in the ability of the souls to go on to full membership.

Judging by conversion relations and journals, it was not uncommon for the believer to experience feelings of inadequacy in comparing his/her spiritual experience with that of other people. Laymen Samuel Loomis and Roger Clap, for instance, both recorded being made uncomfortable by other people's testimonies. "I could not so find as others did, the Time when God wrought the Work of Conversion in my Soul, nor in many respects the Manner thereof," wrote Clap.[100] Loomis similarly complained of "there being ever & anone on in their Relations . . . such things [as] I could not finde to be with me."[101] However, for Loomis and Clap, far from being a disincentive, their sense of a disparity seemed to spur them on to seek God. Taylor suggested how such problems could become themselves part of the solution, through the dialogues between Soul and Saint. Moreover, the use of the form of a poem series particularly affirmed the spiritual rightness of progression. By depicting a relentless spiritual progress, and by using the lyric form to mark each culmination of spiritual experience, Taylor emphasized that the expressive, personalized language in which the believer appropriated salvation was a natural and significant response to grace.

In the same way that Taylor's early poem described the breast being warmed into spontaneous prayer by the Holy Spirit, so the souls in his poem series were driven towards the linguistic expression found in both praise and the procedure of seeking church membership. In his later sermon treatise, *Upon the Types of the Old Testament,* Taylor appears to pun on the membership requirement of the relation in a way that underlined its spiritual significance—only those who have got "a Saving Relation to Christ" may be considered in the "Inward Court" of the Temple, he argued.[102] The relation of one's encounter with Christ was a key part of one's relation to Him. Language, according to Taylor's developing poetics in *Gods Determinations,* could indeed have a spiritual and ecclesiastical role as giving the best available evidence of salvation. Though not mystically powerful in itself, a linguistic response was a fruit that it was appropriate to expect from an infusion of grace. In this tenet were the seeds of Taylor's collision with the views and practices of Solomon Stoddard.

Stoddard, pursuing the logic of the equally Puritan idea that the true spiritual state of an individual was never fully ascertainable, began to argue that while the transformation of conversion was necessary for salvation, the notion of "visible saints," and therefore the church covenant based upon it, was fallacious. In 1688 Stoddard proposed to his Northampton congregation to abolish the requirement of the conversion relation, and by 1690 he had done so. By the end of the century, Stoddard was publicly arguing that the relation was an unnecessary and even harmful rite because it intimidated shy believers. Recent scholarship has emphasized that Stoddard's point of view was not as radical as Taylor liked to portray it, since the conversion relation as practiced in New England (as Stoddard reminded his readers) was itself a fairly recent innovation. Yet for Taylor the membership test was a vital part of the divinely ordained order that the New England Way had uniquely restored to God's church on earth.[103] Further, Stoddard's rejection of the conversion relation, though part of a wider reevaluation of ecclesiology (and, later, sacramental theology), implied a view of the separation between God-given grace and God-given language: "Grace is known only by intuition," leaving no reliable outward marker, Stoddard argued.[104] This view was opposed to the tentative but persistent faith in the link between grace and language expressed by Taylor throughout his poetic Meditations, with their self-conscious attempts to lisp praise and their prayers for grace to sing more sweetly. Stoddard gave the following illustration for his point of view:

> A weak woman is as well satisfied that she loves her child as the wisest man in the land, though she can't make a large discourse upon it, nor prove it by infallible signs, because she feels her love.[105]

A statement with dramatic implications as it stood, Stoddard's comment contained yet more radical possibilities in its ambiguity. Presumably the author's primary meaning was that the woman is "well satisfied that she loves her child" "because she feels her love," but the syntax makes possible (even natural) the reading that because "she feels her love," "she can't make a large discourse upon it." That the comparison was between a woman and "the wisest man in the land," only served to deepen the nuance, since the intensity of a mother's love was potentially more reliable. Thus, the extreme position suggested by Stoddard's championing of those who did not find themselves impelled by their spiritual experience to give a corresponding relation was that the most genuine encounters with the divine may actually make you incapable of discourse.

It was precisely such a view that Taylor's poetic argument in *Gods Determinations* is designed to contradict, through its combination of a progressive formal structure and its links with spontaneous diaristic writings. The argument that "Presumption lies in Backward Bashfulness, / When one is backward though a bidden Guest" was used by Stoddard to justify an open communion, but coming from Taylor's Saint, it celebrated the appropriateness of "Each Ordinance and Instrument of Grace." The apparent overlap in Stoddard's and Taylor's ideas, though leading to contrary conclusions, is not surprising given that they were constructing ways to tackle the same problem, namely, the need to attract more people into church membership.[106] For Taylor, though, a believer's linguistic response (albeit necessarily a humble and self-deprecating one) was a spiritually beautiful and fitting "fruit" of conversion: the relation was a valid harnessing of a grace-given readiness to speak, which Taylor compared elsewhere to that of the Psalmist.[107] As the two poems in the series that directly treat membership convey, the ability of the Soul to overcome feelings of intimidation could be interpreted as evidence that the Holy Spirit had won the victory over human weakness in the soul. As Jonathan Mitchel had put it in 1664, "It cannot be imagined how a person can have had experience of a work of grace, . . . but that he can speak of it, in some way or other, after a savoury manner."[108]

"The Soule Seeking Church-Fellowship" and "The Soul admiring the Grace of the Church Enters into Church Fellowship" illustrate Taylor's sense of the fundamental importance and function of the church covenant. These poems also exemplify how this ecclesiastical formality contributed to Taylor's use of poetic formality. While on the one hand the manuscript format of the poems and their relation to personal musings and idiosyncrasies affirmed the significance of the individual's engagement with God, on the other, the formal and allegorical verse presentation elevated to an eternal importance the spiritual progress depicted. As Taylor portrayed them, the procedures of church membership lay at the intersection of the fully personal and the fully cosmic. These poems enforced Taylor's conviction that (to quote Colacurcio) "these local details are as much a part of God's essential plan as eternal decree or conversion in time."[109] Through his intertwining of literary, spiritual, and ecclesiastical goals in *Gods Determinations,* Taylor highlighted the personal responsibility of the individual before God. But he also marked, through his particular use of poetry, the fact that church order contributed vital form and discipline to the outworking of the personal spiritual journey.

Although the conversion relation was not mentioned by name, its role in protecting the covenant order of the church can be inferred from "The Soule Seeking Church-Fellowship," and "The Soul admiring the Grace of the Church Enters into Church Fellowship." In the first, Taylor described the church as a "Garden fenced in / With Solid Walls of Discipline." The image of the church as an attractive coach was thus replaced by an edifice with walls that loomed over the approaching soul, with an intimidating effect that, Taylor implied, was fitting at this significant stage of the soul's progress.

> Whereby Corruptions are kept out, whereby
>   Corrupters also get not in,
> Unless the Lyons Carkass Secretly
>   Lies lapt up in a Lamblike Skin
>   Which Holy seems yet's full of Sin.
>
> For on the Towers of these Walls there Stand
>   Just Watchmen Watching day, and night,
> And Porters at each Gate, who have Command
>   To open onely to the right.
>   And all within may have a Sight.[110]

According to Taylor's church records, the procedure was that, first, the names of candidates were "publikly propounded in the Assembly," then, if no valid objections were raised, these candidates were called forward on a communion Sunday "to give an account of some of those Experiences of Gods works upon their hearts." Accounts were given by men orally in person, and by women (and by "bashful" men with permission) in written form, to be read aloud by someone else. Once their account had been "propounded to the Church for their judgment" and accepted, they were formally "admitted to the Covenant."[111]

Taylor transcribed the brief relations given by the seven male founding members (including himself) at the official "gathering" of the Westfield church in August 1679. They were unique in content, stylistically personal and occasionally anecdotal. At the same time, they were relatively formal rather than conversational, and were probably recited from memory. Taylor admitted somewhat apologetically, after writing down his own version, that

> This is the Ordere, & most of the matter, onely in some things inlarged, that was then delivered, for although I had drew it up, yet not having committed it verbatim, to my memory before the Elders & Messengers came, & then being something touched in my health: as also somewhat disturbed in my minde, I could not so easily fix it in my minde after.[112]

However, his willingness to write down in his official records "the Order, & most of the matter," being content with "some small variation in the words, & Phrases" demonstrates Taylor's view of the essential quality of the relation: that, as a personal and meaningful story, it arose out of past experience, and did not rely on an authoritatively fixed arrangement of words. It was a form, but not a set form.

Concerning the use of conversion relations as a prelude to membership, we also know that Taylor viewed himself as fully in line with established practice and that he came to consider Stoddard a dangerous innovator. If the elderly John Davenport had been driven to urge that "the Porter look well unto the Doors," in the heat of the debate about the Halfway Covenant, he would have been even more appalled by the trends developing in churches in Edward Taylor's time.[113] Taylor's church register shows that he implemented the Halfway Covenant at Westfield, but it is equally clear that Taylor's support of the Halfway Covenant (like Jonathan Mitchel's) was balanced by a particularly passionate commitment to the "fenced" communion table, and to the strict maintenance of the covenanted church of "visible saints."[114] Both Colacurcio and Patterson have underlined that Taylor's recorded sermons and *Gods Determinations* convey his willingness to recognize as potentially elect even those whose faith was weak; but as Patterson has noted, Taylor combined this attitude of charity and encouragement with a particularly firm allegiance to the demands of the official membership procedure.[115]

In the preamble to the relations of founding members recorded in his "Church Records," there is a clear indication that Taylor was more enthusiastic about the giving of conversion relations than Stoddard and others of his ministerial colleagues. Taylor's account of events is slightly cryptic, but it seems that time constraints (which resulted from problems earlier in the day of the gathering) led the visiting ministers to document the relations rather than listen to them, as Taylor had planned:

> After the profession of our Faith was made, we were called out to give some account of the workings of the Spirit upon our hearts, . . . An account of which so far as time would admit was then personally given in these Relations (here abbreviated) following, the which had, at least some, been read (& doubtless it would have been to more edification) had not the Elders & Messenger of Northampton, & Hadly Churches drove on to the Contrary.[116]

As Patterson has noted, although Taylor stressed the need for "Christian Charity" in judging candidates fit for membership (i.e., allowing for their "humane infirmities"), almost a quarter of his "Foundation Day Sermon" was, nonetheless, devoted to the requirement of the conversion relation. Taylor presented evidence from the Bible and from the practice of the "primitive" church in order to prove that "it is necessary that the Person seeking with any Church of Christ to have Communion, give an account of the workings of Gods Spirit upon his heart, either personally, or by some other, unto that Church." In the revised version, Taylor even rose to the challenge of arguing that the 3,000 people baptized after hearing the Apostle Peter preach in Acts, Chapter 2, proceeded to give their relations before formal admission to the church.[117]

Since Stoddard had not by 1679 advanced radical ideas about the sacrament as a converting ordinance, what was at issue for Taylor was the distinction between halfway and full church members, hence the necessity of the conversion relation. About a month after the gathering of Taylor's church, Stoddard would be wrangling with Increase Mather over this requirement at the 1679 synod.[118] Taylor would have known about Stoddard's views, and although the changes in Stoddard's methods of entering church members in his register from 1677, namely, the elimination of any distinction between halfway and full members, was (as Davis has underlined) probably only a change in Stoddard's recording practice, the change is significant insofar as it signals the direction in which Stoddard's theology was developing.[119] A decade later, in the winter of 1687–88, Taylor heard a rumor that Stoddard "was about to bring all Civilized & Catechised above 14 years old to the Lords Supper, & throwing away all relations of the account of their hope to the church." Taylor expressed his firm opposition in a polite but candid letter, which he recorded in a notebook: "It seems to carry the Interest of Christ from him & to do as the Philistins, to make a Cow to carry the Arke[:] this Cost Uzza deer in the Conclusion."[120] Uzza, though apparently well intentioned, broke a clear ceremonial law. The King James Bible described his fate thus: "he put his hand to the ark: and there he died before God."[121] Although Taylor's tone was more conciliatory in this letter than in any of his future writing against Stoddard's opinions, even at this early stage in the 1680s his perception of the spiritual necessity of the conversion relation was absolute.

As I have suggested, the poetic style of *Gods Determinations* and its manuscript format were evocative of certain characteristics of the conversion relation, for example, in their shared emphases on individualization and on the use of language as a direct response to grace. Yet there was also an implicit contrast between the conscious artistry and tight forms of Taylor's verses, and the more colloquial, prosaic, and spontaneous form of the conversion relation, and this contrast generated a vitalizing and meaningful tension in *Gods Determinations*. As Hammond and other critics have suggested, *Gods Determinations* depicted the progressive victory of desire over fear in the life of the soul; the result of this victory was hope.[122] With this special, personal hope attained, the believer could pass beyond being merely "Civilized & Catechised," that is, beyond being nonscandalous in life and merely able to recite by rote the principles of the faith as learned from an approved catechism. The true believer would surpass the level of rote-learning and recitation, the rite of owning the covenant, and even the words of poems such as Taylor's; such believers were able to proceed to the more advanced stage of reformulation, as they related "the account of their hope" in order to be received into membership.

At the particular moment in the chronology of *Gods Determinations* when the delivery of the conversion relation is represented, the implicit contrast between Taylor's verse style and the comparatively informal style of the relation appears, symbolically, to be at its strongest. In "The Soul admiring the Grace of the Church Enters into Church Fellowship," Taylor described the membership procedure in a particularly distanced and metaphorical way. One effect of this is to emphasize the archetypal quality of the poetic description: it was a model like Shepard's formula, not an example that could impose itself as a rigid set form on another person.[123] This seems to have been Bunyan's purpose in his depiction of the same moment in *The Pilgrim's Progress.* He described Christian's being interviewed by the Porter and then by the Damsel Discretion, upon entry to the Palace Beautiful, representing the church: "Then [Discretion] asked him whence he was, and whither he was going, and he told her. She asked him also, how he got into the way, and he told her; Then she asked him, What he had seen, and met with in the way, and he told her; and last, she asked his name, so he said, It is *Christian.*"[124] Like Taylor, Bunyan seems to have been reticent about scripting this exchange, despite the fact that his prose medium gave him a better opportunity, and despite his allowing Christian to retell his story informally on other occasions. To Congregationalists like Bunyan and Taylor, this moment of testimony was best described in ways that highlighted its significance without trespassing on the freedom of the individual who, spurred by a spiritual desire, had to find his or her own words.[125]

Taylor's poem "The Soul admiring the Grace of the Church Enters into Church Fellowship" gives a schematized account of the contest between desire and fear. This account epitomizes the progress displayed in the poem series as a whole, and also pinpoints this special moment in the series as pivotal: "Converts new / Seing [the Church's] Centinalls of all demand / The Word to shew;" are portrayed as at first standing "between two Passions Crusht / Desire, and Feare."[126] The victory of Desire over Fear is thus depicted as focused on the "demand" to "shew" "The Word":

> Thus are they wrackt. Desire doth forward Screw
> > To get them in,
> But Feare doth backward thrust, that lies purdue.
> > And Slicks that Pin.
> You cannot give the word, Quoth she, which though
> You stumble on't it's more than yet you know.
>
> But yet Desires Screw Pin doth not Slack:
> > It still holds fast.
> But Fears Screw Pin turns back or Screw doth Crack
> > And breaks at last.
> Hence on they go, and in they enter: where
> Desire Converts to joy: joy Conquours Fear.
>
> They now enCovenant with God: and His:
> > They thus indent.
> The Charters Seal's belonging unto this
> > The Sacrament

So God is theirs avoucht, they his in Christ.
In whom all things they have, with Grace are splic'te.[127]

The pivotal nature of this moment is underlined by Taylor's placing the transition in the middle of the poem. The line, "But yet Desires Screw Pin doth not Slack:" begins the third stanza of the six-stanza poem, and the tension is dramatically released two lines later when "Fears Screw Pin turns back or Screw doth Crack." The paralleling of alternatives and the extra internal rhyme of "back" and "Crack" enforces the defeat and breaks the back of the line of verse with the snapping sound of a brittle bone. Through this curious, metaphorical, mechanized depiction of the spiritual and psychological struggle, Taylor succeeded in completely eliding the inward moment of victory with the outward ecclesiastical event of Soul's finally stepping forward for membership. Both were simultaneously represented in the workings of the cosmic machine.

Compared with the dialogue and the praise poems of *Gods Determinations,* Taylor gave this lyric a particularly high level of psychological abstraction. In fact, there is almost a touch of exaggeration in the way in which he stepped carefully around the relation at this crucial point compared with his more straightforward language and spiritual dialectic in earlier poems in the series. In his recorded relation, Josiah Dewy, one of the founding members of Taylor's church, recounted a parallel experience in much more mundane and direct language: "I began to long aft[er] Communion with God in his Ordinances, yet having some fear I forbore about halfe a year" until "I was so convinced of Duty that I durs[t] no longer delay: wherefore I went to the Elders, & made know[n] my desires to joyne to the Church."[128] The action of the poem corresponds to such an experience but its mechanical images, reminiscent of instruments of torture, though visually and physically evocative, are also impersonal. They are less mimetic of speech or personal writing than the images and language of the earlier dialogue poems.

For such sudden poetic distance to dominate just at this precise instant suggests a considered reticence. On the ecclesiastical level, the individual would have been going through some very practical and community-based procedures at this point, procedures that culminated in his or her giving a conversion relation. That Taylor's poetry became most unlike a conversion relation at the very moment when it was temporally closest to it positioned the poem acutely in the role of a literary foil to an alternate ecclesiastical form. Taylor's depiction of the relationship of metaphorical to actual glory in sermon VII of

Christographia, though taken slightly out of context, seems applicable to the relationship his ornate verse bore to the less visible beauty of Congregational church order, as extolled by John Cotton and as exemplified in the conversion relation.[129] Taylor declared: "Grace excells all Metaphors. The varnish laid upon it doth but darken, and not decorate it: its own Colours are too glorious to be made more glorious, by any Colour of Secular glory. Its Heavens Glory upon the Soul."[130] "Grace excell[ed] all Metaphors," and Taylor placed these "Metaphors" carefully so as to invite being spiritually superseded by a personal, grace-inspired relation.

The relation superseded his poetry because it was a more spiritually performative use of language: it could achieve what *Gods Determinations* could only portray, and his poetry's formal beauty was superficial compared with the spiritualized beauty of New England church order. At the same time, the coexistence of the implicit official form of the conversion relation with Taylor's stylized poetic portrayal of the procedure in "The Soul admiring the Grace of the Church Enters into Church Fellowship" captured the mysterious coincidence of God's fixed divine decree with the believer's active choice. The moment when the poetic portrayal was most mechanistic coincided with that point in the story when, from an earthly perspective, the believer would have most appeared to be taking the initiative. Taylor's poetry thus conveyed both sides of the coin, and thereby suggested that the brand of church order to which he was committed was particularly well attuned to the will of God.

In the detail of the poem, the giving of the relation was compacted to a symbolic giving of "the word" (the "go-ahead" as it were), and to the indenting of the covenant: "You cannot give the word, Quoth [Feare]," but two stanzas later:

> They now enCovenant With God: and His:
>   They thus indent.
> The Charters Seal's belonging unto this
>   The Sacrament
> So God is theirs avoucht, they his in Christ.
> In whom all things they have, with Grace are splic'te.[131]

Even though a covenant was by nature a verbal agreement, Taylor substituted the oral ecclesiastical procedure with a schematic legal outline of its spiritual significance. In practice, often the only official documenting would have been that the minister inscribed the new member's name in a church register.[132] Taylor's poetic representation imparted the spiritual importance of the moment, but by doing this through evoking imaginary documents, Taylor endowed what was primarily an oral gesture with a kind of inverted formal significance: it was as meaningful as a legal, documented transaction, but, according to heavenly rules, it was the theologically correct way of arranging church membership and therefore also better than any such written transaction. Thus, by a dialectical play on spiritual value and worldly value, Taylor enhanced the worth of the relation through his use of verse. The way he achieved this through the use of a legal, documentary image to suggest an oral relation epitomized the inverse relationship he constructed between his formally crafted poem series and the less formalized language of church procedures.[133]

By enforcing such a careful sense of distance between itself and the practicalities of the actual membership proceedings, Taylor's poem left conspicuous room for the candidates' own personal formulations. Taylor's schematic description underlined the deep spiritual formality he believed to be expressed in the relation, despite its relatively informal style. Indeed, his figuring covenant membership through the indenting of a document suggests how personalized, unique, and concrete he believed a candidate's admission to membership to be. Indenting a document involved writing it out in duplicate, and then cutting it in half with a wavy or jagged line. It was a legal procedure that ensured each individual a personalized copy, one that visibly showed that individual to be bound in agreement to the other party.[134] The alternating long and short lines of "The Soul admiring the Grace of the Church Enters into Church Fellowship" composed a visual key shape, with deep indentations, and this aptly reflected the legal image it contained.

Moreover, by the procedure of indenting, according to this poem, the believer became "splic'te" with grace to Christ. The interlocking long and short lines, and the rhyme of "indent" and "sacrament," "His" and "this / The Sacrament" bound the new member into fellowship and communion. Citations in the *Oxford English Dictionary* suggest that the word "splice" at this time was still primarily associated with the splicing of ropes for rigging. This involved both a splitting apart of threads and a rejoining to unite different threads. The doubleness of this image therefore enhanced the doubleness of tearing and binding already implied in the indenture image. Through such wordplay, Taylor enforced the paradox of the Massachusetts church membership requirements: they entailed both the making of an individualized personal commitment, and also the abandonment of the self and the soul into an eternal union with Christ. The conversion relation maintained this special tension (in a way that the prescripted profession of faith could not) through the combination of its official ecclesiastical role, and its personal, verbal uniqueness. In the detail of the imagery of "The Soul admiring the Grace of the Church Enters into Church Fellowship," as in *Gods Determinations* as a whole, Taylor thus endorsed and worked to promote these dual qualities of personalization and a formal, eternal significance.

Taylor's Meditations and the Conversion Relation

Read in the light of the relationship between *Gods Determinations* and the conversion relation, Taylor's Meditations appear to have been similarly reflecting the dual qualities that would have made them self-demonstrations of grace. In their expressions of praise and commitment, though very different in form to the conversion relation, they echoed certain aspects of its role: in particular, the balance it achieved between individuality and formula. In this respect, his poetic Meditations were further embodiments of Taylor's belief in the victory of language over silence, as guaranteed by grace:

> Oh! Bright! Bright thing! I fain would something say:
>   Lest Silence should indict me. Yet I feare
> To say a Syllable lest at thy day
>   I be presented for my Tattling here.[135]

Critics have already noted that Taylor seemed to be testing his salvation through writing his Meditations.[136] The sense, in these poems, of the speaker's being called by Christ and ready to respond, and yet acutely aware of his spiritual and linguistic poverty, strongly associates them with the conversion relation. Since Taylor apparently wrote his Meditations in preparation for the Lord's Supper, they had a certain schematic link with the conversion relation, insofar as the relation formed a key part of the procedure of admission to the Lord's Table. Rowe has implicitly illustrated this connection in her analysis of Meditations 2.102–2.111 (the "sacramental series") by arguing that "as meditations in keeping with the tradition of Puritan preparationism, these lyrics become equivalent to the wedding garb." The requirement of the wedding garment was a gospel image frequently borrowed by Taylor to justify the ecclesiastical and spiritual requirements for would-be communicants.[137]

At a time when people around him were beginning to lose faith in the conversion relation, and to shrink back to accepting outward obedience and prescribed professions of faith, Taylor constantly exercised his own experience of God by reformulating that experience and speaking it back to God. Research has shown the extent to which Taylor's poetics were based on a design of playing harmonies over his Biblical texts, using suggestions from works like Keach's *Tropologia*.[138] And yet the identification of authoritative sources for Taylor's imagery does not fully account for his poetic method of deploying it. Despite the scholarly work of Scheick, Craig, Rowe, and others tracing Taylor's use of his sources, and the work of comparativists like Martz and Grabo showing his similarity to other devotional writers and poets, Taylor's adaptation of ideas and images remains resistantly idiosyncratic.[139]

His notorious imagery, particularly for sin and for the Eucharist, indeed drew upon emblems, theological and devotional writings, and of course the Bible, but his insistence on expressing himself in colloquial language and scene-setting makes his style particularly striking. In the following lines, for example, Taylor curiously inserted an "up" after "kneads" and "disht," and made an altar out of a farmhouse kitchen table, and a proud cook out of an angel:

> And he to end all strife
> The Purest Wheate in Heaven, his deare-dear Son
> Grinds, and kneads up into this Bread of Life.
> Which Bread of Life from Heaven down came and stands
> Disht on thy Table up by Angells Hands.[140]

Grabo's comment stands, that although "Taylor's symbols are conventional," "his strange eye for peculiar details, his going one step beyond the convention, and his domesticating his symbols with kitchen details give his symbolism a quaint, sometimes grotesque, individual quality." That Taylor quite intended to give this impression is apparent in the fact that the emphatic verb "grinds" in "Grinds, and kneads up" was added in a later revision to the cited line.[141] Through such insistent quirkiness, Taylor made borrowed tropes unquestionably his own. He reformulated the language, imagery, and concepts that he came across in his reading, in such a way as to make them homely, but also to give them an unique signature quality.

Taylor's sermons and his own conversion relation show him to have been naturally of a much more vivid turn of phrase than all the lay members of his church whose relations survive. Taylor was far more prone to imagery and exclamations of "oh!" Nevertheless, the relations of the lay members display the similar design of appropriating Biblical texts and images and reexpressing them from an uniquely personal and anecdotal perspective. John Ingerson, for example, narrated how one evening, he was "filled with horrour of Conscience": "& my Sins were like mountains ready to sink me down into Hell every moment. & not being able in the night to sleep, was forced to rise up at midnight, & Call up my Father in Law . . ."[142] Another of Westfield's founder members, Josiah Dewy, described in the most vivid terms his inner struggles with the "continuall boylings, & bublings of Corruptions in all my thoughts, words, Duties & performances, which made me with Shame of heart to loath myselfe, & cry out, oh! wretched man that I am, who shall deliver me from this body of death?"[143]

"You cannot give the word, Quoth she, which though / You Stumble on't it's more than yet you know"—as Taylor well knew, verbal stumbling and a measure of uncertainty were marks of the conversion relation, so Fear's warning in *Gods Determinations*, in a paradoxical sense, pointed the way.[144] Samuel Loomis ended his relation with the following conclusion, typical of most of the relations in its hesitancy: "I . . . cannot but declare, that (unless my deceitfull heart beguile me) I have [co]mmonly found the quickening influences of [God] in one place or another untill this day."[145] John Ingerson and John Root confessed their continued sense of helplessness, but "Cast" themselves on Christ together with all their corruptions, in Ingerson's words, "So to leave myselfe with him, let him do, what he would with me." In his Meditations, Taylor expressed his sense of helplessness, and his awareness of what Caldwell described as "the problem of expression" even more directly through his verbal stumbling:

> When, Lord, I seeke to shew thy praises, then
>   Thy shining Majesty doth stund my minde.
> Encramps my tongue, and tongue ties fast my Pen,
>   That all my doings, do not what's designd.
> My speeches Organs are so trancifide
> My words stand startld, can't thy praises stride.[146]

Yet like the conversion relation, Taylor's poem powerfully showed the step of faith being taken, despite the speaker's feeling of verbal impotence.

Moreover, the self-abnegation of Taylor's verse gave it a design that, unlike the self-vaunting poetry of Milton, seemed to allow for the idea that other forms of language were potentially more powerful than itself. In the proem to *Gods Determinations* and in Taylor's early verse celebration of the English language, the decorative quality of his poetic language sometimes tipped over, through trying too hard, into what Wigglesworth might have called an "overweening" style. By contrast, the conversion relation was implicitly given a pivotal importance, as the "word" that the believer had to give in order to join the church in *Gods Determinations*. Even Taylor's Meditations were essentially preparatory to a communion service and sermon, rather than being in themselves the verbal culmination. In this way, through Taylor's idiosyncratic rather than polished verse style, and through its deference to other ecclesiastical verbal forms, Taylor did not put forward poetry unambiguously as the prime form for the expression of spiritual mysteries.

Because of his relatively high respect for the nicer qualities of poetic form, Taylor's poetry is in many ways closer in style to that of the more courtly religious poets associated with British high-Anglican and Catholic traditions. Yet he was nevertheless true to his New England heritage in his belief that an altar of perfectly groomed and dignified speech was often precisely not what God required. Taylor perceived the Pauline paradox of strength in weakness as a vitalizing mystery. As Wigglesworth put it:

> To see a weak man Strong,
>   And Strongest when most Weak;
> To see the Strong through Weakness fall
>   And all their bones to break:
>   This is a *Mystery*
>   A Christian *Paradox;*
> But this ensuing little Key
>   The Cabinet unlocks.[147]

While Taylor's use of verse formality communicated a strong sense of the relationship between church order and the rhythms of life and language, Taylor's poetics were not straightforwardly liturgical. He believed in the rigid framework of church order and the ordinances; but, reworking earlier trends in the New England religious and literary tradition, Taylor used flexibility and personalization of language as a means of tackling the dangers of set forms. Although Taylor's verse had much more poetic formality than the verse of the Bay Psalm Book and *The Day of Doom*, he nevertheless also found stylistic ways to emphasize the spiritual benefits of more spontaneous and personal language, according to the traditions of New England church order.

There was a self-consuming, provisional quality to Taylor's poetic writing, In that as he reminded the reader that it existed under the shadow of a final consummation. *Gods Determinations* had the same eschatalogical dependence as that confessed by the Bay Psalm compilers, in that it explicitly awaited the day when the carriageful of believers arrived to join in the "eternall Halleluiahs" around the throne of God.[148] In the light of this future transformation, as in the event of the Second Coming depicted by Wigglesworth, the ephemerality and evanescence of all material things would be revealed. In *Gods Determinations*, Taylor's poetic style underlined its own provisionality, in deference to its spiritual referents. Far from creating the analogy of a self-sufficient parallel world, the poetry enforced the ethereality of the images and the words used to form them.[149] Taylor's image for the church, for instance, mutated according to its contextual function, from a medieval turreted citadel in one poem, back to a stage-coach in the next, in which the souls "bowle and Swim / to Glory bright."[150] Such shape-shifting and undulating imagery conveys an impression of flux within a fixed framework, and this is reflective of an overall pattern in Taylor's poetry and in the use of the conversion relation he supported.

POETRY AND THE FORMATION OF A PROTO-NATIONAL CULTURE

Monumentalizing, on the other hand, was a growing tendency within early New England literature, illustrated by the publication of funeral elegies, and prose histories, beginning with Nathaniel Morton's *New Englands Memoriall* (1660), and the chronicle poems by John Wilson and Benjamin Tompson mentioned earlier. Taylor's own incomplete "Metrical History of Christianity" suggests that he, too, felt the influence of such writings. Memorializing poetry, like Wilson's *Song of Deliverance*, was linked in some ways to the ecclesiastical halfway stage. In 1626, the invitation of Wilson's narrator, "Come Children, hearken and consider well," was addressed to literal children, but in New England in 1680, the same language would have equally addressed the unconverted adult children, the "rising generation" of New England. But while Wilson's verse, in its emphasis on memory, had the potential of being a foil-like use of language (not unlike that of the Bay Psalm Book, for example), the evidence of Tompson's and other contemporaneous verse suggests a tendency, by this time, to allow or even encourage a kind of petrification at the literary "halfway" stage of monumentalizing and culture–building. The enlivening spiritual encounter and the cosmic role of the covenanted church were even more the focus of Taylor's poem series than of either the Bay Psalm Book or *The Day of Doom;* and this was doubtless because the theological position of requiring a conversion experience and its verbal fruition in the conversion relation was gradually becoming marginal. While Taylor's teaching, according to the extant statistics, was apparently more successful in its time than Stoddard's in that the Westfield church grew to have a relatively high proportion of the local community in membership, Stoddard's teaching gradually became the prevalent orthodoxy in the region. In the two years before Taylor's death in 1729, his successor brought the Westfield church into line and the membership requirement of giving a conversion relation was dropped.[151]

While Stoddard fought to keep conversion central, his rejection of the requirement to give evidence of it fed into other more secularizing trends. By the late seventeenth century, the experience of conversion, with all its mystery and apparently arbitrary spiritual exclusivity, was increasingly being co-opted into the development of a more politicized and proto-national narrative. The emphasis in Taylor's teaching on the need for personal conversion, and the key role of the church in this personal transformation, may have set *Gods Determinations* apart from texts like Wilson's *Song of Deliverance*, but it put it completely out of step with Tompson's *New Englands Crisis*. Images of exclusion and wall-building which served an ecclesiastical function in *Gods Determinations* were used by Tompson to emphasize the formation of a literally fortified community, based unambiguously on racial exclusion. Moreover, this emphasis on solid walls and worldly experience was compounded by the fact that Tompson even secularized his eschatology. For instance, in his prophecy of the resurrection of the colony—its dawning rebirth—he put religious rhetoric to the service of a proto-nationalistic, rather than heavenly goal. His appeal to Christ was to, "in [New England's]

> funeral ashes write thy Name
> So fair all Nations may expound the same:
> Out of her ashes let a Phoenix rise
> That may outshine the first and be more wise.[152]

The phoenix was a symbol for Christ, and in "The Prologue" Tompson mentioned "*New Englands* hour of passion," suggesting that New England (rather than her covenanted churches or even the body of believers) constituted one collective Christic soul.[153]

This idea had been developing in funeral elegies, as Scheick and others have noted; and as Emory Elliott has pointed out, it was natural that the conversion relation should provide "the psychological pattern for other genres," including those "where the subject is the whole community's trauma." Still, in *New Englands Crisis*, which follows the colonial community through suffering and uncertainty to prophetic redemption, the outline of the conversion relation is applied to the literal reconstruction of the colony.[154] Though it invoked "Conclusion," the cited strophe was followed in the poem series by one final narrative section (probably added while the poem was in press). This passage depicts "a fortification of Boston," thereby concluding the series by epitomizing the overall vision in Tompson's work, namely, a hopeful material and earthly future for the resurrected colony:

> A tribe of female hands, but manly hearts
> Forsake at home their pasty-crust and tarts
> To knead the dirt, . . .
> These brave essayes draw forth Male stronger hands
> More like to Dawbers then to Martial bands:
> These do the work, and sturdy bulwarks raise,
> But the beginners well deserve the praise.[155]

The word "Dawber," meaning the one who builds the plaster wall of a house, carried connotations of drawing and painting, which is suggestive of how Tompson envisaged his own poetic image-building as a "Service to [his] Countrey" (as he called it in his brief preface) and part and parcel of the reconstruction process.[156]

Thus, Tompson used poetic form to meld spiritual and national destiny, exploiting the bonding potential of rhyme to pull together a social identity and collective memory, whereas Taylor, on the other hand, nurtured in his poems more "self-consuming" qualities. Tompson's verse contributed to the cultural effort (epitomized by Cotton Mather's *Magnalia* of 1702) to construct an intelligible history of New England, and to build a model of its past to which subsequent generations could aspire. Taylor's "Poeticall" verse abdicated (for the most part) from this kind of memorializing, in the immediate interests of driving the imagined reader beyond its own limited form, towards a more numinous spiritual experience. Tompson, rather like his Boston women, made a beginning to the process of reconstruction, and presented his verses as "brave" "essayes" in the vanguard of the work of building a much more earthly and inclusive community than Taylor's covenanted church. The communal identity envisaged by Tompson was religious, and was based (like that of numerous funeral elegies) on a group retelling of a kind of collective spiritual experience. But Tompson's community "relation" lacked both the inward and the ecclesiastical dimensions of *Gods Determinations.* Tompson's community was inclusive with regard to the white colonists, and its walls were literally made of mud and earth. The earthly community became the point in itself: Tompson's symbolic fortified edifice, unlike Taylor's church, had walls but no wheels.

Taylor's evocative predestinarian stagecoach, and his consciousness of the fruitful potential of the tense relationship between individual spiritual encounter and "solid walls of discipline," were inherited from ministerial forebears that included the Bay Psalm Book compilers and the author of *The Day of Doom.* Like these writers, Taylor applied verse to the needs of the church, and affirmed the goals of the covenant—to encourage people to seek God personally and then to affirm this inward experience communally and verbally. His poetry was a means of promoting both the zeal and the orderliness that Miller described as characteristic of the New England religious endeavor. By being far more personalized in tone, language, and format than the Bay Psalm Book and *The Day of Doom, Gods Determinations* emphasized the role of personal reformulation in religious life, at a time when church and community were leaning increasingly towards public and communal forms that diminished spiritual differences between individual colonists. Taylor's unique poetic style, while far more elevated than that of the Bay Psalm compilers and Wigglesworth, creatively promoted alternative and oral kinds of expression. Its poetics involved an ambiguous continuation of the antiliturgical element of these earlier works, but developed in such a way as to use ritualistic forms to defend a different kind of language, namely, grace-inspired relations, and personal reformulations of religious experience.

The poetic development from the Bay Psalm Book, through *The Day of Doom,* to *Gods Determinations* and *New Englands Crisis,* paralleled the development of the New England church: from an emphasis on communal conformity, with grace as the reward of obedience; to a halfway attempt to be more inclusive; to the dividing of the ways, with a manuscript invitation to personal renewal through joining the covenant sharply contrasting with a public poem which co-opted the significance of church and covenant into its portrayal of proto-national history. It was not exactly a process of secularization, but rather one in which the verse expression of spiritual and ecclesiastical concerns seemed to lose its vital eschatological tension, its sense of the collision of the divine and domestic realms in the locus of New England church order. The self-undermining aspects of the poetry I have considered, including its popular appeal and yet its spiritual exclusivity, its allegiance to the church and yet its dependence upon individual encounter, functioned to direct the reader's attention to a world beyond. By the beginning of the eighteenth century, it had apparently become more pressing to memorialize the earthly past and to build the earthly future of New England. At the same time, the relaxation of church order, particularly in the use of the church covenant, meant that the exciting and uncertain relationship between church forms and poetic form no longer posed such a central challenge or opportunity to writers of New England verse.

Conclusion

In 1982, A. Owen Aldridge found that the New Critical emphasis on "esthetic criteria over ideas and historical relationships" was both persistent and inappropriate in the study of early American texts.[1] Since then, according to Philip Gura, there has been a sea change, and early American literary scholars have "finally . . . made the turn to 'reconstructive' criticism."[2] To Gura's approbation, whereas the ideological research of Miller, Morgan, and Murdock (and to some extent Bercovitch) had constructed a rather monolithic view of early America, and one that centered too much on New England, more recent literary scholarship has highlighted diversity. Critics like Michelle Burnham, Carla Mulford, and David S. Shields, for example, have applied their efforts to what Lee Heller has described as the "historicized recovery" of works previously considered marginal, including works by women, popular works, ephemera, and texts that were circulated rather than published.[3]

Few have condemned what Shields has heralded as "the liberation of the field" to include "a mutable and expanding canon." However, the idea that (to quote Michael P. Clark and Murry Krieger) "'ascetic' dedication to historical reconstruction" may in fact be replacing 'aesthetic' interest in textual analysis" has aroused some concerned voices, and with good reason. Scheick styled his study *Design in Puritan American Literature* as countering the "scholarly tendency to read colonial American works 'historically' as documents principally providing a direct record of their time or 'new historically' as documents primarily representing various kinds of psychological, gender, or political repression in their time." While Scheick's definitions perhaps caricature historical and historicist approaches, his embattled stance is telling. And his point is well made that in certain works Puritans directly "engaged aesthetic concerns that apparently were for them profoundly important." As Clark put it, "To ignore the literary aspects of these texts in favor of their cultural or historical contexts is to strip the texts of the power that shaped the lives of the people who wrote them" and "challenged the expectations and values of the readers who read them."[4]

As I hope my investigation into the relationship between ecclesiastical and poetic forms has confirmed, it is impracticable to try to separate the "literary aspects" of texts from their "historical contexts." Literary endeavor, however humble, inevitably involves a measure of self-consciousness: an author (even a diarist) writes in awareness of other, published texts, and other styles and modes of writing. While Larzer Ziff and Norman Grabo have protested against Gura's emphasis on history and culture partly on the grounds that sociology was not what literary scholars did best, Clark's and Scheick's comments pointedly suggest that a focus on history and culture *rather than* literature is likely to distort the significance that texts had for their contemporary readers.[5] But the efforts of critics like Scheick to reemphasize an aesthetic approach in opposition to the historical or historicist approach risk forcing an artificial dichotomy between the methodologies. While the literary contours of the expanding early American archive make it only sensible to accept Carla Mulford's deliberately loose definitions of literature as "the written record of persons' thinking and activities," and "a body of materials that create and shape cultures," it is equally important to remember that within the early American cultures themselves, written forms were not necessarily so generically amorphous and undifferentiated by literary concerns.[6]

"Humane literature" (to borrow a term from John Norton) had varied and significant connotations for early New England readers and writers.[7] From classical oratory to popular poetry, different kinds of formal speech and writing were evocative of different associations. Religious writers perceived that as a result their chosen genres, forms, and styles had different sets of risks and advantages. Since these risks and advantages depended in part upon how the poets adapted their chosen forms, there are significant benefits to wedding historical and theological considerations to aesthetic and literary ones. Such an approach has at least been necessary to my exploration of how the Bay Psalm compilers, Bradstreet, Wigglesworth, and Taylor, transformed the literary forms they inherited in order to enhance their effectiveness in the New England religious context. I have tried in my research to demonstrate ways in which the polarization of early American literature scholarship into cultural/historical versus aesthetic/literary perspectives might be avoided in order to enhance "reconstructive" criticism, by giving careful consideration to the role played by ideas of beauty and hierarchies of style within the historical literary culture of Puritan New England.

As Clark has pointed out, though, Gura's triumphalistic depiction of the leading critics all heading for the destination of cultural studies is rather selective, as his omission of the work of scholars like Ivy Sch-weitzer and Jeffrey Hammond illustrates. One of the thorny problems with approaches that emphasize literary value is their implicit reli-ance on an unacknowledged, ahistorical framework of so-called con-ventional aesthetics.[8] Although this problem cannot be completely resolved, Schweitzer and Clark have tackled it by constructing clear interpretative methodologies using modern literary theory and apply-ing it to early American texts. Jeffrey Hammond and I have focused more on historicizing literary aesthetics and working to recover the ideas of verbal form and spiritual beauty that were inherent in seven-teenth-century New England church teaching and practices. As Daly's pioneering study claimed, although little New England Puritan writ-ing dealt directly with poetics, aspects of Puritan theological writings had implications for poetry.[9] My work builds on Daly's methodology to incorporate increased awareness of the more popular and per-formative dimensions of early modern writing by addressing church practices, in addition to more theoretical discussions, concerning the use of verbal forms and formality. So, while resisting making cultural connections and observations the goal of my research, I have tried to situate literary value in the colonial religious and cultural nexus that contributed to its development.

In this respect, my investigation of the resistant aesthetic, which was forged (in its various forms) in response to the demands of colonial religious life, follows a similar trajectory to Hammond's work on early New England religious verse. However, whereas Hammond's analysis of the role and functioning of the poetry has verged on the anthropo-logical, because of his willingness to "[subsume] aesthetics under the category of use" (to quote Heller), my work has highlighted the im-portance of notions of attractiveness and literary style to New En-gland church order and poetic form.[10] In view of the importance of these elements to the seventeenth-century poets and their audiences, a strictly utilitarian approach seems to me incomplete. John Cotton's construction of a kind of aesthetic of scriptural obedience (albeit ab-stracted, inverted and even "invisible") involved a defiant adaptation of the values of his Laudian opponents, who passionately pursued an overtly ceremonial application of "the beauty of holiness" proclaimed in Psalm 29, verse 2. The Bay Psalm Book compilers' re-jection of "polishing," Taylor's ambivalent use of ornate verbal deco-ration in his verse, and Mitchel's and Wigglesworth's attempts to cast the verse of *The Day of Doom* as both an allurement and a test further illustrate the extent to which the cultural and religious goals of the verse were entangled with questions of attractiveness and literary form.

Indeed, I have shown how, in each case, the conflict of values within the verse was linked to the fundamental paradox in the Puritan writers' aims, that is, that they sought to communicate a religious message which included the self-undermining idea that human effort (including literary effort) was useless unless activated by the Holy Spirit. Thus, although the crucial ingredient was therefore not itself aesthetic, insofar as it was the independent participation of a personal God, the construction of this arrangement involved a certain reconfiguration of literary design in reaction against high-Anglican ecclesiastical models. Accordingly, this reconfiguration entailed the portrayal of ritualized and highly polished forms of language as less desirable and less spiritually attractive than forms that managed to counter the impression of formality and fixity—qualities associated in New England with spiritual deadness. In examining the links between poetic and ecclesiastical forms in the seventeenth-century colonial context, my research reinforces Shields's assertion of the continuing need for "theological literacy" in early New England literary scholarship.[11] In addition, because the scope of my study spans a variety of texts from works written primarily for church use, to published popular verse, to carefully preserved manuscript poetry, I hope that it illustrates how a more inclusive definition of literature can inform a critical approach that nevertheless maintains an important formalist element.

What Lawrence Buell has described as "cultural studies' leveling of genre hierarchies" presents the literary critic with a problem that is often easiest ignored.[12] As Tompkins has noted, the culturally sensitive critic of popular literature, "instead of asking whether a work is unified or discontinuous, subtle, complex, or profound," will ask "whether it was successful in achieving its aims."[13] While my research has involved considering the writers' aims in the texts I have addressed, the paradoxical nature of these writers' religious aspirations has highlighted the potential disadvantages of limiting the critical project in this way. Since the religious poets I have studied tended to have ideal aims that they did not believe it was fully within the power of their poetry to achieve, the critic who is examining the poems in terms of the "cultural work" they appear to have accomplished successfully risks in some sense being undermined by the material. Hammond has suggestively outlined such cultural work in New England religious verse in terms of the design to transform the reader's "sinful self" into a "saintly self." Yet my research highlights significant authorial hesitancy and ambivalence concerning the role of poetry in pursuing such spiritual goals.

Adapting the tools of literary criticism to suit the artistic dynamics of popular literature such as ballads and metrical Psalters is a difficult task and relatively infrequently undertaken, which doubtless accounts in part for the preference for historical and utilitarian analyses which has accompanied the increasing willingness to address more popular genres in literary studies. David D. Hall's work on popular religious writing has opened up some suggestive avenues for the literary critic. Theorizing his contribution to the "growing interest in colonial popular culture," Hall has suggested that popular culture is particularly accepting of the coexistence of conflicting trends: "We may think of culture as both ordered and disordered. . . . It has multiple dimensions; it presents us with choice even as it also limits or restrains the possibilities for meaning."[14] For New England religious writers, it was especially important to have, and to communicate, an awareness of a certain coexistence of order and disorder in the church, for instance, in the cultural ambivalence of meaning in didactic texts, which would have been expected to have different effects on different readers. Through such authorial ambivalence, New England verse writers could enforce the belief that it was only by God's arbitrary intervention that any human effort bore fruit. This ambivalence informed their stylistic choices, which, as a result, sometimes appeared rather perverse, as the writers themselves well knew. In the Bay Psalm Book, for instance, the compilers' desire to promote the prioritizing of fidelity amongst their readers led them deliberately to turn away from a reader-centered poetic style. In their poetry, Wigglesworth and Taylor also conveyed a marked awareness of the limits of human language, an ambivalence towards the genre of verse, and an acute awareness of its secondary nature as a nonordained, nonecclesiastical form.

As Schweitzer has argued, literary genres like the lyric posed significant problems to pious New England writers, including a problem of spiritual authority.[15] Such problems had no obvious doctrinal resolution and certainly crossed the rather fluid boundaries between popular and more erudite verse—between funeral elegies and Taylor's Meditations, for example. In the examples of didactic religious verse I have considered, the writers addressed such problems in different ways. One common thread, however, was their creation of verse that enforced its own reliance upon a quasi-performative, church-related context. In the Bay Psalm Book this performative context additionally involved music, and, in *The Day of Doom*, an allusion to folksong. Yet these poetic texts and *Gods Determinations* all additionally subordinated themselves to spiritual processes that they could not guarantee to enact or supply, even when performed in their special contexts. Thus, while the authors certainly had a kind of performative ideal for their texts, their antiliturgical stances also enforced the impossibility of ritually securing a powerful spiritual effect. Hence, *Gods Determinations* in many ways served as a foil to the conversion relation precisely by not offering itself as such a spiritually efficacious form of language.

Recognizing the performative context of much of early New England's literary production is important, especially because church teaching stressed the delivery of the spoken word/Word. As I showed in chapter 1, the traditional idea of Puritan New England as an exceptionally word-centered culture needs to be qualified in view of the teaching of the ministers themselves, not to mention the culture of folk religion which Hall has evoked. Richard P. Gildrie has reminded us that "conversation" meant "behavior" in seventeenth-century New England, so in addition to the performativity of texts in ecclesiastical contexts there was a strong nonverbal emphasis on morality and action compared to which verse was trivial verbal play.[16] Yet the link between the spiritualization of aesthetic value and the performative context was complicated by the theological rejection of ritual. While many New England writers and ministers appeared to attribute much to performative aspects, their discomfort with overtly ritualistic religious practices means that their emphasis on the performative value of a text can be understood as a useful way of representing the discrepancy between literary and spiritual power, and of highlighting the intrinsic literary limitations of a text. Since such writers did not believe that any humanly crafted experience (verbal or otherwise) could capture a spiritual event, early New England's religious culture was no more fundamentally performative than it was exclusively centered on the written word. Ecclesiastical and poetic exercises from early New England provide, therefore, a fascinating "scene of negotiation" between these two emphases, to borrow a phrase from Buell's dialogue-debate on literary "borders."[17]

A further element of cross-border "negotiation" represented in the didactic religious verse I have examined is that between the highly educated clergy and the variegated colonial audience they sought to reach. The New England clergy were knowingly addressing a readership many of whom they knew would not respond in an ideal way. Indeed, had they all responded perfectly, then the religious message would have been rendered suspect—not just because of its predestinarian element, but also because of its counteremphasis on the church covenant as something that an individual stepped forward and actively chose to join. Research by Hall, Hambrick-Stowe, and

Cohen has suggested that there was a "bridge" rather than a simple division between popular and clerical piety in early New England, and my research has shown how the ministers' didactic poetry could be a principal locus of this exchange.[18]

As Amory and Hall have shown, the material form of the "colonial book" and its position within a culture contributed to its meaning and connotations and thereby enhanced or even counteracted its internal literary strategies.[19] Each primary text in my case studies (the Bay Psalm Book, *The Day of Doom*, and *Gods Determinations*) had a different publication status and cultural position. These characteristics both reflected and shaped the ongoing dialogue between ministerial authors and ordinary churchgoers as the century developed. The inward-focused church covenant, represented by the ubiquitous semi-official text of the Bay Psalm Book, developed into a more outward-looking covenant with halfway options at the time *The Day of Doom* was published. By the last two decades of the century, when Taylor was minister at Westfield, churches seemed faced with the choice of ecclesiological liberalization or social marginalization, and Taylor's manuscript, *Gods Determinations*, which strongly promoted the church covenant, remained unpublished.

The fact that, after close inspection, it is hard to classify these poetic texts in any satisfactory way as either popular or élite highlights their nature as mediation or "scene[s] of negotiation" on the moving stage of seventeenth-century New England. *The Day of Doom* and *Gods Determinations* were poetic texts that brought together conflicting voices and points of view and thereby captured the diversity of New England society, in a way perhaps not dissimilar to the popular theater in seventeenth-century England. When placed in the context of the colony's ecclesiastical controversies, therefore, these texts speak for themselves in support of the now widely accepted view that a "univocal, monolithic Puritanism" never existed in New England.[20] Yet their ministerial authors brought the voices together in their poems in order to try and exert some control over them and over the reader, in the hope of spurring on the reader's (and by extension society's) progress towards a spiritual and ecclesiastical goal. On the question of whether they were socially inclusive or exclusive, these texts therefore exhibit an intriguing ambivalence.

One feature that I have highlighted as illustrating this perhaps rather surprising equivocation is the tense relationship between poetry and the plain style. It has long been a commonplace of New England Puritan scholarship that the plain style was the favored means of the clergy for "negotiation" with their audiences (and vice versa). But while critics have noted that the plain style was an artful style, insofar as it was designed to convey the complexities of religion to the comprehension of the meanest, its role as a literary icon was still more paradoxical.[21] In chapter 1, I argued that more than a set of stylistic prescriptions, the plain style was an ideal to which almost mystical powers were often ascribed. If this entailed a paradoxical reversal of value, based on the Pauline inversions of wisdom and foolishness, strength and weakness, it also elevated the popularly accessible plain style to spiritual heights, suggesting that "ritual and magic" were less absent from New England religious culture than is commonly thought.[22] As the typical elegiac reference to John Cotton's "seraphic" powers of preaching confirms, the idealization of the plain style in New England religious culture accorded it a position that was occupied in educated high-church circles in England by the more elaborate styles of John Donne, Richard Hooker, and George Herbert, who were all canonized in biographies by Izaak Walton in 1640, 1665, and 1670, respectively.[23]

By its nature poetry was considered to be less plain than prose—so much is clear from the preface to the 1640 Bay Psalm Book. Yet as Wigglesworth's poetry, the Bay Psalms, and late verse by Anne Bradstreet show, poetry could be given some key qualities of plainness. It could thereby occupy a kind of halfway position: that is, it could possess the allure and lyric intensity of verse and yet also have a seriousness and straightforwardness reminiscent of plain-style prose. Even in such cases, however, as the prefatory material suggests, there was a danger of compromise and contamination. Part of the ambivalence within the genre and its halfway position within New England religious culture was certainly a result of what Myra Jehlen and Michael Warner have called "the double-bind of the colonial."[24] According to this "double-bind," literary styles and genres were judged according to the standards of the home country, giving the colonial writer little freedom to develop new native forms without an accompanying sense of inadequacy. What tempered this situation for the seventeenth-century New England writer was that, because the project of religious settlement was made in deliberate competition with the impure English church and society, the provincial limitations of the literary culture were relatively easily turned into features for pride.

Witness, for instance, Thomas Hooker's supposed apology for his "wilderness style":

> That the discourse comes forth in such a homely dresse and course habit, the Reader must be desired to consider, It comes *out of the wildern-*

esse, where curiosity is not studied. Planters if they can provide cloth to go warm, they leave the cutts and lace to those that study to go fine.

As it is beyond my skill, so I professe it is beyond my care to please the niceness of mens palates, with any quaintnesse of language. They who covet more sauce then meat, they must provide cooks to their minde.[25]

Anne Bradstreet, too, while apologizing for her style, also conveyed a subtly ambivalent attitude to the standards of the British poetry she had grown up admiring. Having been driven "from Parnassus in a rage" in her elegy on Sidney, she left his fame "to England's rolls." Later, when describing her "ill-formed offspring" who was being sent out among the public, Bradstreet's own harsh attitude towards her child/book is in fact an anticipation of the cruelty of the critical public which she knew this "child" would inevitably face.[26] Albert J. Von Frank is one of the many critics who have seen in Bradstreet's earlier verse a representative New England nostalgia for the home country, arguing that she turned to British-made poetic forms and allusions in an effort to stave off the encroaching wilderness.[27] Such could also be said of Edward Taylor, whose very sparse references to his frontier surroundings include a handful of "canooes" in Meditation 2.78.[28] Yet as my research has demonstrated, the ecclesiastical attitude to set forms and formality in the colony encouraged a principle of inversion with regard to traditional and ritualistic church conventions, and, as in the example from Hooker's preface, this inversion could be harnessed to the development of colonial pride in an alternative way of doing things.

While the relationship between the colonists and the English literary tradition was of prime importance, the colonial experience gave their adaptation of British literary conventions an air of defiance. The Bay Psalm Book was an explicitly defiant translation; the elaborate verse of *Gods Determinations* was defiantly subordinated to the less eloquent but ecclesiastically ordained form of the conversion relation; and Wigglesworth's *Day of Doom* was written in apparent defiance of certain local and transatlantic readerly expectations. As Wigglesworth's, Mitchel's, Bradstreet's, and Hooker's prefatory anxieties all illustrate, their self-judgment continued to be based partly on the values of the "home" country, where (in their view) literary standards were different and in some sense higher, but where pagan superstition was also more rife. Seen in this transatlantic dimension, early New England's literary culture constitutes neither a primitive incarnation of American culture, nor "something that was exported intact from Europe," but rather "a complicated set of negotiations" between the nations.[29]

To say as much does not diminish the significance of the encounter with the American continent and its peoples, since (as Scanlan has convincingly argued) one outlet for the settlers' anxiety about the native Americans around them was in accentuating their opposition to British versions of paganism, for example, rituals and ceremonial forms that were deemed to be Papist. Roger Williams's poems show that the native cultures provided a model of an alternate society that was available to give greater resonance to the rhetoric of religious and civil disputes between the colonists and in front of their transatlantic audience:

> Truth is a Native, naked Beauty; but
> Lying Inventions are but Indian Paints,
> Dissembling hearts their Beautie's but a Lye
> Truth is the proper Beauty of Gods Saints.[30]

Much of the poetry I have addressed has concerned "the proper Beauty of Gods Saints" and the potential unreliability of appearances and of language. These questions were rendered more acute by the settlers' experience of moving away from a civilization where things and people were more permanently established, or at least gave a more convincing impression of so being.

My research shows, therefore, how the development of religious verse in early New England was built upon the colonial reconfiguring of poetic and ecclesiastical forms and literary values inherited from Britain. Far from staving off the colonial experience, these borrowed forms were remodeled to suit local needs, while the writers still kept one eye fixed on Britain. The self-consciousness and the double standard that this gave the early New England writers was incorporated into their immediate task of writing for a New England audience who shared their dual frame of reference. Moreover, if "colonial discourse" is "a form of writing that, by its very nature, must always promise more than it can deliver," then the colonial experience reinforced the trends that my study has particularly emphasized within New England piety and religious expression, namely, the frustrated but richly aspirational quality of the verse.

The need for spiritual complementation and the self-conscious poetic "halfwayness" that I have examined in early New England verse were reinforced by the colonial situation. These features contributed to a strategy of inverting the limitations of a transplanted, provincial civilization. Yet they also exemplify what Delbanco has described as the "unchanging human heart," because the strong desires for transcendence, clarity, and certainty communicated by the literary designs of the New England religious writers, once understood in their particular context, are recognizable to readers from different cultures.[31] As I suggested in chapter 4, by the end of the seventeenth century, the emphasis on the church covenant as the means of achieving personal and colonial progress was giving way to newer more socially and religiously inclusive (and racially exclusive) trends. By the time Mather wrote his *Magnalia* in 1702, the kind of ecclesiology that had informed the poetic styles of the Bay Psalm Book, *The Day of Doom*, and Taylor's *Gods Determinations* had become marginalized.

As a result of this marginalization, the ecclesiology of the covenanted church in the eighteenth century no longer presented such an immediate analogy for the relationship between the religious poet and his audience, nor such a central focus for spiritual seeking. The gradual reconceptualization of the ecclesiastical and colonial project, illustrated in Tompson's *New Englands Crisis*, for example, was focused more on the *de facto* earthly community of settlers, and this focus on human civilization rather than spiritual and heavenly ideals paved the way for the development of a more integral political identity. However, the loss of the strong ecclesiological basis ironically made the literary culture more vulnerable to provincialization. The resistant aesthetic and the development of defiant antiformal literary forms continued as a significant strand within the literary culture, but at the same time it was ridiculed and avoided by certain self-consciously sophisticated and Anglophilic writers, including Benjamin Franklin, Mather Byles, and Jane Colman Turell. "Go lead the way, my Muse," wrote Jane Colman aged seventeen in 1725, "nor must you stop, / 'Till we have gain'd *Parnassus* shady Top."[32] Michael Wigglesworth must have turned in his grave.

Notes

Introduction

1. Vernon Louis Parrington, "The Puritan Divines, 1620–1720," in *A History of American Literature*, ed. W. P. Trent et al., vol. 1, 31 (Cambridge: Cambridge University Press, 1918).

2. Perry Miller, *The New England Mind: The Seventeenth Century* (Cambridge: Harvard University Press, 1939; reprint, 1954), and *The New England Mind: From Colony to Province* (Cambridge: Harvard University Press, 1953; reprint 1981); Perry Miller and Thomas H. Johnson, eds., *The Puritans*, rev. ed., 2 vols. (New York: Harper and Row, 1963).

3. Michael Winship, "Reconsiderations: Were There Any Puritans in New England?" *New England Quarterly* 74 (2001): 118–38. Cf. Patrick Collinson, *The Religion of Protestants: The Church in English Society, 1559–1625* (Oxford: Clarendon Press, 1983); Peter Lake, *Anglicans and Puritans? Presbyterianism and English Conformist Thought from Whitgift to Hooker* (London: Unwin Hyman, 1988).

4. Larzer Ziff, *Puritanism in America: New Culture in a New World* (New York: Viking Press, 1973); Andrew Delbanco, *The Puritan Ordeal* (Cambridge: Harvard University Press, 1989), Norman Pettit, *The Heart Prepared: Grace and Conversion in Puritan Spiritual Life*, 2d ed. (Middletown, Conn.: Wesleyan University Press, 1989); Charles Lloyd Cohen, *God's Caress: The Psychology of Puritan Religious Experience* (New York: Oxford University Press, 1986); David Leverenz, *The Language of Puritan Feeling: An Exploration in Literature, Psychology, and Social History* (New Brunswick, N.J.: Rutgers University Press, 1980); Charles Hambrick-Stowe, *The Practice of Piety: Puritan Devotional Disciplines in Seventeenth-Century New England* (Chapel Hill: University of North Carolina Press, 1982); Philip F. Gura, *A Glimpse of Sion's Glory: Puritan Radicalism in New England, 1620–1660* (Middletown, Conn.: Wesleyan University Press, 1984); Janice Knight, *Orthodoxies in Massachusetts: Rereading American Puritanism* (Cambridge: Harvard University Press, 1994); Michael P. Winship, *Making Heretics: Militant Protestantism and Free Grace in Massachusetts, 1636–1641* (Princeton: Princeton University Press, 2002); Sacvan Bercovitch, *The American Jeremiad* (Madison: University of Wisconsin Press, 1978), and *The Puritan Origins of the American Self* (New Haven: Yale University Press, 1975); Patricia Caldwell, *The Puritan Conversion Narrative: The Beginnings of American Expression* (Cambridge: Cambridge University Press, 1983); Lisa Gordis *Opening Scripture: Bible Reading and Interpretive Authority in Puritan New England* (Chicago: University of Chicago Press, 2003); David D. Hall, *Worlds of Wonder, Days of Judgment; Popular Religious Belief in Early New England* (New York: Knopf, 1989); Ann Kibbey, *The Interpretation of Material Shapes in Puritanism: A Study of Rhetoric, Prejudice and Violence* (New York: Cambridge University Press, 1986); Jane Kamensky, *Governing the Tongue: The Politics of Speech in Early New England* (Oxford: Oxford University Press, 1997).

5. Ivy Schweitzer, *The Work of Self-Representation: Lyric Poetry in Colonial New England* (Chapel Hill: University of North Carolina Press, 1991), 10–11.

6. Philip F. Gura, "Early American Literature at the New Century," *William and Mary Quarterly*, 3d ser., 57 (2000): 619–20, 607; David Perkins, *Is Literary History Possible?* (Baltimore: Johns Hopkins University Press, 1992), 185.

7. Jeffrey A. Hammond, *Sinful Self, Saintly Self: The Puritan Experience of Poetry* (Athens: University of Georgia Press, 1993), 35.

8. Jeffrey Hammond, *The American Puritan Elegy: A Literary and Cultural Study* (Cambridge: Cambridge University Press, 2000), 44, 45, 47, 68. Hambrick-Stowe also emphasizes devotional functionality in his Introduction to *Early New England Meditative Poetry* (New York: Paulist Press, 1988), 7–62.

9. Stanley E. Fish, *Self-Consuming Artifacts: The Experience of Seventeenth-Century Literature* (Berkeley: University of California Press, 1972); Ursula Brumm, "Edward Taylor and the Poetic Use of Religious Imagery," in *Typology and Early American Literature*, ed. Sacvan Bercovitch, 191–206 (Amherst: University of Massachusetts Press, 1972); Grabo, *Edward Taylor: Revised Edition* (Boston: Twayne, 1988); Hambrick-Stowe, *Practice of Piety*.

10. Robert Daly, *God's Altar: The World and the Flesh in Puritan Poetry* (Berkeley: University of California Press, 1978), 45, 30, 41, 69–81, 134.

11. Kathleen Blake, "Edward Taylor's Protestant Poetic: Nontransubstantiating Metaphor," *American Literature* 43 (1971): 2.

12. Norman S. Grabo, "The Veiled Vision: the Role of Aesthetics in Early American Intellectual History," in *The American Puritan Imagination: Essays in Revaluation*, ed. Sacvan Bercovitch, 24–25 (Cambridge: Cambridge University Press, 1974); Patricia Caldwell, *Puritan Conversion Narrative, 37; Willis Barnstone, "Misalliance of Theory and Practice or Parable of the Bay Psalm Book," Translation Review* 32–33 (1990): 22–26; Hammond, *Sinful*, 6, and *Elegy*, 57, 68. See also Daly, *God's Altar*, 69–80.

13. *The Whole Booke of Psalmes Faithfully Translated into English Metre* ([Cambridge, Mass.], 1640; facsimile reprint, New York: Dodd, Mead, 1903), Sig. **3v. Hereafter referred to as the Bay Psalm Book; Cotton Mather, *Manuductio ad Ministerium* (Boston, 1726; reprint, New York: AMS Press, 1978), 42; Jonathan Mitchel, "On the following Work, and It's Author" (first extant publication in the 1701 edition of *The Day of Doom*, reprinted in *The Poems of Michael Wigglesworth*, ed. Ronald A. Bosco [Lanham, Md.: University Press of America, 1989], 299).

14. The two stanzas of Taylor's "Upon Wedlock and Death of Children," published in Mather's *Right Thoughts in Sad Hours*, are discussed in Thomas H. Johnson, "A Seventeenth-Century Printing of Some Verses of Edward Taylor," *New England Quarterly* 14 (1941): 139–41; Mather, *Manuductio*, 42; Bay Psalm Book, Sig. **3v.

15. The chief anthologies of poetry are: *The First Century of New England Verse*, ed. Harold S. Jantz (New York: Russell & Russell, 1944; reprint, 1962); *Handkerchiefs from Paul*, ed. Kenneth B. Murdock (Cambridge: Harvard University Press, 1927; reprint, 1970); *Colonial American Poetry*, ed. Kenneth Silverman (New York: Hafner, 1968); *Seventeenth-Century American Poetry*, ed. Harrison T. Meserole (New York: Doubleday, 1968), reprinted as *American Poetry of the Seventeenth Century* (University Park: Pennsylvania State University Press, 1985; reprint, 1993).

16. Hammond, *Sinful*, 8, 5.

17. Michael P. Clark, "The Honeyed Knot of Puritan Aesthetics," *Puritan Poets and Poetics: Seventeenth-Century American Poetry in Theory and Practice*, ed. Peter White (University Park: Pennsylvania State University Press, 1985), 68. For Renaissance ar-

guments against poetry, see Russell Fraser, *The War Against Poetry* (Princeton: Princeton University Press, 1970).

18. Hammond, *Sinful*, 13; George Herbert, *The Temple: Sacred Poems and Private Ejaculations* (Cambridge, 1633; facsimile reprint, London: Wells Gardner, 1876), 48; Michael Drayton, "To the Honourable Gentlemen of Englande, true favorers of Poesie," in *Matilda* (1594), reprinted in *The Works of Michael Drayton*, ed. J. William Hebel (Oxford: Basil Blackwell, Shakespeare Head Press, 1961), 1:211.

19. See Roy Harvey Pearce, *The Continuity of American Poetry* (Princeton: Princeton University Press, 1961), 18.

20. According to Thomas Johnson, Taylor owned the second edition: Anne Bradstreet, *Several Poems Compiled with Great Variety of Wit and Learning* (Boston, 1678); see inventory of Taylor's library, 13 January 1729–30, transcribed and annotated in *The Poetical Works of Edward Taylor*, ed. Thomas H. Johnson (New York: Rockland Editions, 1939; reprint, Princeton: Princeton University Press, 1943), 212.

21. Hammond, *Sinful*, 4; John Woodbridge, "Epistle to the Reader," in *The Tenth Muse*, Lately Sprung Up in America (London, 1650), reprinted in *The Works of Anne Bradstreet*, ed. Jeannine Hensley (Cambridge: Belknap Press of Harvard University Press, 1967), 3.

22. Alan B. Howard, "The World as Emblem: Language and Vision in the Poetry of Edward Taylor," *American Literature* 44 (1972): 359–84; William J. Scheick, *Design in Puritan American Literature* (Lexington: University Press of Kentucky, 1992), 55, 62; Grabo, *Edward Taylor: Revised Edition*; John Gatta, *Gracious Laughter: The Meditative Wit of Edward Taylor* (Columbia: University of Missouri Press, 1989), 10, 159 passim. For a detailed account of the debate about Taylor's incongruous imagery, see Raymond A. Craig, "The 'Peculiar Elegance' of Edward Taylor's Poetics," in *The Tayloring Shop: Essays on the Poetry of Edward Taylor in Honor of Thomas M. and Virginia L. Davis*, ed. Michael Schuldiner (Newark: University of Delaware Press, 1997), 76–77.

23. Taylor's English education is not known, but when he enrolled at Harvard he was, unusually, awarded advanced standing. See Thomas Davis, *A Reading of Edward Taylor* (Newark: University of Delaware Press, 1992), 20.

24. See Taylor to Samuel Sewall, 29 September 1696, in Taylor's manuscript Commonplace Book, Massachusetts Historical Society, Boston, printed in "The Pouring of the Sixth Vial: A Letter in a Taylor-Sewall Debate," ed. Mukhtar Ali Isani, *Proceedings of the Massachusetts Historical Society* 83 (1971):125. Francis Murphy notes that Taylor probably knew Chauncy, since they shared a room one night. Chauncy transcribed many poetic extracts into his commonplace book, including verses by Herrick, Cleveland, Beaumont, and Spenser. *The Diary of Edward Taylor*, ed. Francis X. Murphy (Springfield: Connecticut Valley Historical Museum, 1964), 12.

25. Barbara Lewalski, *Protestant Poetics and the Seventeenth-Century Religious Lyric* (Princeton: Princeton University Press, 1979) 388; *Edward Taylor's Gods Determinations and Preparatory Meditations: A Critical Edition*, ed. Daniel Patterson (Kent, Ohio: Kent State University Press, 2003), 80. For another discussion of Taylor and Herbert, see John Gatta, *Gracious Laughter*, 71–72.

26. Silverman's examples of "fervently glad distress" were John Fiske's elegies and the Bay Psalms. See his *Colonial American Poetry*, 127.

27. H. L. Mencken, "Puritanism as a Literary Force," in *A Book of Prefaces* (London: Jonathan Cape, 1922): 205, 208–10.

28. Scheick, *Design*, 34, 23–24.

29. See, for example, Thomas Goddard Wright, *Literary Culture in New England (1620–1730)* (New Haven: Yale University Press, 1920), 92–93.

30. Taylor to Samuel Sewall, 125.

31. For a survey of Herbert's influence, see John T. Shawcross, "Some Colonial American Poetry and George Herbert," *Early American Literature* 23 (1988): 28–51.

32. See Wigglesworth, *Poems*, 9. Richard Crowder highlighted the possible sources for Wigglesworth's knowledge of Christian/pagan syncretism in books in John Harvard's bequest. Some of these works, in spite of being relatively Puritan, made classical references: for example, Wither's "Epithalamia" included references to Vulcan, Minerva, Neptune, Jove, Juno, Hymen, and others. Quarles began his first book of emblems with the careful invocation, "when my Urania sings, / She sings praises of the King of Kings," which still falls short of Wigglesworth's angry radicalism. Richard Crowder, *No Featherbed to Heaven: A Biography of Michael Wigglesworth, 1631–1705* ([East Lansing]: Michigan State University Press, [1962]), 103.

33. Wright, *Literary Culture*, 39, 52 and note. Increase Mather's 1664 library inventory lists a copy of Herbert's poems, and there exists a privately owned copy of the 1675 edition with Increase's Latin inscription.

34. Wright, *Literary Culture*, 54–57, and David Cressy, *Coming Over: Migration and Communication between England and New England in the Seventeenth Century* (Cambridge: Cambridge University Press, 1987), 232–34.

35. The commonplace books are described in Samuel Eliot Morison, *Harvard College in the Seventeenth Century* (Cambridge: Harvard University Press, 1936), 1:125–32, 116. On the college library, see Samuel E. Morison, *The Founding of Harvard College* (Cambridge: Harvard University Press, 1935), 265, 269–70; Wright, *Literary Culture*, 272–93; *The Printed Catalogues of the Harvard College Library, 1723–1790*, ed. W. H. Bond and Hugh Amory, Publications of the Colonial Society of Massachusetts, 68 (Boston: Colonial Society of Massachusetts, 1996).

36. Hugh Amory and David D. Hall, eds., *The Colonial Book in the Atlantic World* (Cambridge: Cambridge University Press,1000), 95.

37. Wright, *Literary Culture*, 121–23. Two of these "garlands" are identifiable as Richard Johnson's *The Crown Garland of Golden Roses* and Thomas Deloney's *Strange Histories; or, The Garland of Delight*, perhaps in their London reprints of 1683 and 1681, respectively.

38. Cressy notes that in 1688 Sewall shipped one barrel and two punchions of books back with him to Massachusetts (*Coming Over*, 212, 233–34); Wright, *Literary Culture*, 61. On early New England books and readers more generally, see Amory and Hall *Colonial Book*, chapters 3 and 4.

39. The third most popular verse style in seventeenth-century New England was that of Herbert's "The Church-porch," as illustrated in Jonathan Mitchel's commendatory verses on *The Day of Doom*, cited below (Shawcross, "Colonial Poetry and George Herbert," 49 n. 14).

40. Gura, "Early American Literature," 602.

41. Lawrence Buell, "Circling the Spheres: A Dialogue," *American Literature* 3 (1998): 477–78. On multilingual, multiethnic trends, see Ada Van Gastel, "Ethnic Pluralism in Early American Literature: Incorporating Dutch-American Texts into the Canon," in *Early American Literature and Culture*, ed. Kathryn Zabelle Derounian-Stodola (Newark: University of Delaware Press, 1992), 109; Gura, "Early American Literature," 610; David S. Shields, "Joy and Dread among the Early Americanists," *William and Mary Quarterly*, 3d ser., 57 (2000): 638. Examples of the "hemispheric perspective" include Walter Mignolo, *Local Histories, Global Designs: Coloniality, Sub-*

altern Knowledges, and Border Thinking (Princeton: Princeton University Press, 2000); and Susan Castillo and Ivy Schweitzer, Eds., *A Companion to* The Literatures of Colonial America: An Anthology (Oxford: Blackwell, 2005).

42. William C. Spengemann, "Discovering the Literature of British America," *Early American Literature* 18 (1983): 7. See also Philip F. Gura, *The Crossroads of American History and Literature* (University Park: Pennsylvania State University Press, 1996), 18, 49.

43. Jeffrey A. Hammond, "Where are we going, where have we been?: Puritan Poetics Reconsidered," *Early American Literature* 22 (1987): 129.

44. Kenneth B. Murdock, *Literature, and Theology in Colonial New England* (Cambridge: Harvard University Press, [1949]; reprint, Westport, Conn.: Greenwood, 1976).

45. Karen E. Rowe, *Saint and Singer: Edward Taylor's Typology and the Poetics of Mediation* (Cambridge: Cambridge University Press, 1986); Hammond, *Sinful*; Schweitzer, *Self-Representation*; Scheick, *Design*; and Craig, "Peculiar Elegance."

46. Lewalski, *Protestant Poetics*, 5 and 31. Craig, "Peculiar Elegance," 96.

47. Mason I. Lowance, Jr., *The Language of Canaan: Metaphor and Symbol in New England from the Puritans to the Transcendentalists* (Cambridge: Harvard University Press, 1980). See also Thomas M. Davis, "The Exegetical Traditions of Puritan Typology," *Early American Literature* 5 (1970):11–50; *Typology and Early American Literature*, ed. Sacvan Bercovitch (Amherst: University of Massachusetts Press, 1972); Karen E. Rowe, "Prophetic Visions: Typology and Colonial American Poetry," in *Puritan Poets and Poetics*, ed. Peter White, 47–66 (University Park: Pennsylvania State University Press). For an interesting theoretical survey of the different literary critical approaches to Puritan typology, see Mitchell Breitwieser, "Early American Antigone," in *Theorizing American Literature: Hegel, the Sign, and History*, ed. Bainard Cowan and Joseph G. Kronick 125–61 (Baton Rouge: Louisiana State University Press, 1991). Scholars of New England gravestone iconography have also explored Puritan theology of figuralism; see, for instance, Dickran Tashjian and Ann Tashjian, *Memorials for Children of Change* (Middletown, Conn.: Wesleyan University Press, 1974).

48. Massachusetts was the most influential and tightly organized colony in church matters. New Haven was also strict, but did not always take part in or agree with decisions made by the Massachusetts synods. Connecticut was different again, and its churches less carefully regulated. For a comparative survey, see Robert G. Pope, *The Half-Way Covenant: Church Membership in Puritan New England* (Princeton: Princeton University Press, 1969).

49. Lewalski, *Protestant Poetics*, 7. See also Ramie Targoff, *Common Prayer: The Language of Public Devotion in Early Modern England* (Chicago: University of Chicago Press, 2001), 73–84.

50. Harold Fisch, *Poetry with a Purpose: Biblical Poetics and Interpretation* (Bloomington: Indiana University Press, 1988; reprint, 1990), 104–36.

51. Robert Frost, "The Figure a Poem Makes," *The Collected Poems of Robert Frost* (London: Longmans, Green, 1939), [i]. Jerome McGann, *Black Riders: The Visible Language of Modernism* (Princeton: Princeton University Press, 1993), 143.

52. Hammond, *Sinful*, 9.

53. Ibid., 19.

54. John Bunyan, *Grace Abounding to the Chief of Sinners* (London, 1666), reprinted in *Grace Abounding with Other Spiritual Autobiographies*, ed. John Stachniewski with Anita Pacheco (Oxford: Oxford University Press, 1998); for example, "This

Scripture also did seem to me to trample upon all my desires," and "These places did pinch me very sore," 20, 50.

55. John Cotton, *A Modest and Cleare Answer to Mr. Balls Discourse of Set Formes of Prayer* (London, 1642), 5.

56. John Bunyan, *The Pilgrim's Progress From This World, to That Which is To Come* (London, 1678), A6r.

57. Wigglesworth, *Poems*, 299, lines 1–6.

58. John Fiske's elegy poem on John Cotton, based on the anagram "O, Honie knott" (in Meserole, *American Poetry*, 187–90), provides an apt image, picked up by Clark, "Honeyed Knot."

59. Michael P. Clark, "The Crucified Phrase: Sign and Desire in Puritan Semiology," *Early American Literature* 13 (1978–79): 287–89.

60. Cotton, *Modest*, 7. For the Calvinist basis of Cotton's verbal iconoclasm, see Kibbey, *Material Shapes*, 44–48. For more on the eroticization of sin, with particular reference to Michael Wigglesworth, see Walter Hughes, "'Meat Out of the Eater': Panic and Desire in American Puritan Poetry," in *Engendering Men: The Question of Male Feminist Criticism*, ed. Joseph A. Boone and Michael Gadden, 102–21 (New York: Routledge, 1990).

61. Hambrick-Stowe, *Practice of Piety*, viii.

62. Cotton, *Modest*, 7.

63. Entry made after Michael Wigglesworth's death in June 1705 in notebook entitled "Michael Wigglesworth & his son Edward," Notebook 3, New England Historic Genealogical Society, Boston.

64. Miller, *The Seventeenth Century*, 300–330, 360–61.

65. Wigglesworth, *Poems*, 55, lines 1417–21.

66. Gordis, *Opening Scripture*, 34–35, 44, 60.

67. *A Platform of Church Discipline Gathered out of the Word of God* (Cambridge, Mass., [1648]), reprinted in *The Creeds and Platforms of Congregationalism*, ed. Williston Walker (New York: Charles Scribner's Sons, 1893), 200.

68. Thomas Shepard, *God's Plot: The Paradoxes of Puritan Piety*, ed. Michael McGiffert (Amherst: University of Massachusetts Press, 1972), 70, 142 and 200.

69. Gura, *Crossroads*, 49.

70. Daly, *God's Altar*, 136.

71. Kathryn Zabelle Derounian-Stodola, ed., introduction to *Early American Literature and Culture* (Newark: University of Delaware Press, 1992), 16.

72. Perry Miller, "A Colonial Dialect," in *Early American Literature: A Collection of Critical Essays*, ed. Michael T. Gilmore (Englewood Cliffs, N.J.: Prentice-Hall, 1980), 30.

73. Kibbey, *Material Shapes*, 8, 11.

74. Clark, "Crucified Phrase," 284.

75. "The significance of fidelity as ensured by literalness is that the work reflects the great longing for linguistic complementation." Walter Benjamin, "The Task of the Translator" (1923), reprinted in *Illuminations*, trans. Harry Zohn (New York: Harcourt, Brace & World, 1968), 79.

CHAPTER 1. THE MEANING OF FORMS

1. Jeffrey A. Hammond, *Edward Taylor: Fifty Years of Scholarship and Criticism* (Columbia, S.C.: Camden House, 1993), on Rowe's work, 108, and on his own, 140; Scheick, *Design*, 1, 30–34.

2. Craig, "Peculiar Elegance," 73, 78; Hammond, *Sinful*, 31 (Hammond's italic); Rowe, *Saint*, 247.

3. Scheick, *Design*, 31; on Wigglesworth, see, for example, Gary Sloan, "Wigglesworth's *The Day of Doom*," *The Explicator* 56 (1998): 64–67. For discussion of this critical tendency to read *The Day of Doom* as if it were a sermon, see my chapter 3.

4. Gura, *A Glimpse*, 7, 11; Knight, *Orthodoxies*, 29–31 passim; Michael Winship, "'The Most Glorious Church in the World': The Unity of the Godly in Boston, Massachusetts, in the 1630s," *Journal of British Studies* 39 (2000): 95–96. The Cambridge Platform and other key documents of New England church history are reprinted in Walker, *Creeds and Platforms*. For detailed overviews of the development of New England church order in the seventeenth century, see Stephen Foster, *The Long Argument: English Puritanism and the Shaping of New England Culture 1570–1700* (Chapel Hill: University of North Carolina Press for the Institute of Early American History and Culture, 1991), David D. Hall, *The Faithful Shepherd: A History of the New England Ministry in the Seventeenth Century* (Chapel Hill: University of North Carolina Press for the Institute of Early American History and Culture, 1972); E. Brooks Holifield, *The Covenant Sealed: The Development of Puritan Sacramental Theology in Old and New England, 1570–1720* (New Haven: Yale University Press, 1974); Miller, *Colony to Province*; Edmund S. Morgan, *Visible Saints: The History of a Puritan Idea* (Ithaca: Cornell University Press, 1963); Pettit, *Heart Prepared*; and Pope, *Half-Way Covenant*.

5. Winship, *Making Heretics*, 8, and "The Most Glorious Church," 95–96. See also Gordis, *Opening Scripture*, 186.

6. From the examination of Anne Hutchinson, in David D. Hall, ed., *The Antinomian Controversy 1636–1638: A Documentary History* (Middletown, Conn.: Wesleyan University Press, 1968), 337.

7. See *Roger Williams, John Cotton, and Religious Freedom: A Controversy in New and Old England*, ed. Irwin H. Polishook (Englewood Cliffs, N.J.: Prentice-Hall, 1967). Two key texts are Williams's *The Bloudy Tenent of Persecution, for Cause of Conscience, Discussed, in a Conference betweene Truth and Peace* (London, 1644), and Cotton's *The Bloudy Tenent Washed, and Made White in the Bloud of the Lambe* (London, 1647). Gordis suggests a connection between Cotton's and Williams's views on toleration and their views on exegesis (*Opening Scripture*, Chapter 6).

8. Thomas Hooker, *The Covenant of Grace Opened* (London, 1649), 42; cf. Sargent Bush, Jr., *The Writings of Thomas Hooker: Spiritual Adventure in Two Worlds* (Madison: University of Wisconsin Press, 1980), 124.

9. Morgan estimates that the conversion relation was a widespread prerequisite by 1636 (*Visible Saints*, 60); Pope suggests 1640 (*Half-Way Covenant*, 3–8).

10. For Hooker's views, see Bush, *Writings of Thomas Hooker*, 59–60, 125. See also Richard Mather, *A Defence of the Answer and Arguments of the Synod met at Boston in the Year 1662* (Boston, 1664); Thomas Shepard, *Church-Membership of Children and their Right to Baptism* (Cambridge, Mass., 1668). What the majority of first-generation ministers thought is hard to establish, and indeed became a bone of contention in the filiopietistic debates of the 1660s. James F. Cooper argues that they agreed in principle with Richard Mather, but in practice only baptized infants of full members; *Tenacious of their Liberties: The Congregationalists in Colonial Massachusetts* (New York: Oxford University Press, 1999, 89–90.

11. Reprinted in Walker, *Creeds and Platforms*, 301–39.

12. Pope, *Half-Way Covenant*, 38–39; Cooper, *Tenacious of their Liberties*, 88–114.

13. Morgan, *Visible Saints*, 143–45; Pope, *Half-Way Covenant*, 239, 269–75. For the case against the 1662 reforms, see John Davenport, *Another Essay for the Investiga-*

tion of the Truth (Cambridge, Mass., 1663); and Charles Chauncy, *Antisynodalia Scripta Americana* (London, 1662). For the case in favor, see Jonathan Mitchel, *Propositions Concerning the Subject of Baptism* (Cambridge, Mass., and London, 1662); John Allin, *Animadversions upon the Antisynodalia Americana* (Cambridge, Mass., 1664); and Increase Mather, *The First Principles of New England, Concerning the Subject of Baptism and Communion of Churches* (Cambridge, Mass., 1675). On Increase Mather's change of heart from opponent to supporter of the reforms, see Robert Middlekauff, *Three Generations of Puritan Intellectuals, 1596–1728* (New York: Oxford University Press,1971), 122–25.

14. Walker, *Creeds and Platforms*, 436. On mass covenant renewals, see Harry S. Stout, *The New England Soul: Preaching and Religious Culture in Colonial New England* (New York: Oxford University Press, 1986), 97; Pope, *Half-Way Covenant*, 241–46.

15. Stout, *New England Soul*, 98.

16. Pope, *Half-Way Covenant*, 245–46.

17. Walker, *Creeds and Platforms*, 457.

18. Ibid., 433; Mather, cited in Solomon Stoddard, *An Appeal to the Learned being a Vindication of the Right of Visible Saints to the Lords Supper* (Boston, 1709), 93.

19. See Thomas M. Davis, Introduction to *Edward Taylor vs. Solomon Stoddard: The Nature of the Lord's Supper*, ed. Thomas M. Davis and Virginia L. Davis (Boston: Twayne, 1981), 4–5, 18–19.

20. Texts in this debate include Increase Mather's *The Order of the Gospel* (Boston, 1700), and *A Dissertation Wherein the Strange Doctrine . . . is Examined and Refuted* (Boston, 1708); and Stoddard's *The Inexcusableness of Neglecting the Worship of God, under A Pretence of being in an Unconverted Condition* (Boston, 1708), and *Appeal to the Learned*. Edward Taylor's writings opposing Stoddard's views, such as "The Appeale Tried," are also relevant though unpublished at the time; see Taylor, *Edward Taylor vs. Solomon Stoddard*.

21. "Anglicization" is a term used by Hall in *Faithful Shepherd*, 272–75; and Stout, *New England Soul*, 127–47. On Colman, see Stout, *New England Soul*, 131. On Timothy Edwards, see Stout, *New England Soul*, 145, 150.

22. Walter J. Ong, *Ramus, Method, and the Decay of Dialogue* (Cambridge: Harvard University Press, 1958), 284.

23. John Cotton, *Singing of Psalmes, a Gospel Ordinance* (London, 1647), 15; Craig, "Peculiar Elegance," 78. Ramie Targoff brings out Cotton's understanding of the demands and function of poetry in Psalm translation (*Common Prayer*, 123–30).

24. Cotton, *Modest*, 4, 37.

25. William Bradshaw, *English Puritanisme* (London, 1605), 2.

26. John Donne, *Poetical works*, ed. Herbert J. C. Grierson (Oxford: Oxford University Press, 1971), 308–18.

27. Targoff, *Common Prayer*; Samuel Hieron, *A Helpe unto Devotion* (London, 1610). I discuss the debate about the Anglican Psalter further in chapter 2.

28. John Donne, to Sir H[enry] G[oodyer]; *Letters to Severall Persons of Honor* (London, 1651), 33.

29. The anti-Marprelate tract, *An Almond for a Parrat* (1590), is widely believed to be by Nashe. See also *Pierce Penilesse his Supplication to the Divell* (1592) and the preface to Greene's *Menaphon* (1589). *The Works of Thomas Nashe*, ed. Ronald B. McKerrow, 5 vols. (Oxford: Blackwell,, 1958). Revised edition, ed. F. P. Wilson.

30. Ibid., 3:283, lines 1588–94.

31. Targoff, *Common Prayer*, 87; on the Sidney-Pembroke Psalter, 76–86.

32. P. G. Stanwood, "Liturgy, Worship and the Sons of Light," in *New Perspectives on the Seventeenth-Century Religious Lyric,* ed. John R. Roberts (Columbia: University of Missouri Press, 1994), 106.

33. Thomas Shepard, *A Treatise of Liturgies, Power of the Keyes, and of Matter of the Visible Church* (London, 1653), 37.

34. Samuel Mather, *A Testimony from the Scripture against Idolatry and Superstition In Two Sermons upon the Example of that Great Reformer Hezekiah, 2 Kings 18.4* (Dublin, 1660; reprint, Boston, 1725), 72; John Cotton, *God's Promise to his Plantation* (London, 1630), 9. Cf. "[T]hey tosse the Psalmes in most place like tennice balles," *An Admonition to the Parliament,* in *Puritan Manifestoes: A Study of the Origin of the Puritan Revolt, With a Reprint of the Admonition to the Parliament and Kindred Documents, 1572,* ed. W. H. Frere and C. E. Douglas (London: SPCK, 1954), 29.

35. Mather, *A Testimony,* 72.

36. Cotton Mather, "Nortonus Honoratus," in *Magnalia Christi Americana: or, the Ecclesiastical History of New-England* (London, 1702; reprint, Hartford, Conn.: Silas Andrus, 1853), 1:302.

37. Judith Maltby has highlighted the tenacity and loyalty of some people to the prayer book in " 'By this Book': Parishioners, the Prayer Book and the Established Church," in *The Early Stuart Church 1603–1642,* ed. Kenneth Fincham (Basingstoke: Macmillan, 1993), 136.

38. Richard Hooker, *Of the Laws of Ecclesiastical Polity, Book V,* ed. W. Speed Hill (Cambridge: Belknap Press of Harvard University Press, 1977), 116–17.

39. Entry for 30 March 1673, in "The Autobiography of Increase Mather," ed. M. G. Hall, *Proceedings of the American Antiquarian Society,* n.s., 71 (1961): 316–17.

40. Cotton, *Modest,* 1.

41. Taylor, *Critical Edition,* 130, lines 1–12.

42. *Edward Taylor's Minor Poetry,* ed. Thomas M. Davis and Virginia L. Davis (Boston: Twayne, 1981), 44–45, 127.

43. Wigglesworth, *Poems,* 72, stanza 21.

44. Ibid., 69, lines 61–64.

45. Ibid., 84, lines 45–48.

46. Ibid., 86, line 107.

47. Herbert, *The Temple,* 34–35, 18.

48. Hammond, *Elegy,* 41, 66. Hammond's examples of rhyme being referred to as ordering or containing grief are especially interesting; see pages 120–26, 208. See also William J. Scheick, "Standing in the Gap: Urian Oakes's Elegy on Thomas Shepard," *Early American Literature* 9 (1975): 301–6, and "Tombless Virtue and Hidden Text: New England Puritan Funeral Elegies," in *Puritan Poets and Poetics,* ed. Peter White, 286–302 (University Park: Pennsylvania State University Press, 1985).

49. David E. Stannard *The Puritan Way of Death: A Study in Religion, Culture, and Social Change* (New York: Oxford University Press, 1977), 108–29.

50. Taylor, *Minor Poetry,* 121.

51. Ziff, *Puritanism,* 119.

52. Scheick, *Design,* 34.

53. Hammond, *Elegy,* 66, 202, 140.

54. Meserole, *American Poetry,* 187–90; Murdock, *Handkerchiefs,* 19, 9–11.

55. "Some Offers to Embalm the Memory of the Truly Reverend and Renowned John Wilson: The First Pastor of Boston, in New England," probably by Benjamin Tompson, in *Benjamin Tompson: Colonial Bard: A Critical Edition,* ed. Peter White (University Park: Pennsylvania State University Press, 1980), 186–88.

56. Scheick, "Tombless Virtue," 297; John William Draper, *A Century of Broadside Elegies* (London: Ingpen and Grant, 1928).

57. Herbert, *The Temple*, 69.

58. Murdock, *Handkerchiefs*, 12–14.

59. Meserole, *American Poetry*, 191, lines 33–36.

60. Ibid., 191, lines 37–44.

61. Nathaniel Ward, *The Simple Cobler of Aggawam in America* (London, 1647), 78.

62. Taylor, *Minor Poetry*, 13–18.

63. Meserole, *American Poetry*, 397–98. See the brief biographical sketch of Tillam in *The Puritans in America: A Narrative Anthology*, ed. Alan Heimert and Andrew Delbanco (Cambridge: Harvard University Press, 1985), 126. For a more detailed account of Thomas Tillam's career as an English radical, see David S. Katz, *Sabbath and Sectarianism in Seventeenth-Century England* (Leiden: E. J. Brill, 1988), 21–47.

64. Cotton, *Modest*, 37, 14.

65. Lowance shows typology being invoked to justify the rejection of Medieval *allegoria* and Old Testament or Roman Catholic ceremonies, but also being applied in a quasi-allegorical way itself in providential readings of New England history, personal salvation stories, and ultimately (by Jonathan Edwards) in interpretations of the book of nature; *Language of Canaan*, 35, 51, and 79.

66. William Ames, *A Fresh Suit Against Human Ceremonies in God's Worship* (Rotterdam, 1633), 1:36.

67. John Owen, *A Discourse of the Work of the Holy Spirit in Prayer* (London, 1682), in *The Works of John Owen*, ed. Thomas Russell (London: Baynes, 1826), 4:92.

68. Hooker, to John Cotton, from Rotterdam, c. April 1633, in *Thomas Hooker: Writings in England and Holland, 1626–1633*, ed. George H. Williams et al. (Cambridge: Harvard University Press, 1975), 297.

69. Hall, *Faithful Shepherd*, 156–59. Hall sees the Antinomian Controversy as a result of Cotton's response to this postmigration spiritual "deadness." On postmigration deadness in conversion relations, see Caldwell, *Puritan Conversion Narrative*, chapter 3; Michael W. Kaufman, *Institutional Individualism: Conversion, Exile, and Nostalgia in Puritan New England* (Hanover, N.H.: Wesleyan University Press, 1998), 36.

70. Cotton, *God's Promise*, 13; and *The Covenant of Gods Free Grace* (London, 1645), 10.

71. Thomas Shepard, *A Treatise of Ineffectual Hearing of the Word* (London, 1652; reprint, 1657), 101.

72. Entry for 30 April 1635, *The Journal of John Winthrop, 1630–1649*, abridged, ed. Richard S. Dunn and Laetitia Yeandle (Cambridge: Belknap Press of Harvard University Press, 1996), 79.

73. Cotton, *Bloudy Tenent*, 65, 83, 176, cited in *Polishook, a Controversy*, 90–91.

74. Cotton, *Singing*, 6.

75. Edward Taylor records his first wife (d. 1689) reciting (or possibly reading aloud) *The Day of Doom* (*Minor Poetry*, 114); Cotton Mather noted that *The Day of Doom* might well "find our Children till the *Day* itself arrive," in *A Faithful Man, Described and Rewarded* (Boston, 1705), 25; Francis Jenks notes that elderly people in the early nineteenth century remembered reciting *The Day of Doom* with their catechisms; review of "Rev. Lyman Beecher's Letters on Infant Damnation," *Christian Examiner* 5 (1828): 537.

76. Horton Davies, *The Worship of the American Puritans 1629–1730* (New York: Lang, 1990), 44, 78, 101–2.

77. Augustine, trans. and cit. in Henry Hammond's preface to his *A Paraphrase and Annotations upon the Books of the Psalms* (London, 1659), A10r.

78. Meserole, *American Poetry*, 397–98.

79. Murdock, *Handkerchiefs*, 7–8.

80. Hammond, *Elegy*, 195; the "boasts of the dead" in Puritan funeral elegies are discussed on pages 129–30. Hammond's examples are Samuel Stone's elegy on William Leet (Jantz, *First Century*, 150), and Samuel Danforth's elegy on William Tompson (Murdock, *Handkerchiefs*, 20).

81. John Cotton, *A Treatise of the Covenant of Grace*, 2d ed. (London, 1659), 37–38.

82. For rhetorical analyses of different ministers' sermon styles, see Emory Elliott, *Power and the Pulpit in Puritan New England* (Princeton: Princeton University Press, 1975); Theresa Toulouse, *The Art of Prophesying: New England Sermons and the Shaping of Belief* (Athens: University of Georgia Press, 1987); Leverenz on Cotton's style in *Language of Puritan Feeling*, 175–85; Bush, *Writings of Thomas Hooker*, 311–14 passim. On the importance of the "aural" world that the sermon inhabited, see Stout, *New England Soul*, 4–5, 34–35. On election sermons as compared to regular preaching, see Stout, *New England Soul*, 74, 92–94.

83. Hammond, *Elegy*, 57.

84. J. Daniel Patterson, "The Homiletic Design of Edward Taylor's *Gods Determinations*," in *The Tayloring Shop: Essays on the Poetry of Edward Taylor in Honor of Thomas M. and Virginia L. Davis*, ed. Michael Schuldiner, 132 (Newark: University of Delaware Press, 1997). See also Miller, *Seventeenth Century*, 239–79.

85. William Perkins, *The Arte of Prophecying* (Cambridge, 1606), reprinted in *Workes of that Famous and Worthie Minister of Christ*, vol. 2 (London, 1617), 673.

86. College Notebook, p. 135, Harvard University Archives, Boston. (This is an enlarged photostat copy of Notebook 4, New England Historic Genealogical Society, Boston.)

87. Wigglesworth, *Poems*, 5.

88. College Notebook, 136.

89. Davies, *American Puritans*, 102–3. See Richard Bernard, *The Faithfull Shepherd*, rev. ed. (London, 1621), 299–300; Perkins, *Arte of prophecying*, 670.

90. Sermon preached at Whitehall, 12 February 1618, in *The Sermons of John Donne*, ed. George R. Potter and Evelyn M. Simpson (Berkeley: University of California Press, 1953–62), 2:171. For literary thoughts on Donne compared with New England writers, see Murdock, *Literature and Theology*, 25–36.

91. Of course, by far the majority of New England sermons were not published. On publication, see Gordis, *Opening Scripture*, 217–18; Babette May Lewis, *Preaching in the First Half Century of New England History* (Hartford, Conn.: American Society of Church History, 1945), 9, 83–85; Everett Emerson, *John Cotton* (New York: Twayne, 1965), 85–86; Winifred Herget, "The Transcription and Transmission of the Hooker Corpus," in *Thomas Hooker: Writings in England and Holland, 1626–1633*, ed. George H. Williams et al. (Cambridge: Harvard University Press, 1975), George Selement, "Publication and the Puritan Minister," *William and Mary Quarterly* 37 (1980): 236–39. Stout describes ministers' books of sermon Notes in *New England Soul*, 34. Unauthorized editions could irritate ministers if they felt their views misrepresented; see Larzer Ziff, Introduction to *John Cotton on the Churches of New England* (Cambridge: Belknap Press of Harvard University Press, 1968).

92. Thomas Goodwin and Philip Nye, prefatory epistle to Thomas Hooker, *The Application of Redemption . . . The First Eight Books* (London, 1656), C4v.

93. Stout, *New England Soul*, 324 n. 5; Karl Keller, "The Example of Edward Taylor," *Early American Literature* 4 (1969): 20–22; Gordis, *Opening Scripture*, 59.

94. Patterson, "Homiletic," 135–36; Hammond, *Elegy*, 56–57. Hammond notes the way in which Mitchel's verses stress links between poem and sermon, but does not weigh Mitchel's sense of the difference of the genre, which is leading him to stress these links. Even Herbert's "A Verse may find him who a sermon flies," implies the use of a significantly different means that is justified by sharing the sermon's goal. For further discussion of Mitchel's and Wigglesworth's prefatory verses and the tension between poem and sermon forms, see chapter 3.

95. Thomas Hooker, *The Application . . . First Eight Books* 205. Cf. Ephesians 2:19–22.

96. Perkins, *Arte of Prophecying*, Bernard, *Faithfull Shepherd*. On the influence of these texts in New England, see Gordis, *Opening Scripture*, chapter 1.

97. Stout, *New England Soul*, 35. Cf. Gordis, *Opening Scripture*, 3, 5 passim.

98. Stout, *New England Soul*, 23.

99. Ibid., 324 n. 5.

100. Kamensky, *Governing the Tongue*, 14.

101. Hall, *Worlds of Wonder*, 42; John Cotton, *Christ the Fountaine of Life* (London, 1651), 181. Kibbey argues further that "Puritans believed written texts were in some way fundamentally dependent for their intelligibility on their incorporation into speech"; *Material Shapes*, 8.

102. *Edward Taylor's "Church Records" and Related Sermons*, ed. Thomas M. Davis and Virginia L. Davis (Boston: Twayne, 1981), 117, 116. For further examples, see Hall, *Worlds of Wonder*, 40–41.

103. *The Diary of Michael Wigglesworth, 1653–1657: The Conscience of a Puritan*, ed. Edmund S. Morgan (New York: Harper and Row, 1965), 108.

104. Perkins, *Arte of Prophecying*, 672.

105. Increase Mather, *The Life and Death of that reverend man of God Mr. Richard Mather, teacher of the church in Dorchester in New-England* (Cambridge, Mass., 1670), reprinted in *Two Mather Biographies: "Life and Death" and "Parentator,"* ed. William J. Scheick (Bethlehem, Pa.: Lehigh University Press, 1989), 61; Scheick, *Design*, 23.

106. Miller, "Colonial Dialect," 27; Edward Taylor, *Christographia*, ed. Norman S. Grabo (New Haven: Yale University Press, 1962), and *Upon the Types of the Old Testament*, ed. Charles W. Mignon, 2 vols. (London: University of Nebraska Press, 1989).

107. Ward, *Cobler;* Edward Johnson, *A History of New-England, from the English planting in the Yeere 1628, untill the Yeere 1652 [The Wonder-Working Providence of Sions Saviour]* (London, 1654); Miller, "Colonial Dialect," 26.

108. Hooker, *Application . . . First Eight Books*, 206. Hooker also develops an image of weakening a potion with too much sugar.

109. Thomas Hooker, *The Soules Implantation* (London, 1637), 65; Cotton Mather, *Psalterium Americanum* (Boston, 1718), vii.

110. John Cotton, *A Brief Exposition of the Whole Book of Canticles* (London, 1642), 112.

111. Emory Elliott, "New England Puritan Literature," in *Cambridge History of American Literature*, ed. Sacvan Bercovitch, 1:247; Taylor, *Critical Edition*, 191, Meditation 1.42, line 4. On the influence of Ramus on the concept of rhetoric as ornament, and the separation of content and style, see Miller, *The Seventeenth Century*, 326–27.

112. Kibbey, *Material Shapes*, 20.

113. Taylor, *Minor Poetry*, 25, 29.

114. College Notebook, 143.

115. Taylor, *Critical Edition*, 158, lines 5–6.

116. Cotton Mather, *Magnalia Christi Americana: or the Ecclesiastical History of New-England*, 2 vols. (London, 1702; reprint, Hartford, Conn.: Silas Andrus, 1853), 1:275.

117. Hammond, *Elegy*, 171. Hammond discusses this intriguing trope of textualization and gives examples of it from a number of Puritan funeral elegies on pages 170–71.

118. Meserole, *American Poetry*, 410–11.

119. E.g., Isaiah 61:1, Matthew 11:5.

120. This impression is one effect of the numerous elegies in Nathaniel Morton's history, *New England's Memoriall* (Cambridge, Mass., 1669).

121. Wigglesworth, *Poems*, 49, lines 1441–44.

122. John Cotton, *The New Covenant, or A Treatise, unfolding the order and manner of the giving and the receiving of the Covenant of Grace to the Elect* (London, 1654), 69.

123. Taylor, *Christographia*, 328, 120.

124. Cotton, *Treatise of the Covenant of Grace*, 199–200. See also Cotton's letter to Thomas Shepard (1636) in Hall, *Antinomian Controversy*, 30. Whereas I highlight the mystical dimension to Cotton's statement, Gordis, in *Opening Scripture*, 40–41, has analyzed how Cotton sought to provide "greater light" through his sermon technique.

125. Taylor, *Critical Edition*, 105, lines 165–54.

126. Ramus argued that logic and rhetoric were one and the same art. He is therefore a key figure behind the development of the ideal of the plain style and the concept of persuasion by clarity. For Ramist influence on New England verse, see, for instance, Alan H. Pope, "Petrus Ramus and Michael Wigglesworth: The Logic of Poetic Structure," in *Puritan Poets and Poetics*, ed. Peter White, 210–26 (University Park: Pennsylvania State University Press, 1985).

127. John Norton, *Abel Being Dead Yet Speaketh* (London, 1658), 13–14. Norton expressed a view of "Divine Eloquence" that was strongly reminiscent of Perkins' ideas, insofar as he emphasized its role of ensuring that the greater glory went to God.

128. *Application of Redemption, The Ninth and Tenth Books*, 2d ed., (London, 1659),57.

129. Taylor, *Christographia*, 120.

130. Meserole, *American Poetry*, 219.

131. For more examples of the trope and a fuller interpretation, see Hammond, *Elegy*, 115–17, 137. The idea that jeremiads carried an affirming message, beyond their negative rhetoric, is endorsed by many scholars, including Stout, in *New England Soul*, 63; and the arguments are presented most fully by Sacvan Bercovitch, *Jeremiad*, 3–30.

132. E.g., Thomas Shepard, Jr.,'s elegy on John Norton, and Francis Drake's on Jonathan Mitchel, in Morton, *Memoriall*, 166, 193.

133. Wigglesworth, *Poems*, 299, lines 11–12.

134. Taylor described and interpreted the Temple in detail in *Types*, 2:409–36.

135. Taylor, *Critical Edition*, 62, lines 411–12.

136. Cotton, *Modest*, 7.

137. Cotton, *Singing*, 51.

138. Thomas Lechford, *Plaine Dealing: or Newes from New-England* (London, 1641), reprinted as *Collections of the Massachusetts Historical Society*, 3d ser., 3 (Cambridge, Mass.: Metcalf, 1833): 114. For an analysis of Lechford's perspective and other early accounts of New England worship, see Robert Neuenschwander, "The Origin and Intent of the Bay Psalm Book" (D.Mus. diss., Northwestern University, 1977), 2–24. Although Cotton condemned Lechford's opinions in *The Way of the Congregational Churches Cleared* (London, 1648), 265, his argument in *Singing of Psalms* was a response to Lechford's criticism.

139. Morgan, *Visible Saints*, 91. See also Daniel B. Shea, Jr., *Spiritual Autobiography in Early America* (Princeton: Princeton University Press, 1968), 91; *The Notebook of the Reverend John Fiske, 1644–1675*, ed. Robert G. Pope, Collections of the Colonial Society of Massachusetts, 47 (Boston: The Society, 1974), xvi. Caldwell argues against the formulaic/stereotype perception of New England relations, in *Puritan Conversion Narrative*, 39–41 passim.

140. David G. Miller, review of *The Self and the Sacred: Conversion and Autobiography in Early American Protestantism*, by Rodger M. Payne, *American Literature* 71 (1999): 798.

141. Thomas Shepard, *The Parable of the Ten Virgins Opened & Applied* (London, 1660), 2:200.

142. Morgan, *Visible Saints*, 92.

143. Taylor, "*Church Records*", 115.

144. See Stoddard, *Appeal to the Learned*, 75. For an account of how Stoddard's views in particular evolved from earlier New England theology, see Holifield, *The Covenant Sealed*, 206–20. Since Miller, scholars have argued against the portrayal of Stoddard as radical and Taylor as conservative in ecclesiastical matters. Emory Elliott, for instance, has argued that the membership requirements (including the conversion relation) were more severely applied in the second generation than at the time of their first instigation, and therefore that Stoddard's rejection of the covenant, and Taylor's active encouragement to the Soul to come forward for membership, as in *Gods Determinations*, were equally innovative responses to the problem both ministers perceived; *Power and the Pulpit*, 37–43, 182–86.

145. Murdock, *Handkerchiefs*, 8.

146. Shipard, *God's Plot*, 73. Poetic examples of this duality of emotional pain and spiritual comfort experienced in bereavement include Wigglesworth's dialogue between Flesh and Spirit, in a poem written after the death of his wife, included in *Meat Out of the Eater or Meditations Concerning the Necessity, End, and Usefulness of Afflictions Unto God's Children* (Cambridge, Mass., 1670), reprinted from the 1689 edition in *Poems*, 231–33; and Taylor's "Upon Wedlock, & Death of Children," *Minor Poetry*, 106–7.

147. Bradstreet, *Works*, elegies on her grandchildren, 235–37, and "To My Dear Children," 240–45. On the persistence of doubt concerning the afterlife in early seventeenth-century literary culture, despite the supposed hegemony of Christian belief, see Robert N. Watson, *The Rest Is Silence: Death as Annihilation in the English Renaissance* (Berkeley: University of California Press, 1994), 3. On the Puritan theology of mourning, including teaching against excessive grieving, see Hammond, 69–100.

148. Moses Fiske's vows of owning the covenant (John Fiske, *Notebook*, 205).

149. Mitchel, "Propositions" (1664), in Mather, *Magnalia*, 2:104.

CHAPTER 2. THE BAY PSALM BOOK

1. Cotton, *Gods Promise*, 8; Meserole, *American Poetry*, 397–98; *New Englands First Fruits* (London, 1643), 23, reprinted in Morison, *Founding*, 443.

2. Sig. **2v.

3. John Milton, "L'Allegro," in *Poems of Mr John Milton, Both English and Latin*, 2 vols. (London, 1645), C2v.

4. Cotton, Mather, *The Nightingale. An Essay on Songs among Thorns* (Boston, 1724), 18, and *Psalterium*, xxiv.

5. Journal, Houghton Library, Harvard University, ms am 929, 8v.

6. Saint Augustine, translated and cited in Hammond, *A Paraphrase*, A10r.

7. "God grant the reformation may never be lost while the Psalms are sung in our churches," *Magnalia*, 1:408; Henry Wilder Foote, *Three Centuries of American Hymnody* (Cambridge: Harvard University Press, 1940), 24. For an annotated bibliography of other works considering the Bay Psalm Book in the context of hymnody, see Barbara Owen, "The Bay Psalm Book and Its Era," *Hymn* 41 (1990): 18–19.

8. "vident enim sacras conciones hoc pacto profundiu descendere in hominum animos," in a letter dated 5 March 1560, Latin and English version in *The Works of John Jewel*, ed. John Ayre (Cambridge: University Press, 1850), 4:1230.

9. Sig. **2v.

10. Theodore Dwight Bozeman, *To Live Ancient Lives: The Primitivist Dimension in Puritanism* (Chapel Hill: University of North Carolina Press, 1988), 344–45 passim; on the Bay Psalm Book, 139–50.

11. Hugh Amory, "'Gods Altar Needs Not Our Pollishings': Revisiting the Bay Psalm Book," *Printing History* 12 (1990): 8.

12. *Records of the Governor and Company of the Massachusetts Bay in New England*, ed. Nathaniel B. Shurtleff, vol. 1, *1628–1641* (Boston: W. White, reprint, 1853; New York: AMS, 1968), 344. While senior ministers John Cotton and Nathaniel Ward were awarded 600 acres each in the same year, and investors and senior magistrates generally received even more, Day's 300 acres well exceeded the base norm of about 50 acres per person. In addition, the grant was processed directly by the General Court rather than one of its local appointees, indicating that the colony was giving Day official recognition (240, 344, passim).

13. *The Whole Booke of Psalmes Faithfully Translated into English Metre*, ed. Zoltán Haraszti (Cambridge, Mass., 1640; facsimile reprint, Chicago: University of Chicago Press, 1956); Zoltán Haraszti, *The Enigma of the Bay Psalm Book* (Chicago: University of Chicago Press, 1956); review of Haraszti's twin volumes by Sidney E. Mead and Ernest R. Sandeen, *The Journal of Religion* 37 (1957): 209.

14. Bay Psalm Book, Sig. **3v; *The Literary History of the United States*, ed. Robert E. Spiller et al., 4th ed. (New York: Macmillan, 1974), 63; Louise Russell Stallings, "The Unpolished Altar: The Place of the Bay Psalm Book in American Culture" (PhD diss., Texas A&M University, 1977), 5. Craig, "Peculiar Elegance," 71.

15. *Magnalia*, 1:407. Although Mather's precise source for this rhyme is unknown, Harold Jantz found a version, with minor differences, on a scrap of paper in Increase Mather's handwriting, indicating that the rhyme was passed down within the family tradition; Jantz, *First Century*, 21.

16. Cotton, *Singing*, 60.

17. Bay Psalm Books, Sig. **2r.

18. Rivkah Zim, *English Metrical Psalms: Poetry as Praise and Prayer, 1535–1601*

(Cambridge: Cambridge University Press, 1987); Philipp von Rohr-Sauer, *English Metrical Psalms from 1600–1660* (Freiburg, Germany: Poppen & Ortmann, 1938); Targoff, *Common Prayer*, 74, 82–83.

19. Thomas Wyatt, *Certayne Psalmes Chosen out of the Psalter of David Commonlye Called thee .vii. Penytentiall Psalmes* (London, [1549]); James I and William Alexander, *The Psalmes of King David translated by King James* (London, 1631).

20. "Vpon the translation of the Psalmes by Sir Philip Sydney, and the Countesse of Pembroke his sister," Donne, *Works*, 319 lines 37–38. For other examples of criticism of Sternhold and Hopkins from a poetic point of view, see Targoff, *Common Prayer*, 82–83.

21. George Wither, *The Psalms Translated into Lyric Verse* (The Netherlands, 1632; reprint, Manchester: Spenser Society, 1881); Francis Rous, *The Psalms of David in English Meeter* (London, 1643); William Barton, *The Book of Psalms in Metre* (London, 1644). A revised version of Rous's Psalter became established in the Church of Scotland, but after the Restoration brought back the Book of Common Prayer to England, Sternhold and Hopkins remained standard in the Church of England until replaced by Nahum Tate and Nicholas Brady, *A New Version of the Psalms of David* (London, 1696).

22. Richard Crashaw, *Steps to the Temple: Sacred Poems, with Other Delights of the Muses* (London, 1646), 27.

23. See the "Argument" introducing the Book of Psalms in the annotated Geneva Bible. *Geneva Bible* (Geneva, 1599; facsimile reprint, Buena Park, Calif.: Geneva Publishing, 1991); Sedulius, *Opus Paschale*, ed. Johannes Huemer, Corpus Scriptorum Ecclesiasticorum Latinorum (Vienna, 1885), x, 176–77. For further references, see Lewalski, *Protestant Poetics*, 7, and Targoff, *Common Prayer*, 65–76.

24. Philip Sidney, *An Apology for Poetry or The Defence of Poetry*, ed. Geoffrey Shepherd (Manchester: Manchester University Press, 1973), 99; Ben Jonson, *Timber, or Discoveries* (London, 1641), reprinted in *Ben Jonson*, ed. C. H. Herford, P. Simpson, and E. Simpson vol. 8 (Oxford: Clarendon Press, 1954), 636. *The Psalms of Sir Philip Sidney and the Countess of Pembroke*, ed. John C. A. Rathmell (Garden City, NY: Doubleday, 1963); John Milton, *Poems; &c. upon Several Occasions* (London, 1673), 130–65.

25. Sig. **4r.

26. Wigglesworth, *Poems*, 299, lines 14–15. For another example, John Wilson's son described his father as "another sweet singer of Israel" who wrote "heavenly verses," in the preface to the (posthumous) Boston edition of John Wilson's *A Song of Deliverance for the Lasting Remembrance of Gods Wonderful Works never to be Forgotten* (London, 1626; reprint, Boston, 1680), [i].

27. George Sandys, *A Paraphrase upon the Psalmes of David and upon the Hymnes Dispersed throughout the Old and New Testaments* (London, 1636), [A]1r; Cotton, *Singing*, 56.

28. Bay Psalm Book, Sigs. **[1]v–**2r.

29. Cotton, *Singing*, 60, and *Modest*, 17. For readings of these treatises that highlight the other side of the argument, i.e., the extent to which Cotton approved the composition and use of devotional poetry, see Targoff, *Common Prayer*, 125–30, Craig, "Peculiar Elegance," 73–74.

30. Norman S. Grabo, "How Bad is the Bay Psalm Book?" *Papers of the Michigan Academy of Science, Arts, and Letters* 46 (1961): 614.

31. Willis Barnstone, *The Poetics of Translation: History, Theory, Practice* (New Haven: Yale University Press, 1993), 57.

32. Donne, *Sermons*, 170–71; George Wither, *Preparation to the Psalter* (London, 1619), 69.

33. *Preparation*, 75. Wither's comments are reminiscent of ministers' discussions of the different effects of sermons and Bible reading on regenerate and unregenerate hearers; see chapter 1 and Gordis, *Opening Scripture*, 44, 60.

34. Cotton, *Singing*, 51. Cotton's references to the ceremonial beauty of Old Testament worship, which Calvinists believed should be replaced by more spiritual (and plainer) New Testament worship, implicitly alluded to the Laudian movement in the 1630s to increase "the beauty of holiness" (Psalm 29:2) by emphasizing (and enforcing) ceremonialism in Anglican liturgical practice. See Peter Lake, "The Laudian Style: Order, Uniformity and the Pursuit of the Beauty of Holiness in the 1630s," in *The Early Stuart Church 1603–1642*, ed. Kenneth Fincham, 161–85 (Basingstoke: Macmillan, 1993).

35. *Singing*, 6.

36. N. H. Keeble, *The Literary Culture of Nonconformity in Later Seventeenth-Century England* (Leicester: Leicester University Press, 1987), 186.

37. Stallings, "The Unpolished Altar," 97, 110–25; Winthrop, *Journal*, 230–34; Bay Psalm Book, Sig. *2r. On the emphasis on unity in writings reacting to the Antinomian controversy, see Gordis, *Opening Scripture*, 160, 167, 185–86. Views diverge on the effects of the crisis: Knight presents the anti-Cottonian faction as victorious, but acknowledges the continued presence of dissenting voices; *Orthodoxies*, 197–99. Darren Staloff argues that it resulted in the cultural domination of ordinary folk by a ministerial/magisterial intelligentsia; *The Making of an American Thinking Class: Intellectuals and Intelligentsia in Puritan Massachusetts* (New York: Oxford University Press, 1998), 72, a claim firmly rejected by Cooper in *Tenacious of their Liberties*, 46–47, 67. Either way, the leaders who stayed emerged from the controversy keen to counteract the bitter division it had involved.

38. Amory, "Gods Altar," 6; Thomas Prince, *The Psalms, Hymns, & Spiritual Songs, of the Old and New Testament, Faithfully Translated into English Metre. Being the New-England Psalm book revised and improved* (Boston, 1758), i. Prince may have been surmising about the number involved, since his account seems otherwise based on Cotton Mather's comments rather than a fresh source (cf. the similar account by Daniel Neal, *The History of New-England* [London, 1720], 1:188). George P. Winship has put the case for the single authorship of John Eliot, *The Cambridge Press 1638–1692: A Reëxamination of the Evidence concerning the Bay Psalm Book and the Eliot Indian Bible* (Philadelphia: University of Pennsylvania Press, 1945), 28–30, but the variety of verse styles makes this unconvincing.

39. For printing statistics, see Winship, *Cambridge*, 34, Amory, "Gods Altar"; Amory and Hall, *Colonial Book*, 106. Amory and Winship have puzzled over the high figure of 1,700 (circa one copy per eight colonists). Winship suggested some copies were exported, Amory that they were sold over several years. The 1651 Psalter was revised, enlarged, and retitled *Psalms, Hymns and Spiritual Songs of the Old and New Testament faithfully translated into English metre for the use, edification, and comfort of the saints in public and private especially in New England*. For details of eighteenth-century revisions and gradual replacement by Isaac Watts's *The Psalms of David Imitated* (1719), see Maxine Thompson Turner, "Three Eighteenth-Century Revisions of the Bay Psalm Book," *The New England Quarterly* 45 (1972): 270–77; and Foote, *Hymnody*, 160.

40. Bush has corrected Haraszti's identification of the draft preface as in Cotton's hand to that of an unidentified scribe, probably a Harvard student on a train-

ing placement, who worked for Cotton in 1640–41; *The Correspondence of John Cotton,* ed. Sargent Bush, Jr. (Chapel Hill: University of North Carolina Press, 2001), 70 n. 8. On Quarles's now lost psalms, see John Josselyn, *Account of two Voyages to New-England* (London, 1674), 19–20; Karl Josef Höltgen, "New Verse by Francis Quarles: The Portland Manuscripts, Metrical Psalms, and the Bay Psalm Book," *English Literary Renaissance* 28 (1998): 128.

41. Cotton to Shepard, between 1 Feb. and 1 June 1636, *Correspondence,* 232; Gordis, *Opening Scripture,* 34, 55, 61, 100–101.

42. Michael Winship, "Most Glorious Church," 92. For primary documents, see Hall, *Antinomian Controversy;* and Cotton, *Correspondence.*

43. Haraszti, *Enigma,* 124 n. 6.

44. Bay Psalm Book, Sigs. **3v–**4r.

45. *A Modell of Christian Charity,* in *Collections of the Massachusetts Historical Society,* 3d ser., 7 (Boston: Little and Brown, 1838), 31–48.

46. Exodus 20:24–25. This and all future Biblical citations are from the 1611 Authorized Version.

47. [A]6r.

48. [A]1r.

49. Wigglesworth, *Poems,* 299, line 7. Six psalms in the Bay Psalm Book are presented in two different metrical versions (51, 85, 100, 117, 133, 138).

50. Bradstreet, verses from the Andover MS (first publ., 1867), *Works,* 292, lines 11–20. Some similarity between these verses and the Bay Psalm Book has been noted by Silverman in *Colonial American Poetry,* 42.

51. *Works,* 237, line 12; Hammond, *Elegy,* 230–31. Hammond's critique of readings of Bradstreet as rebellious and having unpuritan leanings challenges the all too easy imposition of "twentieth-century subjectivities" on the early modern text. (But Hammond's condemnation of anachronism in literary critical approaches to colonial Puritan texts is also paradoxical, since virtually the whole practice of modern literary analysis is anachronistic where such texts are concerned.) For more feminist, radicalizing interpretations of Bradstreet's spiritual struggles, see Ann Stanford, *Anne Bradstreet: The Worldly Puritan* (New York: Burt Franklin, 1974); and Wendy Martin, *An American Triptych: Anne Bradstreet, Emily Dickinson, Adrienne Rich* (Chapel Hill: University of North Carolina, 1984).

52. Craig, "Singing with Grace: Allusive Strategies in Anne Bradstreet's 'New Psalms,'" *Studies in Puritan American Spirituality* 1 (1990): 153; Hammond, *Sinful,* 16. Cf. Rosemary Fithian, "'Words of My Mouth, Meditations of My Heart': Edward Taylor's Preparatory Meditations and the Book of Psalms," *Early American Literature* 20 (1985): 89–119; Beth M. Doriani, "'Then Have I . . . Said with David': Anne Bradstreet's Andover Manuscript Poems and the Influence of the Psalm Tradition," *Early American Literature* 24 (1989): 52–69.

53. Moses Coit Tyler, *A History of American Literature, 1607–1765* (New York: Putnam's Sons, 1878; reprint, Ithaca: Cornell University Press, 1949), 237; Mather Byles, "To Pictorio, on the Sight of his Pictures," in *Poems on Several Occasions* (Boston, 1744), reprinted in *Works,* ed. Benjamin Frankin V (Delmar, N.Y.: Scholars' Facsimiles & Reprints, 1978), 90. Byles was responding to an exhibition of paintings by Smibert, which he saw in 1730; Foote, *Hymnody* 72.

54. Amory analyzes the errata in extant copies of the first edition, including the revision of Ps 19 from "and from presumptuous-sins, let thou / kept back thy servant bee," to "And from presumptuous-sins, kept back / O let thy servant bee," "Gods Altar," 8.

55. Stallings shows, through comparison with Milton, Marvell, and Donne, that the kind of inversions used in the Bay Psalm Book were more acceptable at that stage in the development of the English language, but her statistics also highlight the remarkable frequency in the Bay Psalm Book (one inversion in four or five lines) compared to her other sources ("The Unpolished Altar," 76–78).

56. Sig. *4r.

57. J. H. Dorenkamp, "The *Bay Psalm Book* and the Ainsworth Psalter," *Early American Literature* 7 (1972): 13.

58. The Salem church voted to adopt the Bay Psalm Book in 1667, and the Plymouth church in 1692 (George Hood, *A History of Music in New England with Biographical Sketches of Reformers and Psalmists* [Boston: Wilkins, Carter, 1846; reprint, New York: Johnson Reprint Corporation, 1970], 53–54.)

59. See Amory, "Gods Altar," 5.

60. Irving Lowens, "The Bay Psalm Book in 17th-Century New England," *Journal of the American Musicological Society* 8 (1955): 24; Lorraine Inserra and H. Wiley Hitchcock, *The Music of Henry Ainsworth's Psalter*, I.S.A.M. Monographs, No. 15 (New York: Institute for Studies in American Music, Brooklyn College, City University of New York, 1981), 25. Bozeman has attributed this reduction in metrical variety to the compilers' efforts "to contain the temptations of meter" and thereby produce a more faithful translation; *To Live Ancient Lives*, 147.

61. *The Humble Request . . . to the Rest of their Brethren, in and of the Church of England* (London, 1630), reprinted in *Chronicles of the First Planters of the Colony of Massachusetts Bay, from 1623 to 1636*, ed. Alexander Young (Boston: Little and Brown, 1846), 295. The authorship of the text is uncertain: Winthrop, Dudley, and five others signed it; Thomas Cartwright, *A Replye to an Answere Made of M. Doctor Whitegifte, Against the Admonition to the Parliament* (London, 1573), 1.

62. Higginson, 1629, cited in Cotton Mather is *Magnalia*, 1:362. On the relationship between the churches of New and Old England, see Foster, *The Long Argument*.

63. *Modell*, 45. This duty to exceed the more corrupt English congregations in holiness seems to help shape New England covenant theology, as in Peter Bulkeley's *The Gospel-Covenant*, 2d ed. (London, 1651), 16: "the Lord looks for more from thee, then from other people," cited in Stout, *New England Soul*, 26.

64. Taylor, *Critical Edition*, 177, lines 1–2.

65. Dorenkamp discusses the Psalms as "lesson and prayer," in "Ainsworth Psalter," 3; draft in Haraszti, *Enigma*, 112. The anxiety that the didactic and affective gap between words and feelings could cause in a singer was expressed by one Mrs. Crackbone, "I was afraid to sing because to sing a lie," cited in Kaufman, *Institutional Individualism*, 36.

66. Bay Psalm Book, Sig. **2v.

67. Thomas Sternhold, John Hopkins, William Whittingham, et al., *The Whole Booke of Psalmes* (London, 1562; reprint, 1642).

68. Stallings, "The Unpolished Altar, 236; Ravenscroft included almost all the tunes from previous English Psalters in four-part harmony; Waldo Selden Pratt, *The Music of the Pilgrims: A Description of the Psalm-Book Brought to Plymouth in 1620* (Boston: Ditson, [1921]; reprint, New York: Russell & Russell, 1971), 31.

69. Pratt, *Music of the Pilgrims*, 20.

70. This tune by Louis Bourgeois is familiar to modern congregations with its English text, "All People That on Earth Do Dwell," probably by William Kethe (1561). It is Psalm 100 in Sternhold and Hopkins. Owen, "Bay Psalm Book," 12.

71. Sig. Ll 3v.

72. Lowens notes, however, that despite its wider variety of verse forms overall, Sternhold and Hopkins still had a higher proportion of psalms in common meter than the 1640 Bay Psalm Book; "Bay Psalm Book," 29. Out of a total of 156 psalms (including the 6 in 2 versions) the 1640 Bay Psalm Book has 116 psalms in common meter quatrains (syllabically) 8686, fifteen in short meter quatrains 6686, sixteen in long meter quatrains 8888, six in hallelujah meter 66664444. One psalm (115) has a unique meter of 8-syllable sestets rhyming aabccb; Ps. 85 and Ps. 138 are in sestets 888888, with ababcc rhymes.

73. Sig. **2r.

74. Pratt, *Music of the Pilgraims*, 14–15.

75. Lowens notes, in the 1651 revision, a significant proportional rise in common meter stanzas, stability in long meter, decrease in short meter and hallelujah meter, and only a single example of a different form (888888); "Bay Psalm Book," 26, 29.

76. *Diary of Samuel Sewall 1674–1729*, ed. M. Halsey Thomas (New York: Farrar, Strauss and Giroux, 1973), 2:881. For further discussion of Sewall's comments, see Maxine Thompson Turner, "A History of the Bay Psalm Book" (PhD diss., Auburn University, 1971), 63. Haraszti's findings corroborate Lowens's concerning the deterioration of singing; *Enigma*, 67–68. Thirteen tunes were provided in the 1698 edition of the Bay Psalm Book, whereas the 1640 Bay Psalm Book "admonition" boasted over 40, in theory, to be found in Ravenscroft. See Richard G. Appel, *The Music of the Bay Psalm Book, 9th Edition (1698)*, I.S.A.M. Monographs, No. 5 (New York: Institute for Studies in American Music, Brooklyn College of the City University of New York, 1975), 4–5.

77. See, for instance, John Tufts, *An Introduction to the Singing of Psalm Tunes in a Plain and Easy Method* (Boston, 1726), usually found bound into copies of the Bay Psalm Book; and Thomas Symmes, *The Reasonableness of Regular Singing* (Boston, 1720). The eighteenth-century New England singing school movement is outlined by Leonard Ellinwood, *The History of American Church Music*, rev. ed. (New York: Da Capo Press, 1970), 18–26, and Irving Lowens, *Music and Musicians in Early America* (New York: Norton & Co., 1964), 19–20.

78. For example, Sternhold and Hopkins Psalm 1:3, Psalm 3:4.

79. "Wherefore doth the wicked contemn God? he that said in his heart, Thou wilt not require *it*" (King James Bible, Psalm 10:13).

80. *Enigma*, 41–43.

81. For Hebrew exercises at Harvard, see Morison, *Seventeenth Century*, 1:200–203.

82. Sig. **2r.

83. Sig. **3r.

84. Stallings, "The Unpolished Altar," 157–58.

85. For detailed examples of textual analysis of the sources of individual Psalms, see Haraszti, *Enigma*, 41–55; Stallings, "The Unpolished Altar," 218ff.

86. On the Bay Psalm Book compilers' use of the Ainsworth version, see Dorenkamp, "Ainsworth Psalter," 3–16.

87. Stallings, "The Unpolished Altar," 157–60.

88. "Fruit" is also found in the Geneva version, but "aspe" is not, so it is reasonable to assume that the translator was looking at the 1611 Bible gloss.

89. For Stallings's analysis of Psalms 99 and 199 in relation to the Geneva Bible,

see "The Unpolished Altar," 160, 211–12. But note that 99:3–4 follows the Authorized Version with "justice" rather than Geneva Bible's "equity."

90. Haraszti, *Enigma*, 36; Harry S. Stout, "Word and Order in Colonial New England," in *The Bible in America: Essays in Cultural History*, ed. Nathan O. Hatch and Mark A. Noll, 19–38 (New York: Oxford University Press, 1982); Michael G. Ditmore, "A Prophetess in Her Own Country: An Exegesis of Anne Hutchinson's 'Immediate Revelation,'" *William and Mary Quarterly*, 3d Ser., 57 (2000): 354, and 362 passim on the influence of the Geneva gloss. To complicate things, eight English editions of the A.V. were printed with the Geneva gloss between 1611 and 1715; Christopher Hill, *The English Bible and the Seventeenth-Century Revolution* (London: Allen Lane, Penguin, 1993), 66.

91. Foote, *Hymnody*, 34–35; Barnstone, "Misalliance," 25.

92. Targoff, *Common Prayer*, 71.

93. Sig. **2r.

94. H[enry] A[insworth] *The Book of Psalmes; Englished both in prose and metre. With annotations, opening both the words and sentences, by conference with other scriptures* (Amsterdam, 1612). Ainsworth's Psalter was republished in 1617, 1626, 1639, and 1644. The copy listed in William Brewster's library in Plymouth was a "prose and metre" edition (Wright, *Literary Culture*, 256).

95. Copies of Ainsworth's *Annotations upon the Five Bookes of Moses, and the Booke of the Psalmes* (London, 1622) were recorded in the libraries of the Mathers, John Harvard, and Peter Bulkeley; Wright, *Literary Culture*, 265.

96. "Annotations upon the Book of Psalmes," gathered separately and dated 1617, in *Annotations upon the Five Bookes of Moses, and the Booke of the Psalmes* (London, 1622), C2r.

97. John Cotton accepted that the English Bible was not quite the Word of God as originally given, but he left it to the specially trained minister to "make use of his own gift in examining the truth of the translation which he readeth unto the Church;" *Modest*, 11.

98. Amory attributes the unusual choice of quarto format to the lack of pica font at the Cambridge press; "Gods Altar," 7.

99. Michel de Certeau, *The Practice of Everyday Life*, trans. Steven Rendall (Berkeley: University of California Press, 1984), 134. The connection between Certeau and the Glossa was made by Peter Candler, Jr., "The Liturgy of Interpretation: Memory and the *Glossa Ordinaria*" (paper presented at the annual conference of Anglo-Saxon, Norse and Celtic, Cambridge University, May 2000).

100. On the interplay of hierarchical authority and personal responsibility in popular piety, see Hall, *Worlds of Wonder*, 66–69.

101. Kaufman, *Institutional Individualism*, 36, 96–97; Foster, *The Long Argument*, 174, 184.

102. Benjamin, *Illuminations*, 79.

103. *Gods Promise*, 13.

104. Shepard, *Ineffectual Hearing*, 101; Bradstreet, "Meditation 51," in *Works*, 282.

105. Stephen Foster, "The Godly in Transit," in *Seventeenth-Century New England*, ed. David D. Hall and David Grayson Allen (Boston: Colonial Society of Massachusetts, 1984), 186. Cf. Cooper, *Tenacious of their Liberties*, 7.

106. Mather, *Magnalia*, 1:407; Byles, *Works*, 90.

107. The 1640 preface was reprinted in three undated editions, published in London on behalf of Usher, the Boston bookseller, but it does not seem to be found in any of those printed in America, from 1651 onwards (Winship, *Cambridge*, 100).

In his 1758 revision, Thomas Prince referred to and quoted the "*ancient preface*" as if it were well known (*Psalms*, vi).

108. *Nonconformity*, 135. For similar discussion of the devotional functionality of colonial Puritan poetry, see Hammond, *Elegy*, 45–47, and Hambrick-Stowe, Introduction to *Meditative Poetry*, 7–62.

109. Bradstreet, *Works*, 251–52, 259–69. Only two poems by Bradstreet are extant from later than 1662: "Upon the Burning of our House" (1666), and "As Weary Pilgrim" (1669). Although there is a distinct shift towards simplicity in Bradstreet's late style, this poetic format was not "new" in the sense that Bradstreet had used it in "Upon a Fit of Sickness," written when she was 19 (222). Many critics have celebrated Bradstreet's shift to a simpler, more "parochial" style; see, for instance, Eavan Boland, "Two Worlds," *PN Review* 28 (2001):11–15. For a contrary view of this shift as a "retreat," see Timothy Sweet, "Gender, Genre, and Subjectivity in Anne Bradstreet's Early Elegies," *Early American Literature* 23 (1988): 152–74.

110. Silverman, *Colonial American Poetry*, 42; Hambrick-Stowe, *Meditative Poetry*, 27. See also Craig, "Singing with Grace."

111. "On my son's return out of England. July 17, 1661," Bradstreet, *Works*, 264, lines 31–34.

112. "In Thankful Remembrance For My Dear Husband's Safe Arrival. Sept. 3, 1662," *Works*, 270, stanzas 2 and 4.

113. Hammond, *Sinful*, 18.

114. Wigglesworth, *Poems*, 170–71. The first and third stanzas of Wigglesworth's poem are verses 1–4 and 5–7 of Psalm 130 in the 1651 Bay Psalm Book, and half of Wigglesworth's fourth stanza is Psalm 49:5.

115. Bay Psalm Book, Sig. **2v–**3r.

116. *Meat*, 170–71.

CHAPTER 3. THE HALFWAY COVENANT

1. Samuel Whiting, *A Discourse of the Last Judgment, or Short Notes upon Mat.* XXV (Cambridge, Mass., 1664).

2. Following the designation of the Boston 1701 edition as the "fifth" by Wigglesworth, Bosco posits a second edition immediately after the first, c. 1663–64, *Psalms*, 305. However, such an edition would have oversaturated the colonial market as described by Hugh Amory, who explains the "fifth" edition by counting three intervening London editions, and subtracting the 1662 Cambridge edition because it was privately financed; Amory and Hall, *Colonial Book*, 107–8.

3. Wigglesworth, Notebook 3.

4. Amory and Hall, *Colonial Book*, 107.

5. *Poems*, 9, lines 6–18.

6. Bradstreet, *Works*, 15, line 18. Wigglesworth was more radical than many ministers in his rejection of classical tropes. On the widespread (but generally circumspect) incorporation of classical allusion into Puritan funeral elegies and the "double-talk" of pagan/Christianizing language in the relatively few Latin elegies, see Hammond, *Elegy*, 34–36. On the Latin poetry written by New England Puritan ministers, see Lawrence Rosenwald, "*Voces Clamantium in Deserto*: Latin Verse of the Puritans," in *Puritan Poets and Poetics: Seventeenth-Century American Poetry in Theory and Practice*, ed. Peter White, 303–17 (University Park: Pennsylvania State University

Press, 1985). A selection of Puritan verse is anthologized in *Early American Latin Verse 1625–1825: An Anthology*, ed. Leo M. Kaiser (Chicago: Bolchazy-Carducci, 1984). Apart from funeral elegies, another poetic genre that invited classical allusion was almanac verse, as it dealt with the seasons and often the zodiac. The younger Samuel Danforth's "*Ad Librum*" in the 1686 New England Almanac directly commented on this dilemma: "Forgive me yet, *Good Reader,* If that I / The *Names* impos'd by old Idolatry / On *Months* and *Planets* still reteyn; Because / I'm forc't thereto by cruel Customs Laws," Meserole, *American Poetry,* 486, lines 30–33.

7. "On the following Work, and It's Author," *Poems,* 299, line 9.

8. Ibid., 76, lines 146–48.

9. Ibid., 299, line 4.

10. Thomas Shepard, *The Sincere Convert,* 4th ed. (London, 1646), 98.

11. See Foster, "The Godly in Transit," 175–230; Cooper, *Tenacious of their Liberties,* 88–114.

12. Walker, *Creeds and Platforms,* 301–44. For a brief comparison of the 1648 and 1662 documents, see J. Daniel Patterson, "A Critical Edition of Edward Taylor's 'Gods Determinations'" (PhD diss., Kent State University, 1985), xx–xxi.

13. Jonathan Mitchel, "An Answer to the Apologetical Preface," in *A Defence of the Answer and Arguments of the Synod Met at Boston in the Year 1662,* by Richard Mather (Boston, 1664), 42–43.

14. *Poems,* 15–16, stanzas 20–21.

15. Ibid., 17, lines 209–14.

16. John Milton, "Ad Patrem," line 103, in *Poems, Both English and Latin,* 2:68. Translated "witless populace" in *The Riverside Milton,* ed. Roy Flannagan (Boston: Houghton Mifflin, 1998), 227.

17. *Poems,* 280. stanza 2.

18. Harold Field Worthley, *An Inventory of the Records of the Particular (Congregational) Churches of Massachusetts Gathered 1620–1805* (Cambridge: Harvard University Press, 1970), 341.

19. *Propositions;* "An Answer." Mitchel also wrote a separate manuscript list of "Propositions," transcribed by Cotton Mather and introduced as written by Mitchel "for his own satisfaction on January 4, 1664" (*Magnalia,* 2:102). By the time Mitchel died in 1668, he had become very strongly identified with the Halfway Covenant: his "life," in Mather's *Magnalia,* especially the long introduction written by Increase, reads largely as a propaganda vehicle for the reforms.

20. Chauncy, *Anti-Synodalia;* Davenport, *Investigation.*

21. In a notebook entitled "Liber Sextus Concid . . ." (full title illegible), Wigglesworth took notes, mainly in shorthand, on sermons dated 1653, including many many by Davenport. Notebook 2, New England Historic Genealogical Society, Boston.

22. Printed in Deloraine Pendre Corey, *The History of Malden Massachusetts 1633–1785* (Malden: the author, 1899).

23. *Poems,* xxx.

24. The handwriting is difficult to judge because Wigglesworth's fair copy of the poem is in a more careful hand than he used in his notebooks. Bosco follows Richard Crowder in dating the poem circa 1665, because the script is definitely earlier than that of the elegy on Buncker in 1669. But I think a date not later than 1658 is likely, because of the changes in Wigglesworth's "d" and the similarity or transitional nature of certain letters ("h" and "p") compared with the script of his Harvard orations; *Poems,* xxx; Crowder, *No Featherbed to Heaven,* 320.

25. Notebook 3, 29 January 1661–62.

26. Conclusion of Mitchel's manuscript "Propositions," in Mather's *Magnalia*, 2:104.

27. *Poems*, 81 lines 241–42.

28. Ibid., 31, lines 657–60.

29. Ibid., 27, lines 533–36.

30. Cotton, *Treatise of the Covenant of Grace*, 199–200.

31. *Poems*, 21, lines 343–44; 7, line 96; 78, lines 207–24.

32. Tyler, *History*, 278; Waggoner, "Puritan Poetry," *Criticism* 6 (1964): 297. See also Sloan, "*The Day of Doom*," 64–67.

33. College Notebook, 136.

34. *Poems*, 49, stanza 154. I've corrected the typo of "split" for "spilt" against the London 1673 edition.

35. Ibid., 32, stanza 87.

36. Cotton, *Singing*, 6; draft preface, Haraszti, *Enigma*, 112.

37. *Poems*, 49, line 1242–44.

38. Ibid., 56, stanza 182.

39. F. O. Matthiessen, "Michael Wigglesworth, A Puritan Artist," *New England Quarterly* 1 (1928): 500.

40. Douglas Robinson, *American Apocalypses: The Image of the End of the World in American Literature* (Baltimore: Johns Hopkins University Press, 1985), 37.

41. *Poems*, 47, stanza 147.

42. *Poems*, 73, lines 21-23, 27.

43. College Notebook, 143.

44. Pope, "Petrus Ramus and Michael Wigglesworth," 210–226. Hammond does not highlight divine omniscience as the alternative defining force, but does note that Wigglesworth makes "clear that the ultimate test of doctrine was not human logic but divine;" *Sinful*, 253 n.14.

45. Bush, "Paradox, Puritanism, and Taylor's *God's Determinations*," *Early American Literature* 4 (1969): 50.

46. *Poems*, 28, lines 557–60.

47. Ibid., 33, lines 725–28.

48. Ibid., 56, lines 1447–48.

49. Ibid., 78, lines 222–24.

50. College Notebook, 135.

51. Ibid.

52. *Poems*, 32, 33, stanzas 88 and 90.

53. Ibid., 34, lines 741–44.

54. Ibid., 36, lines 785–86, stanza 101.

55. Richard Bernard advocated the method of "*Sermoncinatio*: or *Dialogismus*, which is, when a question is made, & forthwith readily answered, as if two were talking together" as a device that "stirres up attention, and makes the matter manifest with delight"; and also the method of "Confutation": "because if the truth delivered have any adversaries, they must be confuted first . . . and the errours or heresies be overthrown"; *Faithfull Shepherd*, 304–5, 274.

56. *Poems*, 76, lines 137–144.

57. Thomas Hooker, *A Survey of the Summe of Church-Discipline* (London, 1648), A4v.

58. Hammond, *Sinful*, 41.

59. Pope, "Petrus Ramus and Michael Wigglesworth"; John C. Adams, "Alexan-

der Richardson and the Ramist Poetics of Michael Wigglesworth," *Early American Literature* 25 (1990): 271–88; Harsharan Singh Ahluwalia, "Salvation New England Style: A Study of Covenant Theology in Michael Wigglesworth's *The Day of Doom*," *Indian Journal of American Studies* 4 (1974): 1–12.

60. Samuel Kettell, *Specimens of American Poetry with Critical and Biographical Notices* (Boston: Goodrich, 1829), I:36; John Ward Dean, *Sketch of the Life of Rev. Michael Wigglesworth* (Albany, N.Y.: Munsell, 1863), 10; Tyler, *History*, 277; Corey *Malden Massachusetts*, 225; Daly, *God's Altar*, 132. See also Matthiessen, "A Puritan Artist," 493–504.

61. Whiting, *Discourse*, A6v.

62. Gérard Genette, *Paratexts: Thresholds of Interpretation*, trans. Jane E. Lewin (Cambridge: Cambridge University Press, 1997), 238.

63. Genette, *Paratexts*, 208; *Poems*, lines 1–8.

64. 1 Corinthians 1:20.

65. *Poems*, 7, lines 101–4.

66. *Poems*, 6, lines 57–60; note alluding to *The Day of Doom* as work in progress, Notebook 3, 29 January 1661–62. See also the reference to "my poor labours" in a subsequent note on the sales of the first edition.

67. Ibid., 8, lines 127–28; 7, line 95; Mather, *Faithful Man*, 24.

68. "On the following Work, and It's Author," *Poems*, 300, line 43; Notebook 3, 17 and 18 September 1669.

69. Hammond, *Sinful*, 26, 28; Craig, "Peculiar Elegance," 96.

70. *Poems*, 138, lines 9–12.

71. *Diary*, 99. Hughes has argued that Wigglesworth is "particularly prone to sexual desire when he concentrates most intently on religious obligations," connecting this to the way in which Puritan piety encouraged a desire for God that could be envisioned in images of physical intimacy, but classed acts of sodomy as deeply sinful, 107–15.

72. Whiting, *Discourse*, A7v; Hammond, *Elegy*, 193; Cotton Mather, *The Thoughts of a Dying Man* (Boston, 1697). For discussion of this use of "dying," see Stannard, *Puritan Way of Death*, 77.

73. *Poems*, 300, line 37.

74. From the third point in "Reasons that move me at this time earnestly to desire deliverance from this long continued & increasing weakness are such as these;" Notebook 3.

75. Eva Cherniavsky argues that *The Day of Doom* and Wigglesworth's confessional writing involved an unending rehearsal of abjection and sin rather than the destruction of it all: "In the formulaic recitation of sin, Wigglesworth learns to delight in that which he repudiates"; "Night Pollution and the Floods of Confession in Michael Wigglesworth's Diary," *Arizona Quarterly* 45 (1989): 29–30, 33. For a contextualized discussion of the homoerotic dimension to Wigglesworth's sexual anxiety, see Alan Bray, "The Curious Case of Michael Wigglesworth," in *A Queer World: The Center for Lesbian and Gay Studies Reader*, ed. Martin Duberman (New York: New York University Press, 1997), 205–15.

76. The full title of Herbert's 1633 collection was *The Temple: Sacred Poems and Private Ejaculations*. In imitation, Henry Vaughan's equally measured and polished book of verse, *Silex Scintillans* (London, 1650), was given an identical subtitle.

77. *Literature and Theology*, 145.

78. *Poems*, (1645), 1:8.

79. *Poems*, 12, lines 53–56.

80. Emily Dickinson, *The Complete Poems*, ed. Thomas H. Johnson (Cambridge: Belknap Press of Harvard University Press, 1955; reprint, London: Faber and Faber, 1970), 178, poem 374.

81. 1 Corinthians 2:4–5.

82. Bunyan, *Pilgrim's Progress*, A4r–v.

83. John Ottenhoff, "From Venus to Virtue: Sacred Parody and George Herbert," in *George Herbert: Sacred and Profane*, ed. Helen Wilcox and Richard Todd (Amsterdam: VU University Press, 1995), 59.

84. "A pleasant ballad of the iust man shewing his patience in extremite," registered 1564–65 and transferred in 1624 as "Patient Job," reprinted in *Old English Ballads 1552–1625*, ed. Hyder E. Rollins (Cambridge: Cambridge University Press, 1920), 209–12; "The Scornful Maid," reprinted in *The Pepys Ballads*, ed. Hyder E. Rollins (Cambridge: Harvard University Press, 1929), 1:242–46.

85. Johnson cites Arnold's *Chronicle* (1502) as the source for his version of "Nutbrown Maid"; *A Book of British Ballads*, ed. R. Brimley Johnson (London: Dent, 1912; reprint, 1966), xv, 36–45. For publication details, see Tessa Watt, *Cheap Print and Popular Piety, 1550–1640* (Cambridge: Cambridge University Press, 1991), 41 and note.

86. Watt, *Cheap Print*, 84, 106–11.

87. Ibid., 41n.

88. Tessa Watt's statistics include: 1560–1588, on average 35% of all registered ballads were godly ones; 1588–1625 19%; 1625–1640 9%; Watt, *Cheap Print*, 41, 47.

89. These garlands, which largely concern the lives and loves of British royalty and nobility, are listed on a 1683 import invoice belonging to John Usher, the Boston bookseller; see Wright, *Literary Culture*, 121.

90. *The Winter's Tale*, Act IV, Scene 3; William Shakespeare, *Complete Works*, ed. W.J. Craig (Oxford: Oxford University Press, 1988), 342–43.

91. Sternhold, Hopkins, Whittingham, et al., *Psalms*; Cotton, *Modest*, 32. For more disparaging references to ballad singing made by colonial Puritans, see Cyclone Covey, "Puritanism and Music in Colonial America," *William and Mary Quarterly*, 3d ser., 8 (1951): 385. Commenting on the Great Awakening in the *Pennsylvania Gazette*, Benjamin Franklin reiterated the conventional dichotomy: "instead of Songs and Ballads, the People are every where entertaining themselves with Psalms, Hymns and Spiritual Songs," 12 June 1740, page 2.

92. *Poems*, 11, stanza 1.

93. J. A. Leo Lemay, *"New England's Annoyances": America's First Folk Song* (Newark: University of Delaware Press, 1985), 1. Lemay creates an amalgamated "reconstruction" of this ballad, and describes all the extant texts, 1–3, 88–95. In 1711 Cotton Mather lamented that "the Minds and Manners of many People about the Countrey are much corrupted, by foolish Songs and Ballads, which the Hawkers and Pedlars carry into all parts of the Country," cited in Amory and Hall, *Colonial Book*, 102. In the seventeenth century such items were almost certainly imported, not printed locally; Ibid., 102, 127.

94. Wigglesworth and Seaborn Cotton studied at Harvard as undergraduates from 1647 to 1651. Wigglesworth stayed on as a tutor until 1653; Morison, *Seventeenth Century*, 1:116.

95. *Diary*, 25 June 1653, 27–28.

96. *Poems*, 24, lines 443–48.

97. If "Gods Controversy with New England" was also written by Wigglesworth, it shows him, by contrast, using different stanza forms to distinguish between the

NOTES

voice of the narrator and the voice of God; Ibid., 87–102. That Christ and the souls are both given the same stanza form in *The Day of Doom* is particularly striking in comparison.

98. Ibid., 51, lines 1289–92.

99. For references classing *The Day of Doom* as a children's poem, see Mather, *Faithful Man*, 25; Jenks, Review, 537. Emory Elliott claims that "*The Day of Doom* was primarily intended to teach children several doctrinal truths"; "Puritan Literature," 243. Because the poem addresses so many different groups there are certainly sections that specifically address the situation of children (e.g., stanzas 33, 199, and 200) but neither internal evidence nor Wigglesworth's notebooks support the idea that he was aiming the poem at children.

100. "In slumbring sleep I lay," full title: "A comfortable new ballad of a dreame of a sinner, being very sore troubled with the assaults of Sathan," dated 1624 in the Stationers' Register, *The Pepys Ballads*, facsimiles, ed. W. G. Day (Cambridge: Brewer, 1987), 1:39; "A very godly song, intituled, the earnest petition of a faithfull Christian, being clarke of Bodnam, made upon his death-bed, at the instant of his transmutation," registered 1624. This ballad survived at least from 1624 to 1688; Watt, *Cheap Print*, 106.

101. *Poems*, 41, lines 980–84.

102. Hall, *Worlds of Wonder*, 57.

103. "Day of wrath, that day, / The world will dissolve into burning ash: / As witness David and the Sibyl" (my translation). *Missale Romanum ex decreto sacrosancti concili tridentini*, 4th ed. (Turin: Alfredi Mane, 1922), 125–26. For information on the use and authorship of this chant, see *Dictionnaire d'archéologie chrétienne et de liturgie*, ed. Fernand Cabrol and Henri Leclercq (Paris: Letouzey et Ane, 1920), 4:819–21.

104. *The Pack of Autolycus or Strange and Terrible News of Ghosts, Apparitions, Monstrous Births, Showers of Wheat, Judgments of God, and other Prodigious and Fearful Happenings as told in Broadside Ballads of the Years 1624–1693*, ed. Hyder Edward Rollins (Cambridge: Harvard University Press, 1927; reprint, Port Washington, N.Y.: Kennikat Press, 1969), vii–xvi.

105. "St. Bernard's Vision" was first published in 1613 as a metrical translation from the Latin, by William Crashaw; see Watt, *Cheap Point*, 111.

106. *Worlds of Wonder*, 57.

107. *Poems*, 66, lines 1761–64.

108. Ibid., 63, lines 1685–88.

109. Ibid., 64–65, lines 1739, 1721–23.

110. Ibid., 63–64, lines 1689–90, 1697–98.

111. Joseph Woodfall Ebsworth, ed., *The Bagford Ballads: Illustrating the Last Years of the Stuarts* (Hertford: Austin, 1878), 1:225.

112. "The deadmans song, whose dwelling was neere unto Basing Hall in London"; Day, *The Pepys Ballads*, 2:8. This ballad, registered in 1624, was still available in 1712; Watt, *Cheap Print*, 111.

113. *Dekker His Dreame* (London, 1620), 14.

114. *Dekker*, 40. Compare Milton's "darkness visible." Milton's concoction of such elusive images entailed a comparable rejection of the emblematic approach embodied in *Dekker His Dreame*. However, unlike Wigglesworth, Milton wrote inspired by the possibilities of language to create a mysterious, almost numinous medium to represent the world of spirit, by hovering between materiality and abstraction.

115. Crowder pointed out this similarity in *No Featherbed to Heaven*, 106. As Robinson has observed, the primary source for verbal exchanges between Christ and the judged is Matthew 25; *American Apocalypses*, 55.

116. *Dekker*, 8.

117. Kenneth B. Murdock, ed., Introduction to Michael Wigglesworth, *The Day of Doom or, A Poetical Description of the Great and Last Judgment: with Other Poems* (New York: Spiral, 1929), vii.

118. Daly, *God's Altar*, 134.

119. Bernard, *Faithfull Shepherd*, 344.

120. *Poems*, 29–41, lines 585–86, 733–34, 909–12.

121. Ibid., 41, stanza 122.

122. Whiting, *Discourse*, 140.

123. *Poems*, 57, lines 1487–88.

124. Hammond, *Sinful*, 46.

125. Whiting, *Discourse*, 158. Although different in the form of its presentation, Whiting's argument contained a similar paradox to Wigglesworth's concerning the impossibility of escaping the limits of human fallibility in the process of self-examination. Man's difficulty in preparing for Judgment arises in part from the lack of realistic analogy with human experience: "Men may sometimes be put off with Excuses, but the great Judge will not" (140).

126. Dante Alighieri, *The Divine Comedy, I: Hell*, trans. Dorothy L. Sayers (London: Penguin, 1949), Canto X, Canto XII, 128–113, 142–48.

127. *Dekker*, 51.

128. *Poems*, 56, lines 1443–44.

129. Ibid., 60, lines 1585–96.

130. From a long autobiographical entry made by Edward Wigglesworth after his father's death; Notebook 3.

131. *Poems*, 41, lines 977–79. Isaiah 55:8. See also Romans 11:33: "O the depth of the riches both of the wisdom and knowledge of God! how unsearchable are his judgments, and his ways past finding out."

132. Notably, the title page of *Pilgrim's Progress, Part I* advertized it as "delivered under the similitude of a dream."

133. First printed c. 1620; reprinted in Ebsworth, *Bagford Ballads*, 2:110.

134. Dekker's seven-year slumber corresponded to his almost seven years imprisonment for debt in King's Bench Prison (1613–1619). See George Price, *Thomas Dekker* (New York: Twayne, 1969), 127.

135. *Dekker*, title page.

136. *Diary*, 24 October 1653, 51.

137. Caldwell considers the avoidance of reference to dreams a significant difference between British and New England conversion relations; *Puritan Conversion Narrative*, 14–26.

138. *Poems*, 12, stanza 6.

139. After the 1670 first edition, the next surviving edition of *Meat Out of the Eater* was published in Boston in 1689, calling itself the "Fourth Edition." There were two more editions in 1717 and 1770; *Poems*, 312.

CHAPTER 4. *GODS DETERMINATIONS*

1. Yale University Library, Beinecke Z117 p. 203. The full title is "Gods Determinations touching his Elect; the Elects Combat in the Conversion, and Coming up to God in Christ together with the Comfortable Effects thereof."

2. According to Thomas Davis, an authority on Taylor's manuscripts, the handwriting can be dated to "the early 1680s, perhaps even earlier"; Introduction to *Edward Taylor's Minor Poetry* (Boston: Twayen, 1981), xvi. Evidence of strong parallels with Taylor's 1679 Foundation Day Sermon suggests a window of 1678–81, that is, before Taylor began his Preparatory Meditations; Davis, *A Reading of Edward Taylor*, 27–30. Taylor's only known published verses are two stanzas of "Upon Wedlock, & Death of Children," in Cotton Mather's *Right Thoughts in Sad Hours* (London, 1689), and his elegy on Deacon Dewey, published as a pamphlet in 1713. See Taylor, *Minor Poetry*, 299, and Davis, "Edward Taylor's Elegy on Deacon David Dewey," *Proceedings of the American Antiquarian Society* 96 (1986): 75–84, respectively.

3. Pope, *Half-Way Covenant*, 239, 269–75.

4. "Heads" reprinted in Walker, *Creeds and Platforms*, 455–62; Cooper, *Tenacious of their Liberties*, 153.

5. Mather, cited in Stoddard, *Appeal to the Learned*, 93; *The Necessity of Reformation* (Boston, 1679), reprinted in Walker, *Creeds and Platforms*, 433. For an overview of this stage of the Mather-Stoddard debate, see Davis, *Taylor vs. Stoddard*, 8–10 and notes.

6. *Appeal to the Learned*, 75.

7. *The Defects of Preachers Reproved in a Sermon Preached at Northampton, May 19th 1723* (New London, Conn., 1724), 24.

8. *"Church Records,"* 7–8.

9. See Davis, *Taylor vs. Stoddard*, 1–57, and Holifield, *The Covenant Sealed*, 206–20.

10. Gatta, *Gracious Laughter*, xiv, 207.

11. Ibid., 99, referring to Johan Huizinga, *Homo Ludens: A Study of the Play-Element in Culture* (Boston: Beacon Press, 1955), 10–11; Nathalia Wright, "The Morality Tradition in the Poetry of Edward Taylor," *American Literature* 18 (1946): 18–24. Cf. Davis, *A Reading of Edward Taylor*, 210 n. 28; Patterson, "A Critical Edition," cxxii n. 71.

12. Taylor, *Critical Edition*, 117, lines 2001–6.

13. Taylor did not own copies of the works of these poets, but he may have read them in England. Increase Mather, Taylor's friend and former student, owned copies of *The Temple*. See Wright, *Literary Culture*, 59.

14. *Gracious Laughter*, Gatta, 134; Taylor, *Critical Edition*, 120–21.

15. Jim Egan, *Authorizing Experience: Refigurations of the Body Politic in Seventeenth-Century New England Writing* (Princeton: Princeton University Press, 1999), 100. Egan argues that the rhetoric of the historical narratives that arose from King Philip's War constructed "a national community rather than a religious one." But this is a little misleading because, although emphatically more collective and racial, the sense of colonial identity after the war was still defined in religious terms. Cf. Richard Slotkin and James K. Folsom, eds., Introduction to *So Dreadfull a Judgment: Puritan Responses to King Philip's War, 1676–1677* (Middletown, Conn.: Wesleyan University Press, 1978); Jill Lepore, *The Name of the War: King Philip's War and the Origins of American Identity* (New York: Knopf, 1999), 166–67; Stout, *New England Soul*, 74–75, 80, 92–94.

16. Wilson, *A Song of Deliverance*, reprinted in Murdock, *Handkerchiefs*, 25–26.

17. *New Englands Crisis, Or a Brief Narrative, of New-Englands Lamentable Estate at Present, Compar'd with the Former (but Few) Years of Prosperity* (Boston, 1676). An updated version of this group of poems was printed in London as *New-Englands Tears For Her Present Miseries* (London, 1676).

18. Phyllis M. Jones, "Puritan's Progress: The Story of the Soul's Salvation in the Early New England Sermons," *Early American Literature* 15 (1980): 25.

19. *Minor Poetry*, 5–18; Donald E. Stanford, "Edward Taylor," in *Major Writers of Early American Literature*, ed. Everett Emerson (Madison: University of Wisconsin Press, 1972), 84–85. Taylor's library inventory shows that his interest in English Catholic–Protestant battles continued after his migration; see *The Poetical Works of Edward Taylor*, ed. Thomas H. Johnson (New York, Rockland editions, 1939; reprint, Princeton: Princeton University Press, 1943), 201–20. Though Taylor did not publish topical anti-Catholic poetry in New England, others did; e.g., Benjamin Harris and Richard Steere. See David S. Shields, *Oracles of Empire: Poetry, Politics and Commerce in British America, 1690–1750* (Chicago: University of Chicago Press, 1990), 196–99; Donald P. Wharton, *Richard Steere: Colonial Merchant Poet* (University Park: Pennsylvania State University Press, 1979); Meserole, *American Poetry*, 454–56.

20. Critics have argued that the Indian Wars influenced the allegorical warfare at the beginning of Taylor's composition of *Gods Determinations*. See Davis, *A Reading of Edward Taylor*, 27, referencing Dean Hall, "Edward Taylor: The Evolution of a Poet" (PhD diss., Kent State University, 1977), 146ff.; Patterson, "A Critical Edition," cxiii n. 18; Gatta, *Gracious Laughter*, 102 n. 2; Davis has equated Satan with "King Philip" (*Minor Poetry*, xv). Such influences are highly plausible, but do not diminish the significance of Taylor's turn inwards to psycho-spiritual subject matter in such a crisis. It is noteworthy, too, that Taylor owned a copy of *The Iliad* (Taylor, *Poetical Works*, 215), and that, like his colleagues, he used imagery of spiritual warfare in times of civil peace; e.g., his 1671 elegy on Charles Chauncy which concludes, "In middst of all the Combat pray do we / Inable us, oh Lord, to Shine as Hee;" Taylor, *Minor Poetry*, 35.

21. "*Church Records*", 104–12.

22. John Hoyt Lockwood, *Westfield and its Historic Influences, 1669–1919*, vol. 1 ([Westfield, Mass.]: the author, [1922]), 222–23, 218, 230.

23. "*Church Records*," 174–79. See also Walter L. Powell, "Edward Taylor's Westfield: An Edition of the Westfield 'Town Records'" (PhD diss., Kent State University, 1982), 17–28, 126.

24. "*Church Records*," 5.

25. Gatta, *Gracious Laughter*, 206. Gatta contrasts Taylor's rejection of "nationalized typology" with that of Cotton Mather, qualifying the contrast by noting Taylor's indirect allegiance in his Meditations to the providential mission. See also Lowance on Taylor's application of typological interpretation of Scripture to the individual soul but not to the collective soul of New England; *Language of Canaan*, 89–111. For Puritan interpretations of the war, see Slotkin and Folsom, *So Dreadfull a Judgment*, and Lepore, *The Name of the War*.

26. J. Daniel Patterson, "*Gods Determinations* The Occasion, the Audience, and Taylor's Hope for New England," *Early American Literature* 22 (1987): 64–65.

27. "*Church Records*," 151. Taylor's Foundation Day sermon exists in two versions: one prepared for the official gathering in 1679, but not preached in full because of a lack of time, and one revised and extended circa 1692–93 to respond to Solomon Stoddard's arguments about the Lord's Supper. Davis, Introduction to Taylor, "*Church Records*," xiii–xv, xviii–xxx, xxxviii. Cf. Dean Hall and Thomas M. Davis, "The Two Versions of Edward Taylor's Foundation Day Sermon," *Resources for American Literary Study* 5 (1975): 199–216. This and all future references will be to the 1679 version unless otherwise stated.

28. Walker, *Creeds and Platforms*, 428.

29. Michael J. Colacurcio, "*Gods Determinations Touching Half-Way Membership: Occasion and Audience in Edward Taylor*," *American Literature* 39 (1967): 311, and *Doctrine and Difference: Essays in the Literature of New England* (New York: Routledge, 1997), 31. Patterson strongly contends, against Colacurcio, that the audience of *Gods Determinations* was all-inclusive (see "Occasion," and "Homiletic"). Gatta supports Colacurcio; *Gracious Laughter*, 102.

30. David L. Parker, "Edward Taylor's Preparationism: A New Perspective on the Taylor-Stoddard Controversy," *Early American Literature* 11 (1976–77): 259–78; George Sebouhian, "Conversion Morphology and the Structure of *Gods Determinations*," *Early American Literature* 16 (1981–82): 226–40. See also Robert D. Arner, "Notes on the Structure of Edward Taylor's *Gods Determinations*," *Studies in the Humanities* 3 (1973): 27–29.

31. Gatta, *Gracious Laughter*, 80–81, citing Caldwell, *Puritan Conversion Narrative*. Gatta's brief discussion of the influence of the conversion relation on Taylor's verse is the fullest exploration of this connection so far. See also allusions in Rowe, *Saint*, 197; Patterson, "Occasion," 77; Colacurcio, *Doctrine*, 37. Davis, *A Reading of Edward Taylor*, 26.

32. *Edward Taylor's Treatise Concerning the Lord's Supper*, ed. Norman S. Grabo (East Lansing: Michigan State University Press, 1965), 74.

33. Taylor, *Critical Edition*, 49, lines 9–14.

34. See Dennis H. Barbour, "*Gods Determinations* and the Hexameral Tradition," *Early American Literature* 16 (1981–82): 213–25. On the "manuscript system" and lyric poetry written for circulation among élite communities, see Arthur F. Marotti, *Manuscript, Print, and the English Renaissance Lyric* (Ithaca: Cornell University Press, 1995).

35. *Minor Poetry*, 156.

36. Psalms, in *Minor Poetry*, 44–101; Job paraphrases, 127–210. Interestingly, Davis has noted that metrically Taylor's Psalm paraphrases follow Sternhold and Hopkins rather than the Bay Psalm Book (*Minor Poetry*, 45).

37. Early critics using these epithets include Wallace C. Brown, "Edward Taylor: An American 'Metaphysical,'" *American Literature* 16 (1944): 186–97; and Austin Warren, "Edward Taylor's Poetry: Colonial Baroque," *Kenyon Review* 3 (1941): 355–71. Cf. Rowe, *Saint*, 314–15 n. 3.

38. Such distinctions are tricky, of course. The verse form of Taylor's Meditations, for example, is shared not only with Herbert's "The Church Porch" but also with An Collins's Meditations, designed for a less well educated, more popular audience. Collins's Meditations are more chatty and socially radical than Taylor's, and less complex in imagery and structure. See Collins, *Divine Songs and Meditacions* (London, 1653).

39. Patterson, "Homiletic," 131–50. See also Jean L. Thomas, "Drama and Doctrine in *Gods Determinations*," *American Literature* 36 (1965): 452–62.

40. On Dickson, see Michael Schuldiner, "Puritan Casuistry and the Character of the Three Ranks of Soul in Edward Taylor's *Gods Determinations*," in *The Tayloring Shop*, ed. Michael Schuldiner, 105–30 (Newark: University of Delaware Press, 1997) Gatta also links the Saint/Soul dialogues to the work of other "spiritual physicians" such as Thomas Hooker, William Ames, William Perkins and Timothy Bright; *Gracious Laughter*, 119–22, 125. On Shepard's *Sincere Convert*, see Taylor, *Poetical Works*, 191 n. 1; Gatta, *Gracious Laughter*, 108 n. 9.

41. But Keller also argues that Taylor's concern in his Meditations with preparation and process (as opposed to completion and polish) made publication inappro-

priate for the more private poems, and Keller includes sections of *Gods Determinations* in this category; "Example of Edward Taylor," 5–26.

42. Bush, "Paradox," 61; Stanford, "Edward Taylor," 79; Taylor, "Critical Edition," ix; Hambrick-Stowe, *Meditative Poetry*, 52. Scheick describes *Gods Determinations* as "intended for an audience"; *Design*, 25. For further studies, see Hammond, *Sinful*, 267 n. 9.

43. Colacurcio, "*Gods Determinations*," 313; Hambrick-Stowe, *Meditative Poetry*, 52; Patterson, "Homiletic," 140–41, 146. Cf. Robert Arner, "Proverbs in Edward Taylor's *Gods Determinations*," *Southern Folklore Quarterly* 37 (1973): 1–13.

44. Taylor, *Critical Edition*, 59, lines 317–22.

45. Hammond, *Sinful*, 162–63; Davis, *A Reading of Edward Taylor*, 16.

46. Murphy, "Taylor's Attitude toward Publication," *American Literature* 34 (1962): 393–94; Gatta, *Gracious laughter*, 74–80; Harold Love, *Scribal Publication in Seventeenth-Century England* (Oxford: Clarendon, 1993), 42, 35–46. On the audiences of seventeenth-century American poetry, see Meserole, *American Poetry*, xxi–xxv. Meserole noted, too, that Benjamin Lynde's verses, for example, are known to us only from Lynde's correspondence with Samuel Sewall (491).

47. Hammond, *Sinful*, 162.

48. Taylor's predestinarianism has been debated. Rowe has argued that New England "covenant" theology tempered the predestinarianism of European Calvinism by stressing "the free will with which man participates in the contract" (Rowe, *Saint*, 18); but, as Donald Stanford points out in his Preface to the 1989 paperback edition of *The Poems of Edward Taylor* (Chapel Hill: University of North Carolina Press, 1989), the title "Gods Determinations touching his Elect" is definitive.

49. *Critical Edition*, 62, lines 413–16.

50. Shepard, *Virgins*, 2:6.

51. *Critical Edition*, 61–62, lines 387–96.

52. While "cheapen" meant literally "to bargain for," it had already acquired the figurative sense of "to lower in estimation" by the seventeenth century. *Oxford English Dictionary*, 2d ed., sv. "cheapen."

53. "What presses give birth to with sodden pangs is acceptable, but manuscripts are more venerated," cited in Love, *Scribal Publication*, 152–53; Marotti, *Manuscript*, 44–48.

54. Davis, *A Reading of Edward Taylor*, 38.

55. Charles W. Mignon, "Edward Taylor's *Preparatory Meditations*: A Decorum of Imperfection," *Proceedings of the Modern Language Association* 83 (1968): 1423–28; Alan Shucard, *American Poetry: The Puritans through Walt Whitman* (Boston: Twayne, 1988), 29–31; Donald Junkins "'Should Stars Wooe Lobster Claws?': A Study of Edward Taylor's Poetic Practice and Theory," *Early American Literature* 3 (1968): 88–116; William J. Scheick, *The Will and the Word: The Poetry of Edward Taylor* (Athens: University of Georgia Press, 1974), 129–30; Michael Schuldiner, "Edward Taylor's 'Problematic' Imagery," *Early American Literature* 13 (1978): 92–101. For further discussion, see Lewalski, *Protestant Politics*, 391 and Craig, "Peculiar Elegance," 77.

56. For photographs of a surviving seventeenth-century New England church in Hingham, Mass., see Davies, *American Puritans*, 287–92. When the Ship Meeting House was built at Hingham in 1681, the town was a relatively prosperous port. The interior, though plain, is elegantly paneled and carved in a classical style. Taylor's Westfield church, being inland and close to the frontier, would have been similarly plain, square, and wooden, but also cruder, and probably fortified.

57. Commonplace Book, Massachusetts Historical Society, Boston, P 172, 308.

58. See Gatta, *Gracious Laughter*, 73, 100, 136.

59. *Minor Poetry*, 13–18. St. Bartholomew's day was renowned for the "massacre" of a number of Protestant leaders in France, 24 August 1572.

60. *Doctrine*, 41. Colacurcio associates the first rank of souls with Cotton's teaching, and the second and third with that of Hooker and Shepard, respectively; but he also argues that in practice Taylor collapsed the second and third ranks together completely (40ff.).

61. Colacurcio, "*Gods Determinations*," 302; Patterson, "Occasion," 66–67; Taylor, *Critical Edition*, 13–15.

62. *Critical Edition*, 63, lines 435–42.

63. *Christographia*, 229; *Critical Edition*, 80–82.

64. *Critical Edition*, 15.

65. *Christographia*, 120. I quote this in full in chapter 2.

66. "Laymans Lamentation," in *Minor Poetry*, 15.

67. *Critical Edition*, 66, 75.

68. Ibid., 87–90, 93–105.

69. Taylor did not own any of Cotton's works on liturgy or psalm-singing, but his inventory shows he did own *The Bloudy Tenent Washed* (*Poetical Works*, 206). He also copied from John Cotton's anticeremonial writings (Commonplace Book, MHS P 172).

70. Cotton, *Modest*, 37.

71. "*Church Records*," 112–13.

72. Gatta, *Gracious Laughter*, xiv; Hambrick-Stowe divided his selection of Bradstreet's and Taylor's poetry into "occasional" and "formal" meditative verse; *Meditative Poetry*, 19. Although he borrowed this distinction from Bishop Joseph Hall via Barbara Lewalski, it is problematic. First, the antiliturgical arguments of Cotton and his successors jar with Hall's overall outlook on church order. Second, while Hambrick-Stowe's criticism of Hall's term "deliberate" (as defined against "occasional" or "extemporary" meditations) is quite valid on the grounds that all meditation is deliberate, his substitution of "formal" isn't wholly appropriate for the New England church context. Perhaps this problem with the terms suggests that the distinction itself was in some way compromised or dismantled by poets like Bradstreet and Taylor.

73. *Critical Edition*, 80, lines 929–36.

74. As Francis Murphy noted, these lyrics by Taylor are in perfect syllabic measure and therefore "could have been set to music but they weren't"; "Anne Bradstreet and Edward Taylor," in *The Columbia History of American Poetry*, ed. Jay Parini (New York: Columbia University Press, 1993), 11. On possible musical structure and influences in *Gods Determinations*, see also Grabo, *Edward Taylor: Revised Edition*, 100–107.

75. *Minor Poetry*, 17, 15. On his death, Taylor owned four theological works by Owen, published in the 1670s and 1680s, making him one of Taylor's favorite British theologians. Taylor's continued antiliturgical stance is apparent from notes he made (probably from a book he was reading) on "Reasons why the Service Booke urged upon Scotland, ought to be refused," including the argument that "It quencheth the Holy Spirit: because he gets no imployment" (Commonplace Book, MHS P 172, p. 320).

76. *Minor Poetry*, 15.

77. Rowe, *Saint*, 206.

78. *American Puritanism: Faith and Practice* (Philadelphia: Lippincott, 1970), 117.

79. Gatta, *Gracious Laughter*, 51–59. Scheick, however, has vigorously denied that Taylor's imagery is "free-associative in nature rather than coherent in design"; *Design*, 67.

80. Targoff, *Common Prayer*, 87–88; Herbert, *The Temple*, 174–75, 183. See "The Order for the administration of the Lords supper, or holy communion," *Book of Common Prayer* (London, 1630).

81. Love, *Scribal Publication*, 142, 148.

82. *Worlds of Wonder*, 128. Perhaps Hall was deliberately making a judgment about which diaries could be classed as "great."

83. Shepard, *God's Plot*; Wigglesworth, *Diary; The Diary of Cotton Mather*, Massachusetts Historical Society Collections, 7th ser., 7–8 (Boston: Massachusetts Historical Society, 1911–12); Bradstreet, *Works*, 271–91; Tompson, *Journal*.

84. Journal, 24 Nov 1726, 26 Nov 172[6].

85. *Benjamin Tompson*, 66.

86. Note-taking was a common practice in church, and the ministers' words and arguments were often thus taken down and taken in by members of the congregation. Davies, *American Puritans*, 77 and note. Wigglesworth, while in training for the ministry, took down sermon notes in shorthand; Notebook 2.

87. *Critical Edition*, 92–93, lines 1291–92, 1319–22.

88. Journal, undated entries, p. 1r, 60r. The first excerpt is apparently Tompson's own composition, the second is apparently copied.

89. Tompson eventually signed his name to the marriage covenant he copied out, but not until many years had passed, presumably because the accusatory rhetoric left him feeling far too unworthy! Inscribed on the same page but in a later and trembling hand are the following two notes (I have added punctuation to clarify the sense): "This above writ many years ago, But never signed untill the day mentioned below: 1728"; "Joseph Tompson[i.e., signature]. I am ashamed of my self that i hav so long neglected this Duty of signing untill the 88 year near expireing." I have not yet found the published source of this contract, but Tompson is not unique in incorporating such a document into his notebook. Philip Greven discusses a similar marriage contract in Joseph Bean's journal (entry for 25 June 1741), and cross-references the diary of Benjamin Lyon (entry for 13 July 1765), *The Protestant Temperament: Patterns of Child-Rearing, Religious Experience, and the Self in Early America* (New York: Knopf, 1977), 126 and note. The gender implications of such contracts are discussed in Greven (124–40), and Schweitzer, *Self-Representation*, 21–35.

90. Colacurcio, *Doctrine*, 257 n. 17.

91. *Critical Edition*, 12, lines 1855–60.

92. Amory and Hall, *Colonial Book*, 85; Wright, *Literary Culture*, 121–23.

93. Gatta, *Gracious Laughter*, 115 passim. In a number of dialogue poems in *Meat Out of the Eater* Wigglesworth used this positive method, too, to "echo" the private "turmoil" of the reader, and to turn "the stasis of doubt into an active process of belief"; Hammond, *Sinful*, 69.

94. *Critical Edition*, 99, lines 1475–82.

95. Patterson considers the implication of Saint's interpretation to be that "[t]he desire for grace is . . . a basis for hope and an acceptable sign of election" ("Occasion," 76), and has argued that Taylor's encouragement to the weak in faith was a shift away from stricter standards in response to the problem of declining church membership; "'A Critical Edition," 18–19. But Taylor may have carefully preselected any readers of *Gods Determinations*.

96. Tompson added the note: "Delivered or sent in a manyscript unto her father by Mr hubbert the minister as a cordiall upon that Day that her funerall was," [86r]. Dane died in 1689. For further evidence of scrupulosity as lying behind apparent declension, see Edmund S. Morgan, "New England Puritanism: Another Approach," *William and Mary Quarterly* 18 (1961): 236–42; Pope, *Half-Way, Covenant*, 135–36; Hall, *Faithful, Shepherd*, 251–56. The scrupulosity thesis has been strongly opposed by Darrett B. Rutman, "God's Bridge Falling Down: 'Another Approach' to Puritanism Assayed," *William and Mary Quarterly*, 3d ser., 19 (1962): 408–21; and Bozeman, *To Live Ancient Lives*, 362.

97. Hambrick-Stowe, *Meditative Poetry*, 52.

98. *Critical Edition*, 116, lines 1960–64.

99. Ibid., 80, line 925; 112, lines 1843–66.

100. *Memoirs of Roger Clap. 1630* (Boston, 1844), 24.

101. Taylor, "*Church Records*," 108.

102. *Types*, 1:424–26, 435 (written c. 1693–99).

103. See Gatta, *Gracious Laughter*, 86; and Davis, *Taylor vs. Stoddard*, 8–19. For Stoddard on the relation as an innovation, see his "Arguments for the Proposition," in *Edward Taylor vs. Solomon Stoddard: The Nature of the Lord's Supper*, ed. Thomas M. Davis and Virginia L. Davis (Boston: Twayne, 1981), 83. For an overview of the theological debate, see Holifield, *The Covenant Sealed*, 206–20. For discussions revising the simplistic portrayal of Taylor as conservative and Stoddard as radical, see Parker, "Edward Taylor's Preparationism"; Gatta, *Gracious Laughter*, 84–100; Karl Keller, "The Loose, Large Principles of Solomon Stoddard," *Early American Literature* 16 (1981): 27–41; and Gura, *Crossroads*, 79–94.

104. *Defects of Preachers Reproved*, 17, cited in Davis, *Taylor vs. Stoddard*, 27.

105. Stoddard, *The Tryal of Assurance* (Boston, 1698), 19.

106. Taylor, *Critical Edition*, 111, 115, lines 1841–42, 1930. Taylor made this point in his Foundation Day Sermon: "as it is a fault to enter unprepared, so it is a fault when prepared not to enter"; "*Church Records*," 150. On Stoddard and Taylor as responding to the same pastoral problem, see Elliott, *Power and the Pulpit*, 182–86.

107. The allusion contributes to Taylor's Biblical reasons for requiring the conversion relation, as given in the revised version of his Foundation Day sermon, "A Particular Church is Gods House"; "*Church Records*," 302. This use of the Psalmist cements the connection in Taylor's thought between conversion relations and responses of lyric praise, as found in the "choral epilogue" and in the Meditations.

108. "Propositions," in Mather, *Magnalia*, 2:103.

109. Colacurcio, "*Gods Determinations*," 309–10.

110. *Critical Edition*, 115, lines 1945–54.

111. "*Church Records*," 161; for Taylor's Biblical reasons for giving the church the role of judge, see "A Particular Church is Gods House" (316–17). For a broader outline of the procedure in Massachusetts churches in general, see Morgan, *Visible Saints*, 88–89, but note that Pope's research has qualified the implied view of homogeneous practice; *Half-Way Covenant*, passim.

112. "*Church Records*," 104.

113. Davenport, *Investigation*, 15.

114. For Taylor's implementation of the Halfway Covenant, see Pope, *Half-Way Covenant*, 190–91; and Patterson, "A Critical Edition," xii–xiii, cxii–cxiii. From 1681 onwards, the position is very clear in the church register, with the words "admitted into Full Communion" used in contradistinction to phrases such as "put himselfe [or herselfe] under the Watch of the Church"; "*Church Records*," 162–72.

115. Patterson, "Occasion," 77–79.

116. "*Church Records*," 97. While Taylor alludes here to relations being "read," he also refers to not having memorized his own verbatim (104), so the exact method of presentation he envisaged for the gathering, and what actually happened, is unclear. See page 7 for Taylor's list of the elders and messengers present, including Solomon Stoddard at the head of the Northampton contingent.

117. "*Church Records*," 126–37, 304–5; Patterson, "Occasion," 72–73, 78.

118. Davis, *Taylor vs. Solomon Stoddard*, 8–10. Taylor first came across Stoddard's promotion of the sacrament as a converting ordinance in a copy of a 1690 sermon on Galatians; *Taylor vs. Stoddard*, 192–47. It was this idea that inspired Taylor's most vehement anti-Stoddardean writing and preaching, including his treatise on the Lord's Supper.

119. "*Church Records*," 128–37; Davis details and discusses the changes in Stoddard's church records; *Taylor vs. Stoddard*, 4–5.

120. *Taylor vs. Stoddard*, 63–64, discussed in Davis's introduction, 10–12. Stoddard's *The Safety of Appearing at the Day of Judgment* had been published in Boston in 1687.

121. 1 Chronicles 13:10.

122. Hammond, *Sinful*, 93. Scheick finds the dilemma of hope versus fear an "underlying schema" providing "an autonomous inner dynamic" in "The Jawbones Schema of Edward Taylor's *Gods Determinations*," in *Puritan Influences in American Literature*, ed. Emory Elliott, 38–54 (Urbana: University of Illinois, 1979). Patterson endorses Scheick's reading; "Occasion," 73; Davis highlights how the centrality of the dichotomy between hope and fear links *Gods Determinations* with the "Foundation Day Sermon" that Taylor preached in 1679; *A Reading of Edward Taylor*, 29.

123. Shepard, 2:200: "Thus I was humbled, then thus I was called, then thus I have walked, though with many weaknesses since, and such special providences of God I have seen, temptations gone through, and thus the Lord hath delivered me, blessed be his Name, &c." I discuss this formula in chapter 1.

124. *Pilgrim's Progress*, 52.

125. For a different and more liturgical approach, see Cotton Mather's poem "Conversion Exemplified" in *Agreeable Admonitions for Old & Young* (Boston, 1703), revised and reprinted as "The Covenant Consented to" in *A Monitor for the Children of the Covenant*, Boston, 1715 and 1725, and *Baptismal Piety*, 1727. See *Cotton Mather's Verse in English*, ed. Denise D. Knight (Newark: University of Delaware Press, 1989), 38–40. Mather's melding of first person lyric expression with theological didacticism anticipated the popular verses and hymns of Isaac Watts. Paradoxically, the prevalence of Watts's style of verse in early eighteenth-century New England was influenced by the role of personal testimony in the churches, originally part of the reaction against prescribed liturgy. See Shields, *Oracles of Empire*, 211.

126. The sharp intensity of the dilemma portrayed in this poem renders suspect Colacurcio's account of this transitional moment, as bringing a "new round of anxieties" which are "mostly social"; *Doctrine*, 37.

127. *Critical Edition*, 116–17, lines 1977–94. The period after "indent" is inappropriate according to modern punctuation. As Gerhard T. Alexis notes concerning a similar instance in a stanza in "Christs Reply," "Taylor is anything but consistent in this regard, and a period may appear where a comma would be found in a similar construction elsewhere . . . so the period does not mean that there is a

complete statement up to that point"; "A Keen Nose for Taylor's Syntax," *Early American Literature* 4 (1969): 98.

128. *"Church Records,"* 112.

129. Gatta has made a similar *via negativa* argument for Taylor's aesthetics and the inverse relation, for instance, of his flamboyant poetic depictions of music and decoration to the plain-style worship of his Westfield church; *Gracious Laughter,* 73, 100, 134–36.

130. *Christographia,* 253.

131. *Critical Edition,* 117, lines 1989–94.

132. The seven original members of the Westfield church signed a founding document, and later members and halfway members had their names written in the register; *"Church Records,"* 159–73.

133. On the historical privileging of script over orality in legal transactions, see Love, *Scribal Publication,* 159.

134. *Oxford English Dictionary,* 2d ed., s.v. "indent" verb, II.2 *trans.*

135. Meditation 1.21, *Critical Edition,* 157, lines 7–10.

136. See Hammond, *Sinful,* 146; Gatta, *Gracious Laughter,* 80–81.

137. Rowe, *Saint,* 222. The evidence of *Gods Determinations* goes against Rowe's interpretation that, for Taylor, the formal processes of joining the church were "mere preliminaries," 218. Taylor's paralleling of some aspects of the conversion relation in his Meditations illustrates that "[t]he stages that characterized the believer's first conversion—repentance and the experience of grace—also characterized the process of meditation and prayer throughout life"; Hambrick-Stowe, *Practice of Piety,* 166; applied to Taylor, 207–8. See also Cohen, *Gods Caress,* 104.

138. Craig, "Peculiar Elegance," 83–96.

139. Louis L. Martz, Foreword to *The Poems of Edward Taylor,* ed. Donald E. Stanford (New Haven: Yale University Press, 1960), xiii–xxxvii; see Grabo on Taylor and the mystics in his *Edward Taylor,* 40–83.

140. Meditation 1.8, *Critical Edition,* 140, lines 20–24.

141. Draft reads: "The Purest Wheate in Heaven, his deare-dear Son / Doth knead up there into this Bread of Life." For further discussion, see Donald Junkins, "Edward Taylor's Revisions," *American Literature* 37 (1965): 145. For details of the handful of poems that exist in multiple versions, and the revisions visible in Taylor's manuscripts, see Junkins, "Edward Taylor's Revisions," 137; Taylor, *Poems,* 506–8. See also Taylor, *Minor Poetry,* 285–329.

142. *"Church Records,"* 116.

143. Ibid., 110. Cf. Romans 7:24.

144. *Critical Edition,* 117, lines 1981–82. For the explicit acceptance by English ministers of "broken language, and bad and low expressions" in conversion relations, see Geoffrey F. Nuttall, *Visible Saints: The Congregational Way 1640–1660* (Oxford: Blackwell, 1957), 110. Gatta makes a potentially allied point about Taylor's use of "stumble on't," namely, that in Taylor's portrayal of the conversion relation as a game of "Password," the taunts ironically help Soul by betraying how close is the word being sought, which Gatta takes to be the Bible, on which the Soul should rely; *Gracious Laughter,* 138–89.

145. *"Church Records,"* 108. Another candidate confessed, "I have searched to see whether I loved God's company or no and I have found indeed my opposition against it. Yet I have found in some poor measure that God hath helped me to take delight in his will"; Wigglesworth, *Diary,* 121. Morgan judged that relations were

expected to mention imperfections in order to mark sufficient humility to suggest grace; *Visible Saints*, 91.

146. Meditation 2.43, *Critical Edition*, 284, lines 1–6. The application of Caldwell's phrase to Taylor's Meditations is Gatta's; *Gracious Laughter*, 80–81.

147. "Strength in Weakness," lines 5–12, from "Riddles Unriddled, or Christian Paradoxes," in *Meat Out of the Eater*, *Poems*, 189; The "key" referred to the verses that this particular poem introduced.

148. Bay Psalm Book, Sig. **4r.

149. Perhaps it is fair to say that Bunyan's texts have proved right the suspicions of New England ministers about the power of language to seduce the reader to an unspiritual contentment in its own charms, since, as critics have long observed, the symbolic world that Bunyan created in *The Pilgrim's Progress* is so self-sufficient that the allegorical story can be read novelistically.

150. *Critical Edition*, 117, lines 1996–97.

151. Pope, *Half-Way Covenant*, 252–57; Caldwell, *Puritan Conversion Narrative*, 84, 99; Gatta, *Gracious Laughter*, 95; Davis, *Taylor vs. Stoddard*, on the vote to make relations optional, 47, on Stoddard's membership figures in the 1670s, 4–5. Patterson calculates that in Westfield in 1680, there were approximately thirty-one church members and seventy children, equivalent to about half of the village's 200 or so residents ("Occasion," 69), and Davis notes that throughout Taylor's ministry, Westfield had an unusually high proportion of communicant church members: about one in three town inhabitants, at the turn of the century; introduction to *"Church Records,"* xxxiv.

152. *Benjamin Tompson*, 98, lines 587–90.

153. Ibid., 85, line 73.

154. Scheick, "Standing in the Gap," 302; and "Tombless Virtue," 290; Slotkin and Folsom, *So Dreadfull a Judgment*, 212; Elliott, "Puritan Literature," 1:206.

155. *Benjamin Tompson*, 98–99, lines 599–601, 611–14.

156. "To the Reader," *Benjamin Tompson*, 83.

CONCLUSION

1. A. Owen Aldridge, *Early American Literature: A Comparatist Approach* (Princeton: Princeton University Press, 1982), 14.

2. Gura, "Early American Literature," 607.

3. Michelle Burnham, *Captivity and Sentiment: Cultural Exchange in American Literature, 1682–1861* (Hanover, N.H.: University Press of New England, 1997); *Only for the Eye of a Friend: The Poems of Annis Boudinot Stockton*, ed. Carla Mulford (Charlottesville: University Press of Virginia, 1995); David S. Shields, *Oracles of Empire*, and *Civil Tongues and Polite Letters in British America* (Chapel Hill: University of North Carolina Press for the Institute of Early American History and Culture, 1997); Lee Heller, "Conceiving the 'New' American Literature," *Early American Literature* 29 (1994): 85.

4. Shields, "Joy and Dread," 636; Michael P. Clark, "The Persistence of Literature in Early American Studies," *William and Mary Quarterly*, 3d ser., 57 (2000): 641, alluding to Murray Krieger, "My Travels with the Aesthetic," in *Revenge of the Aesthetic: The Place of Literature in Theory Today*, ed. Michael P. Clark (Berkeley: Univer-

sity of California Press, 2000), 208–36; Scheick, *Design*, 1; Clark, "Persistence," 645–46.

5. Larzer Ziff, "Text and Context," *William and Mary Quarterly*, 3d ser., 45 (1988): 348–49; Norman S. Grabo, "So Who Killed Literary History?," *William and Mary Quarterly*, 3d ser., 45 (1988): 342–44.

6. Carla Mulford, "The Ineluctability of the People's Stories," *William and Mary Quarterly*, 3d ser., 57 (2000): 628. Mulford goes on to affirm that "the historical grounding of scholars has brought about a more complicated sense of what art might have been for early writers" (629).

7. Norton, *Abel*, 13.

8. Gura, "Early American Literature," 611; Clark, "Persistence," 645; Schweitzer, *Self-Representation;* Hammond, *Sinful;* Heller, "Conceiving," 85.

9. Daly, *God's Altar*, 43.

10. Heller, "Conceiving," 85; Hammond, *Elegy*, 8.

11. Shields, "Joy and Dread," 639.

12. Buell, "Circling the Spheres," 482.

13. Jane Tompkins, *Sensational Designs: The Cultural Work of American Fiction, 1790–1860* (New York: Oxford University Press, 1986), 38.

14. Hall, *Worlds of Wonder*, 3–4.

15. Schweitzer, *Self-Representation*, 37, 80.

16. Richard P. Gildrie, *The Profane, the Civil, & the Godly: The Reformation of Manners in Orthodox New England, 1679–1749* (University Park: Pennsylvania State University Press, 1994), 2.

17. Buell, "Circling the Spheres," 471.

18. Hall, *Worlds of Wonder;* Hambrick-Stowe, *Practice of Piety;* Cohen, *God's Caress*.

19. *Colonial Book*.

20. Shields, "Joy and Dread," 636. Cf. Elliott, "New England Puritan Literature," 184.

21. Miller, "Colonial Dialect," 26.

22. Hall, *Worlds of Wonder*, 20. As I discuss in my Introduction, Hall and Hammond have particularly highlighted the effectively ritualistic elements of Puritan culture, but without always emphasizing the ways in which the colonists tried to keep their practices distinct from what they believed to be the idolatrous ritualism of high-Anglican and Catholic churches.

23. Collected together in Izaak Walton, *The Lives of Dr. John Donne, Sir Henry Wotton, Mr. Richard Hooker, [and] Mr. George Herbert* (London, 1670).

24. *The English Literatures of America, 1500–1800*, ed. Myra Jehlen and Michael Warner (New York: Routledge, 1997), xix.

25. Hooker, *Survey*, A4v.

26. *Works*, 191, lines 83, 91, and "The Author to Her Book," *Works*, 221, line 1.

27. Albert J. Von Frank, *The Sacred Game: Provincialism and Frontier Consciousness in American Literature, 1630–1860* (Cambridge: Cambridge University Press, 1985), 15–21.

28. *Critical Edition*, 350, line 32.

29. Thomas Scanlan, *Colonial Writing and the New World, 1583–1671: Allegories of Desire* (Cambridge: Cambridge University Press, 1999), 2.

30. Roger Williams, *A Key into the Language of America* (London, 1643), reprinted in Meserole, *American Poetry*, 183.

31. *The Puritan Ordeal,* 6.

32. Jane Colman Turell, *Memoirs of the Life and Death of the Pious and Ingenious Mrs. Jane Turell* (Boston, 1735), 75; reprinted in facsimile in *Poems of Jane Turell and Martha Brewster,* ed. Kenneth A. Requa (Delmar, N.Y.: Scholars' Facsimiles & Reprints, 1979).

Works Cited

Adams, John C. "Alexander Richardson and the Ramist Poetics of Michael Wigglesworth." *Early American Literature* 25 (1990): 271–88.

Ahluwalia, Harsharan Singh. "Salvation New England Style: A Study of Covenant Theology in Michael Wigglesworth's *The Day of Doom*." *Indian Journal of American Studies* 4 (1974): 1–12.

Ainsworth, Henry. *The Book of Psalmes; Englished both in prose and metre. With annotations, opening both the words and sentences, by conference with other scriptures.* Amsterdam, 1612.

———. *Annotations upon the Five Bookes of Moses, and the Booke of the Psalmes.* London, 1622.

Aldridge, A. Owen. *Early American Literature: A Comparatist Approach.* Princeton: Princeton University Press, 1982.

Alexis, Gerhard T. "A Keen Nose for Taylor's Syntax." *Early American Literature* 4 (1969): 97–101.

Allin, John. *Animadversions Upon the AntiSynodalia Americana.* Cambridge, Mass., 1664.

Ames, William. *A Fresh Suit Against Human Ceremonies in God's Worship.* Rotterdam, 1633.

Amory, Hugh. "'Gods Altar Needs Not Our Pollishings': Revisiting the Bay Psalm Book." *Printing History* 12 (1990): 2–14.

Amory, Hugh, and David D. Hall, eds. *The Colonial Book in the Atlantic World.* Cambridge: Cambridge University Press, 2000.

Appel, Richard G. *The Music of the Bay Psalm Book, 9th Edition (1698).* I.S.A.M. Monographs, No. 5. New York: Institute for Studies in American Music, Brooklyn College of the City University of New York, 1975.

Arner, Robert D. "Notes on the Structure of Edward Taylor's *Gods Determinations*." *Studies in the Humanities* 3 (1973): 27–29.

———. "Proverbs in Edward Taylor's *Gods Determinations*." *Southern Folklore Quarterly* 37 (1973): 1–13.

Barbour, Dennis H. "*Gods Determinations* and the Hexameral Tradition." *Early American Literature* 16 (1981–82): 213–25.

Barnstone, Willis. "Misalliance of Theory and Practice or Parable of the *Bay Psalm Book*." *Translation Review* 32–33 (1990): 22–26.

———. *The Poetics of Translation: History, Theory, Practice.* New Haven: Yale University Press, 1993.

Barton, William. *The Book of Psalms in Metre.* London, 1644.

Bay Psalm Book (see separate entries under Wilberforce Eames, Zoltán Haraszti, and *Whole Booke of Psalmes*).

Benjamin, Walter. *Illuminations*. Trans. Harry Zohn. New York: Harcourt, Brace & World, 1968.

Bercovitch, Sacvan. *The American Jeremiad*. Madison: University of Wisconsin Press, 1978.

————. *The Puritan Origins of the American Self.* New Haven: Yale University Press, 1975.

————, ed. *Typology and Early American Literature*. Amherst: University of Massachusetts Press, 1972.

Bernard, Richard. *The Faithfull Shepherd*. Rev. ed. London, 1621.

Blake, Kathleen. "Edward Taylor's Protestant Poetic: Nontransubstantiating Metaphor." *American Literature* 43 (1971): 1–24.

Boland, Eavan. "Two Worlds." *PN Review* 28 (2001): 11–15.

Bond, W. H., and Hugh Amory, eds. *The Printed Catalogues of the Harvard College Library, 1723–1790*. Publications of the Colonial Society of Massachusetts, 68. Boston: Colonial Society of Massachusetts, 1996.

Book of Common Prayer, and Administration of the Sacraments, and other Rites and Ceremonies of the Church of England. London, 1630.

Bozeman, Theodore Dwight. *To Live Ancient Lives: The Primitivist Dimension in Puritanism*. Chapel Hill: University of North Carolina Press, 1988.

Bradshaw, William. *English Puritanisme*. London, 1605.

Bradstreet, Anne. *Several Poems Compiled with Great Variety of Wit and Learning*. Boston, 1678.

————. *The Tenth Muse, Lately Sprung Up in America*. London, 1650.

————. *The Works of Anne Bradstreet*, ed. Jeannine Hensley. Cambridge: Belknap Press of Harvard University Press, 1967.

Bray, Alan. "The Curious Case of Michael Wigglesworth." In *A Queer World: The Center for Lesbian and Gay Studies Reader*, ed. Martin Duberman. 205–15. New York: New York University Press, 1997.

Breitwieser, Mitchell. "Early American Antigone." In *Theorizing American Literature: Hegel, the Sign, and History*, ed. Bainard Cowan and Joseph G. Kronick. 125–61. Baton Rouge: Louisiana State University Press, 1991.

Brown, Wallace C. "Edward Taylor: An American 'Metaphysical.'" *American Literature* 16 (1944): 186–97.

Brumm, Ursula. "Edward Taylor and the Poetic Use of Religious Imagery." In *Typology and Early American Literature*, ed. Sacvan Bercovitch. 191–206. Amherst: University of Massachusetts Press, 1972.

Buell, Lawrence. "Circling the Spheres: A Dialogue." *American Literature* 3 (1998): 465–90.

Bunyan, John. *Grace Abounding to the Chief of Sinners*. London, 1666. Reprinted in *Grace Abounding with Other Spiritual Autobiographies*, ed. John Stachniewski with Anita Pacheco. Oxford: Oxford University Press, 1998.

————. *The Pilgrim's Progress From This World, to That Which is to Come*. London, 1678.

Burnham, Michelle. *Captivity and Sentiment: Cultural Exchange in American Literature, 1682–1861*. Hanover, N.H.: University Press of New England, 1997.

Bush, Sargent, Jr. "Paradox, Puritanism, and Taylor's *God's Determinations.*" *Early American Literature* 4 (1969): 48–66.

———. *The Writings of Thomas Hooker: Spiritual Adventure in Two Worlds.* Madison: University of Wisconsin Press, 1980.

Byles, Mather. *Poems on Several Occasions.* Boston, 1744. Reprinted in *Works,* ed. Benjamin Frankin V. Delmar, N.Y. Scholars' Facsimiles & Reprints, 1978.

Cabrol, Fernand, and Henri Leclercq, eds. *Dictionnaire d'archéologie chrétienne et de liturgie.* 15 vols. Paris: Letouzey et Ane, 1907–53.

Caldwell, Patricia. *The Puritan Conversion Narrative: The Beginnings of American Expression.* Cambridge: Cambridge University Press, 1983.

Candler, Peter, Jr. "The Liturgy of Interpretation: Memory and the *Glossa Ordinaria.*" Paper presented at the annual conference of Anglo-Saxon, Norse and Celtic, Cambridge University, May 2000.

Cartwright, Thomas. *A Replye to an Answere made of M. Doctor Whitegifte, Againste the Admonition to the Parliament.* London, 1573.

Castillo, Susan, and Ivy Schweitzer, eds. *A Companion to* The Literatures of Colonial America: An Anthology. Oxford: Blackwell, 2005.

Certeau, Michel de. *The Practice of Everyday Life.* Trans. Steven Rendall. Berkeley: University of California Press, 1984.

Chauncy, Charles. *Anti-Synodalia Scripta Americana.* London, 1662.

Cherniavsky, Eva. "Night Pollution and the Floods of Confession in Michael Wigglesworth's Diary." *Arizona Quarterly* 45 (1989): 15–33.

Clap, Roger. *Memoirs of Roger Clap. 1630.* Boston, 1844.

Clark, Michael. "The Crucified Phrase: Sign and Desire in Puritan Semiology." *Early American Literature* 13 (1978–79): 278–93.

———. "The Honeyed Knot of Puritan Aesthetics." In *Puritan Poets and Poetics: Seventeenth-Century American Poetry in Theory and Practice,* ed. Peter White. 67–83. University Park: Pennsylvania State University Press, 1985.

———. "The Persistence of Literature in Early American Studies." *William and Mary Quarterly,* 3d ser., 57 (2000): 641–46.

Cohen, Charles Lloyd. *God's Caress: The Psychology of Puritan Religious Experience.* New York: Oxford University Press, 1986.

Colacurcio, Michael J. *Doctrine and Difference: Essays in the Literature of New England.* New York: Routledge, 1997.

———. "*Gods Determinations Touching Half-Way Membership:* Occasion and Audience in Edward Taylor." *American Literature* 39 (1967): 298–314.

Collins, An. *Divine Songs and Meditacions.* London, 1653.

Collinson, Patrick. *The Religion of Protestants: The Church in English Society, 1559–1625.* Oxford: Clarendon Press, 1983.

Cooper, James F. *Tenacious of their Liberties: The Congregationalists in Colonial Massachusetts.* New York: Oxford University Press, 1999.

Corey, Deloraine Pendre. *The History of Malden Massachusetts 1633–1785.* Malden: the author, 1899.

Cotton, John. *The Bloudy Tenent Washed and Made White in the Bloud of the Lambe.* London, 1647.

———. *A Brief Exposition of the Whole Book of Canticles.* London, 1642.

————. *Christ the Fountaine of Life*. London, 1651.

————. *The Correspondence of John Cotton*, ed. Sargent Bush, Jr. Chapel Hill: University of North Carolina Press, 2001.

————. *The Covenant of Gods Free Grace*. London, 1645.

————. Draft preface to the Bay Psalm Book. In Zoltán Haraszti, *The Enigma of the Bay Psalm Book*. 107–15. Chicago: University of Chicago Press, 1956.

————. *God's Promise to his Plantation*. London, 1630.

————. *A Modest and Cleare Answer to Mr. Balls Discourse of Set Formes of Prayer*. London, 1642.

————. *The New Covenant, or A Treatise, unfolding the order and manner of the giving and receiving of the Covenant of Grace to the Elect*. London, 1654.

————. *Singing of Psalmes, a Gospel Ordinance*. London, 1647.

————. *A Treatise of the Covenant of Grace*. 2d ed. London, 1659.

————. *The Way of the Congregational Churches Cleared*. London, 1648.

Covey, Cyclone. "Puritanism and Music in Colonial America." *William and Mary Quarterly*, 3d ser., 8 (1951): 378–88.

Craig, Raymond A. "The 'Peculiar Elegance' of Edward Taylor's Poetics." In *The Tayloring Shop: Essays on the Poetry of Edward Taylor in Honor of Thomas M. and Virginia L. Davis*, ed. Michael Schuldiner. 68–101. Newark: University of Delaware Press, 1997.

————. "Singing with Grace: Allusive Strategies in Anne Bradstreet's 'New Psalms.'" *Studies in Puritan American Spirituality* 1 (1990): 148–69.

Crashaw, Richard. *Steps to the Temple: Sacred Poems, with Other Delights of the Muses*. London, 1646.

Cressy, David. *Coming Over: Migration and Communication between England and New England in the Seventeenth Century*. Cambridge: Cambridge University Press, 1987.

Crowder, Richard. *No Featherbed to Heaven: A Biography of Michael Wigglesworth, 1631–1705*. [East Lansing]: Michigan State University Press, [1962].

Daly, Robert. *God's Altar: The World and the Flesh in Puritan Poetry*. Berkeley: University of California Press, 1978.

Dante Alighieri. *The Divine Comedy, I: Hell*. Trans. Dorothy L. Sayers. London: Penguin, 1949.

Davenport, John. *Another Essay for the Investigation of the Truth*. Cambridge, Mass., 1663.

Davies, Horton. *The Worship of the American Puritans 1629–1730*. New York: Lang, 1990.

Davis, Thomas M. "Edward Taylor's Elegy on Deacon David Dewey." *Proceedings of the American Antiquarian Society* 96 (1986): 75–84.

————. "The Exegetical Traditions of Puritan Typology." *Early American Literature* 5 (1970): 11–50.

————. Introduction to *Edward Taylor's "Church Records" and Related Sermons*, ed. Thomas M. Davis and Virginia L. Davis. Boston: Twayne, 1981.

————. Introduction to *Edward Taylor's Minor Poetry*, ed. Thomas M. Davis and Virginia L. Davis. Boston: Twayne, 1981.

————. Introduction to *Edward Taylor vs. Solomon Stoddard: The Nature of the Lord's Supper*. ed. Thomas M. Davis and Virginia L. Davis. Boston: Twayne, 1981.

———. *A Reading of Edward Taylor.* Newark: University of Delaware Press, 1992.

Day, W. G., ed. *The Pepys Ballads,* facsimiles of the Pepys ballad collection, Magdalene College, Cambridge. 5 vols. Cambridge: Brewer, 1987.

Dean, John Ward. *Sketch of the Life of Rev. Michael Wigglesworth.* Albany, N.Y.: Munsell, 1863.

Dekker, Thomas. *Dekker His Dreame. In which, beeing rapt with a Poeticall Enthusiasme, the great Volumes of Heaven and Hell to Him were opened, in which he read many Wonderful Things.* London, 1620.

Delbanco, Andrew. *The Puritan Ordeal.* Cambridge: Harvard University Press, 1989.

Deloney, Thomas. *Strange Histories; or, The Garland of Delight.* London, 1681.

Derounian-Stodola, Kathryn Zabelle, ed. *Early American Literature and Culture.* Newark: University of Delaware Press, 1992.

Dickinson, Emily. *The Complete Poems,* ed. Thomas H. Johnson. Cambridge: Belknap Press of Harvard University Press, 1955. Reprint, London: Faber and Faber, 1970.

Ditmore, Michael G. "A Prophetess in Her Own Country: An Exegesis of Anne Hutchinson's 'Immediate Revelation.'" *William and Mary Quarterly,* 3d ser., 57 (2000): 349–92.

Donne, John. *Poetical Works,* ed. Herbert J. C. Grierson. Oxford: Oxford University Press, 1971.

———. *The Sermons of John Donne,* ed. George R. Potter and Evelyn M. Simpson. Vol. 2. Berkeley: University of California Press, 1955.

Dorenkamp, J. H. "*The Bay Psalm Book* and the Ainsworth Psalter." *Early American Literature* 7 (1972): 3–16.

Doriani, Beth M. "'Then Have I . . . Said with David': Anne Bradstreet's Andover Manuscript Poems and the Influence of the Psalm Tradition." *Early American Literature* 24 (1989): 52–69.

Draper, John William. *A Century of Broadside Elegies.* London: Ingpen and Grant, 1928.

Drayton, Michael. *The Works of Michael Drayton,* ed. J. William Hebel. Vol. 1. Oxford: Basil Blackwell, Shakespeare Head Press, 1961.

Eames, Wilberforce, ed. *The Whole Booke of Psalmes Faithfully Translated into English Metre.* [Cambridge, Mass.], 1640. Facsimile reprint, New York: Dodd, Mead, 1903.

Ebsworth, Joseph Woodfall, ed. *The Bagford Ballads: Illustrating the Last Years of the Stuarts.* Vol. 1. Hertford: Austin, 1878.

Egan, Jim. *Authorizing Experience: Refigurations of the Body Politic in Seventeenth-Century New England Writing.* Princeton: Princeton University Press, 1999.

Ellinwood, Leonard. *The History of American Church Music.* Rev. ed. New York: Da Capo Press, 1970.

Eliott, Emory. "New England Puritan Literature." In *Cambridge History of American Literature,* ed. Sacvan Bercovitch, Vol. 1. 169–306. Cambridge: Cambridge University Press, 1994.

———. *Power and the Pulpit in Puritan New England.* Princeton: Princeton University Press, 1975.

Emerson, Everett. *John Cotton.* New York: Twayne, 1965.

Fisch, Harold. *Poetry with a Purpose: Biblical Poetics and Interpretation.* Bloomington: Indiana University Press, 1988. Reprint, 1990.

Fish, Stanley E. *Self-Consuming Artifacts: The Experience of Seventeenth-Century Literature.* Berkeley: University of California Press, 1972.

Fiske, John. *The Notebook of the Reverend John Fiske, 1644–1675*, ed. Robert G. Pope. Collections of the Colonial Society of Massachusetts, 47. Boston: Colonial Society of Massachusetts, 1974.

Fithian, Rosemary. "'Words of My Mouth, Meditations of My Heart': Edward Taylor's Preparatory Meditations and the Book of Psalms." *Early American Literature* 20 (1985): 89–119.

Foote, Henry Wilder. *Three Centuries of American Hymnody.* Cambridge: Harvard University Press, 1940.

Foster, Stephen. "The Godly in Transit." In *Seventeenth-Century New England*, ed. David D. Hall and David Grayson Allen. 185–238. Boston: Colonial Society of Massachusetts, 1984.

———. *The Long Argument: English Puritanism and the Shaping of New England Culture 1570–1700.* Chapel Hill: University of North Carolina Press for the Institute of Early American History and Culture, 1991.

Franklin, Benjamin. *Pennsylvania Gazette*, 12 June 1740.

Fraser, Russell. *The War Against Poetry.* Princeton: Princeton University Press, 1970.

Frere, W. H., and C. E. Douglas, eds. *Puritan Manifestoes: A Study of the Origin of the Puritan Revolt, With a Reprint of the Admonition to the Parliament and Kindred Documents, 1572.* London: SPCK, 1954.

Frost, Robert. *The Collected Poems of Robert Frost.* London: Longmans, Green, 1939.

Gatta, John. *Gracious Laughter: the Meditative Wit of Edward Taylor.* Columbia: University of Missouri Press, 1989.

Genette, Gérard. *Paratexts: Thresholds of Interpretation.* Trans. Jane E. Lewin. Cambridge: Cambridge University Press, 1997.

Geneva Bible. Geneva, 1599. Facsimile reprint, Buena Park, Calif.: Geneva Publishing, 1991.

Gildrie, Richard P. *The Profane, the Civil, & the Godly: The Reformation of Manners in Orthodox New England, 1679–1749.* University Park: Pennsylvania State University Press, 1994.

Gordis, Lisa. *Opening Scripture: Bible Reading and Interpretive Authority in Puritan New England.* Chicago: University of Chicago Press, 2003.

Grabo, Norman S. *Edward Taylor.* New Haven, Conn.: College and University Press, 1961.

———. *Edward Taylor: Revised Edition.* Boston: Twayne, 1988.

———. "How Bad is the Bay Psalm Book?" *Papers of the Michigan Academy of Science, Arts, and Letters* 46 (1961): 605–15.

———. "So Who Killed Literary History?" *William and Mary Quarterly*, 3d ser., 45 (1988): 342–44.

———. "The Veiled Vision: The Role of Aesthetics in Early American Intellectual History." In *The American Puritan Imagination: Essays in Revaluation*, ed. Sacvan Bercovitch. 19–33. Cambridge: Cambridge University Press, 1974.

Greven, Philip. *The Protestant Temperament: Patterns of Child-Rearing, Religious Experience, and the Self in Early America.* New York: Knopf, 1977.

Gura, Philip F. *The Crossroads of American History and Literature.* University Park: Pennsylvania State University Press, 1996.

———. "Early American Literature at the New Century." *William and Mary Quarterly,* 3d ser., 57 (2000): 599–620.

———. *A Glimpse of Sion's Glory: Puritan Radicalism in New England, 1620–1660.* Middletown, Conn.: Wesleyan University Press, 1984.

Hall, David D., ed. *The Antinomian Controversy 1636–1638: A Documentary History.* Middletown, Conn.: Wesleyan University Press, 1968.

———. *The Faithful Shepherd: A History of the New England Ministry in the Seventeenth Century.* Chapel Hill: University of North Carolina Press for the Institute of Early American History and Culture, 1972.

———. *Worlds of Wonder, Days of Judgment; Popular Religious Belief in Early New England.* New York: Knopf, 1989.

Hall, Dean. "Edward Taylor: The Evolution of a Poet." Ph.D. diss., Kent State University, 1977.

Hall, Dean, and Thomas M. Davis. "The Two Versions of Edward Taylor's Foundation Day Sermon." *Resources for American Literary Study* 5 (1975): 199–216.

Hambrick-Stowe, Charles E., ed. Introduction to *Early New England Meditative Poetry: Anne Bradstreet and Edward Taylor.* New York: Paulist Press, 1988.

———. *The Practice of Piety: Puritan Devotional Disciplines in Seventeenth-Century New England.* Chapel Hill: University of North Carolina Press, 1982.

Hammond, Henry. *A Paraphrase and Annotations upon the Books of the Psalms.* London, 1659.

Hammond, Jeffrey A. *The American Puritan Elegy: A Literary and Cultural Study.* Cambridge: Cambridge University Press, 2000.

———. *Edward Taylor: Fifty Years of Scholarship and Criticism.* Columbia, S.C.: Camden House, 1993.

———. *Sinful Self, Saintly Self: The Puritan Experience of Poetry.* Athens: University of Georgia Press, 1993.

———. "Where are we going, where have we been?: Puritan Poetics Reconsidered." *Early American Literature* 22 (1987): 114–32.

Haraszti, Zoltán, ed. *Bay Psalm Book: A Facsimile Reprint of the First Edition of 1640.* Chicago: University of Chicago Press, 1956.

———. *The Enigma of the Bay Psalm Book.* Chicago: University of Chicago Press, 1956.

Heimert, Alan, and Andrew Delbanco, eds. *The Puritans in America: A Narrative Anthology.* Cambridge: Harvard University Press, 1985.

Heller, Lee. "Conceiving the 'New' American Literature." *Early American Literature* 29 (1994): 83–90.

Herbert, George. *The Temple: Sacred Poems and Private Ejaculations.* Cambridge, 1633. Facsimile reprint, London: Wells Gardner, 1876.

Herget, Winifred. "The Transcription and Transmission of the Hooker Corpus." In *Thomas Hooker: Writings in England and Holland, 1626–1633,* ed. George H. Williams et al. 253–70. Cambridge: Harvard University Press, 1975.

Hieron, Samuel. *A Helpe unto Devotion.* London, 1610.

Hill, Christopher. *The English Bible and the Seventeenth-Century Revolution.* London: Allen Lane, Penguin, 1993.

Holifield, E. Brooks. *The Covenant Sealed: The Development of Puritan Sacramental Theology in Old and New England, 1570–1720*. New Haven: Yale University Press, 1974.

Holmes, Nathaniel. *Gospel Musick*. London, 1644.

Höltgen, Karl Josef. "New Verse by Francis Quarles: The Portland Manuscripts, Metrical Psalms, and the Bay Psalm Book." *English Literary Renaissance* 28 (1998): 118–41.

Holy Bible, Containing the Old and New Testaments Translated [. . .] By His Majesty's Special Command. London, 1611.

Hood, George. *A History of Music in New England with Biographical Sketches of Reformers and Psalmists*. Boston: Wilkins, Carter, 1846. Reprint, New York: Johnson Reprint Corporation, 1970.

Hooker, Richard. *Of the Laws of Ecclesiastical Polity, Book V*. ed. W. Speed Hill. Cambridge: Belknap Press of Harvard University Press, 1977.

Hooker, Thomas. *The Application of Redemption, The First Eight Books*. London, 1656.

———. *The Application of Redemption . . . The Ninth and Tenth Books*. 2d ed. London, 1659.

———. *The Covenant of Grace Opened*. London, 1649.

———. *The Soules Implantation*. London, 1637.

———. *A Survey of the Summe of Church-Discipline*. London, 1648.

———. *Writings in England and Holland, 1626–1633*, ed. George H. Williams et al. Cambridge: Harvard University Press, 1975.

Howard, Alan B. "The World as Emblem: Language and Vision in the Poetry of Edward Taylor." *American Literature* 44 (1972): 359–84.

Hughes, Walter. " 'Meat Out of the Eater': Panic and Desire in American Puritan Poetry." In *Engendering Men: The Question of Male Feminist Criticism*, ed. Joseph A. Boone and Michael Gadden. 102–21. New York: Routledge, 1990.

Huizinga, Johan. *Homo Ludens: A Study of the Play-Element in Culture*. Boston: Beacon Press, 1955.

Inserra, Lorraine, and H. Wiley Hitchcock. *The Music of Henry Ainsworth's Psalter*. I.S.A.M. Monographs, No. 15. New York: Institute for Studies in American Music, Brooklyn College of the City University of New York, 1981.

James I and William Alexander. *The Psalmes of King David translated by King James*. London, 1631.

Jantz, Harold S., ed. *The First Century of New England Verse*. New York: Russell & Russell, 1944. Reprint, 1962.

Jehlen, Myra, and Michael Warner, eds. Introduction to *The English Literatures of America, 1500–1800*. New York: Routledge, 1997.

Jenks, Francis. Review of "Rev. Lyman Beecher's Letters on Infant Damnation." *Christian Examiner* 5 (1828): 537.

Jewel, John. *The Works of John Jewel*, ed. John Ayre. Vol. 4. Cambridge: University Press, 1850.

Johnson, Capt. Edward. *A History of New-England, from the English planting in the Yeere 1628, untill the Yeere 1652 [The Wonder-Working Providence of Sions Saviour]*. London, 1654.

Johnson, R. Brimley, ed. *A Book of British Ballads*. London: Dent, 1912. Reprint, 1966.

Johnson, Richard. *The Crown Garland of Golden Roses.* London, 1662.

Johnson, Thomas H., "A Seventeenth-Century Printing of Some Verses of Edward Taylor." *New England Quarterly* 14 (1941): 139–41.

Jones, Phyllis M. "Puritan's Progress: The Story of the Soul's Salvation in the Early New England Sermons." *Early American Literature* 15 (1980): 14–28.

Jonson, Ben. *Timber, or Discoveries* (London, 1641). Reprinted in *Ben Jonson*, ed. C. H. Herford, P. Simpson, and E. Simpson. Vol. 8. 555–649. Oxford: Clarendon Press, 1954.

Josselyn, John. *Account of two Voyages to New-England.* London, 1674.

Junkins, Donald. "Edward Taylor's Revisions." *American Literature* 37 (1965): 135–52.

———. "'Should Stars Wooe Lobster Claws?': A Study of Edward Taylor's Poetic Practice and Theory." *Early American Literature* 3 (1968): 88–116.

Kaiser, Leo M., ed. *Early American Latin Verse 1625–1825: An Anthology.* Chicago: Bolchazy-Carducci, 1984.

Kamensky, Jane. *Governing the Tongue: The Politics of Speech in Early New England.* Oxford: Oxford University Press, 1997.

Katz, David S. *Sabbath and Sabbatarianism in Seventeenth-Century England.* Leiden: E. J. Brill, 1988.

Kaufman, Michael W. *Institutional Individualism: Conversion, Exile, and Nostalgia in Puritan New England.* Hanover, N.H.: Wesleyan University Press, 1998.

Keeble, N. H. *The Literary Culture of Nonconformity in Later Seventeenth-Century England.* Leicester: Leicester University Press, 1987.

Keller, Karl. "The Example of Edward Taylor." *Early American Literature* 4 (1969): 5–26.

———. "The Loose, Large Principles of Solomon Stoddard." *Early American Literature* 16 (1981): 27–41.

Kettell, Samuel. *Specimens of American Poetry with Critical and Biographical Notices.* 2 vols. Boston: Goodrich, 1829.

Kibbey, Ann. *The Interpretation of Material Shapes in Puritanism: A Study of Rhetoric, Prejudice and Violence.* New York: Cambridge University Press, 1986.

Knight, Janice. *Orthodoxies in Massachusetts: Rereading American Puritanism.* Cambridge: Harvard University Press, 1994.

Krieger, Murray. "My Travels with the Aesthetic." In *Revenge of the Aesthetic: The Place of Literature in Theory Today*, ed. Michael P. Clark. 208–36. Berkeley: University of California Press, 2000.

Lake, Peter. *Anglicans and Puritans? Presbyterianism and English Conformist Thought from Whitgift to Hooker.* London: Unwin Hyman, 1988.

———. "The Laudian Style: Order, Uniformity and the Pursuit of the Beauty of Holiness in the 1630s." In *The Early Stuart Church 1603–1642*, ed. Kenneth Fincham. 161–85. Basingstoke: Macmillan, 1993.

Lechford, Thomas. *Plaine Dealing: or Newes from New-England.* London, 1641. Reprinted in *Collections of the Massachusetts Historical Society*, 3d ser., 3. Cambridge, Mass.: Metcalf, 1833: 55–128.

Lemay, J. A. Leo. *"New England's Annoyances": America's First Folk Song.* Newark: University of Delaware Press, 1985.

Lepore, Jill. *The Name of the War: King Philip's War and the Origins of American Identity.* New York: Knopf, 1999.

Leverenz, David. *The Language of Puritan Feeling: An Exploration in Literature, Psychology, and Social History.* New Brunswick, N.J.: Rutgers University Press, 1980.

Levy, Babette May. *Preaching in the First Half Century of New England History.* Hartford, Conn.: American Society of Church History, 1945.

Lewalski, Barbara. *Protestant Poetics and the Seventeenth-Century Religious Lyric.* Princeton: Princeton University Press, 1979.

Lockwood, John Hoyt. *Westfield and its Historic Influences, 1669–1919.* Vol 1. [Westfield, Mass.]: the author, [1922].

Love, Harold. *Scribal Publication in Seventeenth-Century England.* Oxford: Clarendon, 1993.

Lowance, Mason I., Jr., *The Language of Canaan: Metaphor and Symbol in New England from the Puritans to the Transcendentalists.* Cambridge: Harvard University Press, 1980.

Lowens, Irving. "The Bay Psalm Book in 17th-Century New England." *Journal of the American Musicological Society* 8 (1955): 22–29.

———. *Music and Musicians in Early America.* New York: Norton & Co., 1964.

Maltby, Judith. "'By This Book': Parishioners, the Prayer Book and the Established Church." In *The Early Stuart Church 1603–1642,* ed. Kenneth Fincham. 115–37. Basingstoke: Macmillan, 1993.

Marotti, Arthur F. *Manuscript, Print, and the English Renaissance Lyric.* Ithaca: Cornell University Press, 1995.

Martin, Wendy. *An American Triptych: Anne Bradstreet, Emily Dickinson, Adrienne Rich.* Chapel Hill: University of North Carolina, 1984.

Martz, Louis L. Foreword to *The Poems of Edward Taylor,* ed. Donald E. Stanford. New Haven: Yale University Press, 1960.

Mather, Cotton. *Agreeable Admonitions for Old & Young.* Boston, 1703.

———. *Baptismal Piety.* Boston, 1727.

———. *Cotton Mather's Verse in English,* ed. Denise D. Knight. Newark: University of Delaware Press, 1989.

———. *The Diary of Cotton Mather.* Massachusetts Historical Society Collections, 7th ser., 7–8. Boston: Massachusetts Historical Society, 1911/12.

———. *A Faithful Man, Described and Rewarded.* Boston, 1705.

———. *Magnalia Christi Americana: or, the Ecclesiastical History of New-England.* 2 vols. London, 1702. Reprint, Hartford, Conn.: Silas Andrus, 1853.

———. *Manuductio ad Ministerium.* Boston, 1726. Reprint, New York: AMS Press, 1978.

———. *A Monitor for the Children of the Covenant.* Boston, 1715.

———. *The Nightingale. An Essay on Songs among Thorns.* Boston, 1724.

———. *Psalterium Americanum.* Boston, 1718.

———. *Right Thoughts in Sad Hours.* London, 1689.

———. *The Thoughts of a Dying Man.* Boston, 1697.

Mather, Increase. "The Autobiography of Increase Mather," ed. M. G. Hall. *Proceedings of the American Antiquarian Society,* n.s., 71 (1961): 271–360.

———. *The First Principles of New England, Concerning the Subject of Baptism and Communion of Churches*. Cambridge, Mass., 1675.

———. *The Life and Death of that reverend man of God Mr. Richard Mather, teacher of the church in Dorchester in New-England*. Cambridge, Mass., 1670. Reprinted in *Two Mather Biographies: "Life and Death" and "Parentator,"* ed. William J. Scheick. Bethlehem, Pa.: Lehigh University Press, 1989.

Mather, Richard. *A Defence of the Answer and Arguments of the Synod Met at Boston in the Year 1662*. Boston, 1664.

Mather, Samuel. *A Testimony from the Scripture against Idolatry and Superstition In Two Sermons upon the Example of that Great Reformer Hezekiah, 2 Kings 18.4*. Dublin, 1660. Reprint, Boston, 1725.

Matthiessen, F. O. "Michael Wigglesworth, A Puritan Artist." *New England Quarterly* 1 (1928): 493–504.

McGann, Jerome. *Black Riders: The Visible Language of Modernism*. Princeton: Princeton University Press, 1993.

Mead, Sidney E., and Ernest R. Sandeen. Review of *The Bay Psalm Book: A Facsimile Reprint of the First Edition of 1640* and *The Enigma of the Bay Psalm Book*, by Zoltán Haraszti. *Journal of Religion* 37 (1957): 209.

Mencken, H. L. "Puritanism as a Literary Force." In *A Book of Prefaces*. 197–283. London: Jonathan Cape, 1922.

Meserole, Harrison T., ed. *Seventeenth-Century American Poetry*. New York: Doubleday, 1968. Reprinted as *American Poetry of the Seventeenth Century*. University Park: Pennsylvania State University Press, 1985. Reprint, 1993.

Middlekauff, Robert. *Three Generations of Puritan Intellectuals, 1596–1728*. New York: Oxford University Press, 1971.

Mignolo, Walter. *Local Histories, Global Designs: Coloniality, Subaltern Knowledges, and Border Thinking*. Princeton: Princeton University Press, 2000.

Mignon, Charles W. "Edward Taylor's *Preparatory Meditations:* A Decorum of Imperfection." *Proceedings of the Modern Language Association* 83 (1968): 1423–28.

Miller, David G. Review of *The Self and the Sacred: Conversion and Autobiography in Early American Protestantism*, by Rodger M. Payne. *American Literature* 71 (1999): 798–99.

Miller, Perry. "A Colonial Dialect." In *Early American Literature: A Collection of Critical Essays*, ed. Michael T. Gilmore. 22–33. Englewood Cliffs, N.J.: Prentice-Hall, 1980.

———. *The New England Mind: From Colony to Province*. Cambridge: Harvard University Press, 1953. Reprint, 1981.

———. *The New England Mind: The Seventeenth Century*. Cambridge: Harvard University Press, 1939. Reprint, 1954.

Miller, Perry, and Thomas H. Johnson, eds. *The Puritans*. Rev. ed. 2 vols. New York: Harper and Row, 1963.

Milton, John. *Poems; &c. upon Several Occasions*. London, 1673.

———. *Poems of Mr. John Milton, Both English and Latin*. 2 vols. London, 1645. Facsimile reprint, Menston, England: Scolar Press, 1970.

———. *The Riverside Milton*, ed. Roy Flannagan. Boston: Houghton Mifflin, 1998.

Missale Romanum ex decreto sacrosancti concili tridentini. 4th ed. Turin: Alfredi Mane, 1922.

Mitchel, Jonathan. "An Answer to the Apologetical Preface." In Richard Mather, *A Defence of the Answer and Arguments of the Synod Met at Boston in the Year 1662.* Boston, 1664.

———. "Propositions." 1664. In Cotton Mather, *Magnalia Christi Americana: or, the Ecclesiastical History of New-England.* Vol. 2. 102–4. London, 1702. Reprint, Hartford, Conn.: Silas Andrus, 1853.

———. *Propositions Concerning the Subject of Baptism and Consociation of Churches,* and *Propositions.* Cambridge, Mass., and London, 1662. Reprinted in *The Creeds and Platforms of Congregationalism,* ed. Williston Walker. 301–44. New York: Scribner's Sons, 1893.

Morgan, Edmund S. "New England Puritanism: Another Approach." *William and Mary Quarterly* 18 (1961): 236–42.

———. *Visible Saints: The History of a Puritan Idea.* Ithaca: Cornell University Press, 1963.

Morison, Samuel E. *The Founding of Harvard College.* Cambridge: Harvard University Press, 1935.

———. *Harvard College in the Seventeenth Century.* 2 vols. Cambridge: Harvard University Press, 1936.

Morton, Nathaniel. *New England's Memoriall.* Cambridge, Mass., 1669.

Mulford, Carla. "The Ineluctability of the People's Stories." *William and Mary Quarterly,* 3d ser., 57 (2000): 621–34.

———, ed. *Only for the Eye of a Friend: The Poems of Annis Boudinot Stockton.* Charlottesville: University Press of Virginia, 1995.

Murdock, Kenneth B., ed. Introduction to Michael Wigglesworth, *The Day of Doom or, A Poetical Description of the Great and Last Judgment: with Other Poems.* New York: Spiral, 1929.

———, ed. *Handkerchiefs from Paul.* Cambridge: Harvard University Press, 1927. Reprint, 1970.

———. *Literature and Theology in Colonial New England.* Cambridge: Harvard University Press, [1949]. Reprint, Westport, Conn.: Greenwood, 1976.

Murphy, Francis. "Anne Bradstreet and Edward Taylor." In *The Columbia History of American Poetry,* ed. Jay Parini. 1–15. New York: Columbia University Press, 1993.

———. "Taylor's Attitude toward Publication." *American Literature* 34 (1962): 393–94.

Nashe, Thomas. *The Works of Thomas Nashe,* ed. Ronald B. McKerrow. Revised edition, F. P. Wilson. 5 vols. Oxford: Blackwell, 1958.

Neal, Daniel. *The History of New-England.* London, 1720.

Neuenschwander, Robert. "The Origin and Intent of the Bay Psalm Book." D.Mus. diss., Northwestern University, 1977.

New Englands First Fruits. London, 1643. Reprinted in S. E. Morison, *The Founding of Harvard College.* Cambridge: Harvard University Press, 1935.

Norton, John. *Abel Being Dead Yet Speaketh: or, The life and death of that deservedly famous man of God, Mr John Cotton, late teacher of the church of Christ, at Boston in New-England.* London, 1658.

Nuttall, Geoffrey F. *Visible Saints: The Congregational Way 1640–1660.* Oxford: Blackwell, 1957.

Ong, Walter J. *Ramus, Method, and the Decay of Dialogue.* Cambridge: Harvard University Press, 1958.

Ottenhoff, John. "From Venus to Virtue: Sacred Parody and George Herbert." In *George Herbert: Sacred and Profane,* ed. Helen Wilcox and Richard Todd. 49–61. Amsterdam: VU University Press, 1995.

Owen, Barbara. "The Bay Psalm Book and Its Era." *Hymn* 41 (1990): 12–19.

Owen, John. *A Discourse of the Work of the Holy Spirit in Prayer.* London, 1682. In *The Works of John Owen,* ed. Thomas Russell. Vol 4. London: Baynes, 1826.

Parker, David L. "Edward Taylor's Preparationism: A New Perspective on the Taylor–Stoddard Controversy." *Early American Literature* 11 (1976–77): 259–78.

Parrington, Vernon Louis. "The Puritan Divines, 1620–1720." In *A History of American Literature,* ed. W. P. Trent et al. Vol. 1. 31–56. Cambridge: Cambridge University Press, 1918.

Patterson, J. Daniel. "A Critical Edition of Edward Taylor's 'Gods Determinations.'" Ph.D. diss., Kent State University, 1985.

———. "*Gods Determinations:* The Occasion, the Audience, and Taylor's Hope for New England." *Early American Literature* 22 (1987): 63–81.

———. "The Homiletic Design of Edward Taylor's *Gods Determinations.*" In *The Tayloring Shop: Essays on the Poetry of Edward Taylor in Honor of Thomas M. and Virginia L. Davis,* ed. Michael Schuldiner. 131–50. Newark: University of Delaware Press, 1997.

Pearce, Roy Harvey. *The Continuity of American Poetry.* Princeton: Princeton University Press, 1961.

Perkins, David. *Is Literary History Possible?* Baltimore: Johns Hopkins University Press, 1992.

Perkins, William. *The Arte of Prophecying. Workes of that Famous and Worthy Minister of Christ.* Vol. 2. 643–73. London, 1617.

Pettit, Norman. *The Heart Prepared: Grace and Conversion in Puritan Spiritual Life.* 2d ed. Middletown, Conn.: Wesleyan University Press, 1989.

Polishook, Irwin H., ed. *Roger Williams, John Cotton, and Religious Freedom: A Controversy in New and Old England.* Englewood Cliffs, N.J.: Prentice-Hall, 1967.

Pope, Alan H. "Petrus Ramus and Michael Wigglesworth: The Logic of Poetic Structure." In *Puritan Poets and Poetics,* ed. Peter White. 210–26. University Park: Pennsylvania State University Press, 1985.

Pope, Robert G. *The Half-Way Covenant: Church Membership in Puritan New England.* Princeton: Princeton University Press, 1969.

Powell, Walter L. "Edward Taylor's Westfield: An Edition of the Westfield 'Town Records.'" Ph.D. diss., Kent State University, 1982.

Pratt, Waldo S. *The Music of the Pilgrims: A Description of the Psalm-Book Brought to Plymouth in 1620.* Boston: Ditson, [1921]. Reprint, New York: Russell & Russell, 1971.

Price, George. *Thomas Dekker.* New York: Twayne, 1969.

Prince, Thomas. *The Psalms, Hymns, & Spiritual Songs, of the Old and New Testament, Faithfully Translated into English Metre. Being the New-England Psalm book revised and improved.* Boston, 1758.

Robinson, Douglas. *American Apocalypses: The Image of the End of the World in American Literature.* Baltimore: Johns Hopkins University Press, 1985.

Rohr-Sauer, Philipp von. *English Metrical Psalms from 1600–1660.* Freiburg, Germany: Poppen & Ortmann, 1938.

Rollins, Hyder E., ed. *Old English Ballads 1552–1625.* Cambridge: Cambridge University Press, 1920.

———, ed. *The Pack of Autolycus or Strange and Terrible News of Ghosts, Apparitions, Monstrous Births, Showers of Wheat, Judgments of God, and other Prodigious and Fearful Happenings as told in Broadside Ballads of the Years 1624–1693.* Cambridge: Harvard University Press, 1927. Reprint, Port Washington, N.Y.: Kennikat Press, 1969.

———, ed. *The Pepys Ballads.* Vols. 1 and 2. Cambridge: Harvard University Press, 1929.

Rosenwald, Lawrence. "*Voces Clamantium in Deserto:* Latin Verse of the Puritans." In *Puritan Poets and Poetics,* ed. Peter White. 303–17. University Park: Pennsylvania State University Press, 1985.

Rous, Francis. *The Psalms of David in English Meeter.* London, 1643.

Rowe, Karen E. "Prophetic Visions: Typology and Colonial American Poetry." In *Puritan Poets and Poetics,* ed. Peter White. 47–66. University Park: Pennsylvania State University Press, 1985.

———. *Saint and Singer: Edward Taylor's Typology and the Poetics of Mediation.* Cambridge: Cambridge University Press, 1986.

Rutman, Darrett B. *American Puritanism: Faith and Practice.* Philadelphia: Lippincott, 1970.

———. "God's Bridge Falling Down: 'Another Approach' to Puritanism Assayed." *William and Mary Quarterly,* 3d ser., 19 (1962): 408–21.

Sandys, George. *A Paraphrase upon the Psalmes of David and upon the Hymns Dispersed throughout the Old and New Testaments.* London, 1636.

Scanlan, Thomas. *Colonial Writing and the New World, 1583–1671: Allegories of Desire.* Cambridge: Cambridge University Press, 1999.

Scheick, William J. *Design in Puritan American Literature.* Lexington: University Press of Kentucky, 1992.

———. "The Jawbones Schema of Edward Taylor's *Gods Determinations.*" In *Puritan Influences in American Literature,* ed. Emory Elliott. 38–54. Urbana: University of Illinois Press, 1979.

———. "Standing in the Gap: Urian Oakes's Elegy on Thomas Shepard." *Early American Literature* 9 (1975): 301–6.

———. "Tombless Virtue and Hidden Text: New England Puritan Funeral Elegies." In *Puritan Poets and Poetics,* ed. Peter White. 286–302. University Park: Pennsylvania State University Press, 1985.

———. *The Will and the Word: The Poetry of Edward Taylor.* Athens: University of Georgia Press, 1974.

Schuldiner, Michael. "Edward Taylor's 'Problematic' Imagery." *Early American Literature* 13 (1978): 92–101.

———. *Gifts and Works: The Post-Conversion Paradigm and Spiritual Controversy in Seventeenth-Century Massachusetts.* Macon, Ga.: Mercer University Press, 1991.

———. "Puritan Casuistry and the Character of the Three Ranks of Soul in Edward

Taylor's *Gods Determinations."* In *The Tayloring Shop,* ed. Michael Schuldiner. 105–30. Newark: University of Delaware Press, 1997.

Schweitzer, Ivy. *The Work of Self-Representation: Lyric Poetry in Colonial New England.* Chapel Hill: University of North Carolina Press, 1991.

Sebouhian, George. "Conversion Morphology and the Structure of *Gods Determinations." Early American Literature* 16 (1981–82): 226–40.

Sedulius. *Opus Paschale,* ed. Johannes Huemer. Corpus Scriptorum Ecclesiasticorum Latinorum. Vienna, 1885.

Selement, George. "Publication and the Puritan Minister." *William and Mary Quarterly* 37 (1980): 219–41.

Sewall, Samuel. *Diary of Samuel Sewall 1674–1729,* ed. M. Halsey Thomas. 2 vols. New York: Farrar, Strauss and Giroux, 1973.

Shakespeare, William. *Complete Works,* ed. W. J. Craig. Oxford: Oxford Unversity Press, 1988.

Shawcross, John T. "Some Colonial American Poetry and George Herbert." *Early American Literature* 23 (1988): 28–51.

Shea, Daniel B., Jr. *Spiritual Autobiography in Early America.* Princeton: Princeton University Press, 1968.

Shepard, Thomas. *God's Plot: The Paradoxes of Puritan Piety,* ed. Michael McGiffert. Amherst: University of Massachusetts Press, 1972.

———. *The Parable of the Ten Virgins Opened & Applied.* 2 vols. London, 1660.

———. *The Sincere Convert.* 4th ed. London, 1646.

———. *A Treatise of Ineffectual Hearing of the Word.* London, 1652. Reprint, 1657.

———. *A Treatise of Liturgies, Power of the Keyes, and of Matter of the Visible Church.* London, 1653.

Shields, David S. *Civil Tongues and Polite Letters in British America.* Chapel Hill: University of North Carolina Press for the Institute of Early American History and Culture, 1997.

———. "Joy and Dread among the Early Americanists." *William and Mary Quarterly,* 3d ser., 57 (2000): 635–640.

———. *Oracles of Empire: Poetry, Politics, and Commerce in British America, 1690–1750.* Chicago: University of Chicago Press, 1990.

Shucard, Alan. *American Poetry: The Puritans through Walt Whitman.* Boston: Twayne, 1988.

Shurtleff, Nathaniel B., ed. *Records of the Governor and Company of the Massachusetts Bay in New England, 1: 1628–1641.* Boston, W.W. 1853. Reprint, New York: AMS, 1968.

Sidney, Philip. *An Apology for Poetry or The Defence of Poetry,* ed. Geoffrey Shepherd. Manchester: Manchester University Press, 1973.

Sidney, Philip, and Mary Sidney Herbert. *The Psalms of Sir Philip Sidney and the Countess of Pembroke,* ed. John C. A. Rathmell. Garden City, N.Y.: Doubleday, 1963.

Silverman, Kenneth, ed. *Colonial American Poetry.* New York: Hafner, 1968.

Sloan, Gary. "Wigglesworth's *The Day of Doom." The Explicator* 56 (1998): 64–67.

Slotkin, Richard, and James K. Folsom, eds. *So Dreadfull a Judgment: Puritan Responses to King Philip's War, 1676–1677.* Middletown, Conn.: Wesleyan University Press, 1978.

Spengemann, William C. "Discovering the Literature of British America." *Early American Literature* 18 (1983): 3–16.

Spiller, Robert E., et al., eds. *The Literary History of the United States*. 4th ed. New York: Macmillan, 1974.

Stallings, Louise Russell. "The Unpolished Altar: The Place of the Bay Psalm Book in American Culture." Ph.D. diss., Texas A&M University, 1977.

Staloff, Darren. *The Making of an American Thinking Class: Intellectuals and Intelligentsia in Puritan Massachusetts*. New York: Oxford University Press, 1998.

Stanford, Ann. *Anne Bradstreet: The Worldly Puritan*. New York: Burt Franklin, 1974.

Stanford, Donald E. "Edward Taylor." In *Major Writers of Early American Literature*, ed. Everett Emerson. 59–91. Madison: University of Wisconsin Press, 1972.

———, ed. Preface to *The Poems of Edward Taylor*. Chapel Hill: University of North Carolina Press, 1989.

Stannard, David E. *The Puritan Way of Death: A Study in Religion, Culture and Social Change*. New York: Oxford University Press, 1977.

Stanwood, P. G. "Liturgy, Worship and the Sons of Light." In *New Perspectives on the Seventeenth-Century Religious Lyric*, ed. John R. Roberts. 105–23. Columbia: University of Missouri Press, 1994.

Sternhold, Thomas, John Hopkins, William Whittingham, et al. *The Whole Booke of Psalmes*. London, 1562. Reprint, 1642.

Stoddard, Solomon. *An Appeal to the Learned being a Vindication of the Right of Visible Saints to the Lords Supper*. Boston, 1709.

———. "Arguments for the Proposition." In *Edward Taylor vs. Solomon Stoddard: The Nature of the Lord's Supper*, ed. Thomas M. Davis and Virginia L. Davis. 67–86. Boston: Twayne, 1981.

———. *The Defects of Preachers Reproved in a Sermon Preached at Northampton, May 19th 1723*. New London, Conn., 1724.

———. *The Safety of Appearing at the Day of Judgment, In the Righteousness of Christ: Opened and Applied*. Boston, 1687.

———. *The Tryal of Assurance*. Boston, 1698.

Stout, Harry S. *The New England Soul: Preaching and Religious Culture in Colonial New England*. New York: Oxford University Press, 1986.

———. "Word and Order in Colonial New England." In *The Bible in America: Essays in Cultural History*, ed. Nathan O. Hatch and Mark A. Noll. 19–38. New York: Oxford University Press, 1982.

Sweet, Timothy. "Gender, Genre, and Subjectivity in Anne Bradstreet's Early Elegies." *Early American Literature* 23 (1988): 152–74.

Symmes, Thomas. *The Reasonableness of Regular Singing*. Boston, 1720.

Targoff, Ramie. *Common Prayer: The Language of Public Devotion in Early Modern England*. Chicago: University of Chicago Press, 2001.

Tashjian, Dickran, and Ann Tashjian. *Memorials for Children of Change*. Middletown, Conn.: Wesleyan University Press, 1974.

Tate, Nahum, and Nicholas Brady. *A New Version of the Psalms of David*. London, 1696.

Taylor, Edward. *Christographia*, ed. Norman S. Grabo. New Haven: Yale University Press, 1962.

———. Commonplace Book. Massachusetts Historical Society, Boston.

———. *The Diary of Edward Taylor*, ed. Francis X. Murphy. Springfield: Connecticut Valley Historical Museum, 1964.

———. *Edward Taylor vs. Solomon Stoddard: The Nature of the Lord's Supper*, ed. Thomas M. Davis and Virginia L. Davis. Boston: Twayne, 1981.

———. *Edward Taylor's "Church Records" and Related Sermons*, ed. Thomas M. Davis and Virginia L. Davis. Boston: Twayne, 1981.

———. *Edward Taylor's* Gods Determinations *and* Preparatory Meditations: *A Critical Edition*, ed. Daniel Patterson. Kent, Ohio: Kent State University Press, 2003.

———. *Edward Taylor's Minor Poetry*, ed. Thomas M. Davis and Virginia L. Davis. Boston: Twayne, 1981.

———. *Edward Taylor's Treatise Concerning the Lord's Supper*, ed. Norman S. Grabo. East Lansing: Michigan State University Press, 1965.

———. Letter to Samuel Sewall, 29 September 1696. In "The Pouring of the Sixth Vial: A Letter in a Taylor-Sewall Debate," ed. Mukhtar Ali Isani. *Proceedings of the Massachusetts Historical Society* 83 (1971): 123–29.

———. *The Poems of Edward Taylor*, ed. Donald E. Stanford. New Haven: Yale University Press, 1960.

———. "Poetical Works." Beinecke Rare Book and Manuscript Library, Yale University.

———. *The Poetical Works of Edward Taylor*, ed. Thomas H. Johnson. New York, Rockland editions, 1939. Reprint, Princeton: Princeton University Press, 1943.

———. *Upon the Types of the Old Testament*, ed. Charles W. Mignon. 2 vols. London: University of Nebraska Press, 1989.

Thomas, Jean L. "Drama and Doctrine in *Gods Determinations*." *American Literature* 36 (1965): 452–62.

Tompkins, Jane. *Sensational Designs: The Cultural Work of American Fiction, 1790–1860*. New York: Oxford University Press, 1986.

Tompson, Benjamin. *Benjamin Tompson: Colonial Bard, A Critical Edition*, ed. Peter White. University Park: Pennsylvania State University Press, 1980.

———. *New Englands Crisis, Or a Brief Narrative, of New-Englands Lamentable Estate at Present, Compar'd with the Former (but Few) Years of Prosperity*. Boston, 1676.

———. *New-Englands Tears For Her Present Miseries*. London, 1676.

Tompson, Joseph. Journal. ms am 929. Houghton Library, Harvard University.

Toulouse, Theresa. *The Art of Prophesying: New England Sermons and the Shaping of Belief*. Athens: University of Georgia Press, 1987.

Tufts, John. *An Introduction to the Singing of Psalm Tunes in a Plain and Easy Method*. Boston, 1726.

Turell, Jane Colman. *Memoirs of the Life and Death of the Pious and Ingenious Mrs. Jane Turell*. Boston, 1735. Reprinted in *Poems of Jane Turell and Martha Brewster*, ed. Kenneth A. Requa. Delmar, N.Y.: Scholars' Facsimiles & Reprints, 1979.

Turner, Maxine Thompson. "A History of the Bay Psalm Book." Ph.D. diss., Auburn University, 1971.

———. "Three Eighteenth-Century Revisions of the Bay Psalm Book." *The New England Quarterly* 45 (1972): 270–77.

Tyler, Moses Coit. *A History of American Literature, 1607–1765.* New York: Putnam's Sons, 1878. Reprint, Ithaca: Cornell University Press, 1949.

Van Gastel, Ada. "Ethnic Pluralism in Early American Literature: Incorporating Dutch-American Texts into the Canon." In *Early American Literature and Culture,* ed. Kathryn Zabelle Derounian-Stodola. 109–21. Newark: University of Delaware Press, 1992.

Vaughan, Henry. *Silex Scintillans.* London, 1650.

Von Frank, Albert J. *The Sacred Game: Provincialism and Frontier Consciousness in American Literature, 1630–1860.* Cambridge: Cambridge University Press, 1985.

Waggoner, Hyatt H. "Puritan Poetry." *Criticism* 6 (1964): 291–312.

Walker, Williston, ed. *The Creeds and Platforms of Congregationalism.* New York: Charles Scribner's Sons, 1893.

Walton, Izaak. *The Lives of Dr. John Donne, Sir Henry Wotton, Mr. Richard Hooker, [and] Mr. George Herbert.* London, 1670.

Ward, Nathaniel. *The Simple Cobler of Aggawam in America.* London, 1647.

Warren, Austin. "Edward Taylor's Poetry: Colonial Baroque." *Kenyon Review* 3 (1941): 355–71.

Watson, Robert N. *The Rest Is Silence: Death as Annihilation in the English Renaissance.* Berkeley: University of California Press, 1994.

Watt, Tessa. *Cheap Print and Popular Piety, 1550–1640.* Cambridge: Cambridge University Press, 1991.

Wharton, Donald P. *Richard Steere: Colonial Merchant Poet.* University Park: Pennsylvania State University Press, 1979.

Whiting, Samuel. *A Discourse of the Last Judgment, or Short Notes upon Mat. XXV.* Cambridge, Mass., 1664.

Whole Booke of Psalmes Faithfully Translated into English Metre. [Cambridge, Mass.], 1640.

Wigglesworth, Michael. *The Day of Doom.* London, 1673.

———. *The Diary of Michael Wigglesworth, 1653–1657: The Conscience of a Puritan,* ed. Edmund S. Morgan. New York: Harper and Row, 1965.

———. *Meat Out of the Eater or Meditations Concerning the Necessity, End, and Usefulness of Afflictions Unto God's Children,* Cambridge, Mass., 1670.

———. *The Poems of Michael Wigglesworth,* ed. Ronald A. Bosco. Lanham, Md.: University Press of America, 1989.

Wigglesworth, Michael, and Edward Wigglesworth. Notebooks 2, 3, and 4. Wigglesworth Family Papers (Mss. 71). R. Stanton Avery Special Collections Department, New England Historic Genealogical Society, Boston.

Williams, Roger. *The Bloudy Tenent of Persecution . . . Discussed, in a Conference betweene Truth and Peace.* London, 1644.

———. *A Key into the Language of America.* London, 1643.

Wilson, John. *A Song of Deliverance for the Lasting Remembrance of Gods Wonderful Works never to be Forgotten.* London, 1626. Reprint, Boston, 1680.

Winship, George Parker. *The Cambridge Press 1638–1692: A Reëxamination of the Evidence concerning the Bay Psalm Book and the Eliot Indian Bible.* Philadelphia: University of Pennsylvania Press, 1945.

Winship, Michael P. *Making Heretics: Militant Protestantism and Free Grace in Massachusetts, 1636–1641.* Princeton: Princeton University Press, 2002.

———. "'The Most Glorious Church in the World': The Unity of the Godly in Boston, Massachusetts, in the 1630s." *Journal of British Studies* 39 (2000): 71–98.

———. "Reconsiderations: Were There Any Puritans in New England?" *New England Quarterly* 74 (2001): 118–38.

Winthrop, John. *The Journal of John Winthrop, 1630–1649* (abridged), ed. Richard S. Dunn and Laetitia Yeandle. Cambridge: Belknap Press of Harvard University Press, 1996.

———. *A Modell of Christian Charity.* In *Collections of the Massachusetts Historical Society,* 3d ser., 7. 31–48. Boston: Little and Brown, 1838.

Winthrop, John, Thomas Dudley, et al. *The Humble Request [. . .] to the Rest of their Brethren, in and of the Church of England.* London, 1630. Reprinted in *Chronicles of the First Planters of the Colony of Massachusetts Bay, from 1623 to 1636,* ed. Alexander Young. 293–99. Boston: Little and Brown, 1846.

Wither, George. *Preparation to the Psalter.* London, 1619.

———. *The Psalms Translated into Lyric Verse.* The Netherlands, 1632. Reprint, Manchester: Spenser Society, 1881.

Worthley, Harold Field. *An Inventory of the Records of the Particular (Congregational) Churches of Massachusetts Gathered 1620–1805.* Cambridge: Harvard University Press, 1970.

Wright, Nathalia. "The Morality Tradition in the Poetry of Edward Taylor." *American Literature* 18 (1946): 18–24.

Wright, Thomas Goddard. *Literary Culture in New England (1620–1730).* New Haven: Yale University Press, 1920.

Wyatt, Thomas. *Certayne Psalmes Chosen out of the Psalter of David Commonlye Called thee .vii. Penytentiall Psalmes.* London, [1549].

Ziff, Larzer. Introduction to *John Cotton on the Churches of New England.* Cambridge: Belknap Press of Harvard University Press, 1968.

———. *Puritanism in America: New Culture in a New World.* New York: Viking Press, 1973.

———. "Text and Context." *William and Mary Quarterly,* 3d ser., 45 (1988): 348–49.

Zim, Rivkah. *English Metrical Psalms: Poetry as Praise and Prayer, 1535–1601.* Cambridge: Cambridge University Press, 1987.

Index

predestination, 144–45, 203–4, 210; and Halfway Covenant, 68; *Day of Doom*, 27, 124, 129–30, 155; funeral elegies, 69; *Gods Determinations*, 26–28, 70, 168, 194, 247 n. 48; sermons, 66, 69

preparationism, 26, 27, 196

Presbyterianism, 36, 38, 122, 158

Prince, Thomas, 86

print culture, 15, 17–19, 181, 211; ballads, 140–41, 142–43, 147–48, 241 n. 93; Bay Psalm Book, 78, 86, 106, 232 n. 39; *Day of Doom*, 114–15; *Gods Determinations*, 167–70; sermon publication, 55, 57, 226 n. 91

psalmody, metrical, 24, 70–71, 76–99, 104–7, 110; critical approaches, 209; didacticism in, 52–53; replacing ungodly ballads, 141–42. *See also* Bay Psalm Book; Cotton on psalm-singing; ordinances; Psalter and psalm versions

Psalms, Book of, 22, 77, 78, 80–82, 84–85, 187; Augustine, 77–78; Luther, 106

Psalters and psalm versions, 80–84, 103, 231 n. 21; Sandys, 83, 89–90, 93; Taylor, 165–66. *See also* Ainsworth; Bay Psalm Book; Sternhold and Hopkins

Puritanism: affections in, 26–28, 55, 67, 83, 96, 114, 131; colonial circumstances, 33, 78–79, 108; rationality and its limits, 11–12, 27–28, 83, 126–32, 155; spiritual experience, 26–28, 53–55, 60, 66, 67, 68, 73–74, 77, 96, 106–7, 108–9, 171–75, 179–88, 249 n. 89; outward conformity, 33–34, 35, 36, 37, 50–52, 54, 108, 109, 121–26, 155. *See also* church order; conversion; covenant

Quarles, Francis, 87

Ramus, Petrus, 67, 227 n. 111, 228 n. 126

Ravenscroft, Thomas, 95, 97

reading: Bible, 84–85, 102; Psalms 77, 106–7; reader in *Day of Doom*, 116, 124–135, 149–53; reader in *Gods Determinations*, 166–70, 174, 178, 181–84, 195; sermons, 60

reconstructive criticism, 12–14, 31, 205, 206, 207

ritualism: Anglican, 44–45, 81, 82, 85, 207–8, 214; Puritan, 158–60; in Taylor, 160, 164–65, 166, 199, 203; in other New England verse, 13, 14, 22, 45–46, 48, 212, 254 n. 22

Robinson, Douglas, 127

Root, John, 174, 198

Rous, Francis, 81; Rous Psalter, 81, 84, 231 n. 21

Rowe, Karen E., 21, 31, 196

Rutman, Darrett B., 177

Sandys, George, 83, 89–90, 93

Scanlan, Thomas, 214

Scheick, William J.: critical approaches, 31, 32, 205–206; funeral elegies, 45, 46, 47, 202; puritan poetics, 16–17, 21, 61

Schweitzer, Ivy, 12, 21, 207, 209

Separatism, 33, 94, 95, 104

sermon, 57, 161; and *Day of Doom*, 24, 65, 68–69, 116–17, 126–36, 150, 155; and *Gods Determinations*, 166–67, 173; as ordinance, 56–61, 164; Bible in, 58, 59, 64; in church service, 52–69; influence on other verse, 17, 53–55, 58–69, 92, 111–13, 182–83, 210–11; modern criticism, 55, 226 n. 82; performative context, 64–65, 66; publication, 55, 57, 226 n. 91; style and design, 58–63, 132–33, 144, 150, 239 n. 55; theory, 23–24, 28, 55–69, 130, 133, 173. *See also* plain style

Sewall, Samuel, 18, 19, 97–98

Shakespeare, William, 141

Shepard, Thomas, Sr., 26, 34, 40–41, 116, 169; Antinomian Controversy, 87; Bay Psalm Book, 79; conversion relation, 71; journal, 28, 73–74; spiritual experience, 51, 108, 109

Shepard, Thomas, Jr., 34, 69, 87

Shields, David S., 205, 208

Sidney, Mary, 82

Sidney, Philip, 82, 139

Silverman, Kenneth, 16–17, 110

Sloan, Gary, 133

Spengemann, William, 20

Stallings, Louis Russell, 86, 101